A BLESSING OF YEARS

Lawrence Joseph Cardinal Shehan

A Blessing of Years

The Memoirs of
Lawrence Cardinal Shehan

University of Notre Dame Press
Notre Dame & London

BX
4705
.S6126
A37
1982

Library of Congress Cataloging in Publication Data

Shehan, Lawrence, Cardinal, 1898–
  A blessing of years.

  1. Shehan, Lawrence, Cardinal, 1898–
2. Catholic Church—Maryland—Baltimore—Bishops—
Biography. 3. Baltimore (Md.)—Biography. I. Title.
BX4705.S6126A37 1982 282'.092'4 [B.] 82-19965
ISBN 0-268-00667-9

With deep affection and total loyalty
I dedicate this book to
Pope John Paul II

Contents

The University of Notre Dame Press gratefully acknowledges the generous suppport of The Marion I. & Henry J. Knott Foundation, Incorporated, Baltimore, Maryland in the publication of *A Blessing of Years: The Memoirs of Lawrence Cardinal Shehan*.

Acknowledgments

IN THE PREPARATION OF THIS BOOK, I sought and received advice and assistance from many persons. It is not possible to name each of them, but I should like to express particular appreciation to the following, each of whom made a special contribution to my efforts:

Archbishop Borders, who continually encouraged me during the entire period when this book was in preparation.

Bishop Austin Murphy, for his unfailing support and encouragement, and for his assistance in reconstructing some of the events recounted in the book.

Bishop Frank Stafford, for his kindness in reviewing certain chapters and in offering the benefit of his experience, particularly in connection with Associated Catholic Charities.

Bishop Frank Murphy, who was so helpful during the Second Vatican Council and became my secretary after the Council.

Monsignor Porter J. White, whose assiduous attention to detail and excellent memory were of immeasurable help, especially in that part of my memoirs which deals with the Second Vatican Council.

Miss Mary Elizabeth (Betty) Sweeney, my secretary of many years, for her assistance in researching much of the material needed for this book, her careful attention to detail, her willingness to assume responsibility for the preliminary typing of the manuscript, and her supervision of the typing of later versions.

Mrs. William (Dorothy) Leonard and Mrs. Edwin (Jeanne) Trexler, for their patience and thoroughness in typing many revisions of each chapter of the manuscript.

ix

I wish also to express appreciation to the following publishers for permission to quote from their material: To America Press for excerpts from *The Documents of Vatican II*, ed. Walter M. Abbot, S.J.; to the National Catholic News Service for excerpts from the *Council Daybook*; to Our Sunday Visitor Press for excerpts from *The Catholic Almanac*; to *Time* for the excerpt from " 'It's Like Shooting God.' "

Prologue

MY LIFE HAS SPANNED ALL THE years of the more than eight decades of the twentieth century. My memories go back to its very beginning. I have some vivid recollections of early childhood and what it was like to grow up in Baltimore in a typical Catholic family during those placid and pleasant years that followed the dawn of the century and came to a rude ending with the outbreak of World War I. I also have vivid memories of the sad years of that war and the epidemic of influenza that swept through the country in the winter following the war's end, probably taking more American lives than had been lost on the field of battle. My priestly (as distinguished from episcopal) ministry began during what have been characterized as years of unprecedented prosperity, 1923-29, and came to a close shortly after the end of World War II. Thus they included the years of the Great Depression, 1929-41, and those of the Second World War, 1941-45.

My memories of the years following the Second World War begin with my rather reluctant acceptance of the office of Bishop—reluctant, not because of my unwillingness to serve, but because I was convinced that I lacked certain physical and intellectual qualities which I considered important for one who carries the weight of that office. The memories that follow include my eight years (1945-53) as Auxiliary Bishop of Baltimore—two under Archbishop Curley and six under Archbishop Keough. Then came my eight years (1953-61) as first Bishop of Bridgeport, the second "southerner" to be appointed to a northern diocese. After returning to Baltimore to become Archbishop, I was immediately immersed in the important program of high school construction initiated by Archbishop Keough, and also within the first year departed for the opening of the Second Vatican Council, whose four periods I attended, and in which I participated to the degree of my ability and opportunity.

1

Before the end of the Council, I found myself all unexpectedly elevated to the rank of Cardinal. In that capacity, I headed the papal delegation to Istanbul to preside, with the Greek Orthodox Patriarch Athenagoras, over the memorable ecumenical service on December 7, 1965, the day before the Second Vatican Council celebrated its solemn closing. Finally, toward the very end of my ministry as Archbishop of Baltimore, I was appointed by Pope Paul VI to be Papal Legate to the Melbourne Eucharistic Congress.

Are my recollections of these eventful years worth recording? The reader will have to be the judge. One thing I would emphasize: this book in no sense is meant to be a history of the time. It is simply the record of my memories, checked for accuracy when that has been possible. For my purpose, it seems important to include in this Prologue two things: a brief sketch of the Baltimore in which I grew up during the early 1900s and a description of the Catholic Church in Baltimore during that same period.

At the dawn of the twentieth century, Baltimore shared the prosperity, the optimism, the bright expectations that seemed to be prevalent throughout the country. Its commerce, banking, and shipping, which constituted its main business, were all flourishing. Its financial institutions might be said to have been almost glutted with assets, as was soon to become evident. To the observant and thoughtful person of the time, Baltimore presented a strange paradox. The city possessed considerable wealth. Within the previous decades it had become first the home of The Johns Hopkins University, and later of The Johns Hopkins Hospital and Medical School. It already had such institutions of culture and education as the Peabody Conservatory of Music and the George Peabody Library. Through the generosity of two of its wealthy citizens, the general public had access to the extensive collection of books and valuable services of the Enoch Pratt Free Library, and to the Walters Collection of fine art, which was housed in a handsome gallery. In this same city, however, existed grossly unsanitary conditions that would have been tolerated in no other city of its size and financial resources in the whole country. Those shocking conditions arose from two main causes: the lack of even the faintest resemblance to a system of sewerage and sewage disposal; and a water supply that was one of the worst, from the point of view of both quantity and quality, in the country. Such conditions can only be explained by a sort of public apathy that probably arose during the Civil War when Baltimore was the only "occupied" city of the country, and lasted down to the early years of the twentieth century. During those years, Baltimore had passed through some very difficult times. In spite of them, and in spite of the city's grave physical defects, as I have already observed, its banking business, commerce, and shipping survived, and during the last years of the nineteenth century on into the twentieth, they were flourishing. Then suddenly disaster struck, threatening to bring it all to an end.

One of the most vivid memories of my childhood is that of standing with my parents at a southern window of a darkened second story bedroom of our home on Kennedy Lane watching the leaping flames rise above the skyline into the expanse of blood-red sky, more than two miles away. It was Sunday, February 7, 1904, and this was the Baltimore Fire.

As usual that Sunday morning downtown Baltimore was deserted except for the watchmen who made their regular rounds to see that all was well with the great warehouses, banks, and other financial institutions that comprised that important section of the city. Perhaps an occasional policeman huddled in a doorway on the sheltered side of the street, trying to protect himself from the biting northwest wind. One of the watchmen observed smoke rising from the sidewalk grating in front of the large warehouse of the J. Hurst Company on Hopkins Place at German (now Redwood) Street. He sounded the alarm, and within minutes firemen from the nearest fire station arrived with their apparatus, ready to extinguish what they presumed to be a small basement fire. When the firemen attempted to enter, they found their way blocked by dense smoke and heated gases, for the fire had already eaten its way into the packs of inflammable dry goods readied for shipment to retail merchants of the South. A second alarm was sounded, but before additional equipment arrived, the front wall of the building had been blown out by the steadily mounting pressure, leaving the whole interior open to the driving wind. In a matter of minutes the entire building was aflame. The fire, lashed by the wind, spread rapidly to adjoining buildings.

While the morning was still young, it was apparent that the city was faced with a disaster beyond the capacity of the local fire department. Signals of distress were sent to other cities. Soon men and equipment were on their way by special trains from York and Hanover, from Washington, Philadelphia, and Wilmington, and even from New York. As

they arrived and began their work, it became evident that the confla-
gration was totally out of control. Each additional hose attached to the
hydrants lowered the pressure of the whole system, and the piddling
streams of water were without effect. So intense was the heat and so
immediate the danger that the firemen were driven from the streets,
forced to leave their equipment behind to be destroyed. In an effort to
contain the fire, expert dynamiters were brought in, and one after
another a series of large buildings fell. But the embers, lifted by the
heat, were flung by the high wind across the empty space and promptly
ignited new fires. Relentlessly, on a half-mile front reaching from Fayette Street south to the harbor, the wall of flames swept eastward,
destroying everything in its path.

The fire raged all through Sunday night and all day Monday until it
reached Jones Falls. Then the wind died; there was nothing left to burn.
About 140 acres of closely built structures, numbering, according to
the official count, 1,343, were completely ruined. All that remained,
with the exception of a few low compact banks, were two "skyscrapers."
The rest had been ruined beyond all hope of salvaging. The whole area
was covered with smoldering rubble. The financial loss has been re-
liably estimated at $150 million. When it is considered that the best
daily papers then sold at one cent per copy, as compared with fifteen or
twenty cents today, the reader can get some idea of the financial loss
which the city sustained in the year 1904. Other losses, such as busi-
nesses ruined or seriously interrupted, personal careers suddenly ended
or irreparably injured, are beyond estimation.

The mood of the city immediately after the fire was then one of
deep pessimism. In a spell of depression, the promising and able young
mayor, Robert McLane, shot himself. Fortunately, E. Clay Timanus,
the Republican President of the City Council, who succeeded automatically, proved to be a man of intelligence and vigor. His first official
act was to summon the City Council. After a brief discussion (there was
really nothing to discuss, for the plight of the city was self-evident) a
motion was made to begin the work of rebuilding immediately. It
carried unanimously, and the mayor was authorized to appoint a Burnt
District Commission that would have extraordinary powers. As chairman, Mayor Timanus appointed Colonel Sherlock Swann. The Commission's first decision, made seemingly with the approval of the whole
city, was to straighten, widen, and properly pave, according to the best
standards of the day, the narrow and tortuous streets of the area. Here
and there the commission ran into some opposition, but it resolutely
stuck to its plans and ultimately achieved its basic purpose.

Encouraged by the prompt action of public officials, a steadily increasing number of merchants and financiers decided to rebuild their places of business on a larger and more substantial scale than those which they had lost. Within a few days most of the major firms had found temporary offices. Some of the local insurance companies were not able to meet the full amount of the policies they had written and were forced into bankruptcy. But the outside companies paid in full, and this, together with the capital the Baltimore banks had under their control, was sufficient to finance the new construction.

One of the most prompt and important decisions made by the city government, with the approval of the people of Baltimore, was to extend the water system to ensure an adequate supply for all the city's needs and to construct a modern filtration and water treatment plant. Equally important was the decision to install a modern system of sewerage and sewage disposal. Before long, typhoid, once the scourge of Baltimore, became an almost forgotten disease. A new era of prosperity began to make itself felt, and the people began to speak of the fire not as a disaster, but as a blessing in disguise.

Not long ago a person who had recently come to Baltimore to assume a prominent position, said to me: "Baltimore impresses me as a series of individual neighborhoods bound loosely together by a rather weak city government." It is easy to exaggerate the weakness of the central city government. Certainly in the period immediately after the Great Fire, the city government, under the able leadership of Mayor Timanus did not show itself to be either weak or ineffectual in rebuilding the area that had been devastated; just as the city government under the present able and vigorous Mayor, William Donald Schaefer, has not shown itself weak or ineffective in the renewal of the downtown district, the beautification of the harbor area, the development of Harbor Place, and the restoration of an increasing number of neighborhoods. On the other hand, it would be difficult to exaggerate the importance of the neighborhood in the life of Baltimore. This was particularly true during the early years of this century.

Baltimore's neighborhoods during that period were stable and influential. Their individualizing characteristics were determined largely by their ethnic origin, which in turn reflected the history of immigration in the nineteenth century. The first to arrive in significant numbers were the Irish; their first parish, St. Patrick's, was established in 1792, just three years after the Diocese of Baltimore was founded, and

was located at the north end of Fells Point, site of the original town of
Baltimore. How stable was this area as an Irish neighborhood is indicated by the fact that the present church was erected in 1898 to take the
place of the old.

Next after those early Irish came the Germans, probably during
the troubled times that began after Napoleon, having won the famous
battles of Austerlitz in 1805 and Jena in 1807, undertook to redraw the
map of Germany. They came in increasing numbers and settled in East
Baltimore, where the Catholics among them established the great parish of St. James (1833); then further east and to the south, St. Michael's
(1852); Holy Cross in South Baltimore (1858); Sacred Heart still further
east in Highlandtown (1873); and Fourteen Holy Martyrs in West Baltimore (1870). Of course, not all, nor perhaps even the majority, of the
German immigrants were Catholic. The long list of Lutheran churches
found in the current telephone directory bears witness to the large
number of Protestants among the great influx of German immigrants
of the nineteenth century.

The second and largest wave of Irish immigrants arrived after the
tragic Irish potato famine, 1845-47. They settled in several areas: in
East Baltimore in the old Tenth Ward, where the Church of St. John the
Evangelist was erected in 1853 to serve their needs; in Canton, just
north of the wharf of that name, where the parish of St. Brigid was
erected in 1854; in Locust Point, across the harbor from Canton, where
St. Lawrence O'Toole (1859), now Our Lady of Good Counsel, was
built, and in South Baltimore, with its St. Mary, Star of the Sea (1868).
Meanwhile, three important parishes were brought into existence to
care for the needs of a mixed German and Irish population: St. Martin's
(1865), St. Ann's (1873), St. Paul's (1888).

The Italians settled in "Little Italy," where St. Leo's was established in 1881. During the last quarter of the century, the Poles—like
the Irish almost exclusively Catholic—began to come in great numbers
and settled in southeast Baltimore in an area stretching from East
Baltimore Street south to the harbor. There they founded three large
parishes: St. Stanislaus (1879), Holy Rosary (1887), and St. Casimir
(1902). Meanwhile, the Bohemians had also settled in East Baltimore
and established the parish of St. Wenceslaus in 1872. All of these ethnic
neighborhoods remained stable and effective throughout the early years
of the 1900s and some of them far beyond, even to the present day.

There were, of course, other stable neighborhoods that had no
very distinctive ethnic qualities: neighborhoods like Waverly (where

both my maternal great-great grandparents and my paternal grand-parents had settled and on the outskirts of which I was born and raised), Homestead, Hampden, Woodberry, West Baltimore, Irvington. All these neighborhoods remained virtually unchanged after the fire, though their main streets gradually were properly paved. Of course the reconstruction of the burned out downtown area provided employment for workers, both skilled and unskilled, who lived in these areas.

The city's neighborhoods were generally made up of long lines of red brick row houses, two or three stories high, which lined both sides of the street. Often the twenty or more houses making up individual blocks were of identical design and appearance. Since the brick of the Baltimore area was porous, the fronts of all the houses and the sides of the corner houses were painted a standard deep red and pencilled with thin lines of white paint to resemble the mortar jointure of the bricks. Custom demanded that the few steps leading to the front entrance of each house be white, preferably of white marble from the quarries to the north of the city, or at least of wood painted white, and that the window frames also be painted white; The "front steps," furthermore, were kept immaculately clean. As a result the appearance of the city was rather monotonous, but not unpleasant. I have heard it said that in those days Baltimore more closely resembled English towns than any other city in the United States.

One advantage that arose from this multitude of row houses was that it permitted the average Baltimore families to own solid, comfortable homes at a very reasonable cost. How reasonable the cost could be was illustrated by the experience of my own parents shortly before my birth, in the late 1800s. Following their marriage (1893), they had moved into a small red brick row house on Greenmount Avenue near Twenty-fifth Street, which they had rented from my mother's uncle and aunt, Tilghman and Caroline (Aunt Lena, to us) Schofield. My father's modest business must have flourished during the late years of the nineteenth century for the 1897 land records of Baltimore show that, in that year before my birth, my parents purchased the house for the princely sum of $500. Two years later, the record shows they purchased (for protection, I suppose, and perhaps for investment) the identical adjoining house for $650. On each of them, the sellers placed an irredeemable ground rent of $100. Home ownership in Baltimore was a strong and almost universal tradition. The average frugal Baltimorean could see no sense in lining the pockets of a landlord by paying a monthly rent for a house he and his family intended to live in for many years, perhaps for the rest of his life. Thus tradition gave stability to the neighborhoods and was reflected in the stability and the conservative tone of the city as a whole.

The monotonous appearance of Baltimore neighborhoods was somewhat relieved by the possession of three magnificent parks. The most beautiful of these, as I remember it in the early 1900s, was Druid Hill Park in the northwestern section of the city. The city government had purchased the property in the middle of the nineteenth century. Through the park wound a picturesque roadway. Its broad lawns were well kept; its trees had been carefully preserved; it was a favorite place for family picnics. Particularly pleasing to children was its modest zoo. Clifton Park in northeast Baltimore, the second of the three parks, was acquired in the late 1900s as a bequest of Johns Hopkins, whose summer home, popularly known as the "Mansion House," was located here. Its landscape was more monotonous than Druid Hill, but it provided a more varied practical use with its many tennis courts, two baseball diamonds, a football field, and finally a golf course. The third park, located in the southeastern section of Baltimore, is Patterson Park. Although smaller, it was the most used of the parks, because on its four sides are found some of the most densely populated neighborhoods of the city.

A fourth park, Federal Hill in South Baltimore, is much smaller than the other three, but worthy of mention because of its historical importance to the city and because its green slope, rising rather abruptly from the water's edge, provides a most picturesque landscape and the best view of the whole harbor and of the city itself. Federal Hill was the site where the Union Army encamped during the whole of the Civil War.

Besides these more extensive parks, the city was dotted with a number of small parks. The most noteworthy of these and perhaps the most prestigious of all Baltimore parks is what in the early part of the nineteenth century was called "Howard's Park" and came later to be called "Mount Vernon Square." In the middle is Baltimore's most famous landmark, the Washington Monument, a noble rounded marble shaft which rises to a height of 160 feet. Hamilton Owens, former editor of the *Baltimore Sun* and author of the excellent history entitled *Baltimore on the Chesapeake*, calls it one of the most beautiful structures of the world. Most Baltimoreans would agree with him.

Such was the Baltimore that I knew during the early years of the twentieth century. It was a good city in which to live, a good city in which to spend one's childhood and to grow up, a good city in which to raise a family. It was a city for which I developed a deep love during those early years, a love which has persisted undiminished during all the years since, in spite of all the changes, some of them regrettable, that have taken place.

Of particular importance to me personally was the character of the Catholic Church of Baltimore and the quality of its life during the early years of the present century. First, it was a living, developing Church. Although it was already far more than one hundred years old, there was no sign of death or decay at its center or in any of its important parts. It is true that the conversion of residential neighborhoods into areas of commerce and industry and the shifting population in the inner city caused a lessening of Church activity in some of the once-important older parishes. This, however, was more than compensated by the development of newer parishes. Moreover, the strong ethnic spirit tended to preserve some of the older parishes which otherwise would have been adversely affected. The movement of growth and development would greatly increase during the next decade, 1920-1930, as manifested by the multiplication of parishes and parochial schools.

Second, it was a Church that was deeply conscious of its historic past. Here in Baltimore under John Carroll, the Church in the United States had its beginnings. When Carroll was appointed first Bishop in the United States, in 1789, the very year that the Constitution of the United States was enacted, Baltimore was chosen as his see city. One of the first things he did was to take steps toward the founding of St. Mary's Seminary, the oldest and for many years the leading seminary in the country. In 1806 Carroll was finally able to plan and begin the erection of his cathedral church. With great foresight he chose as architect Benjamin Henry Latrobe, one of the leading architects of that time. How well Latrobe, with the support first of Carroll and later of Archbishop Maréchal, designed and built was made evident recently when the old Baltimore Cathedral was chosen as an outstanding example of early American church architecture to be depicted on one of the four American Architecture commemorative postage stamps. In it have been held the seven Provincial Councils —national in scope, since Baltimore was then the only metropolitan see in the United States—and the three Plenary Councils, all presided over by the Archbishops of Baltimore. In that line of ten Archbishops were found, after Carroll and Maréchal, such outstanding churchmen as Samuel Eccleston, Francis P. Kenrick, Martin J. Spalding, James Roosevelt Bayley, and James Cardinal Gibbons.

The most famous and influential of that line was the last mentioned, who became Archbishop of Baltimore in 1877. Gibbons first came into national prominence as President of the Third Plenary Council in 1884, and largely as a result of his outstanding performance, he was named Cardinal in 1887. He ruled the See of Baltimore until his death in 1921. Although he never stepped out of his role of Catholic churchman, he was the dominant figure of the city of Baltimore and the state of Maryland during the years of the late nineteenth and the early twentieth century. It was in the figure of Gibbons as a symbol of the history of the Archdiocese that the Church of Baltimore was kept vividly conscious of its historic past.

Since these are personal memories rather than a history of the time, I may be excused if I recall my first meeting with the famous Cardinal when I was a child about eight years old—a meeting which is not important in itself, but illustrates at once the approachability of Gibbons and the confidence and affection in which he was held even by the children of the Archdiocese. For us, he stood for all that was noble and good.

My childhood meeting with the Cardinal arose from the fact that my grandfather Shehan had established a modest dairy business at 2 Kennedy Lane, less than two blocks from St. Ann's Church and rectory. In the spring of 1903 our own family had moved into the large red brick house next to my grandfather's home and place of business. My grandmother ran what might be called a home dairy shop where she sold milk, cream and other dairy products to customers in the immediate neighborhood. When I was about seven years old, it became part of my daily chores to deliver milk and cream to St. Ann's rectory early each morning in time for breakfast. Thus I came to know quite well Miss Teresa Kraemer, the housekeeper of the rectory. One Sunday in the spring, probably in May of 1906, it was announced at the nine o'clock children's Mass that the Cardinal was coming that day to preside at the eleven o'clock Mass and to administer the Sacrament of Confirmation to the young people of the parish. Immediately after the Mass I went to the back door of the rectory and entered the kitchen without knocking, just as I was accustomed to do when making my daily delivery. "Miss Teresa," I said, "do you think I could meet the Cardinal, get his blessing, and kiss his ring?" "Oh, yes," she said, "if you come here about one o'clock and wait here in the kitchen with me, I'll take you into the hallway and introduce you to the Cardinal as he and the priests come out from dinner, and I know he will be glad to give you his blessing and let you kiss his ring." When I returned at the suggested time, she did just what she had promised. As soon as we heard the diners rise from the table, she took me into the hallway, approached the Cardinal as he came out first, and said: "Your Eminence, this little boy delivers our milk and cream every morning in time for breakfast. He would like to get your blessing and kiss your ring." Some of the priests naturally laughed at my childish presumptuousness, but not the Cardinal. He made me feel that to him the matter was as serious as it was to me. He took my hand into his own, asked me my name, what grade I was in; he hoped I would always be a good boy. Then he told me to kneel, gave me his blessing, and presented his ringed hand to be kissed, patted me on the head, and dismissed me. I could not have cared less about the laughter of the priests. I had gotten what I came for, and more—a memory that is still more vivid in my mind than things that happened yesterday and the day before.

Later I would meet him briefly at times when he came to St. Charles College and St. Mary's Seminary for the celebration of special feasts, and finally I was sent to accompany him on one of his afternoon walks in the spring after I had been informed that I was to go to Rome to finish my course in Theology. That was the last time I saw him, for he died the following Holy Thursday—March 24, 1921. Always he had been the same. I cannot say that in these comparatively few brief contacts with him I ever really came close to him, but throughout all the years of my childhood and youth I was conscious of him as the most important person not only in the Church I had already come to love, but in the city in which I was growing up.

How revered he was, and how widespread and strong was his influence was shown by the great public testimonial which was given to him by his fellow citizens of the city of Baltimore and the state of Maryland on the occasion of the fiftieth anniversary of his ordination to the priesthood and the twenty-fifth anniversary of his cardinalate, at the Fifth Regiment Armory, June 6, 1911. The first suggestion of such a celebration came from James Baldwin, editor of the *Baltimore Sun*. It was planned and carried out by a committee of civic leaders. On that afternoon, an estimated crowd of 20,000 persons gathered in the Armory for the civic celebration. By special train from Washington came President Taft; Vice President James S. Sherman; Champ Clark, Speaker of the House of Representatives; members of the Cabinet; large delegations from both houses of Congress. Chief Justice White of the Supreme Court came from his home in New Orleans; former President Theodore Roosevelt came from his home in Oyster Bay, New York. Practically every important man in the governments of the United States, the state of Maryland, and the city of Baltimore was present on the huge platform. Seldom, if ever, has any person, churchman or layman, received such a tribute from his fellow citizens of the city, state, and nation as Gibbons received on that occasion. Yet it was said of him in the commemorative book on the reception,"There was not in all the thousands a more unassuming man than he who was the central figure of the demonstration." The whole celebration is described by John Tracy Ellis in his excellent two-volume *Life of James Cardinal Gibbons* (1952), which long since has been recognized as one of the most important works—in my judgment the best—in the field of American Church history.

It would be a mistake, of course, to look upon Catholic life in the Archdiocese of Baltimore as simply centering in or dominated by Cardinal Gibbons. In fact, it was not in keeping with his character to exercise "domination." Active leadership and wise guidance, yes—but not domination. The whole Archdiocese was extremely proud of and loyal to him, and it may truly be said that it was suffused with his spirit. But the vitality of the archdiocese was for the most part centered in its parishes. Each of these parishes had its own parochial school, its own Holy Name Society, Sodality of the Blessed Virgin Mary, and St. Vincent de Paul Society. Each was characterized not only by an intense religious interest and activity, but also by an equally in-tense loyalty to the parish on the part of its people. This strong parish life was, of course, not confined to the city of Baltimore, but extended to the city of Washington, our nation's capital, which was then part of the Baltimore Archdiocese, and to parishes found in the many smaller towns and villages spread throughout the entire territory of the arch-diocese, which then included the whole of the "Western Shore" of Maryland and the District of Columbia.

Throughout all these parishes there was real pride in Cardinal Gibbons as their leader, and great loyalty to him. His spirit seemed gently to permeate the whole archdiocese down to the end of his life. It was remarkable how many of our non-Catholic brethren shared with us this sense of reverence and affection. When he died, at the age of eighty-six, the *Baltimore Sun* carried on its front page a truly noble pen-and-ink sketch of Gibbons robed in mitre and cope, clasping his pastoral staff in his left hand, hovering over the city of Baltimore with his right hand outstretched in benediction. I count it a singular grace that I spent my entire childhood and youth, took my first steps toward the priesthood, and went on to the age of maturity, under his beneficent influence.

1. Early Memories

MY EARLIEST MEMORIES ARE CENTERED in my family and in our home on Greenmount Avenue. To us, our little house, set back from the street by a small well-kept lawn, seemed very attractive with its front wall painted red, pencilled with thin white lines, and the frames of its door and windows painted white. There the first four of my parents' six children (I being the third) were born, under the supervision of John Brooke Boyle, our family doctor, for whom we had great affection and for whom my brother Brooke was named.

My memories of our life in that home are generally somewhat vague but almost uniformly happy: waiting with my father in the early morning as he paged through the daily newspaper while my mother finished preparations for the family breakfast; pleasant days spent with my older brother Tom, my sister, Mary, and our mother, who in spite of her care of my younger brother Dan and her many household chores, always found time to answer our countless questions and look after our every need; frequent visits to our widowed grandmother Schofield who lived on Cottage Avenue, little more than a city block away; less frequent but equally enjoyable visits to our grandparents Shehan, whose home and dairy were located on Kennedy Lane, about three times as far but still within easy walking distance, where Thanksgiving and Christmas dinner soon became part of the family ritual. I suppose we always went to the Shehans because our grandmother Schofield, with the help of her two maiden daughters, had rather recently taken responsibility for the rearing of the six children of her oldest son, Carroll, whose wife had died in childbirth. Carroll managed the flour mill at Orange Grove on the Patapsco, some distance upstream from Ellicott City. The mill burned down in the early 1900s and was never rebuilt. undoubtedly because the mills of Maryland, whose flour had been a staple export from Baltimore, could no longer compete

with those that served the great wheat fields of the Midwest. Twice
yearly thereafter, he would organize large Sunday family picnics to
visit the ruins of the old mill; in the spring, allegedly to gather wild
flowers that grew abundantly in the woodland between the terminus of
the Catonsville trolley line and Orange Grove; and in the fall to collect
chestnuts. These became important events in our young lives, but this
would come later, after we had moved from our Greenmount Avenue
home.

As soon as I was old enough, my father began to take me, with my
older brother and sister, every Sunday to the seven o'clock Mass at
St. Ann's Church, while my mother would remain home with our younger brother to prepare breakfast for us on our return. After washing the
dishes and tidying the dining room and kitchen, she would go off to a
later Mass alone. This meant that our father was with us all day
practically every Sunday. He would read the Sunday newspaper and
then occupy himself with various things—checking his business accounts, carrying on the correspondence required by his modest business, and making needed repairs to the house. But his very presence, to
me at least, gave to Sunday a special air of contentment and even happiness. Outwardly he was never a conspicuously religious man, but in
many ways he gave evidence of deep religious conviction and a strong
attachment to the parish of St. Ann. In childhood, both he and my
mother had seen the erection of that parish church through the generosity of Captain William Kennedy, an enterprising and successful sea
merchant, and they had attended the parish school from its beginning.
They remained deeply attached to the memory of Father William
Bartlett, their first pastor, a convert from Quakerism and much loved
by his whole parish, who had died shortly after my birth. They were
also strongly attached to his assistant, Father Lawrence McNamara,
their contemporary in St. Ann's School and the first priest produced
by the parish. It was his name they gave me at baptism.

The external practice of our religion, as well as our affections, was
centered in St. Ann's Church and remained there all through our childhood and youth. There all of us, like our parents before us, would
attend the eight grades of elementary school. By the time my powers
of observation and memory were sufficiently developed to know and retain what was happening, Tom had already entered the first grade.
Each evening after supper, as my mother was washing the dishes and
straightening the dining room and kitchen, with such help as my sister
and I could give, the first thing my father did was to hear the catechism lesson of Tom, who was then using the beginners' Little Balti-

more Catechism. This he would do for each of us as we came to that period of our development. After catechism would come the spelling lesson, the arithmetic tables, or whatever other tasks of memory had been assigned. Although he was a busy and practical man and reasonably successful, and although this must sometimes have been a boring task, he never gave the slightest indication that it was an unusual or unreasonable thing to expect of him. Evidently, to him the hearing of our catechism lesson was an important contribution to our religious education. Incidentally, it gave him a practical test of our progress in reading ability, since obviously a child cannot memorize exactly what he has not read correctly. But the best thing that he and my mother did to promote our religious education and development was to provide a home life that was built upon their firm religious and moral convictions and was pervaded by a strong attractive religious spirit.

Another thing I remember about my father during those early years was the way we missed him when he was obliged to be away from home on rather extended business trips. When he was asked about his occupation, he answered simply that he was a traveling salesman. In the 1900 and 1904 Polk Directory, he is listed as "agent." As I remember his business life, today he would probably be called by the more high-sounding title of sales representative of the J. W. Goddard Company of New York, a firm dealing in tailors' supplies: linings, canvas, buttons, and everything else tailors may use, except the woolen cloth. The territory for which he was responsible was Baltimore and Washington, Western Maryland, West Virginia, and the southeastern states as far down as Jacksonville and Tampa, Florida. His main business was in Baltimore, where his headquarters were located in a downtown office building, and in Washington, where he went every Monday. He made two comparatively brief annual trips to Western Maryland, West Virginia, and Roanoke, Virginia. Twice a year he made extended trips through the southern states, beginning with the cities of Richmond and Norfolk. These occupied about one month each in the spring and fall, and it was during these times that we especially missed him. Preparation for these trips required rather extended correspondence which he carried on in his own virile, flowing, and easily legible handwriting at his old-fashioned rolltop desk, placed in the corner of my parents' bedroom where the light was best. While he was away, he sent letters home regularly once a week addressed to my mother, but meant for all of us.

Many years later, when my mother died, we found among her effects a number of these letters which she had carefully preserved.

One in particular comes to my mind. It was written in a southern town on Palm Sunday afternoon. He had attended Mass at the plain little parish church that was neatly kept, but showed signs of poverty. It was the Mass before which the palms are blessed and carried in procession and at which the Passion of Our Lord is, or was then, regularly chanted. There everything seemed so different. Instead of the stripped fronds of palm we used at home, there were simply twigs of pine. There was no music either in the procession or at the Mass. The priest himself read the Passion and after it gave a brief but interesting sermon. After Mass, my father had gone to the sacristy to speak with the priest, a young man from the North who had chosen to come to this missionary diocese. He was finding the work difficult, but was not at all discouraged. When my father had returned to the hotel, a plain but decent establishment, he had glanced through the local paper and had written letters to customers he planned to visit later in the week. Then he had taken his Sunday dinner alone. After completing this letter he would take it with the others to the railroad post office in order to send them off as soon as possible. He had intended then to take a walk through the town, but it was already beginning to rain, and he looked forward to a long, lonely afternoon. How he wished he were back home! He would make every possible effort to be with us for Easter.

There was no attempt at literary style. In his own plain and simple way, however, it was well written. But the important thing was that it seemed permeated with thoughtfulness and affection for us all. No wonder, then, that we always welcomed him home from these trips with delight. It was not that he was any closer or dearer to us than our mother. I suppose it was simply a case of "absence makes the heart grow fonder."

My father, whose name was Thomas Patrick, was the third child and oldest son of Irish immigrant parents. His father, Daniel Shehan of Limerick, and his mother, Mary Kelly of Galway, met for the first time on the boat that brought both of them from Ireland during those difficult years that followed the great potato famine. The blight first appeared in 1845; it increased to the proportion of national disaster in 1846 and came to a tragic climax in 1847. Its results were felt for many years later. Between 1845 and 1855, the population of Ireland decreased from 8,500,000 to 6,500,000 as a result of "starvation, pestilence and emigration"; before the end of the nineteenth century, it had been cut in half.

Mary's younger brother, John J. Kelly, had come to this country some years earlier, shortly after the 1845-47 tragedy. Settling in Baltimore, he apparently had prospered almost from the beginning, and according to family accounts, later became Treasurer of Loyola Building and Loan Association (now Loyola Federal). After the death of his parents, he decided to bring his sister Mary, their younger sister Brigid, and their brother Martin to this country. It was undoubtedly he who persuaded and enabled both Mary Kelly and Daniel Shehan to come directly to Baltimore after landing in New York. Presumably, it was through his influence that Daniel was able to secure enough capital to set up a small dairy business on Jenkins Lane in what might be called the southernmost part of Waverly. Daniel and Mary were married on February 22, 1857, in the Church of St. John the Evangelist at Valley and Eager Streets.

My mother's maiden name was Anastasia Dames Schofield. Her father was Charles Henry Schofield, of English descent, a convert to the Catholic Church, who died a year or so before my birth. Her mother's maiden name was Barbara Elizabeth Dames. How my mother acquired the name Anastasia, that of the martyr which appears in the Roman Canon of the Mass, I never knew. She herself never used it except on those rare official documents where it was required. To herself and to all her relatives and friends, even to her mother, she was simply "Nan." All I need say about her is that to all of us she was both lovely and lovable, as she was to all who knew her. She and my father were deeply devoted to each other, and remained so throughout life. The American founders of her family, Augustus Dames of Potsdam in Prussia and Dianna Borgus of Amsterdam in Holland, had come to this country some fifty years before the arrival of our Irish grandparents, probably during those troubled times that followed Napoleon's victories.

Having come to Baltimore, Augustus and his wife settled upon a plot of about two acres on a little country road (later Montpelier Street) off Quaker's Lane (later Montebello Avenue, now Loch Raven Boulevard) in the northern part of Waverly. Augustus served in the War of 1812, probably having been inducted by reason of his previous military training in Prussia. His name appears in the U.S. military roster of that war. Presumably, he saw action in the Battle of North Point. After his release from the army, he returned to the little home (originally, according to family tradition, a log cabin) which he had built on Montpelier Street. There he and his wife raised their family. My grandmother, Barbara Elizabeth, was the daughter of his son William, who is said to have been one of the founders of St. Mary's parish, Govans. The name of his son, John Dames, is the first that appears on the baptismal register of St. Mary's. Long before my birth, the Dames home, through various additions, had become a large, rambling frame house. During my childhood it was occupied by my mother's widowed aunt, Emma Dames Green, and her grown daughter and four sons. I remember very well that, when I was between the ages three and four, our family spent the hot summer months there, a refuge from the heat and the by now cramped quarters of our Greenmount Avenue home.

After the birth of their fourth child, my parents began to find the Greenmount Avenue house too small for comfort, particularly in view of further increases which could be expected in the normal course of events. About that time the large reddish brick house at 3 Kennedy Lane, next to our grandparents' house and dairy, became vacant. It had been built as a summer house by a wealthy New York merchant named Fugle. After his death, his widow decided to return to New York. She was willing to lease the property at a very moderate price to a family that could be trusted to take care of it. The advantages of the property were: the spaciousness of both house and grounds; its state of good repair; its relative nearness to St. Ann's Church and School, which my older brother had already entered; the moderate rental which was being asked; and, last but not least, its proximity to the home and dairy of my grandfather. The one big disadvantage was its lack of any modern facilities except for running water in its small back kitchen and in the bathroom immediately above. But anyone familiar with the history of Baltimore before the fire knows that such conditions were found in many, if not most, homes of this city then and for some time thereafter.

To my parents, the advantages must have easily outweighed the disadvantages. So, after finding a suitable tenant for the Greenmount Avenue house, my father signed a lease for the Kennedy Lane property in the spring of 1903. We were all delighted with it. We children were especially pleased with the size of the grounds, which afforded all the room we could want to play and to move about freely and would give us the opportunity to have a much desired dog. The house was L-shaped, with our general living quarters in the long arm of the L, which ran parallel and conveniently close to the corresponding portion of our grandparent's house. The short arm of the L was formed by a room unusually large for a private residence and must have been used by our more wealthy predecessors as a sort of ballroom, but was soon dubbed our "playroom." This, with its correspondingly large bedroom above, was to be closed off during the cold months because of the difficulty of keeping it properly heated. I give it special mention, however, because it played an important role in our lives as long as we lived on Kennedy Lane.

Our house was situated well back from the Lane, leaving us a large unobstructed yard that could be used for a number of games and sports. Though not large enough for a regular baseball diamond, it afforded plenty of space for an adaptation of the game then popular among young boys. My older brother, Tom, a large, handsome boy and a good natural athlete, that summer proved also to be a good organizer of juvenile sports. Our home, and particularly our yard, became a favorite gathering place for our numerous cousins and friends. When the number was large enough to choose sides, or when a game could be arranged with a neighboring team, the players would go across the front lawn and through the gate in the fence that separated our property from the field in front, which was large enough to stake out a diamond and have a regular game. This field belonged to the owner of our house. It was not included in my father's contract of lease, but by arrangement with the owner, my grandfather used it for the grazing of the two horses he kept for his dairy business. Generally, however, it was available for our use.

In the evenings as darkness came on, after we had had a full active day and my mother had completed all her household chores, it was pleasant to sit with her on the front porch and watch the moon in its various phases rising in the east and the fireflies flickering in the lilac, althea, and orange blossom bushes, of which there was a great profusion along the north and south edges of the front lawn and terraces. As the time to go to bed approached, she would often have us join her in song. Her favorites were the Stephen Foster melodies, many of which were then popular. She also could intersperse these with some of the more recent songs, but these for the most part seemed less attractive than the older ones. Generally, we ended by singing one of gone from about eight in the morning to rather late in the evening. As I look back through the mists of so many years, the days of that summer seem like one long, happy dream, filled with sunshine and merriment.

During the latter part of August, my mother organized our first all-day outing at Tolchester Beach. Since it was the first, it entailed rather elaborate preparations, from the acquiring of proper bathing apparel down to the packing of the very last item of food. We would be gone from about eight in the morning to rather late in the evening. As was usual in almost everything we did, cousins and intimate friends joined us for the excursion. One of my mother's maiden sisters agreed to go along, assuming responsibility of preparing part of the food and helping her to supervise the whole group.

We all agreed to meet on the "Louise," an old paddle-wheel steamer, at her berth at the Light Street wharf. The first arrivals staked out for us a desirable location on the top deck from which we would be able to see everything worthwhile.

The most memorable part of the whole excursion was, for me, my first sight of and trip through the harbor. As the "Louise" backed out of her berth, the Light Street wharf appeared dirty and shabby, but once she had turned around, all sorts of interesting things began to come into view. There on the right was the steeple of the Star of the Sea Church with the lantern which at night served as a beacon for boats coming into the harbor; then the green slopes of Federal Hill where the Union troops of occupation had been encamped all during the Civil War. On the left, Fells Point at the foot of Broadway, part of the original town of Baltimore; then the Canton wharf, and near it St. Brigid's Church, where Father Lawrence McNamara was then pastor; then on the right again, the Fairfield Shipyard, where several large vessels were in drydock, having their hulls scraped, repaired, and painted; then, in Curtis Bay, the freight terminal of the B & O and Western Maryland Railroads, with its great piles of coal from the mines of Western Maryland and West Virginia, and its grain elevators where wheat and corn from the Midwest were stored. Next came Fort McHenry; then Sparrows Point, whose steel mills, already busy, were to play so important a role in the city's subsequent history; finally, the Seven-foot Knoll Lighthouse almost immediately ahead, a sign that we were now leaving the harbor and in a few moments would be out in the open Chesapeake. It had taken the better part of an hour to wend our way through the harbor, and it would take the better part of another hour to reach our destination.

The two fastest runners from among the older boys had been instructed to take their places close to the exit from the boat and, as soon as the gangplank was put in place, they raced down the pier and up over the hill to occupy one of the desirable pavilions immediately overlooking the water. Soon the rest of us came trudging along with the hampers of food and the extra articles of clothing.

One surprise of the day was that my mother discovered that my older brother was already able to swim. Sheepishly he admitted that under the pretense of going to play baseball he had actually gone off to a swimming hole in Herring Run with some of his friends. Naturally, he was duly reprimanded. In any event, Tom had learned to swim and had introduced a tradition into the family that all of us would follow—not, however, at the Herring Run swimming hole.

My father joined us, coming down on the afternoon boat. He took me with the older boys over to the amusement park. We had a ride on the merry-go-round and the roller coaster, and he gave the older boys a chance to compete at the shooting gallery. We walked over to look at the little lake and decided that next year a row on the lake might be more fun than a visit to the amusement park. Then we returned to the pavilion for our supper of fried chicken, rolls, and layer cake. When supper was over and things cleared away, it was time to take the boat back home. It was getting dark by the time we passed the Seven-foot Knoll and the lantern was already flashing. The harbor was far more picturesque at night with the lights flickering on two shorelines and reflected on the smooth surface of the harbor. It had been a long, pleasant day. Tolchester from then on became an annual event of late August.

With summer drawing to a close, Tom began to sigh regretfully that the time to return to school was fast approaching. Mary began to prepare excitedly for the beginning of her school days. And I began to wonder: why couldn't I become a schoolboy like Tom.

Early in September, school reopened. My brother had been promoted to the third grade; my sister entered the first at St. Ann's parochial school. Each evening at supper, she would tell us the interesting things that happened in school. "Sister Cantia said this"—"Sister Cantia said that." After she had finished whatever homework she had to do, she began to teach me some of the things she had learned: the alphabet, the basic Arabic numerals, to scribble my name, to read a few simple words from her primer.

That year the cold weather came early—this was to be the winter of the Great Fire. With the coming of the cold weather, my younger brother turned sickly and peevish and seemed to require most of my mother's attention. Moreover, we all began to see our wonderful Kennedy Lane home in a different light. It was spacious indeed, but it was also cold and drafty. I grew lonely and restless, and I began to torment my parents with the question, "Why can't I go to school, too?" No doubt my sister had kept her teacher informed about the wonderful progress her younger brother was making under *her* instruction and how he wanted to come to school. Sister Cantia finally told her that if she would bring me to school a certain Saturday morning as Christmas approached, she would talk to me. The result of that meeting was that Sister said that if I would come in when school reopened after the Christmas holidays, she would give me a trial in the first grade. I was elated, for I felt that I was as good as accepted!

Meanwhile, my parents, sensing, no doubt, that our spirits seemed to be drooping, decided to make something very special of Christmas. My father purchased a large Christmas tree which he erected in the big cold playroom. On the Sunday before Christmas, after breakfast, he lit a fire in the Latrobe stove of that room and invited us to help him trim the tree. There we found laid out in boxes the ornaments he had used in trimming our former small trees, in addition to some new ones he had purchased for this occasion. Using a stepladder, he attached the star to the top of the tree and proceeded to place the proper ornaments on the upper branches; then we were allowed to help him trim the lower branches. Over it all, my father cast a generous sprinkling of tinsel. After the tree had been trimmed, large sheets of brown paper were placed around its foot, and on these was spread a thick layer of dark green sawdust to create the semblance of a garden. In this we placed a motley collection of animals gathered over the past few years: lions and tigers; a den of foxes; a small flock of sheep; a couple of giraffes—all dwelling in peaceful harmony as if it were Paradise itself. The chief ornament of the garden was, of course, the crib, with Mary and Joseph bending over it, the shepherds already kneeling and holding out their offering of lambs. Over the crib, suspended from the lower branches, hovered cardboard angels. In the distance, outside the garden, the three Wise Men on camels made their way reverently toward the crib. Only the tiny Infant was missing. He would not be placed in the manger until Christmas morning. The Kings would not arrive at the crib until we had reached the last day of the Christmas celebration. It was all very crude, I am sure, but to us it was wonderful! We were gazing across the centuries with our imagination, and perhaps with the beginnings of faith.

The next day, my father gave each of us a dollar to add to the little hoard that we had saved during the year for our Christmas shopping. My older brother went off alone; he would walk downtown and back to save the carfare. My mother left our younger brother next door at my grandmother's. He would be content to stay there—particularly with my grandfather, whose name he bore. The year before, my grandfather had been stricken with partial paralysis, causing him to turn his dairy business over to his son John. He was a lovable old man, and my brother, everybody admitted, was a lovable little boy. From the beginning they had developed a strong fondness for each other. About two years later I remember my grandfather calling for him frequently during Lent to take him off to the 8:30 Mass. On one such occasion, Dan asked a question that was never forgotten in the family and was often used to tease him: "Mama, shall I wash my hands or wear my gloves?" (As a matter of fact, washing one's hands could be an unpleasant task on cold days unless there was a kettle of hot water on the stove to add to the cold water in the basin.)

My mother, sister, and I had an enjoyable day doing our Christmas shopping. We took the Greenmount Avenue trolley at Twenty-second Street, got off at Fayette and Howard, and walked north to Lexington Street, in the very heart of the shopping district. Even more enjoyable than the making of our purchases was looking at the fantastic Christmas displays in the windows of all the large department stores, and some of the decorations within. Instead of having regular lunch, my mother took us to the Lexington Market, where we sat at a counter and had doughnuts and hot chocolate, itself a special treat. It was a memorable day, my first real visit to downtown Baltimore.

On Christmas Eve, after returning from work, my father made a fire in the playroom. That night, after the stove was fully aglow, he would carefully bank the fire with coal. We were sent off early to bed, since we were to rise in time to go to the five o'clock Mass, which some years before had been substituted for the traditional Midnight Mass, because certain overly enthusiastic merry-makers had caused disturbances in several parishes. After we had retired, our parents laid out our presents at the foot of the Christmas tree just outside the garden.

Next morning we left for church early enough to claim the seats we were to occupy, four in my grandfather's pew next to the north wall of the church, and two in my parents' own pew just a little to the rear. Mass started promptly. My parents thought that the music was magnificent, as well they might, for it must have been one of the Haydn Masses, which I was to learn later were especially beloved by our pastor, Father (later Monsignor) Cornelius F. Thomas. It was he who read as the Gospel narrative the Nativity story from St. Luke, and delivered the sermon, appropriately short for that early hour. My parents received Holy Communion—even my brother Tom was not

considered old enough to receive, for those were the days before the
liturgical reforms of Pope Pius X (hence also the Haydn music). After
Mass, we paused outside the church to exchange greetings with friends
and acquaintances, then off to home.

After laying aside our overcoats and caps, we were taken into the
playroom, now pleasantly warm, to discover our presents. There was a
sweater for each of us, probably made by our grandmother Schofield,
who was expert with the knitting needles, articles of clothing needed
by us, and as a special gift from our parents: a bicycle for my older
brother, roller skates for my sister and me, and a toy fire engine for
our younger brother. We were all delighted, particularly my older
brother with his bicycle. There was a big hug and kiss for our parents—
even from Tom, who thought he was getting too big for that kind of
nonsense. He took his bicycle out into the yard immediately to try it out.
My sister and I had to try out our skates on the front porch. Meanwhile,
my mother had been preparing breakfast—beefsteak with a special to-
mato gravy beloved by my father; all the buckwheat pancakes we
could eat; coffee for our parents, made with the roasted beans freshly
ground in my mother's coffee mill; milk for the rest of us. We were told
to eat well for there would be only one other meal that day, turkey
dinner in the late afternoon. In the late morning, my father took my
sister and me to visit first our grandparents Shehan and then our
grandmother Schofield, carrying our little gifts for each of them. A
gentle spirit of Christmas pervaded both homes, but not nearly the
intensified spirit that existed in our own. There was no tree in either;
but prominently displayed on the living room mantels, each had its
crib and its decorations of holly. There were cookies and milk and small
gifts from our maiden aunts. We felt no need for lunch when we returned home. There were plenty of activities to occupy us until we
would be called to dinner.

The roast turkey was our first, amply filled with stuffing, with
plenty of giblet gravy (another of my father's favorites) to pour over it.
The gravy even made the mashed potatoes and the sprouts (kale) taste
good. For dessert, we had mince pie for the first time, for before
Christmas my mother had made up a batch of mincemeat from her
mother's recipe. My older brother surprised us all, to say the least, by
casually remarking that it would have been nice to have some ice
cream on top of the pie. My father casually replied that he would have
to be content this time with a second piece of pie. Tom's voracious
appetite never ceased to astound us. But after all, the poor boy was

growing fast, and he had had a hard day, riding his bicycle all around the neighborhood to show it off to his best friends.

The Christmas season came to an end for us on New Year's night, with a family party to which our grandparents, uncles and aunts and close cousins were invited. The Three Kings that day had arrived prematurely at the crib. By evening, all three Latrobe stoves were pleasantly aglow. My mother had baked up large batches of sugar cookies and gingersnaps. My father had churned up a full can of home-made ice cream with cream from my grandfather's dairy. Several aunts providentially (by previous agreement, I am certain) arrived with layer cakes covered with chocolate and coconut icing.

My brother, with the help of two cousins of about the same age, even arranged some informal entertainment. He himself was develop-ing a good voice and did not hesitate to lead off with one of his favorite songs. Then he introduced his performing "stars" with mock solemnity. Each of us had his or her little piece to recite or song to sing. The hit of the show, however, was a scene of the previous summer which had actually taken place between my little brother and an older cousin, Mary Agnes Schofield, which they were induced to repeat. As she took up her teasing of him, going further than she had done previously, he did not need to simulate his former rage; with tears in his eyes, he yelled out at the top of his voice: "You spit-devil!" It ended with her taking him in her arms, kissing him, and assuring him that she was only fooling, to the clapping of hands and laughter of the whole audience. The "show" ended with the singing of "O Come All Ye Faithful," led by our fourteen-year-old cousin, Elsie Schofield, in her much-admired soprano voice. After the show came the refresh-ments—the ice cream, cookies, and layer cakes. All agreed that it was a truly enjoyable evening. Christmas tradition had been established at 3 Kennedy Lane.

After the first of the year, when St. Ann's School reopened, Sister Cantia received me kindly. She assigned me to the desk which from then on would be mine, and gave me the primer I would be using and a small pink-covered beginner's catechism. The first few days were ex-citing, I suppose because different, but I soon realized that school did not measure up to all my expectations. For one thing, I had missed the systematic introduction that the teacher had given the rest of her class, and I found it difficult to make up that loss. Again, while the teacher was as kind and attentive as she could be, she had, as I remember it, some fifty other children under her care, and so she had little time to give to my particular needs and problems. I also found that there was no advantage in being the youngest and one of the smaller members of the class. However, the die had been cast, I had no intention of quitting. Moreover, my father, who seemed to be as anxious as I that I should not fail once I had started, proved to be a good teacher and helped me a great deal in the evenings.

I must say that I found nothing very exciting or stimulating in the lower grades of school. Our teachers, School Sisters of Notre Dame, were all good, well prepared, and dedicated to their work. As far as I can remember there was not a poor or even mediocre teacher in the group. I went forward quietly, doing fairly well and making satisfactory progress, at least according to my report cards. But that is about all I can say concerning my first six years of schooling. I suppose there is not much a teacher can do unless the student is prepared to receive what he or she gives. The truth is that I did not seem prepared to derive any special profit from what my teachers were prepared to offer.

Then, quite suddenly, when I entered the seventh grade, a great change occurred within me. I suppose the basic cause was that my mind had been slowly, almost imperceptibly, maturing. But, also, a new and excellent teacher, Sister Euthemia, appeared on the scene. She was to be my teacher for the next two years. During that school year, moreover, another important event took place that had a deepening effect on my religious thought and life. As I passed my twelfth birthday I became eligible to receive the Holy Eucharist for the first time. This was the spring of 1910, and Pope Pius X's decree on the early reception of the Eucharist was not to appear until August. I was therefore a member of the last group that was required by Church discipline to wait until after my twelfth birthday. In preparation for that, I chose as my confessor and spiritual guide Father Bart Hartwell, who also was to have a real influence on me then and in the future. I liked all the priests at St. Ann's, but I found it easier to confide in him, particularly concerning the problems of adolescence which I had begun to experience. One thing coincidental to my preparation for my First Communion was the importance my father attached to that coming event. He decided that I should have a tailor-made suit for the occasion. From one of his customers he obtained a beautiful piece of blue cloth of fine texture with barely perceptible tiny green stripes. He took me to a German tailor whose shop was in the vicinity of St. James Church and gave precise instructions as to how he wanted the suit made. He also accompanied me when I went for the "fitting." I was deeply impressed that he should take all this time and trouble. Not only did it reveal to me the importance he attached to the coming event, but also and especially his deep interest in and affection for me. Everybody at home agreed that it was a beautiful suit. I preserved it with a care I have never given to any other clothes, and I was to wear it again, carefully cleaned and pressed, when I was confirmed by Cardinal Gibbons the following year. It may seem strange that I should remember so well the clothes I wore at my First Communion and at Confirmation. But that suit had a special sign value: I was no longer a child. I was now a young man with the rights and responsibilities of my newly acquired status.

The change that had taken place in me began to bear fruit after I had entered the eighth grade. In the late fall, the committee promoting Catholic participation in the celebration of Maryland Day (March 25) issued notice of a competition open to all members of the eighth grade of Catholic schools throughout the archdiocese. When Sister Euthemia saw that I was really interested, she pointed out the material I would need and actually borrowed for me from our pastor a copy of Monsignor (later Bishop) William T. Russell's *Maryland, Land of Sanctuary.* So I went to work on my essay, and it was chosen to represent St. Ann's School in the contest. Later, on Maryland Day, it was announced that I had won the second prize for my paper.

Later that spring, an even more significant thing happened. Father Hartwell had once asked me if I had ever thought that I would like to become a priest. I answered that I had thought of it vaguely, but I knew that my father, with five others to educate, could not afford to send me to St. Charles College, the preparatory seminary for the archdiocese. Some time later, Father sent for me and said there was to be an examination for entrance into St. Charles, and a scholarship was being offered to the one judged best qualified. He thought I ought to take the exam, and I assured him I would be glad to do so. When I told my father of this conversation, his reaction was one of flat opposition; I was too young to think seriously of a vocation to the priesthood, much less to enter a junior preparatory seminary. "Finish your high school and then we can talk about what you're going to do." A few evenings later, our pastor paid us one of his rare visits—to speak with my father and mother. He told them bluntly, as was his way, that he thought they ought to let me take the examination. Still my father strongly objected; I was simply too young to be making any such decision. "But," replied the pastor, "he would not be making any decision about his future life.

Why not let him take the examination, see how he does? If he passes the examination and if, as hardly seems likely, he should win the scholarship, it will be up to you and your wife to decide whether or not he accepts it." My father gave in, but reluctantly.

So, on a Saturday morning I went to St. Mary's Seminary for what turned out to be a rather pleasant ordeal. The instructions I had received from Sister Euthemia were an excellent preparation for the test. I had little difficulty with the written part. The oral questioning was conducted by Fathers Berkeley and Jepson, both Sulpician priests. They seemed chiefly interested in my ability to construe English sentences, in the books I had read and what I thought of them, in my general knowledge of American and English literature, and in why I thought I would like to study for the priesthood. I spent the greater part of the morning at the seminary, which seemed rather stark and bleak, with young men in cassocks passing from time to time through the long bare corridor. I left a little before noon, not knowing how I was to be rated by the examiners. Within ten days, however, my pastor was notified that not only had I passed the examination, but I was also being offered a full six-year scholarship, four years of high school and two years of college. My pastor wrote to inform my parents, but he assured them that the decision was left entirely to them, with no attempt to influence them one way or the other.

Quite naturally I was elated at the outcome. I definitely wanted to accept the scholarship, although I believe I tried to express my desire in a way that would not offend my parents. My mother, I felt, was silently on my side, feeling that it was an opportunity that I ought not to miss, but she later made it clear that the final decision was up to my father. He again expressed grave doubts, for he still felt I was too young to leave home and go to a boarding school where all my associates would be older boys—and in this I later felt that he was fundamentally right.

All other arguments, however, were against him. He was still burdened with a debt from the purchase of a large three-story red brick house on Twenty-fifth Street which he had acquired just before we moved from Kennedy Lane and which seemed to suit our purposes admirably. The price he had judged was quite satisfactory, but the necessary renovations were costly—a new central hot water heating system; the entire interior to be repainted, and the construction of new front steps of Beaver Dam marble to bring our house into general conformity with the rest of the neighborhood. My sister's high school education also had to be provided for. Besides, if he were to send me to one of the three private Catholic high schools (Calvert Hall, Loyola, or Mount St. Joseph), he could hardly do less for my three younger brothers, who would be coming along at two-year intervals.

What finally brought him to consent was, I believe, the fact that my older brother, who by his own choice had entered public high school, announced his intention of quitting school at the end of the term and going to work. Because he failed to qualify for the "A" course he wanted to take, he had gradually lost all interest in school. He felt that he was simply wasting his time. My father was not only displeased, he was hurt. He wanted him at least to finish high school. But my brother was now fully grown. Moreover, on his own initiative, through the help of my father's first cousin who held a responsible position in the Federal Bureau of Printing and Engraving in Washington, he had the promise of a job in which, with hard work, he could advance. He was intelligent and had a mind of his own. He gave all indications of being a thoroughly good young man and doubtless, under a direct command from my father, would have obeyed. But on further thought, my father concluded that under the circumstances it was better not to insist. At the same time, he did not want this sort of thing to happen to me. So in the end he decided to consent to the kind of education on which, by this time, I had set my heart.

One thing further happened which I believe reconciled him to this decision. On graduating from St. Ann's School, I was awarded the Kennedy medal for general excellence, an honor which he himself had won a generation before.

With my graduation from St. Ann's, my school days in Baltimore city had come to an end.

2. Student for the Priesthood

ON A WINDY ST. PATRICK'S DAY—March 17, 1911—St. Charles College, Ellicott City, Maryland, was destroyed by fire. The impressive old building had been erected on a property fifteen miles west of Baltimore, a gift to the Sulpician priests from Charles Carroll of Carrollton, then the last surviving signer of the Declaration of Independence. This property had been part of the Carroll estate and was close to Doughoregan Manor, the Carroll family mansion. The few brick walls of the college left partially standing were so heavily damaged that they could not possibly be used as a part of any new structure. The only available place the college could reopen and resume its program without a ruinous delay was an estate called Cloud Cap, near Catonsville, which was owned by the Archdiocese of Baltimore and used by the St. Vincent dePaul Society as a summer camp for poor children of Baltimore.

On the Cloud Cap property there were already two spacious buildings that could be used by the college. The larger of these had a rough-hewn stone basement and first story, which could accommodate the dining room and kitchen, and a superstructure of wood covered with brown shingles, which could serve as the main college dormitory and infirmary. The other building, an oblong frame structure painted gray, that looked as if it might have been one of those country boarding houses used by many Baltimore families to escape the heat of the city, was soon to house the president's office and provide living quarters for a number of faculty members. To the front-left of the refectory, two large frame buildings were rapidly erected: the first, a combination study hall and chapel, with the sanctuary separated from the main body by a draw curtain; the second of these, two stories high, contained a recreation center, a bookstore, and additional dormitory space. On a hilltop about a quarter of a mile away was another large summer boarding house which could serve as temporary quarters of the Junior

Division. With almost heroic effort, these buildings were readied so that the college reopened, resumed its program, and completed the school year before the end of June. Such was the new St. Charles to which I was to go early in September 1911.

On the day set for the opening of the college, my father was away on one of his periodic business trips; I was accompanied, therefore, by my mother. Taking the Catonsville trolley on Greenmount Avenue, we rode through the downtown section of the city and then west on Frederick Avenue until we reached Paradise Avenue, east of Catonsville. There we alighted and began to walk to the college, I carrying the brown leather suitcase my father had bought for me, my mother carrying the umbrella the catalogue had advised students to bring. That umbrella was to be the source of embarrassment to me for a long time. It was a perfectly good umbrella, but it had a strange-looking short curved handle of highly polished light yellow wood, the like of which I have never seen. My father probably knew precisely what he was doing when he purchased it, for rarely, if ever, did any student borrow it; it never became confused with other umbrellas; if it disappeared for a day or two, it was sure to turn up—in fact, it seemed almost impossible to lose it. It was still mine when I graduated, in practically as good condition as on the day I entered.

Together my mother and I walked leisurely south on Paradise Avenue, turned into Maiden Choice Lane, and within about a half hour came to a large black-and-white sign on the left side of the road notifying us that this was St. Charles College. Passing through the modest entrance, we saw rising before us the large dining room and dormitory building—no architectural masterpiece, indeed, but pleasant looking among the trees in the bright September sunshine. On arrival, we were referred immediately to the office of the president, where Father F. X. McKenny welcomed me to the college and saw that I was properly registered. He told me that my spiritual director would be Father Philip Blanc, whom I should try to meet later that day. After a few words of encouragement to me, Father McKenny told my mother she might accompany me to the Junior Division, where I would be living and studying. This was reached by a dirt road that ran south from the college property, through the midst of Zaiser's dairy farm. The main building of the Junior Division was a large yellow frame structure which contained the chapel and sacristy, dormitory space for about forty students, and bedroom-studies for three resident faculty members, including the prefect. On the rear had been added a two-story appendage containing a large lavatory with about twenty washbasins with cold running water, a trunk room, a furnace room, and on the second story three private bathrooms with old-fashioned bathtubs. Near the south side of the main building another large frame building had been erected—a combination of study-hall and recreation center, heated by a large cast-iron pot-bellied stove.

After having seen the quarters where I would be living, my mother decided to start for home. As I accompanied her to the Frederick Avenue car-stop, we had very little to say to each other. Words just would not come. We both seemed to realize that things would never be the same again; I believe we feared to give expression to our feelings. When at last the streetcar approached, she bade me a fond farewell and assured me that she and my father would come to see me every visiting Sunday. She entered the car and was gone.

As I walked back to the college, I was lonely and thoughtful. What would the future be like without the constant support of my parents and the company of my brothers and sister? It was then I began to realize how much a part of my life they were. I had been away from my family only once in my life, on a visit to my cousins, but that week had been filled with pleasant activity and I knew that at the end of it I was to go back home. It was entirely different now.

When I arrived at the Junior Division, almost immediately the prefect, Father Bioletti, sensing, I suppose, my thoughts and feelings, introduced me to a group of "old-comers" who were standing around chatting about their vacation experiences and planning a baseball game for the afternoon. One in particular stands out from that group in my memory. He was a large, handsome, dark-complexioned boy with a shock of dark brown hair falling over his right brow. The reason I can still see him so clearly is that he was soon to become my closest friend and was to remain so throughout life. This was Joe Ells of Ellicott City. He was almost two years older than I.

It was near lunchtime now, so I walked over to the refectory with Ells. He asked about my family and home, and told me about his parents and older sister and his home. Did I play baseball? Not very well, but I would like to learn. After lunch, when Ells and his friends, having gathered up some of the newcomers, went off to play ball, I went over to the Senior Division to see if I could meet Father Blanc. I found him in his room in the gray faculty building. He, too, received me kindly and inquired about my family, my previous education, my main interests. It was evident, however, that he had read the report my pastor had sent in. He assured me that he was pleased to take me under his direction, and appointed a time for me to come each week to make my confession and receive any direction he thought I would need. I left, pleased that I would be under his direction and convinced that I would find it easy to tell him whatever was on my mind.

Classes began next morning. Father Blanc was to be our teacher of Latin: Ernest Theroux, a layman, was our teacher of English and history; Father Bioletti, our teacher of French; Father George Harrig, algebra; Father Marcetteau, our teacher of chant as well as choir director for the whole college. In each class we were given the textbook we were to use: Bennett's *Latin Grammar*, John Bannister Tabb's *Bone Rules of the English Language*, an American history whose author I do not remember, Fraser and Squair's *French Grammar*, Wentworth's *Beginner's Algebra*, and a book of plain chant which we would use in our weekly class and at High Mass and Vespers on Sundays. All of our teachers seemed experienced and let us know what was expected of us. It was evident that we would get down to serious study with no delay. These first days were filled with a kind of excitement and expectation: there seemed to be little time left for thinking of home.

After a few days, however, the homesickness, the first pangs of which I had felt during that lonely walk back to the college after leaving my mother, returned with increasing acuteness. It came to a climax during one afternoon study-period. As I gazed off into space in a sort of daydream, memories and yearnings came flooding into my mind and heart. Finally I lost control. I put my head into the crook of my arm on my desk and sobbed silently. In a moment, at the thought of the scene I would make of myself as the crybaby of the whole community, I was able to regain control. As I took my handkerchief from my pocket, I stealthily gazed around. Fortunately, I was in the last row; nobody seemed to have observed. But the keen eye of Father Bioletti, who was supervising the period from his raised desk up front, had not missed what had happened. After a few moments, he sought some occasion to go to the recreation center in the rear. As he passed by my desk, he cast an inquiring glance at me as if to say: Are you all right?

Ells, whose desk was also in the rear row, two places from mine, had also noticed. During recreation period he took me for a walk on the grounds. When we were beyond the hearing of other students, he said: "You're homesick, aren't you?" "Yes," I replied. "I'm awfully homesick," and I almost sobbed again. "Well," he said, "don't be discouraged and don't give up." Then he told me that the previous year he had gone through the same thing. He had actually telephoned to his father to come up (he was then at the old college) and get him. His father had driven from Ellicott City with his horse and buggy. After listening to Joe's troubles for a while, he said to him, "I haven't come up to take you home. I've come to tell you to stay and finish out the year. You made the choice. I've paid your tuition; now I am telling you to stay and do your best. If at the end of the year you still feel you want to leave, you know that we shall be glad to have you back home with us. But now I'm advising you to stay." So he did stay, and he came to like the college. He did well in his studies, and helped to develop one of the best baseball teams the Junior Division ever had. "So," he repeated, "don't be discouraged and don't quit. You'll be all right. Things will get brighter." Then he made an observation that, even then, I thought unusual coming from a boy less than two years my senior. "I see you don't receive Communion every morning." "I have never received more than once a week," I said. "Why don't you talk to Father Blanc and ask him what he thinks about your receiving every day?"

That evening after supper I did seek out Father Blanc and asked him about daily Communion. Without any hesitation, he approved. I then told him how homesick I had been. He walked up and down with me for a while in front of the refectory and gave me much the same kind of encouragement I had received from Ells. Then he said abruptly: "Run along now. The Juniors must be together at recreation by this time and they will be wondering where you are." I did run along as rapidly as I could, and with a heart much lighter than it had been for some days. I was not really alone. There were people here who did care. It was like a burst of sunshine after a gloomy day.

Another thing of some importance happened to me during the first weeks at St. Charles. That year warm weather lasted well into October. Father Bioletti arranged for us to use the swimming pool of nearby Mount St. Joseph's College on holiday mornings when it was not being used by their own students. During the previous summer while on a two-week family outing at a cottage near Tolchester Beach, I had made a crude beginning in the "art" of swimming. At least I had taught myself to "dog paddle," as we called it, and had learned how easy it was to stay afloat simply by turning over on my back and gently moving my hands and feet. Observing my clumsy efforts, Ells undertook to teach me how to strike out with my arms and to coordinate with them a rhythmic kick of legs and feet. Eventually I developed a certain skill which was to make swimming a lifelong source of healthful and relaxing enjoyment.

Thus, during my first year at St. Charles a strong friendship developed between Ells and myself. Late in that school year, Father Bioletti summoned each of us separately. Just what he said to Ells I never learned; but he told me, gently but firmly, that he thought I was seeing too much of Ells and that I ought to associate more generally with the members of the community. I was somewhat mystified, but Ells knew what he meant: he was referring to the danger of what the Rule euphemistically called "particular friendships." Later on, comparing notes, we both thought his admonition was due to what the students at times referred to as "Frenchy" suspicions. In any event, we both took the admonition in good part and followed his instructions. At the end of that school year, Ells was transferred to the Senior Division. From then on our ways diverged widely. Our genuine friendship, however, was to endure throughout life without a single misunderstanding of any importance. Many years later, when he died after a long painful illness, I was asked by my successor, Archbishop Borders, to give the homily at his funeral Mass.

One other thing which was to have a lasting effect on me was the fact that, largely due to Father Bioletti, I developed a strong liking for some of the best of English and American literature. One afternoon in early winter, noticing me searching rather perplexedly through our still meager library, he handed me Sir Walter Scott's *Ivanhoe*, saying:"Why don't you try this?" I became engrossed in it, and when I had finished and went to return it, he said: "Why not try James Fennimore Cooper's *Deerslayer*?" Again I found his suggestion most apt, and for many months following, long holiday afternoons that otherwise would have been almost unbearably boring were filled with interest by the *Leather Stocking Tales*. When I had finished them, I turned to Scott's *Waverley* novels. I must admit that I tired of them long before I reached their end. Meanwhile, Father Blanc came to my rescue by lending me Dickens' *David Copperfield*. Besides being my director and teacher, Father Blanc was the librarian in charge of assembling and cataloging the new library which was to replace that destroyed by fire. From him I had no difficulty obtaining any of the standard works of English literature. Soon I was to find Dickens far more interesting than either Scott or Cooper, and before I had finished the course at St. Charles, I had read practically all of Dickens and also the major works of Thackeray:

Henry Esmond, The Virginians, Vanity Fair, Colonel Newcomb, and *Pendennis.* Thus, during that first year at St. Charles I developed an interest and a habit that ultimately brought me a wide acquaintance with much of English and American literature.

Moreover, our instructors in English at St. Charles were excellent: after Ernest Theroux, Father Edward Coyle in the third year of high school, relieved during his illness by Father George Gleason; Father McKenny in the fourth; Father Harrigan in the first year of college (class of poetry); and Father Coyle again in the second (class of rhetoric). Under their guidance I became as familiar as one could reasonably expect of a person of such years with the more important works of the principal English authors—not only the fiction I have mentioned, but also the major plays of Shakespeare and some of his sonnets; some of the epic poetry of Milton and the didactic poetry of Pope; a number of the shorter poems of Dryden; much of the lyrical poetry of Wordsworth, Coleridge, Shelley and Keats; as well as the works of Tennyson and Browning. Boswell's *Life of Samuel Johnson,* a copy of which I had received as a prize, had given me a taste for biography. From the more modern era, I came to know Chesterton's *Heretics, Orthodoxy,* and a number of his essays; some of the writings of Belloc; and the slender volume of poetry and prose of Francis Thompson. I don't wish to give the impression that I covered this wide field thoroughly, but only that St. Charles offered the opportunity and the encouragement to read rather extensively, and my own inclinations led me, as far as I was able, to take advantage of this opportunity. I should add that at no time in the course was the importance of the practice in English composition to be overlooked.

While the college was developing its physical plant, facilities for sports were quite limited. For a time, Ells attempted to get me interested in baseball, but, until a slight defect in my vision was discovered and corrected, my batting average was miserable and my ability in handball was no better. By the time I had glasses, my contemporaries who were athletically inclined had advanced so far ahead of me that there was little incentive to try to catch up with them. Meanwhile, the college did acquire some good tennis courts and its own outdoor swimming pool, and of these I made good use.

During my years at St. Charles, judging from the report cards my father carefully preserved, I made satisfactory progress in my studies. The course we followed differed from that found in the standard high school and junior college by the special emphasis placed on the study of Latin and Greek. From the beginning of the first year of high school, one hour each day was devoted to Latin. From the second year on through the rest of the course, four periods a week were given to Greek, English, mathematics, and to French or German: two periods to history, one hour each to elocution, Christian Doctrine, and plain chant. The seriousness with which Latin and Greek were treated can be judged by the texts that were required reading during the six-year course, once the basic groundwork had been laid. In Latin, these texts included Caesar's *Gallic Wars;* Vergil's *Eclogues, Georgics,* and *Aeneid;* Cicero's *Orations;* Horace's *Ars Poetica* and *Odes;* Quintilian's *Institutio Oratoria.*

Much the same pattern was followed in the course of Greek. Basics one year, followed by Xenophon's *Anabasis,* sections of Homer's *Iliad* and *Odyssey,* a play of one of the three great dramatists: Aeschylus, Sophocles, or Euripides (our class read Sophocles' *Antigone*), Demosthenes' *On the Crown,* and one or more of the *Philippics.* The other courses were comparable to those of other high schools and junior colleges of the time. According to present-day standards, the main defect was the lack of courses in physics and chemistry; but these were deliberately deferred to the first two years of the major seminary.

When I returned from summer vacation in September 1912 to begin my second year, I found that two significant changes had occurred in the Junior Division. Father Bioletti had been transferred to the Sulpician Preparatory Seminary at Menlo Park, California, and Joe Ells had gone over to the Senior Division. Father Eugene Saupin, who had been at St. Charles for some years since first coming from France, had been appointed to take Father Bioletti's place. He was a rather stern-looking man who, while seeming to lack Father Bioletti's warmth of personality and leadership in the development of athletic activities, brought other qualities of equal or greater value. I was to spend the next two years under him in the Junior Division. Many years later, at the time of his death, I wrote of him: "Of all the men with whom I had close acquaintance, he came closest to the ideal of what I might call perfect justice."

That second year brought to St. Charles several students for the Archdiocese of Baltimore who were to prove lifelong friends. First among these was John Russell, of approximately my own age, nephew of Monsignor William T. Russell, who was then pastor of St. Patrick's parish in Washington, D.C., and later Bishop of Charleston, S.C. John's family lived in St. Elizabeth's parish in Baltimore, near Patterson

Park, on whose frozen lake he had developed an extraordinary skill in skating. He was a young man of exceptional intelligence and a combination of qualities that destined him to become an outstanding member of the student body. With him came his friend Jerome Sebastian, from St. Patrick's parish in Washington. He was somewhat older than John and I, and far enough advanced in his studies to enter the third year high at St. Charles. He was assigned to the Senior Division, where he promptly struck up a friendship with Joe Ells. Here, too, I should mention Joseph Kennedy of Washington, who although several years our elder and therefore assigned to the Senior Division, yet was in our class and became one of that lasting circle of priest-friends. Finally, to this group two years later was to be added Mitchell Cartwright, whose brother John was then studying for the priesthood at the North American College in Rome, and Joseph M. Nelligan, the son of one of Baltimore's most influential citizens, John J. Nelligan, president and later chairman of the board of the Safe Deposit and Trust Company. Slight of build and pleasant of countenance, Joe stood out in any group by reason of his flaming red hair. After ordination, and following an apprenticeship as associate to Bishop McNamara in the parish of St. Gabriel in Washington, Joe was to return to Baltimore and become chancellor to Archbishop Curley, a capacity in which he served for many years. Washington, Joe was to return to Baltimore and become Chancellor to both the Archbishop and his fellow priests, in the history of the archdiocese. This circle of friends formed at St. Charles, by no means consciously exclusive, was to prove lasting in every sense of the word.

The 1913-14 school year was made memorable by the addition to the teaching staff of two young American priests of exceptional character and ability: Eugene Harrigan of Baltimore and George Gleason of Providence. Both had completed their course of theology at St. Mary's Seminary, had been ordained priests of the Archdiocese of Baltimore, and had immediately become candidates for the Society of St. Sulpice with the intention of fulfilling their year of Solitude (preparation for entrance into the Society) at the House of St. Austin in Washington. I had met Eugene Harrigan shortly after his ordination and during the summer had become friendly with him. About the middle of November he wrote to me that his friend George Gleason had become sick and his doctor recommended that he leave Solitude, temporarily at least, for the period of recuperation. He was to come to St. Charles and Father Harrigan suggested that I meet him at the streetcar stop and accompany him to the college, which he had never visited. Perhaps I can best describe my first impression of Father Gleason by quoting from a sermon I was invited to preach many years later at his funeral Mass.

One cold November afternoon in the year 1913, a young priest . . . alighted from the trolley car at Frederick Road and Paradise Avenue, and was met by a student of the fourth Latin Class of the College . . .

What the student saw was a young man of medium height who, by reason of his slim, erect figure, gave the impression of being somewhat taller than he actually was. In appearance he was extremely youthful, very fair, handsome in a rather delicate sort of way, with a pleasant open smile and with a charm that put one immediately at ease and invited friendly conversation.

Later in the talk, I was to speak of one of his main characteristics: his outstanding musical talent:

That talent had made itself manifest early in his life. By the time he entered St. Charles College he was already an accomplished pianist. During the years that followed he made himself a highly proficient organist. Throughout the years of both college and seminary training, he placed that talent generously at the disposal of the two institutions and their students. The willingness with which he gave of himself and his talent combined with the charm of his personality and the gift of accurate, humorous but kindly mimicry, made him a most welcome member of any group.

The young man's musical talent was greatly enhanced by the possession of a voice of singular beauty. In volume it was not a great voice. But it was unerringly true; it had a bell-like clarity and a haunting purity of tone that made it an almost perfect instrument for the rendition of the Church's chant. To hear him, during the many years that voice retained all the freshness of youth, sing any of the great chants of the Church was indeed an experience to be treasured.

In view of this special talent it was not strange that within weeks of his arrival at St. Charles, Father Gleason was asked to take over the direction of the college choir—then badly in need of such supervision. Within the years that followed (that is between 1914 and 1918) I think it is no exaggeration to say that he

developed one of the finest choirs any junior seminary ever possessed and one few major seminaries could equal.

The following spring (1914) Father Eugene Harrigan, for a similar
reason, followed in the footsteps of his friend George Gleason and came
to join the community of St. Charles, and it was there that both he and
Father Gleason finished out their year of Solitude and at the end were
received into the Society of St. Sulpice. Like that of Gleason, the
appointment of Harrigan was supposed to be only temporary. Soon,
however, under the circumstances of the times, the value of the service
that each was able to render to the college was so great that neither
was ever to leave for another assignment until his death—Harrigan,
August 7, 1936; and Gleason, November 9, 1955.

The circumstance that made the coming of both Gleason and Harrigan of such great importance was the sudden outbreak of World War I
and its almost immediate effect on the college. The Archduke of Austria,
Francis Ferdinand, was murdered at Sarajevo in Serbia June 28, 1914.
Serbia failed to meet the demands of Austria for satisfactory repara-
tions. Just one month later, therefore, Austria-Hungary declared war
on Serbia, who appealed for help to her ally, Russia. Immediately,
Russia ordered the mobilization of part of her army on her southern
border; Germany came to the rescue of her ally, Austria, and declared
war on Russia and, by implication, on France, Russia's ally, July 29.
Germany demanded free passage of her forces through Belgium to
deliver a quick blow against her traditional enemy, France. Belgium
refused and, as a nation, rose to repulse the German invasion. This
brought England, guarantor of the sacredness of Belgium's borders,
immediately into the war. Thus within the incredible span of nine days
(July 28-August 6, 1914), the principal nations of Europe were em-
broiled in World War I.

Although the Belgian resistance won precious time for France and
England, yet from the beginning her gallant efforts were no match for
the efficient and ruthless German war machine. The plight of France
was immediately evident as the main object at which that machine
was directed. A call to the colors for regular military service went out
from Paris and eventually reached every French Sulpician priest who
was within the age group affected. Father Blanc's call came before the
end of the 1914 vacation. He answered it promptly and was soon on his

way to France. Father Saupin's call (by reason of his age, I suppose) did not come until the following year.

After Father Blanc's departure, I had chosen to make my weekly confession to Father Saupin and to look to him for such spiritual guidance as I should need. The relationship I had developed toward Father Saupin during the two years I spent under him as the prefect of the Junior Division can perhaps be best illustrated by an incident which occurred between the time of the departure of Father Blanc and his own later summons to serve France during that time of growing peril. The intellectual tone under the shadow of the war as it went on and on everywhere became more and more somber. I myself seemed to become more pensive and introspective. One evening during this period, as I knelt in prayer at Benediction of the Blessed Sacrament, I seemed to grow oblivious of all around me and to see into the very depths of my soul and heart, and what I saw there I did not like—all the sins, the weakness, and failure of my past life. A sea of doubt arose within me—doubt not about the Church or any of her fundamental teaching, or even about our way of life at the college, but doubt about myself. What right had I to presume that I was called to the priesthood? What right had I to suppose that I could make any worthwhile contribution to the Church's life, or even that I would always remain faithful? Each step that I had taken in life, each serious choice I had made, had seemed the right—almost the inevitable—one at the time, but had I done anything more than to take the line of least resistance? In the light I now saw myself, did I have the courage to leave and seek another objective in life?

Such were the questions that surged through my mind all during Benediction and the night prayers that followed. As I lingered on in the chapel, the conviction grew in me that I must go to Father Saupin and try to tell him all that was in my mind. He listened to me patiently, and after putting a few probing questions to me, took his purple stole from the top drawer of his desk, bade me kneel and renew my sorrow for all that was sinful in what I had told him, imposed upon me a suitable penance, and pronounced over me the words of absolution. Then, while I was still on my knees he gave me a most fatherly talk about the mercy of God and the sinfulness in the hearts of all of us, reminded me how the ignorance of youth diminishes what now seems our guilt, and told me that I should never go back over the past this way again, that if

I were to continue to do so, a scrupulosity that would be really harmful could easily develop. The important thing now, he assured me, was to develop a real trust in the goodness and mercy of God and in the grace won for us by Our Lord and Savior. When I left him that evening I felt that I was a changed person. As I glanced at my watch on my way to the study hall, I realized how short was the time the whole episode had taken. Yet, even now that experience seems to me one of the most important things that happened to me during the six years I spent as a student at St. Charles; and the image of Father Saupin still stands out in my mind as one of Christlike compassion.

Not long after that, Father Saupin received his call to France, and, like Father Blanc, he promptly responded. Life at the college, for me at least, was bound to be very different without these two men to whom I owed so much. Their teaching positions, however, were competently filled by the two priests already mentioned, George Gleason and Eugene Harrigan. The year Father Saupin left was, moreover, marked by the arrival of a third young American Sulpician priest, Father Benjamin J. Tennelly, a native of Kentucky. With Father Saupin, our Latin class (then in the fourth high) was reading Vergil's *Aeneid*. Tennelly was able to take up where Saupin left off. He proved particularly encouraging to me in my Latin studies. He was to continue at St. Charles only the few remaining months of that school year, but during those months he went out of his way to encourage me. I was to meet him again as Professor of Sacred Scripture (which was his real forte) in St. Mary's Seminary, Baltimore.

It was characteristic of such teachers as Blanc, Harrigan, Gleason, and Tennelly that they were men of broad learning and culture with special teaching ability who, to meet a special need, were able to go beyond the particular field they had made their own. Thus, with the spirit of cooperation that existed among the faculty, I believe it safe to say that in a number of subjects the instruction was excellent and in no subject, as far as I can remember, could it be called less than satisfactory.

Lest I seem to picture the faculty of St. Charles as perfect and myself as a sort of model student, let me tell of one difficulty I had with one member of the faculty which came from a most unexpected source. In our fourth year of high school, we had as our professor of elocution and public speaking Father Eugene Harrigan. As our first assignment he gave us the option of delivering a speech of our own composition, or some other that we should choose. Since I could think of no subject on which I wished to give a speech to my classmates, I chose from our Jenkins *Handbook* an excerpt from Edmund Burke's *Reflections on the French Revolution* which I thought I might present fairly well. It was the scene in which the author contrasts Marie Antoinette as he saw her in the year 1774, "shining like the morning star," and the tragic scene of her trial and death in 1794.

The piece was fairly short, within our time limit. Its progression of thought and its cadenced language made it easy to memorize and to deliver. When I finished my presentation, there was a moment of ominous silence. Everyone, including myself, seemed to sense that something must be wrong. Then without saying a word about the manner of delivery, Father Harrigan launched into what I can only describe as a diatribe against Burke and his political philosophy in general and in particular his defense of the *ancien régime* and hatred of the French Revolution. I could interpret his remarks only as a most severe criticism of my poor judgment in having chosen a selection from such a work of such an author. My defense, if I had been given an opportunity to make one, would have been that I was not delivering a speech on political philosophy but a simple piece of elocutionary rhetoric. If the piece were as bad as he claimed, it should never have appeared in a handbook prepared by the revered first President of St. Charles. It seemed to me that Harrigan was being as one-sided in his attack on Burke as he claimed that Burke was one-sided in his hatred of the French Revolution.

The incident in itself was no doubt trivial, and it finds a place here only because it came at a particularly important time in my personal development. It proved painful, not merely because it caused me deep embarrassment, but also because it seemed to bring to an end, temporarily at least, a friendship which I had treasured and had hoped would be lasting. At the end of his criticism of Burke Father Harrigan simply passed on to the next student whose turn it was to speak. Later, I feared that any word or gesture on my part would have been met with a fresh rebuff and perhaps another outburst of sarcasm.

In spite of my rebuff and my altered relationship to Father Harrigan, life went on quite normally for me. The following spring, Michael Cuddy, a classmate, and I entered the college tennis tournament and advanced as far as the semifinals before we were eliminated. I enjoyed the use of the swimming pool when the weather was favorable. During most of the rest of my free time I pursued my interest in English literature.

What clouded my final year at St. Charles (1916-1917) was the apprehension that the United States would ultimately be drawn into the war. Ever since the sinking of the *Lusitania* (1915) with the loss of life to American passengers, the possibility that the United States would be drawn into the conflict had grown. Provocation after provocation had been given when submarines interfered with American shipping. President Wilson, however, had persistently clung to the hope that he, as head of a neutral power, could bring about peace between the warring nations. With the announcement by Germany of her intention to make unrestricted use of the submarine, the President decided that he could wait no longer. Finally came the United States' declaration of war on April 6, 1917. In his war message, Wilson made abundantly clear that the step was inevitable. All effective opposition to such a move had by this time virtually disappeared.

Although the official entrance of the United States into the titanic struggle seemed to raise the morale of the Allied Powers, the outcome was by no means certain, owing to the increasing effectiveness of the German submarines. During the months while the United States was making ready her troops, military equipment, and transport vessels, both the convoy system and listening devices for the discovery of the presence of submarines had been perfected. In the fall, when hundreds of thousands of American troops and their necessary equipment and supporting materiel began to pour safely into the Atlantic and Mediterranean ports of France, it became evident that the fate of Germany was sealed and the victory of the Allies was assured, although the Armistice was not to be signed until November 11, 1918.

Meanwhile, under the war clouds of 1917 and wartime uncertainty, my course at St. Charles was coming to an end with apparent calm on the surface. My relationship to Father Harrigan seems to have improved considerably, since at the time of the declaration of war I remember being one of a group of the seniors who were invited to meet with him in his study to discuss the President's war message. He had high praise for both its contents and its style.

The college catalogue of 1917 shows that three members of the class were graduated with highest honors (*summa cum laude*): Robert Navin of Cleveland, John Twiss of Boston, and Lawrence Shehan of Baltimore. I was chosen to deliver one of the two student speeches—that in English. John Twiss delivered the Latin speech. The address to the graduates was given by Bishop William T. Russell, who had become Bishop of Charleston the previous March.

Looking back over my six years at St. Charles, I would say that they were years of real happiness. I finished my course with few regrets, none of them serious. Even my unexpected painful brush with Father Harrigan and his subsequent coolness served to teach me lessons that I needed to learn at that time. When we had occasion to meet later in life, he always treated me with courtesy and even friendliness. From all other members of the faculty I had received only support and encouragement. I always felt a deep affection for the college. Years later, it was with real sorrow that I saw the changed condition of the times make necessary first the closing down of its high school department and the ultimate abandonment of the college.

During the whole six years that I spent there, I never wavered in the least in my desire to become a priest, nor did I see in those students who became my lifelong priestly friends any such wavering. As a consequence, when I finished my course there, I simply took for granted that I would continue my studies in the major seminary in Baltimore and that the day would come when I would be ordained a priest of the Holy Roman Catholic Church.

When I entered St. Mary's Seminary, in September 1917, it was the oldest and also the largest seminary in the United States, and one of the most venerable Catholic institutions in the country. I enrolled in the Department of Philosophy, of which Father Joseph Bruneau, S.S., was the director. A native of France, he was ordained in the Society of St. Sulpice there in 1889. After serving in other seminary positions in the United States, he was named director of the House of Philosophy at St. Mary's in 1909 and remained there until the time of his death in 1933. He had the reputation of being a very strict but just disciplinarian and may be said to have been respected and feared, rather than loved, by most students. Personally, however, I was to find that beneath an austere appearance he had a warm and generous heart and many other lovable qualities. He was my spiritual director during my three years at St. Mary's Seminary, and later, when I returned from Rome after completing my studies, I asked him to serve me in the same capacity.

During my first year, our main subject of study was philosophy (logic and ontology). Next in importance was science (chemistry and physics). In Scripture, our professor followed very closely the textbook, *Introduction to the Old Testament*, by Father Francis Gigot. At

the time we might have been said to be still living under the shadow
of Modernism. Some thought that Gigot was too far advanced, but
Father Daniel Duffy found no difficulty with him. In fact, my criticism
of Father Duffy would have been that he adhered too closely to Gigot's
text and accepted everything he said without any question. Our professor of Church history followed no text but spoke from notes. However, we had available to us several sets of *The Catholic Encyclopedia*
and I came to own one of my own, a gift from Father Bruneau. Generally speaking, this was adequate for answering important questions
in Church History.

Our main professors in both philosophy and in science during the
first year were certainly competent, though in my opinion not very
interesting and certainly not inspiring. This may have been due as
much to the subject matter as to the personal qualities of the persons
involved. I was interested in philosophy, as I was also in the sciences,
but from the beginning I felt that I had not the type of mind that would
enable me to become an outstanding philosopher. Again, because of
my intention of becoming a priest, I would not expect to become deeply
involved in the physical sciences, although I recognized their importance to any well-educated person in the modern world.

A strange and disturbing thing happened to me during my first
term at the seminary. I should begin by saying that St. Mary's had a
rather strict and conservative system of marking examinations. If
one scored nine out of a possible ten points, he had done well, and anything beyond that was considered extraordinary. In our first inter-term
examination I scored the unusually high mark of 9.5. The list of students' scores was never posted, but was given to faculty members in
order that the student might obtain his marks from his spiritual
director, who thus would have the occasion to discuss with him his
attitude toward studies and the reasons behind his success or failure. In
any event my unusually high mark was soon known to all the faculty
and later to many of the students. In consequence, some who should
have known better began to treat me as a sort of boy-wonder in the field
of philosophy. Shortly thereafter our professor requested that I tutor a
very earnest young man who had done poorly. This I willingly undertook, but the whole thing was embarrassing to me because, as I have
said, deep within myself I realized that I did not have the type of
speculative mind to live up to that reputation.

Soon, however, things more than righted themselves. In the mid-
term exam, which of course was far more important and for which I

had prepared very carefully, we were given a rather general topic to treat. If one were to stick close to the mere outline of our text, the subject could have been treated in a half-hour or less, or one could spend the full two hours that our schedule allotted to the examination. The professor had given us no indication that he wanted a brief treatment—although common sense should have told me that with fifty or more papers to correct, he would prefer as brief a treatment as was possible. In any event, common sense seems to have deserted me. I chose to give the fuller treatment for which I felt prepared; in fact I wrote an essay of some six or seven pages. For my trouble I received what I considered the paltry score of 7. It was the lowest mark I had received in any examination since I had entered St. Charles. The first intimation that something had gone wrong came when my name was not read out among those on the list of the first third, which was always done at the beginning of the first "spiritual reading" after the examination had been corrected and scored. I, who had earlier led the pack, had fallen far back among the herd. The full impact came later that evening when I learned my actual mark from Father Bruneau. It came as a severe shock to me. How could I have achieved 9.5 in my first exam and fallen down so badly in the second, much more important one, for which I had prepared so carefully? Had I missed the point? Had I overprepared? It took me some time to recover and regain my equilibrium. Father Bruneau helped me a great deal, first by his sympathetic understanding, but also by making me realize that this was not the end but only the beginning of my career and that, if I persevered there would be plenty of time to make up for the seeming failure. But, most of all, he helped me to realize that far more serious than the failure was the way I was reacting to my disappointment. In any event, I regained my equanimity and in fact finished the school year quite well.

Some time later, in Wilfred Ward's *Life of John Henry Newman,* I read how young Newman, as a student at Oxford, prepared most assiduously for an examination on which he pinned high hope, and how, when he went up to take it, he failed miserably. My own experience, it seemed to me, enabled me to know somewhat how Newman must have felt. But I was no Newman, and I am afraid I did not learn my lesson so well as he did his.

That whole first year in the seminary stands out in my mind as a rather dreary time. It was not only failure in the examination that caused my spirit of depression, although it certainly helped to add to my gloom; but my health seemed to decline. I had already begun to lose weight, perhaps because the quality of the seminary fare was affected by wartime rationing; I had trouble getting the proper amount of sleep, and over us all there hung the pall of World War I, which went on and on, now for the fourth year.

Shortly after the mid-year break Father Bruneau induced me to consult the seminary physician. Within a comparatively short time, by following the doctor's directions, my loss of weight ceased, and by means of a prescription he gave me I returned to normal sleep. As I remember, it was one of the then rather recently discovered barbiturates—"Amytal" is the name that lingers in my memory. He assured me that it was harmless and nonhabit-forming, and that apparently was the opinion of doctors at that time. Within the next few years, however, members of the medical profession changed their minds on the subject. As a result of further research they decided that barbiturates are habit-forming and their use has been carefully restricted. In any event Amytal helped to bring me through a difficult period of my life. Nevertheless, the school year 1917-1918 stays with me as a less-than-happy memory.

Far different was the year that followed, due principally to the two professors who were the dominant influence during that time: Father Jules Baisnée and Father Arsene Boyer. Both were French, as their names indicate. Father Boyer had come to this country shortly after the French government enacted the 1904 law motivated by unfriendliness toward the Church, particularly Catholic religious orders and societies. The priests of the Society of St. Sulpice must have felt the effects of the legislation immediately, for at that time a number of French Sulpicians came to the United States—much to the advantage of St. Mary's Seminary and St. Charles College in Baltimore, Dunwoodie Seminary in New York, and Brighton Seminary in Boston, all of which the Sulpicians had administered since the late years of the nineteenth century. When I came to know Father Boyer as my professor of biology he was already an old man. His mind had remained active and keen. He had the reputation of an excellent teacher and a scientist of recognized distinction. It was said that he had made one or more authenticated botanical discoveries which officially bear his name. He was also a truly lovable character whose very presence was a valued asset of the seminary community.

Father Jules Baisnée, a much younger man, had come to the United States in 1907. He was thoroughly grounded in Scholastic philosophy, particularly as it had been adapted to the conditions of the day under the influence of Cardinal Mercier and Pope Leo XIII, and he was deeply convinced of its truth and value. He had also read widely in modern philosophy and was familiar with the literature that stemmed from the so-called Enlightenment of Voltaire, Rousseau, Diderot, and the Encyclopedist, as well as with the positions of Comte and his many followers, the schools of Hegel and Kant, and the modern materialistic atheism of which Marx was the leading exponent. At the time he was teaching us he had a particular interest in the American pragmatist William James, and also in Darwin, and his theory of evolution. His broad interest in modern philosophy had not weakened in the least his firm commitment to Scholastic philosophy as adapted and applied to modern conditions. His classes were always lively and relevant. He also had a deep concern for students who showed themselves to be genuinely interested in philosophy. For them he conducted afternoon seminars, during which he could go deeper into contemporary Scholasticism and treat other modern philosophies in more detail.

The progress that I felt I made under the influence of Father Baisnée did much to offset the discouragement I had experienced during my first year. Furthermore, in November 1918, World War I ended, and the joy that filled this country over that event seemed to brighten our entire surroundings. I remember that year as a happy and successful one. As we completed the term and I prepared to enter the School of Theology, I felt that I was advancing in a rather straight line toward my goal, the priesthood.

After the end of that school year, Father Baisnée invited me, together with a mutual friend, Eugene Kraemer, to join him in a rather prolonged visit to Camp St. Mary. The camp, established and conducted by a small group of seminary professors, was beautifully situated on Long Lake in the Adirondack Mountains. We found the water still too cold for swimming, so we decided to take a canoe trip. Going to the west end of the lake, we entered the Racquet River and hence to Racquet Lake; thence on into beautiful Blue Mountain Lake. The trip, as I recall, took four full days, and at night we camped out in the open.

Later, since the weather continued to be fair, we decided on a second trip. This time we made our way to the east end of the lake, entered the upper reaches of the Racquet River, portaged about half a mile around the rapids, and came finally to the Saranac Lakes. When we reached the town of Saranac, we visited a Sulpician priest, Father Burke, who was recuperating at a sanatorium conducted by the Sisters of Mercy. The Sisters were most hospitable, invited us to take dinner with Father Burke, who was ambulatory by that time, and to spend the night in their comfortable lounging chairs on their spacious porch. The next day we took a bus over to Lake Placid, where we visited my uncle, formerly manager of the Belvedere Hotel in Baltimore. After recuperating at Saranac from a bout with tuberculosis, he had taken the position of manager of Lake Placid Inn. When he learned that we were on our way to climb White Face Mountain, which rose from the shore of Lake Placid, he had a fine box lunch prepared for us. The climb was not difficult; the trail was well blazed and offered no particular hazards. We ate our luncheon on the spacious flat rock formation at the top and then stretched out for a rest in the warm, pleasant sunshine. Though the climb had not been strenuous, it was an exhilirating experience.

That summer I must have reached the peak of my physical strength. One afternoon in early August, when the water had become pleasantly warm, Kraemer and I decided to swim across Long Lake—the distance of about a half mile. A fellow camper offered to accompany us in a rowboat and to pick us up on the opposite shore. On reaching our destination, Kraemer and I decided to turn around and swim back. We both made it safely, but I must admit that I was truly tired at the end. It was the farthest I ever swam—in fact, the only distance-swim I ever attempted.

In September, on returning to St. Mary's Seminary I began the first year of the four-year course of theology. I was delighted to learn that I was to have Father Blanc, my old friend and director at St. Charles, as my professor of fundamental moral theology, and Father Tennelly as my Scripture professor in the introduction to the New Testament. In the class on fundamental dogma (apologetics) I found the subject matter most interesting, potentially the most interesting of that year, but the professor, though certainly experienced and competent, was deadly repetitious.

Father Wendell Reilly was to teach us Hebrew. Among all the Sulpicians, he was undoubtedly the best prepared in the field of Scripture. Acknowledged to be an excellent student, he had spent three years at the Ecole Biblique in Jerusalem at the time Père M.-J. Lagrange was the head of that institution and had taken his doctorate in Sacred Scripture at the Pontifical Biblical Institute at Rome. By reason of his dull flat voice, his halting manner of speech, and his inability to maintain good order, he was generally considered a poor teacher for any class that would exceed five or six. One day, for a reason he never expressed, he asked me if I would prefer to take private instruction from him. Naturally, I jumped at the opportunity. Beginning with the first few chapters of Genesis, I would prepare a certain section under his direction. Then on a given evening each week, we would walk up and down together and discuss the section appointed. He did not need a text before him, for he evidently had the whole of Genesis (or at least the more important portions of it) firmly in his memory. This we continued for the rest of that year. Unfortunately, I was never able to derive full profit from the experience, since I have never had the opportunity to pursue higher Scripture studies.

Thus my first year in the School of Theology passed pleasantly, and I believe profitably. In the spring of that year, Father Edward Dyer, director of the school, sent for me and informed me that there was an archdiocesan burse, unused, at the North American College in Rome. If I wished to go and finish my studies there, I was free to do so. I had long desired to be able to complete my studies in Rome and had hoped that when John Cartwright had completed his studies and was ordained there I might be chosen to take his place. Since the war was then in progress, that was beyond possibility. I now readily availed myself of the opportunity. The previous year John Russell and Robert Navin, my classmates at St. Charles, had gone; their presence made me all the more desirous to follow. Before I left Father Dyer's study he informed me that on a certain afternoon I was to go to Cardinal Gibbons' residence on North Charles Street and was to accompany him on his regular afternoon walk. His final words to me were: "Young man, have you read *The Faith of Our Fathers*?" "No," I replied. "I would advise you to do so before you go for that walk." Understandably, I did so.

Thus, on the given afternoon I was at the Cardinal's residence at the appointed time. Within a few minutes he appeared, wearing his customary frock coat and a red skullcap, and carrying a flat beaver clerical hat such as was then worn in Rome. After greeting me, he said: "We shall walk north on Charles Street to Mount Royal Avenue, then we shall go east to Calvert Street and then south. We shall stop at the Shrivers' house. Mrs. Shriver's sister is ill, and I must pay her a visit." Cardinal Gibbons was then in his eighty-sixth year. His mind was clear, his step firm. Everyone who passed us gave him a friendly greeting, and to each he responded with equal friendliness. We chatted about a number of things: about the seminary; about my proposed trip to Rome. Sure enough, at one point he asked: "Young man, have you read *The Faith of Our Fathers*?" "Yes, Your Eminence, I have, and I found it very interesting," I was happy to respond. We made a short visit to the Shriver home, and then we walked back to his residence. I knelt and asked his blessing and kissed his ring. I noted that his slender hand, although now slightly wrinkled, was still as beautiful as it always appears in his pictures. It was the last time I saw him, for he died on Holy Thursday of the following year—March 24, 1921.

3. Rome: North American College, 1920-23

IN THE EARLY SUMMER OF 1920, through the Baltimore agent of the Fabre Line, I made a tentative reservation for the least expensive suitable accommodation on the steamship "Patria," which was scheduled to sail from New York to Naples in mid-September. Meanwhile, Father John Coady, whom I had know since St. Charles days, had decided to go to Rome about the same time to seek a doctorate in Sacred Theology at the Angelicum University. "Could we arrange to travel together?" Yes, I would be very happy to do so if he would accommodate himself to my very restricted budget.

We planned to meet on the boat on the day of departure, since I had to go to Brooklyn two days before sailing for a very important piece of business—my first significant apostolic endeavor since I had started to study for the priesthood. My cousin Elsie Schofield had married William Bolton, the eldest son of a wealthy Brooklyn family. Bill had expressed the desire to become a Catholic, but much to Elsie's distress, had been unable to arrange for instruction at their own large busy parish. Could I be of help? Ed Sweeney, a fellow seminarian from Brooklyn, gave me the name of a Jesuit father he had known from college days who could be counted on to undertake the task. I called on him and was able to make the necessary arrangements. It was a happy choice. Bill became one of the most devoted Catholics of our clan.

On the appointed day, Coady and I met on the boat. He was accompanied by his two sisters, who evidently were not pleased at the humble quarters he and I would be sharing with two other young men we had not yet met. I was accompanied by my father and Elsie. As was always her way in such situations, Elsie brought to a happy end the confrontation (so embarrassing to my father) about the suitability of our accommodations. She had been to Europe in the early summer of the year with the Boltons. With all the authority of a seasoned traveler, she undertook to point out every good feature of our quarters: they were neat, clean, the berths were as comfortable as would be found in any of the staterooms. Besides, we would be spending most of our time on deck, and we would be served the same meals as those who had paid top prices for the best staterooms. All this, she expressed in such a pleasant and jovial way that no one could take offense. Happily, due to Elsie, in the end we all agreed that it was far more sensible for two healthy young men to travel this way than to pay probably twice as much for more luxurious quarters, which I, of course, could not afford.

With the usual tugboat help, our ship was soon moving from its berth out into the ever-impressive New York harbor. Before long we were passing the Statue of Liberty and out into the high seas. It proved to be a very delightful voyage. We had brought along Italian grammars, books of conversational Italian, and some suitable reading. Father Baisnée had given me as a parting gift Newman's *Essay on the Development of Christian Doctrine*. Coady, as soon as he boarded, had the foresight to reserve well-placed deck chairs shielded from the direct sun. With the exception of some thundershowers and rough seas for a couple of days, the passage was calm and enjoyable.

Our two cabinmates were pleasant and interesting. One was the son-in-law of the minister of the Methodist Church on the Via Quirinale in Rome, where he was going to join his wife and little son. Confidentially, he told us that he was an agnostic, ever since his college days (at Harvard, I believe). He loved to engage us in conversation on the foundations of religious belief and to explain why he felt that he could no longer believe. Coady had a good, clear mind and was just as disputatious as the young man. Fresh from Father Baisnée's and Father Brianceau's theology courses, I was glad to join in the conversations and try to measure the effect of the arguments of natural religion and fundamental theology against the foundations of his unbelief. Though we did not succeed in demolishing his convictions, these conversations added a great deal to the interest of the voyage. Coady and I were eager, also, to acquire enough Italian to carry on at least a little conversation with the natives, so we spent a good deal of our time on this attempt. The voyage was by the southern route, with brief stops at the Azores and at Gibralter, and then on to Naples.

It was traditional in Rome at that time for Pontifical Universities to start classes on St. Charles Day, November 4. Since that was almost a month away, Coady and I decided to stay some days in Naples before going on to Rome, and we put up at one of the beach-front-hotels—

the Royal, if I remember correctly. From our waterfront room, the beautiful Bay of Naples, with the city's always busy and interesting harbor, was plainly visible, and rising across the blue waters of the bay was Mount Vesuvius, crowned with its wreath of vapors. The city was fascinating to us both. Not knowing whether we would ever have the opportunity to return, we did the best we could to see everything—the splendid National Museum, the Cathedral, the narrow, winding, and noisy streets. The season of the famous San Carlo Opera House had not yet begun, but the smaller and less famous one (the Politiamo is the name that seems to stick in my memory) was offering *Aida* the day after our arrival. We managed to get two inexpensive seats far up in the gallery and hear the tenor loudly jeered for not reaching Neapolitan standards in the aria "Celeste Aida" and the young soprano who sang the title role just as loudly cheered.

The highlight of our stay in Naples was the trip we made to Sorrento. Starting quite early one morning, we went first to Vesuvius, ascended as far as we could by cable car, climbed on foot to the top of the cone to look down on the boiling lava below. Since it was still well before midday when we had completed the descent, we decided to go on to Pompei to see the uncovered ruins of that ancient city which had been so completely buried by the great volcanic eruption of 79 A.D. Sallust has given as an indication of the deterioration of Roman society the fact that the common people were content with bread and circuses ("panem et circenses"). But perhaps a more significant sign of Roman decadence was evident here in the streets and houses of Pompei, and in the then generally locked Pompeian room of the National Museum of Naples.

Since we were bent on reaching Sorrento before the end of the day we left Pompei in time to have a brief late luncheon at a nearby restaurant and resumed our journey. The summer holiday had ended and the later season was still some time away, so, at the Tramontano Hotel, which had been recommended to us, we were assigned to a large commodious room facing the Gulf of Salerno, almost breathtaking in its beauty in the light of the late afternoon sun. Dinner would not be served until the customary hour of eight o'clock, so we had plenty of time to swim in the clear blue water off the beach owned by the hotel. As we sat on the balcony and watched the sunset, we could see the villa of Marion Crawford, author of *Ave Roma Immortalis!* (a "must" for every student of the North American College) and the then still-popular Saracinesca novels, whose scene is laid mostly in Rome. During those days we visited the sleepy town of

Sorrento and the ancient and picturesque city of Amalfi—built, as it
appeared, on the side of a cliff—with its historic Cathedral of St.
Andrew. After three pleasant days, we returned to Naples by way of
the famous Amalfi Drive. We were now anxious to get on to our destination, so the following day we took the train for Rome.

Rome! Ave Roma Immortalis! "Lo the dome, the vast the wondrous dome—Christ's mighty shrine that soars above His martyr's
tomb." Naturally, the first place I visited was that tomb.

I was happy to find my friends and classmates, Russell and Navin,
at the North American College, then situated on the Via dell'Umilta,
whose location can be best described as at the foot of the Quirinal Hill
within the distance of three American city blocks from the Trevi foun-
tain. After the new students had time to settle down, we had a brief
spiritual retreat, given by the elderly Father Walmsley, S.J. I am sure
the retreat inspired many pious thoughts and good resolves, but the
only words of which I have an accurate memory are those of the
strange jingle the retreat master repeated several times:

> I do not love thee, Dr. Fell,
> The reason why I cannot tell,
> But this alone I know full well,
> I do not love thee, Dr. Fell.

How Father Walmsley worked it into his talks I do not remember,
except perhaps to illustrate our unreasoning reaction to certain persons and things. But I have just now discovered that the little ditty is
to be found, big as life, in that repository of many strange sayings,
Bartlett's Familiar Quotations, where it is attributed to Thomas (Tom)
Brown (1663-1704).

The day following the retreat we began our classes. We attended
the Pontifical University of Propaganda. Our main courses were:
dogmatic theology, under Dr. Borghingini-Duca (later first Papal Nun-
cio to Italy, and Cardinal), whose fluent and clear Latin had a pleasant
musical lilt; moral theology under Dr. Pabin, O.P.; Scripture, Dr.
Ernesto Rufini (later Cardinal Archbishop of Palermo), sometimes
criticized by present-day Scripture scholars as an arch-conservative.
The lecture system was followed in all of these courses, and Latin was
the prescribed language in all classes. In fact, it was probably the only
system possible in such a university where the large classes were
made up of students from many parts of the world. Each of these professors prepared his classes with great care and delivered his lectures

with corresponding clarity. It took time to get used to Pabin's French accent in his pronunciation of Latin, but once we had become attuned to this, he was perhaps the clearest and the easiest to follow of all our professors. All things considered, this turned out to be one of the most enjoyable years, and perhaps the most profitable, in my preparation for the priesthood. It was in the spring of this, my first school year in Rome that we received the sad news that Cardinal Gibbons had died after forty-four years as Archbishop of Baltimore. Many months were to pass before we were to learn of the appointment of his successor. I ended by passing my examination for the baccalaureate and by being awarded a prize in a competitive examination in moral theology. This was reported in the Baltimore press, bringing me letters of congratulations from my former professors and others, as if the prize were much more important than it actually was. Of greater practical significance to me was that it pleased the rector of our college greatly, as he always anxious for the American students to make a good showing at the university. This, however, as we shall see, was partly responsible for bringing about one result which I considered unfortunate.

One of the most serious difficulties I found that first year was that of adjusting to the "camerata" system that then prevailed in all seminaries in Rome. This meant that the entire student body was divided into groups of from eight to twelve, according to the number of rooms available on a given corridor or within a certain section of the house. To preside over each camerata the rector appointed a prefect, a fellow student who, in general, was responsible for the group. Second in command was the beadle, whose regular duty was to decide the route to be followed by the group in traveling to any place, e.g., to and from class and on compulsory walks. My main personal objection was that, since all the other members had spent at least one year at the college and had visited most of the places of interest, they were now inclined to consider a satisfactory walk a visit to the Pincio or to the Borghese Park, where the group was permitted to disperse and meet again at a set time to return to the college. As a consequence, during that year I had very limited opportunities to visit places of real interest to me. The whole system seemed unreasonable in the case of young men in their early twenties, as were all the members of our camerata.

A second difficulty, which had nothing to do with the camerata system, arose from the limited quantity and quality of food generally available to the ordinary people of Rome and hence to the college during the years immediately following World War I. The piece of coarse bread and cup of coffee, which regularly constituted breakfast, hardly seemed adequate sustenance for a morning of two one-hour classes followed by a study period lasting up to the midday meal. Meats generally were of inferior quality and limited mostly to veal, unless recourse was had to the horsemeat then advertised in many butcher shops of Rome but abhorrent to most, if not all, Americans. However, I had been forewarned about the restrictions of the Italian diet at that time and had come prepared to accept them willingly. Nevertheless, as a result of the character of the diet and the rather demanding schedule, I, who had never been robust, began to experience a loss of weight, the full consequences of which were not manifest until the following year.

In the early part of July, in order to escape the intense and humid summer heat of Rome, the entire student body and faculty moved out to the Villa Santa Catharina, pleasantly situated in the Alban Hills near Castel Gandolfo, site of the papal villa. Life there proved to be a welcome contrast to the final month of the school year in the college. The grounds of the Villa were beautiful with their towering umbrella pines, abundant shrubbery, and well-kept winding pathways. There were several fairly good tennis courts with a reasonable opportunity to play. There was also plenty of time for reading. But time soon began to hang heavy on the hands of all of us. Russell and a group of eight or ten compatible classmates and lower classmen soon began to plan a trip to Andermatt in Switzerland, where he had stayed with his uncle and the rector the previous summer. I gladly accepted their invitation to join them. Fortunately, before I had left for Rome, my father's uncle, John J. Kelly, had given a dinner to honor me and had presented me with a purse of at least three hundred dollars in gold—a princely sum in those days—which proved useful during my two summers abroad.

In August we proceeded to carry out our plan. To stretch our funds as far as possible, we traveled third class, stopping at Milan long enough to visit its beautiful cathedral, with its multitude of lacelike spires and the Monastery of St. Ambrose, where the DaVinci fresco of the *Last Supper* is preserved. Thence we went north into Switzerland through the famous St. Gotthard tunnel, as far as Göschenen. There we found a van waiting to take our baggage up the steep four- or five-mile road to our destination. Andermatt then was little more than a village situated in the middle of a fairly spacious plain in the predominantly Catholic canton of Uri. Its most conspicuous feature was the Catholic church and the Franciscan Monastery attached to it. Russell, who had come to know the manager of the Muller Hotel, had arranged a very satisfactory rate for our group, which was to stay for at least two weeks.

The highlight of that time was a walking trip which we began after first taking a horse-drawn van to Gletsch, some ten miles distant. Then we crossed the Rhone glacier with the help of two guides and descended the Reuss River valley on foot to Altorf, where we took the lake steamer to the city of Lucerne. After a two-day stay there, we took the train back to Göschenen. At the end of our Andermatt sojourn we returned by way of Lake Como, stopping at beautiful Bellagio for a few days. We were back at the Villa by mid-September.

Whereas my first year in Rome was the most happy and, hopefully, the most profitable stage of my journey to the priesthood, my second year turned out to be my most difficult and painful one. To begin with, when the list of appointments was read out, I found that I was named prefect of one of the cameratas. If there was ever a job I did not want, it was that one. In the first place, I have never enjoyed the exercise of authority. I found it particularly difficult and even distasteful when it involved fellow students in the way the camerata system required. Yet, once the appointment had been made and announced, I saw no way to get out of it. My camerata was composed of excellent young men, all newcomers except Leo Dubarry of Detroit, who was appointed beadle. He had been at the college for two years and had an excellent knowledge of Rome. Three of the men were from Philadelphia: John Rowan, Ryan Hughes, and Joseph Martin; Abel Caillouet of New Orleans (who was to become Auxiliary Bishop there) Wendell Nold from Houston, Texas (who was to become Bishop of that diocese); Thomas Tobin from Portland, Oregon; John Flynn from Helena, Montana. None of them was ever the source of any difficulty, and with all of them I felt that I became friends—close friends with some. Still, I found such exercise of authority not to my liking.

The position of prefect, moreover, could be time-consuming. For example, one of the members developed dental trouble, which required a series of weekly visits to the dentist. It fell to me to accompany him, to wait while he was being treated, and to return with him. This always happened on holiday mornings, when I could have profitably devoted my time to studies.

Studies themselves were becoming somewhat of a worry. As I had passed my baccalaureate examination and this year all of my close friends in the class would be going up for the licentiate, I desired very much to do so, too. If I neglected to take the examination or if I failed, I would be ineligible for the doctorate the following year and would simply be out of things, separated, as it were, from my friends, waiting for the finish in a desultory sort of way.

To make matters worse, I began to have grave difficulty in sleeping. The depths were reached when I developed acute nervousness, part of which took the form of an annoying scrupulosity. The spiritual director of the college to whom I had gone for direction and help finally must have concluded that my case was hopeless, and said it was his opinion that I should quit and go home. As I sat there for a moment thinking of the past, I said to him that up to the present I had thought I was fulfilling the will of God and had been encouraged every step along the way. In spite of my present difficulties, might it not still be God's will? His reply was: "What do you know about God's will?" I could only answer: "Nothing. I shall do as you have advised."

I went straight to the rector's office, found him in, and told him what had happened. I said I was ready to leave as soon as I could pack my belongings and arrange my transportation. In a very calm voice, he told me to sit down for a few moments and asked if I could tell him just what had happened. I related as completely, but as succinctly as I could, the source of the trouble as I saw it and just what had taken place. At the end he gazed out the window for a moment or two; then facing me he said: "I want you to do two things. I want you first to see the house doctor" (who had the reputation of being one of the best diagnosticians in Rome). "I know he is in the house at the present time, and he can be here in a few moments. Secondly, I would advise you to change your spiritual director and, although you are free to choose whomever you wish, I would recommend Father John O'Rourke" (a Jesuit who came to the college periodically to make himself available for the hearing of Confessions). "I have great confidence in his judgment. Meanwhile, put off your final decision for the present." With that he rang for the portiere and asked him to find the doctor and tell him that the rector would like to see him as soon as he was free. Already I felt a sense of relief. At least I would not have to startle my parents with a cablegram saying that I had quit and I would not have to appear on their doorsill, a man twenty-three years old, penniless, and without any plans for the future.

Soon the doctor appeared. The rector in his fluent Italian told him my story and asked him to give me a physical examination. Since the doctor had his stethoscope and blood pressure gauge with him, he indicated he could examine me immediately. The rector offered his bedroom for the purpose, and there I had the first full physical examination I had received since childhood. He found my pulse, my blood pressure, my lungs quite normal. He used the rector's scale to get my exact weight and observed, what must already have been quite plain to him, that I was seriously underweight. As I dressed, he made a short record of his findings and wrote out two prescriptions. Then he said, handing me the prescriptions, "One of these medicines should help to improve your appetite. The other, taken before going to bed during the next two weeks, should help you to get your normal amount of sleep. This second prescription cannot be refilled. If, after a month, you are still having difficulty with sleep, see me on one of my visits to the college. It is obvious that you ought to have a minor but painful operation. But this is not urgent. I could arrange for it during early July at a *casa di cura* near Lake Nemi not far from your summer villa, if you so wish." I assured him that I did so wish, and that I would make it a point to see him before the summer to report the effect of his prescriptions and find out about arrangements for the operation.

By this time the rector had returned to his office. After receiving the doctor's findings and recommendations, the rector simply added a few words of encouragement and advised me to put off any final decision about the future until we could see what would be the effect of the medicines, the operation, and the change of direction.

Both medicines seemed to have the desired effect. I began to sleep quite soundly; my general health seemed to improve; my acute nervousness and scrupulosity gradually disappeared. I finished the school year quite well. I went up for my licentiate examination and passed without any special difficulty—although, I am sure, not with flying colors. Last, but not least, with the opening of the villa season, my job as prefect came to an end.

Shortly after the beginning of the villa season, I went to the *casa di cura* at Nemi, as I had planned, and had my operation. The rector advised me to remain until the healing process was complete. As I recall, I stayed there about ten days. The casa overlooked the lake, which shone like a brilliant sapphire, delicately set in the dark green of the heavily wooded slopes that rise above it. After I was there about a week, Russell came over to visit me, bringing the news that he, I, and other members of the class had been called to the subdiaconate on August 6, the Feast of the Transfiguration.

At that time, the reception of subdiaconate was the hour of decision, for it was then one took upon himself the obligation of permanent celibacy. As things had happened, I almost felt as if the decision had been taken out of my hands. Here was the call of the Church, issued by my Archbishop. My own inclination and all my training seemed to indicate that I was destined for a celibate life, whether in or out of the priesthood. So I had not the slightest hesitation in accepting the call, trusting that the grace of God would enable me to fulfill the obligation. It was with a sense of deep gratitude and total commitment that I was ordained a subdeacon on that Feast of the Transfiguration.

Something unforeseen happened on the night before our ordination. Russell, myself, and the rest of our class (ten in all, as I recall), having made our retreat at one of the religious houses in Rome, as was customary, stayed at the college that night in order to be on time for the early morning ceremony. Instead of going out to a restaurant that night, the two senior members, who prided themselves on knowing all the college customs, suggested that we take our evening meal together in the college refectory. Since all of the staff were at the Villa, we entrusted our "seniors" to order the meal for us at a nearby restaurant that had a catering service. The meal had been ordered at 8 P.M. but unfortunately the caterer was rather late in completing his preparations. When we were finally summoned, we found the head table, usually reserved for the rector and members of the staff, very nicely arrayed with clean linens and two candelabra, which gave a rather festive appearance to the table.

The meal was indeed quite a plain Roman dinner, but to show that they knew how things should be done, our "seniors" had ordered for dessert Italian spumoni and Asti Spumante. We proceeded leisurely, for we had the whole evening before us, and were just taking our dessert when in walked two American priests in ordinary priestly garb with no signs of special rank upon them. One was tall, robust, handsome, the other slim, gray-haired, and slightly above medium height. They came forward to greet us and no doubt to see what was going on. They turned out to be Archbishop Michael J. Curley, appointed to succeed Cardinal Gibbons only the previous November as Archbishop of Baltimore, and Monsignor Louis Stickney, his secretary. To them, the table with its fine linen cloth, its candelabra, and its two bottles of Asti Spumante at this rather late hour must have appeared as the ending of a sort of banquet—a strange way for ten young men to be preparing to receive subdiaconate the next morning. These were hardly the circumstances Russell and I would have chosen for our first meeting with our newly appointed Archbishop. However, both Curley and Stickney greeted us cordially, and the Archbishop expressed special pleasure at meeting both Russell and myself. Stickney excused himself to go to his room, but the Archbishop accepted the invitation to sit down and have a glass of the Spumante with us. One of our class was a particularly loquacious individual who prided himself on keeping current with all important happenings in the American Church. Soon he undertook to engage the Archbishop in a lively discussion about a much-disputed event that had happened recently in the Church back home. I am sure the Archbishop thought this presumptuous, as did all the rest of us. After a few moments, the Archbishop, pointedly remarking on the lateness of the hour, rose to retire. This was a signal for all of us to rise. Our presiding host asked the Archbishop to say the grace and give his blessing. Our meeting with him ended on a pleasant note.

All would have been well, but the night was hot and sultry. Our loquacious classmate invited two or three of his friends to retire for a breath of fresh air to the roof terrace, where they continued their discussion with unmuted voices. Unfortunately, the terrace was within hearing distance of the rector's quarters, which the Archbishop was occupying. After a few moments, in a loud ringing voice came: "Silence! Go to bed!" there was no mistaking the voice and the authority with which it spoke. Silence immediately reigned, and continued throughout the house for the rest of the night.

The next morning after subdiaconate ordination and breakfast, Russell and I called at the Archbishop's quarters. He greeted us cordially, bade us be seated. He made no reference to the previous evening, but inquired about our health, our progress at the university and our plans for the rest of the summer. On learning that both of us had received our licentiate and hoped during the next year to go on for the doctorate, he warned us against attempting too much and working too hard. He told us about his own experience during his fourth year at the Propaganda; how, from overconcentration on his studies for the doctorate, he had been taken ill and, after early ordination, had to return to Ireland to recuperate fully before going on to the missions in Florida (this was back in 1904, long before the beginning of the Florida boom.) He ended with these unforgettable words: "As your Archbishop, I would rather have a live donkey than a dead doctor."

Before leaving, Russell and I knelt to receive his blessing. We were both glad that we had come together to pay our respects and say good-bye. We were also pleased to be assured that he would attach no great importance to our success or failure to receive the doctorate.

After that Russell left to make final arrangements for his trip, first to Andermatt to meet his uncle, and then on to Oberammergau to see the Passion Play; I, to meet Bill O'Connor and make preparations for our own summer trip which would also end at Oberammergau. O'Connor had been sick the previous summer when Russell and I had been in Switzerland, but we both knew his great desire to see that country before he would return to the States. Russell suggested that we join him at Andermatt. This we agreed to do, but I also wanted to get at least a glimpse of Florence, that most interesting of cities. We decided to stop for a few days in Florence and then go on to Andermatt. When we got to Florence, however, O'Connor seemed as eager to show me the treasures of art he had explored leisurely the previous summer as I was to see them. Consequently, we stayed there longer than we had planned and when we arrived in Andermatt, the Russells were already getting ready to leave. We were now in mid-August; there was a chill in the air; the days were getting perceptibly shorter. However, O'Connor and I did what we had planned to do, and then decided to leave for Munich and Oberammergau.

The regular time of the Passion Play should have been 1920—at the end of the decade. That, the town of Oberammergau decided, was too soon after the ending of World War I to make all the preparation necessary, so the performance was postponed to 1922. Great crowds had been flocking to the little town all summer long. Munich itself was still crowded when we arrived. The earliest performance for which we could obtain tickets was two days away. Meanwhile, since all the hotels were crowded, we found accommodations in a very good pension recommended to us by some fellow students of the college who were leaving just as we were arriving. We spent our time in the excellent Municipal Museum, the Marienkirche, and other places of interest. On the afternoon of the second day, we took the train to Oberammergau to make sure we would be on time for the performance the following morning. We found ourselves assigned to a large double room in a very decent pension. The only meal served there, however, was a continental breakfast. So after washing off the soot acquired in the train ride from Munich, we went out to seek a restaurant for our evening meal. After that we walked through the town, looking through some of the souvenir shops for suitable mementos of our visit and stopping at the parish church. We did not stay long, for we would return in the morning for Mass and Communion. Everywhere we were struck by the courtesy of the people. Many of them spoke English. But O'Connor, while he could not be said to be fluent, had retained enough German from what must have been excellent high school and college courses to carry on a very creditable conversation. Practically all of the people we met were proud to have some part to play or something to contribute, either directly or indirectly, to the production of the Passion Play. So after an interesting and enjoyable evening stroll, we returned to our pension to finish our Office for the day and prepare for bed, leaving word to be awakened in time for the morning Mass. When we arrived at the church, it was already beginning to fill. Most, if not all present, received Communion For this completely Catholic town, the presentation of Our Lord's Passion was apparently a genuine religious experience.

The morning performance began at nine and ran until about noon, when there was a break for lunch. It resumed promptly at two and again ran to the late afternoon. I believe that we both found the whole performance deeply impressive—but somewhat drawn-out by the rather frequent tableaux representing mystical and prophetic scenes from the Old Testament—interruptions necessary, no doubt, to give an opportunity to make shifts of scenery. Anton Lang, who had won fame by his portrayal of the Christus in the 1910 performance, was still in his prime, and he gave a special note of religious realism to the whole production.

On our return trip, we had intended to spend some days in Munich. But even before our trip to Oberammergau we had found Munich a depressing place. The German mark had been steadily decreasing in value since the beginning of the year. In Italy we had become used to the changing value of the lira, but there, after each sudden decline, there had been a rather steady recovery; here the decline was relentless. The result was an increasing pessimism among all classes of people. The day after our return from Oberammergau saw a dramatic plummet in the mark's value. Before we left Munich, it had fallen to about six hundred to the dollar. I shall never forget the distress of the woman who ran our pension. She was the widow of a German

Army officer who had been killed in World War I, and her pension since then had been the main source of her livelihood. So real and so pitiful was her distress that O'Connor and I decided to pay our bill in American money, pool whatever surplus U.S. currency we had with us, retain only what we needed to get back to Rome, give her what we could, and leave by the first train on which we could find accommodations. But how many persons throughout all Germany were experiencing sufferings as great as or even greater than our widowed hostess? What we had seen was but the beginning of the wild inflation and the series of events which finally, some ten years later, were to lead to the triumph of Hitler and the Nazi Party.

Meanwhile, a second distressful event occurred. Even while we were in Oberammergau, O'Connor began to raise sputum that was speckled with blood. When we returned to Munich the tiny specks had turned into a definite streak, and the streak seemed to increase day by day. We were now convinced that he needed expert advice and treatment. The only place we could think of was the *casa di cura* of the Blue Nuns at Fiesole, outside Florence. The previous summer, while the rest of us were in Switzerland, O'Connor had spent many weeks there recuperating from what had been considered a heavy, persistent cold. Now on our way south from Munich, we headed as directly as possible toward the *casa* of the Blue Nuns. From the railroad station in Florence we took a taxicab directly to their door. When the Sisters saw O'Connor, they greeted him like a long-lost son. On hearing his story, however, they showed signs of alarm. They insisted that he go immediately to bed. They had no resident physician, but they knew precisely the doctor who could give him the most effective help and the best advice. If he could not be reached that evening, he would certainly be at the *casa* early the following day. Now they would see that O'Connor would get a hot nourishing meal and a good night's sleep. Meanwhile, I would occupy one of their guest rooms and could join the rest of their guests in the dining room for the evening meal.

The doctor did come the next morning. He gave O'Connor as complete an examination as he could make under the circumstances. If the blood was coming from the lung and if the cause was tuberculosis, as one would have to assume for the present, the only remedy known at that time was complete rest. There was no better place in the world where the patient could be than where he actually was. He, the doctor, would come in daily to observe his condition. Within a few days he could tell whether it would be safe for O'Connor to travel to Rome, where he could then go to the Blue Nuns' hospital for a more thorough examination, a more exact diagnosis, and a plan of treatment. Meanwhile, the patient should simply relax and await developments within the next few days.

Although I remained apprehensive about O'Connor's condition, the days of waiting passed pleasantly enough. I was within easy walking distance of the city of Florence. All I had to do was to go down the hill from the small plateau on which Fiesole was located to be within a short distance of the Arno River. Crossing one of the bridges, I could be within the heart of the city in a very short time. Each morning after Mass and breakfast, I brought myself up to date in the recitation of the Office, visited O'Connor, and then was off to the city, where I would spend most of the day visiting the great galleries and other places of interest. In the late afternoon, I would return in time to have another visit with O'Connor. On the fourth day, the doctor told O'Connor he thought it was safe now to return to Rome. We had planned to go first to the Villa, so that O'Connor could give the rector the written report and recommendations of the doctor. When we reached Rome, we found that there was a strike on and the tram to Castel Gandolfo was not operating. So we decided to go by taxicab directly to the hospital of the Blue Nuns. They readily accepted O'Connor as a patient, and the Sister Superior telephoned to the rector at the Villa, informing him of what had happened. The following day, the Castel Gandolfo trolley line resumed operation and I was able to return to the Villa.

That year of 1922 had been one of increasing unrest throughout Italy. Particularly throughout the industrial north, in cities like Milan, Turin, Genoa, Leghorn (Livorno), Bologna, there had been repeated strikes. Public transportation was often adversely affected, both train service and local streetcars. Especially during the latter part of the summer, for days there would be no tramway service between the Villa Santa Catharina and Rome. The national and local governments seemed powerless to deal with the condition. There was even talk of a national shutdown of industry. In the absence of any strong governmental action, groups of Fascists, made up of veterans of World War I, under the leadership of Benito Mussolini, undertook to break strikes by violence. After their initial success, the Fascist power was said to be substantially subsidized by the wealthy industrialists of the north. In the frequent violent conflicts between the Fascists and the Socialists and other workers' parties, generally it was the better-armed and better-financed Fascists who prevailed. Hence they kept growing in numbers and strength. Because of the increasing unrest, our Villa Santa Catharina at Castel Gandolfo was closed earlier than usual and the entire student body and faculty moved back to the college on the Via dell'Umiltá before the middle of October.

On October 24, at the call of Mussolini, the Fascists met in convention in Naples. There they chose a quadrumvirate who served notice on the king that unless the Fascist party were taken in as part of the government, there would be a takeover of the government itself by force. Meanwhile, Mussolini had gone from the Naples convention to Milan, making known to the king where he could be reached. On October 28, Mussolini gave the word to Fascist groups that they should march on Rome. These met no resistance by the army, and very little from Socialists and other groups.

We were instructed during these critical days to remain within the college and not to venture out on the streets of Rome. On October 28, we heard sporadic rifle shots, and there were reports of violent confrontations in various parts of Rome, but there was no evidence of anything resembling a great revolutionary uprising. A commercial gunsmith's shop in the basement of the college building was broken into, and the hunting rifles that had been there for sale were removed, but that was the only semblance of violence in the area surrounding the college. I remember being in the room occupied temporarily by O'Connor in the late afternoon of the 28th, looking out the window and seeing small groups of black-shirted Fascists calmly walking through the street below with rifles over their shoulders, but that was all.

The next day Mussolini was invited by the king to come to the Quirinal. He arrived by the night train from Milan October 30, and was requested by the king to form a new government. This he did, inviting individuals from other parties, whom he knew he could control, to accept membership in the Cabinet in order to give the semblance of a coalition government, while he reserved for himself the key portfolios. Within the next day or two, the Fascist troops were withdrawn and the regular police took over their ordinary task of preserving public order. From October 30 on, Mussolini was the virtual dictator of Italy, although it was several years before he could so consolidate his position as to be able publicly to assume a title corresponding to the authority he exercised. Everywhere, including the press, he was simply called "Il Duce."

As I remember events of that time, within the early days of November Rome had resumed the appearance of "business as usual." The University of Propaganda reopened its doors on November 4. Soon

it became the boast of the Fascist party that "the trains run on time"—
something that had not been ordinary at least since World War I.

For me personally the one thing of supreme importance in the year
1922 was that on December 23 I was ordained to the priesthood. It was
now more than eleven years since I started on my way as a young boy
just past thirteen. I was now twenty-four years old. As I knelt before
the ordaining prelate and received the imposition of hands and heard
him read over me the words of the form of ordination, I had a firm
belief that I received from him that priesthood which Christ Himself
had instituted at the Last Supper. I have that same belief today, sixty
years later.

The circumstances under which I was ordained were the simplest
imaginable. At seven in the morning, I was accompanied by a young
priest-classmate, Jerry Coyle of Philadelphia, who had been ordained
the previous summer by virtue of the fact that he had served as
sacristan of the college for the past three years. He had offered to
serve me as the customary assistant priest, so he and I went by a
typical old Roman horse and carriage to the Lateran Seminary, where
my ordination was scheduled to take place. Originally, the place of the
ceremony had been announced as the Basilica of St. John Lateran,
but so great was the number of candidates for all orders from first
minor orders up to priesthood that the class had to be divided. Since
my surname comes so far down the alphabet, I was assigned to the
second group, who were to be ordained in the chapel of the Lateran
Seminary. Archbishop Joseph Palica was to be the ordaining prelate.

The ceremony began at 8 a.m.; it did not end until 1 p.m. John
Russell had postponed his ordination until the early summer in order
to be ordained by his uncle. He joined Coyle and myself some time
before that part of the ceremony in which my ordination was to take
place. On the way home, he, Coyle, and I stopped at a restaurant to
have a simple breakfast of toast, eggs, and coffee. During the afternoon some of my friends came to my room to offer congratulations
and to receive my priestly blessing. That was all there was by way of
celebration. I took my regular place in the college dining room that
evening as if nothing had happened. Hopefully, the event had all the
greater spiritual significance by reason of its simplicity. The following
day, Sunday, I offered Mass at one of the side altars of the main
chapel of the college, with Mitchell Cartwright assisting. On Christmas,
after attending the Solemn Midnight Mass, I again offered Mass pri-

vately later in the day at one of the altars of the college chapel. It was only on Tuesday that I was able to offer Mass at the tomb of St. Lawrence and on Wednesday at one of the altars near the tomb of St. Peter.

Little of special moment happened between New Year's Day and the end of the school year. Several months passed before my turn came to offer the Sunday Solemn Mass for the college community. During those months, I continued to attend class at the university, and in my spare time I concentrated as much as possible on preparation for the coming doctoral examination, which came only after the completion of the course in late June or early July. Both John Russell and I passed our exams and received the doctorate of Sacred Theology.

Now that I had been ordained and had received the doctorate, I was free to depart from Rome at any time. However, since John Russell was to be ordained in the college chapel on Sunday, July 8, I decided to remain for the ceremony. Meanwhile, Father George Gleason arrived on his summer vacation. From Rome he intended to go to Lourdes, then to Paris—or, rather, Issy les Molyneaux, headquarters of the Sulpician Fathers, just outside Paris. When he learned that I, too, intended to go to Lourdes and finally to Paris, he asked me if I would care to make the journey north in his company. I was delighted at the invitation.

The day after Russell's ordination, Gleason and I took the train to Genoa, where we stopped for a day or two, since neither of us had ever visited that city. From there we went on as directly as possible to Lourdes. Knowing that Lourdes at that season was likely to be overcrowded, Gleason had made previous arrangements to stay at a large pension conducted by some French Sisters known to the Fathers of St. Sulpice. When they learned that I had made no previous reservation, the Sisters told me that they had vacant a small hall room which left much to be desired, but they would be pleased to have me stay with them, if I so wished. I assured them that I would be glad to accept any accommodation they could make available. The inconvenience caused by the overcrowded condition of Lourdes was more than compensated by the privilege of being part of this great gathering of ardent devotees of Mary, many of whom were suffering from serious afflictions from which they no longer hoped for medical or surgical relief.

Some years ago, Ruth Cranston, a convert to the Church who had become deeply interested in the phenomenon of Lourdes, wrote a book which she entitled *The Miracles of Lourdes*. In it she tells of many medically attested cures whose records she had carefully studied, interviewing as many of the subjects as possible. She has not the slightest doubt about the miraculous character of these cures. Perhaps her most significant chapter, however, is titled "The Real Miracles of Lourdes." Even greater than the cures attested by the *Bureau des Contestations*, she claims, are the deepening of faith, the growing compassion, the increase of courage and patience that have resulted in those who went to the shrine seeking cures but came away, not with what they had originally sought, but with something much better: the spiritual benefits they derived from their experience at Lourdes.

During our stay, we were able to offer Mass at the Grotto, participate in one of the huge candlelight processions, make the outdoor Stations of the Cross, and be present for the daily procession of the Blessed Sacrament. By far the best thing that happened to me that summer was this pilgrimage made in the company of George Gleason.

From Lourdes we took the night train to Paris, and on the advice of Gleason I accompanied him to Issy. He thought that I would find it more satisfactory to stay there rather than to be alone in a Paris hotel. At the Sulpician house we found Father Bruneau from St. Mary's Seminary in Baltimore, who had no hesitation in assuring me that I would be welcome. He introduced me to the superior, and then took me to the *économe*, who assigned me a room which would be mine as long as I cared to stay.

Since I had not yet said Mass and expressed the desire to do so, Father Bruneau summoned a young American seminarian who would take care of me. The young seminarian turned out to be John Ryan of Portland, Maine, whom I had known some eight years before, when he was just beginning his studies at St. Charles College. After serving my Mass, Ryan brought me to the refectory for breakfast. While Gleason and I were eating, he sat down at the table and took a cup of coffee with us. Gleason knew Ryan much better than I did, since he had been his prefect on the Junior Division and his teacher during first-year Latin. When Ryan learned that Gleason was leaving for Solesmes later that day, while I was staying on at Issy, he offered to serve my Mass each day and to act as my guide around Paris. During the past two years he had become fluent in French.

The following day Ryan took me first to see the Cathedral of Notre Dame and then to the nearby Sainte-Chapelle, second only to Chartres in the delicate beauty of its stained-glass windows. For the next several days he was my almost constant companion. Together we visited the Louvre, the Champs Elysées, the Arc de Triomphe, the Eiffel Tower, Sacré Coeur on Montmartre. He knew a number of good but inexpensive restaurants frequented by the American students where we could have luncheon. He had not yet had an occasion to visit Chartres, so on a bright sunny morning we took the train out to see the great cathedral with its magnificent windows. During these days I grew very fond of Ryan, and a real part of my regret at leaving Paris was my parting with this kind, thoughtful and intelligent young man. It is strange that I was never to see him again; yet as I write these lines so many years later, many pleasant memories of him rise before my mind when I recall my first visit to Paris.

In London, as contrasted to Paris, I was alone and lonely. On arrival I went first to the Cathedral of Westminster, where I was greeted graciously and assured I would be welcome there to celebrate daily Mass. I spent most of my time visiting the chief points of interest: Westminster Abbey, St. Paul's Cathedral, the British Museum, the Tower where St. John Fisher and St. Thomas More were imprisoned, near which they were beheaded. In the Tate Museum I was particularly interested in seeing the Turner paintings so much admired by John Ruskin. It was a pleasant few days that I spent there, but I was pleased when at last the time arrived to take the train to Southampton, where I boarded the steamship that brought me back to the United States.

As our ship docked, I found my father and the Boltons waiting for me. What a joy to see them again after an absence of just about three years. My mother did not come because she thought it better to wait at home and prepare an evening dinner for the whole immediate family as a proper way of welcoming me home. Besides the suitcase I carried with me, I had only my trunk—the same I took with me the day I entered St. Charles. It required little time to locate the trunk and have it sent to St. Patrick's Church in Washington, where I had been assigned.

Bill Bolton had made arrangements for a luncheon for four in the main dining room of the Pennsylvania Hotel, and my father had made reservations on the two o'clock train to Baltimore. We had therefore no time to lose. The luncheon was my first American meal in three years, and was a most pleasant occasion for all of us. The Boltons had plenty of news to tell of their four children and some of our mutual New York and Brooklyn friends.

My father and I arrived at the station in ample time and we were soon on our way back home. It must have been about six o'clock when the train pulled into Baltimore. My younger brothers, Brooke and Dan, had jointly purchased an automobile, the first any member of our family ever owned. Dan was waiting for us in the station. Although I believe all of us had a strong family bond, we were a singularly undemonstrative family—and Dan was almost extremely so. But even he seemed to break down on this occasion. For the first and only time in my life he kissed me on the cheek and I kissed him in return. Brooke, seated at the wheel of the car, was much more casual. "Hi, Larry!" he said, extending his right hand, as if it were only last week that he had seen me. "Hi, Brooke," I said in return, trying to express as much joy as I could in that simple greeting.

Within fifteen minutes we were home. How happy my mother was to see me! And Mary, too. I had never seen my father in such a relaxed and joyful mood. He had completed the main work of his life. With my ordination and appointment to St. Patrick's, he had reared and educated his family, and in his eyes all were doing well. Tom who had gone to Philadelphia to live and carry on his business, was already fairly successful and raising a fine family of four children. Mary, since the days of World War I, had held a responsible government position, living most of the time in Baltimore and commuting to Washington each day. So far as I could see, she showed no interest in marriage, or the "religious life." She was devoted to our parents and would remain so as long as they lived—just as she was devoted to her brothers and their families, but above all to the Church. Dan had graduated from dental school more than a year before and was well on his way to building up a flourishing practice in dentistry. Brooke, like Tom, had quit high school before completing the course, but in the world of business he seemed to do well from the beginning. Eventually, he was to become Baltimore District Manager of the Crown Central Petroleum Company, a position he continued to hold to the time of his retirement. My youngest brother, William, having graduated from Calvert Hall, obtained a good position with the C&P Telephone Company and later switched to the B&O Railroad, where he became Manager of Freight Traffic.

That evening I put in a telephone call to Monsignor Thomas, now my pastor, to let him know that I was back home and would come over to Washington to see him the next day. He welcomed me home and thanked me for the call. He knew that after a three-year absence I would be busy about many things in Baltimore, so it would not be necessary for me to come to Washington the next day. Although he would not be able to attend my First Solemn Mass at St. Ann's this coming Sunday, Father John Cartwright would represent him. He advised me, however, to call on Archbishop Curley the next day to let him know that I was back home and ready to start to work. He would expect me at St. Patrick's on the Friday of the following week to take up my duties by hearing Confessions Saturday afternoon and evening. I would be celebrant at the High Mass at eleven on Sunday and either he or Cartwright would preach.

The Solemn Mass in my home parish went well. Since my parents were lifelong members of St. Ann's, they had a host of friends. The church was crowded. Father Mallon, the pastor, preached at the Mass, predicting a bright future for me but appropriately reserving his best remarks for my parents. The reception at our home that evening was a delight to me but particularly to my parents and one of our happiest family celebrations.

4. Years of Joy and Years of Sorrow, 1923-41

ON THE FRIDAY FOLLOWING my First Solemn Mass at St. Ann's, I went to Washington by train and reported to Monsignor Thomas at St. Patrick's rectory at Tenth and G Streets, N.W. He welcomed me and showed me to my quarters on the second floor. These consisted of a small bedroom and bath immediately in back of the suite traditionally reserved for the Archbishop of Baltimore when he visited Washington. In back of the bedroom there was a large common room, furnished with comfortable chairs and containing a pool table, which was frequently used during the period the priests spent together after the midday meal. To the rear of this was my study, which was a converted square solarium or closed-in sunporch, bright and airy in the summer and well heated during the winter. Much of my life was spent in this pleasant room for the next six or seven years.

Among the other members of the household was Father Francis Hurney, who was then about thirty-five years old. He had been ordained shortly before the United States became involved in World War I and had volunteered to serve in the Armed Forces as a Navy chaplain. Another assistant, Father John K. Cartwright, like myself was a native of St. Ann's parish, had graduated from St. Charles, and had been sent to the North American College in Rome in 1911, the year I started my studies for the priesthood. He had remained there until June 1917 when, after his ordination to the priesthood, he received his doctorate in Sacred Theology and returned as assistant in our parish of St. Ann in Baltimore. Three years later, Monsignor Thomas had asked for his appointment to St. Patrick's. I had known him slightly as a boy, but we were to become close friends during the six or seven years we spent together at St. Patrick's. He was extremely intelligent, well read, and an excellent speaker. In addition to his duties in the parish, he served as professor of Church history at the Sulpician Seminary, just opposite The Catholic University. By nature he was witty and gracious. He had a host of friends in Washington. He always had a number of prospective converts under instruction, who generally also became his loyal followers. The final clerical member of the household was Father John Graham, a very intelligent man, then in his fifties, who while residing at St. Patrick's was serving as chaplain to St. Vincent's Orphanage. Each morning an automobile from the institution would call for him in time for him to offer Mass and would bring him back after breakfast.

Mary Hayes, an elderly woman, was housekeeper and had held that position for many years. She was assisted by a younger woman, Julia Martin, who was very devoted to her; an ancient black woman, Lucy, who claimed to have been born in slavery and was an excellent cook; and finally a pleasant young black maid, Mamie Robinson. These took excellent care of us. The rectory was a gray stone building, large in comparison to most rectories of that time, superbly designed and constructed. It was a happy household.

My regular duties at St. Patrick's were to say early Mass in the church, to hear confessions on Saturday afternoons and evenings and again on Wednesday afternoons, and on Sundays to offer one or two Masses according to need and give the homily at each. Moreover, I was henceforth to be the spiritual director of the parish conference of the St. Vincent dePaul Society, which meant that I should attend the weekly meetings and would also try to take care of the spiritual needs of the poor who came and answer emergency calls for material help until the lay members could make the usual home calls and provide for continuing assistance where it was needed. Another of my duties was to give religious instruction to the boys at St. Joseph's Orphanage, then located on H Street between Ninth and Tenth, a mere block away from the rectory.

St. Patrick's was the oldest parish in the city of Washington. For a time, there was a dispute as to whether it or Holy Trinity parish in Georgetown had the right to be called the oldest. But at the time of its founding, Georgetown was a separate village on the edge of the District of Columbia and therefore not a part of the then existing city of Washington; so in that sense at least, St. Patrick's was the oldest. It went back to the foundation of the See of Baltimore, 1789. It was at the very heart of the city, and all of the streetcar lines either passed close by or came within several blocks of the church and rectory. This and the fact that it was the church nearest to the large government office buildings and to the principal downtown stores made St. Patrick's a favorite place for confessions for many of the people of Washington. There were five confessionals in the church. At least four of them were occupied every Saturday afternoon and evening, and often the penitents came in an unbroken stream during the whole time. The fifth confessional was reserved for Monsignor Thomas, already in his sixties, who took his place there when the penitents were particularly numerous. The administration of the Sacrament of Penance was for all of us our single most important and taxing duty. On that first Saturday afternoon I entered the confessional with a great deal of trepidation. I soon learned, however, that the hearing of confessions was not in itself a very difficult duty. Seldom did one come across very perplexing problems. Many penitents needed encouragement and guidance ("counseling," to use the modern word), and some needed consolation. But all of us realized that if we were not ready to give those things, we had no right to be there.

My first year at St. Patrick's passed happily but uneventfully. I was kept reasonably busy, but I had time for some reading. All the members of the household were kind and most considerate. In the spring of 1925, the Holy Year, John Cartwright was asked by James Nolan, the Washington representative of the French Line, to lead a pilgrimage to Rome. Cartwright, having consulted the Superior of the Sulpician Seminary, asked me to substitute for him in his absence as professor of Church history. I was naturally most pleased to have him place such confidence in me. I gladly consented and threw myself heart and soul into the work.

So successful did Cartwright's pilgrimage prove that Nolan decided to organize another in the fall. Doubtlessly on the advice of Cartwright, because I had been so recently in Rome and would be familiar with all the chief places of interest, Nolan asked me to lead the pilgrimage. Archbishop Curley and Monsignor Thomas both consented. The pilgrimage would set sail from New York late in September.

Early in August, however, I was able to get time off between Sundays, so I decided to visit my friend, Father Bill O'Connor, in Liberty, New York. He had recuperated from the tuberculosis he suffered in Italy and was now an assistant at St. Peter's Church. On Monday I went to Baltimore to have dinner with my parents and then take the night train to New York. Monday afternoon my brother Dan suggested that, when he had finished his day's work at the office, we go for a swim in Beaver Dam Quarry near Timonium. After a pleasant and vigorous swim, just as I was getting out of the water I coughed and noticed a streak of blood in my sputum. Except for a slight lingering cough, I had noticed nothing that would indicate anything wrong. Both Dan and I decided that we should not alarm our parents, that I ought to go on to Liberty. The few days of rest and relaxation would probably be good for me.

I took the night train, had a fairly comfortable sleep, said Mass at the Church of St. Francis near the station, made a few purchases for my proposed pilgrimage, and started for Liberty by train in the early afternoon. Bill O'Connor met me at the station, took me to the rectory, and showed me to my room. No sooner had I entered the bathroom to wash up after my dusty train ride than I coughed rather violently and experienced what I can only describe as a massive hemorrhage. Preserving the remnants of the blood in the wash basin, I quickly called O'Connor and showed him what had happened. He said: "Here, get in bed and lie there." He helped me to get undressed and into my pajamas and put me to bed. "Lie still there and don't move. I'll call Dr. Peter Dzworski, the best specialist in Liberty." The doctor was a Jewish convert who had married an Irish Catholic nurse and lived within a block of the church. Within a short time he was there, gave me a brief examination, and told me for the present I would simply have to lie flat on my back and wait until he could make a more thorough examination of my lungs. Meanwhile he would leave a prescription which would quiet my nerves and help me to sleep. One thing he could tell me, however—it would not be safe for me to lead any pilgrimage to Rome in the fall. How long would it be before he could make a definitive diagnosis of what was wrong? That would depend upon my reaction to such treatment as he could give. Until such an examination were made, we would have to assume that tuberculosis was the root of the trouble. I would have to count on many months of recuperation.

As I lay there my mind was full of distress. Here I was, less than two years launched on what I had hoped would be my life's work, for which I had prepared for twelve years. All my hopes and plans, which only yesterday had seemed so bright, lay in the dust. After two weeks on my back, since there had been no recurrence of hemorrhage, the doctor allowed me to sit up for a little while, increasing the time each day. At the end of the third week, my brother Dan came up to see me. Once I saw him, I decided to go back with him if he would take me. My present position was intolerable. I was almost a complete invalid in a rectory I had never visited before, which was not prepared to care for an invalid such as I was proving to be. There were plenty of sanatoria in the area, but I would not have been happy in any of them. The doctor agreed that it would be better for me to go back home. "You have near you in Baltimore the most eminent lung specialist in the United States. He is Dr. Victor Cullen at State Sanatorium, Maryland, near Sabillasville. I would advise you to get in touch with him immediately and place yourself entirely in his hands. If you continue to improve as you apparently have for the past three weeks, you most probably will be all right."

The next day, after I had thanked the pastor of St. Peter's, Bill O'Connor, and the housekeeper for their great kindness to me, Dan and I began our train journey back home. There I lost no time in getting in touch with Dr. Cullen. After a few days' rest, I made an appointment to go to State Sanatorium, about two hours from Baltimore by automobile, carrying with me Dr. Dzworski's brief report and the X-Ray he had taken of my lungs during the last few days in Liberty. After examining the X-Ray, sounding my lungs as thoroughly as he could, and taking more tests, Dr. Cullen told me that, as far as he could determine, the upper left lobe of my lung was affected. If the lesion could be covered over with scar tissue, I probably would be able to go back to work after some months—six would be the minimum. "Meanwhile," he said, "I don't think you would want to stay here at the sanatorium"; and with that I agreed. "The best place for you to be would be over at Mount St. Mary's. Why don't you go there and stay? You could be driven up here once a week for me to check your condition." I replied that I would be glad to follow his instructions, but I had never visited Mount St. Mary's and did not know a single person in the place. "That will be no difficulty." And with that he reached for his telephone. "Father Bradley," he said to the President, "I have a young priest here who has a case of incipient tuberculosis. The best place for him to recuperate would be at the Mount." "Send him over," was the unhesitating reply.

So I went. I was welcomed by Monsignor Bradley, and shown to my room and bath on the second floor of the seminary building. I would take my meals in the priests' dining room nearby. He would arrange to have a lounge chair and blanket placed on each of the broad porches of both the seminary and the Administration Building so that I could rest in the fresh air and sunshine any time of the day. The use of both the seminary and the college libraries would be mine. There I would remain six months. It was then that I first came to know the hospitality and true Christian charity that seemed to be the soul of the Mount. I still vividly remember for their great kindness to me Monsignor Bernard J. Bradley, the President; Monsignor John L. Sheridan, Vice President; Monsignor Joseph (Doc) Tierney; Fathers Peter Coad, John O'Neill, Elwood Berry, and William F. Culhane. Nor should I forget Hugh Phillips, protegé of Monsignor Thomas, who after his ordination became librarian there and much later served briefly as President.

Thus I began what seemed like my slow journey back to health. But what of the future? Would I ever be fit for any real work? Monsignor Thomas used to quote to me an alleged saying of Cardinal Gibbons in his advanced years: "The way to live a long life is to acquire some ailment while still young and learn to take care of yourself." It may not be a perfect prescription, but in both his case and mine it has seemed to work.

In early March, about six months after I learned that I was suffering from tuberculosis, Monsignor Thomas visited me one afternoon at the Mount. From the beginning he had been most solicitous, but now he came to see for himself how I was coming along and to say that he was holding my place open and would be glad to have me back when the doctor would say it was safe for me to come. Dr. Cullen had already indicated that I was now ready to return, so long as I would follow his instructions and could come to him for periodic check-ups. Monsignor thought I ought to wait until the Lenten season had ended and suggested that I return for Easter.

A strange thing happened shortly before Monsignor's visit. Bishop O'Mahoney of Sioux Falls, an alumnus of the Mount, the former spiritual director of the North American College who had administered to me the spiritual shock of my life, appeared for a few days' visit, looking for priestly candidates for his diocese. He was very cordial and spoke to me as if nothing had ever happened between us. Having learned why I was at the Mount and that my recovery was progressing satisfactorily, one day he invited me to come out to his diocese to work. The climate was good, and he had need of priests; he could see that I would be properly placed. This somewhat amazed me. Had he been serious when he had advised me to quit and go home? Or had he used this tactic to shock me into some common sense? Had he foreseen that what did happen would happen? In any event, it was good to learn that the future was not altogether closed to me. I assured the Bishop that I would give his kind invitation serious thought. However, given any other choice, I would not have wanted to live and work in Bishop O'Mahoney's diocese. So, when Monsignor Thomas invited me to return to Washington and Dr. Cullen had given his opinion that it would be safe, I wrote to the Bishop expressing my thanks for his kind thoughtfulness, but telling him that under the circumstances I had decided that I should return to the post where I had been so happy.

Easter Sunday 1926 was a joyous day for me. The Easter celebration then was in striking contrast to the renewed Resurrection liturgy as we have it today. The vigil service, the lighting of the new fire, the blessing of the paschal candle and the baptismal water, the reading of the Twelve Prophecies and the *Exultet,* the Vigil Mass itself, all in Latin of course, were rather quietly celebrated Saturday morning, with comparatively few in attendance. The afternoon and evening were given over to "Easter confessions." The real parish celebration of Easter then was the Solemn Mass late Sunday morning. At St. Patrick's there was a long tradition of fine church music at all times, but particularly for the feasts of Christmas and Easter and at the Pan-American Mass on Thanksgiving Day. This Easter was no exception. Monsignor Thomas celebrated the Mass; Father John Cartwright gave an excellent Easter sermon; the rest of the household attended. To me, after my recent experience of many months, the Mass was a beautiful Resurrection hymn. How many reasons had I to be thankful to God for all the mercies He had bestowed upon me! Might I always be faithful!

After the Mass a number of the friends I had made during the previous two years in the parish stopped at the rectory to tell me that they were pleased to have me back with them again. They noted how much stronger and healthier I looked than during the time before my illness. The next day I resumed my parish duties where I had left off eight months before. It was indeed a time of joy and happiness.

During the many years that were to follow (1926-41), allowing always for my primary affection for my parents, I have no hesitation in saying that one of the most important persons in my life was Monsignor Cornelius F. Thomas, pastor of St. Patrick's. Like myself, Thomas was a native Baltimorean. He was born and raised in St. Peter's parish and received his elementary education in the parochial school. There he met Father William Reardon, and it was probably under his influence that Thomas began his studies for the priesthood at St. Charles College in Ellicott City. Most of Thomas' happy memories of boyhood and youth seemed to center around the parish of St. Joseph in Texas, Maryland—a small town some ten miles north of Baltimore—where Father Reardon had become pastor. With him, Thomas had spent most of his summer vacations working in that parish.

Both at St. Charles and later at St. Mary's Seminary, Thomas built for himself an enviable reputation as an able and promising student. After ordination to the priesthood, his first assignment was to St. Patrick's in Washington. Father Jacob Walter, much beloved by his parishioners because of his dedication to them and his great charity, had been pastor there since before the Civil War. He had acquired a certain fame as the priest who had ministered to Mrs. Mary Surratt during her imprisonment and accompanied her to the gallows after she was convicted as an accomplice in President Lincoln's assassination. To the end, Father Walter maintained steadfastly that the accusation was false and her execution was totally unjust. I mention him here, not only because Thomas spoke of him frequently, but also because he was still a living tradition in the parish when I arrived.

After three years with Father Walter at St. Patrick's, Thomas was appointed, to his great satisfaction, pastor of his beloved parish of St. Joseph in Texas, but he was not permitted to stay there long. Probably on the advice of the Abbé Magnien, head of St. Mary's Seminary, who seemed to have been consulted by Gibbons on the appointments of all young priests, he was brought into the old Cathedral. In due course, he became Chancellor of the Archdiocese (1891–95) and later rector of the Cathedral (1895-1900), serving Cardinal Gibbons efficiently and devotedly. On the death of Bishop Thomas Becker of Savannah in July 1899, it must have been Gibbons who placed Thomas' name on the *terna* sent to the Holy See in preparation for the naming of Becker's successor. Here it must be said that while Thomas served Gibbons and the archdiocese fruitfully and efficiently, he was very outspoken, and some who did not agree with him found his personality abrasive. In any event, soon an AP dispatch from Rome carried the report that Cornelius F. Thomas had been appointed Bishop of Savannah. So definite did the report seem that some of Thomas' friends presented him gifts in view of his presumed coming consecration. Months passed and still the official appointment was not forthcomong. At length, almost a year after Becker's death, the Vatican announced that Benjamin J. Keily had been named Bishop of Savannah.

Thomas made no secret of his disappointment and embarrassment over this turn of events. He judged, moreover, that his position at the

Cathedral was no longer tenable. Meanwhile, the death of Father William Bartlett on April 6, 1900, made vacant the pastorate of St. Ann's in Baltimore, to which our family belonged. According to Thomas, he requested this post and his request was granted. He did not allow his disappointment to embitter him or in any way decrease his productivity. His work, as pastor of St. Ann's, later as founder and editor of the Baltimore *Catholic Review*, as pastor of St. Patrick's in Washington, his duties as the ecclesiastical superior of the Religious Women of the archdiocese, his organization and conduct of the archdiocesan Tribunal, evidence the busy life he continued to live almost to his death in 1941. Such was the pastor with whom I spent more than seventeen of the best years of my life. To me he was always a kind, considerate, and most thoughtful friend.

After the promulgation of the Code of Canon Law (Pentecost Sunday, 1918), it became necessary for the Archbishop of Baltimore to establish an ecclesiastical tribunal. As so often happened, it was to Thomas that Gibbons turned, appointing him *Officialis* and entrusting him with the task of organizing the court. This meant he had to choose a number of Prosynodal Judges; a Notary, who would also be actuary or secretary, to keep the minutes of meetings and whose signature would be necessary to make valid any document of the Tribunal; a Defender of the Bond who might also serve as Promoter of Justice; and a number of Advocates, knowledgeable young priests who would help petitioners to draw up and present their cases to the Tribunal. From the organization of the Tribunal down to my arrival, Father John Barrett, who preceded me as assistant at St. Patrick's, had served as Notary. At that time he had been appointed by Archbishop Curley as Superintendent of Schools and pastor of St. John the Evangelist parish in Baltimore. For several years, however, he continued to serve as the Secretary-Notary of the Tribunal. As his duties in Baltimore increased, he found the frequent trips between the two cities too time-consuming and asked to be relieved of his Tribunal work. At that point, not long after my eight-month sick leave, Monsignor Thomas asked me to undertake that responsibility. I pointed out to him that I was no expert in canon law but that I would be glad to undertake any obligation he thought I could fulfill. Virtually all the cases the Tribunal handled involved the validity of marriages and since all the provisions of the code on marriage were adequately covered in the tract *On Marriage*, he felt that I could satisfactorily perform the duties. Thus

I became involved in the work of the Tribunal—an involvement which
would last for many years.

   When I had arrived at St. Patrick's, September 1923, the country
had entered what seemed to many to be the greatest period of prosperity in its history. That prosperity had its beginning in the spirit of
exhilaration, of expansion, of progress, that arose immediately after
the end of World War I. However, with the collapse of President
Wilson in the summer of 1919 and his subsequent period of almost complete isolation, a cloud of uncertainty seemed to rest over the country.
Spirits were again buoyed when Harding and Coolidge were inaugurated as President and Vice President in March 1921, but it was not
long before another cloud appeared in the form of rumors of unethical
conduct on the part of some of Harding's Cabinet, particularly the
Secretaries of the Departments of Interior and Justice. When Harding
died suddenly on a western trip in the summer of 1923 and Coolidge
succeeded him August 6, the country immediately reacted as if they
had acquired in Coolidge the kind of President the country needed—
honest, straightforward, not burdened with the political and social
ideals of Wilson that made many apprehensive, and not tied to the
kind of "bossism" that had almost proved fatal to Harding. Even in
appearance he looked like a plain Yankee Puritan with the virtue which
that suggested. Each Sunday morning when his duties as President did
not require him to be elsewhere, we could see him from the side
windows of St. Patrick's rectory, with his gracious wife, arriving at the
First Congregational Church on the northeast corner of Tenth and G
Streets, N.W., immediately opposite our rectory. The people had liked
the way he had handled the Massachusetts police strike as Governor,
and they liked the way he had conducted himself as Vice President.
During the presidency of Coolidge, which lasted from August 6,
1923, to March 4, 1929, the national prosperity seemed to come to
full flower. Mining, industry, commerce transportation, finance were
all flourishing. The mood of the country became one of unbounded
optimism. The people seemed convinced that there was no limit
to progress, prosperity, and increasing material wealth. In terms of
dollars the national wealth was measured at about seven billion in
1830, twenty-five billion in 1870, sixty-five billion in 1890, three
hundred fifty billion in 1920; early in 1929 is was approaching four
hundred fifty billion.
   Yet there were certain signs that all was not well with the social

fabric of the country. The value of farmland, which had been greatly inflated during World War I, sank rather rapidly until it had fallen below the prewar level—and it stayed there. Continuing surplus crops kept the price of farm products suppressed to a degree that was completely out of harmony with the seeming prosperity of the rest of the country. The Eighteenth (Prohibition) Amendment and the Volstead Act gave rise to some ugly phenomena: bootlegging, rum-running, the ubiquitous speakeasy, organized crime on an unprecedented scale, widespread and growing disrespect for law. Moreover, there was increasing evidence of maldistribution of national wealth and annual income. The rich were growing richer but the poor were becoming poorer. Unemployment was steadily increasing. More and more individuals and families were sinking below the poverty level into abject and hopeless pauperism.

This last phenomenon was affecting the work of the St. Vincent de Paul conference of St. Patrick's parish. As spiritual director, certain duties brought me face to face with the poor. Emergency requests for such basic needs as food and rent often came directly or were referred to me to handle as best I could until the lay members could be reached to make home visitations. Fortunately, Monsignor Thomas was generous almost to a fault and would allow no one to go hungry or to be evicted so long as there was a dollar in the treasury. But there were many parishes in and near Washington less fortunate than St. Patrick's. There were other cities like Baltimore, now predominantly industrial and more sensitive to the effects of unemployment, where conditions were worse than in Washington.

This phenomenon of the growing number of the poor and underprivileged alongside the increasing general prosperity of the times led to greater attention to the needs of the poor and to the service rendered to them. Because of this situation, Monsignor John O'Grady, professor of social work at The Catholic University, with the approval of the Archbishop of Baltimore and the support of a number of prominent business and professional men, organized the Catholic Charities of Washington to coordinate the work of existing agencies, to supplement that work where necessary, and to bring to it the skills of a staff of professionally trained social workers. Monsignor O'Grady understandably became Director. During the 1920s the volume of work of the Catholic Charities, the staff, and the demands made upon it, steadily increased. Meanwhile, Monsignor O'Grady's position as both professor at The Catholic University and as Executive Secretary of the National Conference of Catholic Charities made it increasingly difficult for him to fulfill all that was expected of him as the Director of the local organization. Accordingly, early in 1929 he asked Archbishop Curley to appoint a Washington priest to serve as his Assistant Director.

Two circumstances probably led the Archbishop to think of me: first, as the Director of the St. Vincent de Paul Conference I had shown an interest in working with the poor and this had brought me into frequent contact with the office of Catholic Charities, and, second, I lived close to the office, then located on F Street near Seventh. I had no professional training in social work, however, and no previous experience that would qualify me to direct an agency staffed by professional social workers and governed by a board composed of prominent business and professional men. In spite of these limitations, the Archbishop appointed me Assistant Director in June 1929. That was in the third month of the Hoover Administration, when despite evidence of a growing need among the poor and underprivileged, the country still showed signs of great prosperity.

President Hoover began his term of office March 4, 1929, amid all the signs of national prosperity and unbounded optimism. To all but a few, that prosperity and optimism seemed to be established on a firm and enduring basis. I have already mentioned several flaws in that picture. But now appeared another and fatal defect. The country was seized with a veritable mania for speculation. The prices of stocks soared to fantastic heights. Billions of dollars were drawn from the banks into Wall Street for brokers' loans to carry margin accounts. In the midsummer of 1929, about 300 million shares of stock were being carried on margin.

Then in October 1929, the market broke. The wild rush to buy gave way to an even more precipitous rush to sell. On October 29, 1929, 16,410,030 shares were thrown on the market for what they would bring. In countless cases, savings of a lifetime were wiped out.

At first, political and financial officials treated the matter as a mere spasm in the market. President Hoover and Secretary of the Treasury Mellon stated that business was sound and predicted that a great revival of prosperity was "just around the corner." In January, the President declared that the trend of business was upward, in March that the crisis would be over in sixty days, in May that we had passed the worst and would recover rapidly. Secretary Mellon saw "nothing in the present situation that warrants pessimism." As the months passed, however, it became evident that we had entered a period of deep depression.

No one can say that the President and Congress were indifferent to the plight of the country, but the persistent expressions of optimism from the President and the Secretary of the Treasury made it almost impossible for Hoover to take prompt and adequate measures to relieve the distress of the growing numbers of the poor. A whole year went by before Hoover appointed a committee of the Cabinet to formulate measures to relieve unemployment (October 1930). In December he placed before Congress a vast program for road construction, public buildings, flood control, and airways development. As a result, he signed twenty-two bills appropriating $300 million for loans by the Federal Farm Board for emergency construction and drought relief. In October 1931, under his urging the bankers of the country formed a $500 million pool to help rescue the weaker banks from failure. On January 22, 1932, he signed a bill creating the $2 billion Reconstruction Finance Corporation, empowered to make loans to banks, insurance companies, agricultural associations, railroads, and other industries. But these measures were neither prompt enough nor sufficient to meet the vast need that had developed. It was almost as if an inexorable law of nature were at work with which nothing could interfere. In the mid-term election, a Democratic majority was created in both houses of Congress; House of Representatives 220 to 214, Senate 48 to 47. In the presidential election of 1932, Roosevelt defeated Hoover by huge popular and electoral majorities.

Almost immediately after the election, Hoover invited Roosevelt to confer with him on measures that might ease the situation during the four months before the latter would take office. Roosevelt, however, refused to commit himself to policies before the power and responsibility were actually in his hands. During that interim period industry, commerce, and banking ground down to a virtual standstill.

How did the poor survive the four terrible years from 1929 until 1933? That they suffered and suffered greatly no one will deny; that their number increased daily is beyond question. But out of the suffering and need there was born among the people of this country a great spirit of generosity, a willingness to share. Here I must pay tribute to the devotion of the members of the St. Vincent de Paul Conferences of many parishes and to the generosity of many pastors; in our own parish of St. Patrick, men like John Madigan, our President, Fred Thuee, William Cogger, the Moriarity brothers, John Mahoney—and, above all, the unbounded generosity of Monsignor Thomas; and to the board of directors of Catholic Charities: Frank Weller, Arthur May, Adam Weschler, Dr. Henry Crosson, Caesar Aiello, George O'Connor, M. X. Wilberding, Allen Pope, Michael Calnan, who stayed with us so loyally during those difficult times; to the staff: Gertrude Marron, Elizabeth Mulholland, Helen Richards, Florence Murray, Margaret Wallace, Mareta Reddington, and others who served as caseworkers during the period when Catholic Charities of Washington was under my charge. I pay tribute not only to their devotion, but also to their frequent ingenuity in searching out means to meet the needs of the poor. Nor dare I overlook the Sisters of the three children's institutions of the Baltimore Archdiocese: the Daughters of Charity of St. Ann's and St. Vincent's, and the Sisters of the Holy Cross of St. Joseph's. A very special tribute is due to Mary Merrick and her devoted board of the Christ Child Society.

Finally, I must pay tribute to Monsignor John O'Grady, who had the foresight to found the Washington Catholic Charities in the early 1920s, who served as its Director so many years and was so profoundly interested not only in the immediate problem of charity, but also in the whole field of social welfare and the problems of government.

To be Assistant Director of Catholic Charities during those distressful times was no enviable position. During those very months when the mania of speculation was at its height, Washington was in the process of organizing its Community Chest. During World War I the efficiency of central fund-raising campaigns for the financing of charitable and social service agencies had brought about the formation of Community Chests in a number of cities in this country. Monsignor O'Grady, however, was opposed on principle to the participation of Catholic charitable groups in such a central-financing organization, and in this he had strong backing: Monsignor Keegan of New York, Monsignor Edwin Leonard of Baltimore, Monsignor Butler of St. Louis, Monsignor Loftus of Buffalo—all heads of strong diocesan organizations of Catholic Charities and prominent figures in the National Conference of Catholic Charities.

For some years the boards of some of the more prominent organizations of charity and social service had resisted the idea of a Washington Community Chest: the Associated Charities of Washington, the YMCA, the YWCA, the Salvation Army, the United Jewish Charities. But as the number of appeals to these and many other organizations serving the poor increased, a growing number of influential Washingtonians, some of them lay board members of such organizations, began to think differently. A number of these individuals joining together decided to ask the National Organization of Community Chests to make a survey of the feasibility and advisability of a Washington Community Chest. Mr. Elwood Street, who had directed the Community Chest in St. Louis, came to Washington in the summer of 1929 to examine the situation. As a result of his survey, the Council of Community Chests gave their opinion that a Community Chest of Washington, D.C., was not only feasible but also highly desirable. In the end, Street was employed to organize the Washington Community Chest and to conduct its first city-wide campaign.

From the beginning, Monsignor O'Grady continued his firm opposition to the participation of the Catholic Charities in the Community Chest and its projected campaign. But in his organization of Charities he had enlisted the support of a number of Catholic business and professional men of the city, whose names I have already mentioned. Many, if not all, of these laymen had come to the conclusion that not only was the participation of the Catholic Charities important but necessary if it were to continue to exist in the face of one large centralized financial campaign. They decided that they could not accept the decision of Monsignor O'Grady as final and that they would appeal to Archbishop Curley. Frank Weller, a prominent Washington lawyer and the President of Catholic Charities; Arthur May, head of Washington's largest wholesale hardware supply company; Adam Weschler, the city's leading auctioneer and Catholic Charities Treasurer, and James Colliflower, head of the largest fuel company, formed a committee representing the lay members of the board. Weller as President made an appointment to see the Archbishop. He then telephoned to Monsignor O'Grady to invite him to accompany them. Learning that he was out of town and would not return until too late, Weller invited me to go with them. I replied that since I had been appointed O'Grady's assistant so recently and knew his mind so well it seemed improper for me to accompany them on such a mission. They saw my point of view and readily accepted it.

From their point of view, their conference with the Archbishop was completely satisfactory. They convinced him of the soundness of their judgment in the matter and assured him that they not only could but would guarantee that the agency would continue to be conducted as a completely Catholic organization without undue interference from the outside. What Catholic Charities would have to do was to promise genuine support of the Campaign and meet certain standards of social work—standards that the organization already met, since it was a member of the Washington Council of Social Agencies. The Archbishop then and there decided that Catholic Charities would participate if the Community Chest wished the agency to become a member on the terms they had presented. He told them that he would inform Monsignor O'Grady of his decision. The graciousness with which O'Grady accepted the Archbishop's decision is worthy of note. As for myself, the Archbishop's decision was "a consummation devoutly to be wished," since I had no desire actively to participate in a financial campaign of our own that, under the circumstances, would seem to be doomed to failure before its start.

In spite of the Depression that began the very year the Community Chest of Washington was organized and conducted its first campaign, the organization proved to be successful and reached its goal during that and the ensuing years. This meant, of course, that the continued existence of the Washington Catholic Charities was assured, so long as we remained a member. It did not mean, however, that we were out of trouble. Monsignor O'Grady had always gone on the principle that the relief budget of the Charities should be kept at a minimum, and that responsibility for such relief should be placed whenever possible on the parish conferences of the St. Vincent de Paul Society. Therefore we entered the Chest with the same budget for the year 1930 as we had operated on during the prosperous year of 1929. As I recall conditions of that time, the direct effects of the Depression were not painfully evident in Washington during the last two months of 1929. Owing to the continued effect of the large government payroll, they never did become so bad as in other large cities that were predominantly industrial, where the effects of unemployment were felt immediately. But after the beginning of 1930, conditions in the rest of the country were soon reflected in Washington. Many of the workers in the federal government felt it necessary to share their incomes with impoverished relatives back home. With the decline in federal revenue, various departments were constrained to economize and severely limit their number of workers. When vacancies occurred, the positions were filled only when absolutely necessary, and when there were openings, these were generally not available to Washingtonians because of their total lack of political influence. Construction work virtually ceased. Business everywhere declined. Soon, therefore, there were increasing evidences of deep poverty. Among the most pathetic was the appearance of strong, able-bodied men selling apples on the downtown street corners.

Often they were beautiful red apples, surplus products, no doubt, of the apple-growing Northwest, and numbers of people stopped to buy them, but as a means of livelihood this was scarcely more than a last measure to stave off starvation. Besides, the busy corners of Washington were strictly limited in number.

For the whole country, the years from 1930 to 1933 were indeed sorrowful times. They were particularly sad for those who worked in an agency like Catholic Charities. The policy of keeping our relief budget at a minimum and placing the main responsibility for direct help on the parish conferences was a good one in the twenties, but it seemed to smack of the doctrinaire when one tried to extend it into the thirties. For one thing, Church revenues were generally among the first to experience the adverse effects of the Depression. I suppose all of us did what we could personally, but there was very little I was able to do on the meager income of an assistant in the thirties. When I was appointed to the agency in 1929, no remuneration was contemplated, just as Monsignor O'Grady had never received any, so none went into the 1930 budget and thus it continued for some years until the Director of the Chest insisted that I should at least receive enough to cover expenses incurred by the job. But my needs were minimal. It was many years before I owned an automobile. Monsignor Thomas was, as usual, his generous self in making available his own car when I had need for one; later my sister, whose office was quite close to St. Patrick's, used to leave her car in the yard of the rectory in the morning and pick it up after work so that I could have the use of it when necessary. Besides clothing and a fee for the barber twice a month, I had no real needs. The only difficulty was that I could do little for those who really needed help.

When on May 12, 1933, President Roosevelt signed the Federal Emergency Relief Bill providing $500 million for direct relief of poverty, half of it an outright gift to the states and the district, and half of it to the states on a matching basis, a great load was lifted from the shoulders of all of us at Catholic Charities. It must be said, however, that even then we were not out of trouble. The Great Depression lasted down to the year 1941, when the United States entered World War II. Meanwhile, I had been appointed director of Washington Catholic Charities in 1938 to succeed Monsignor O'Grady.

Before bringing to a close these memories of the sorrowful years of the Great Depression, I must recall the death of my parents. A tragic event for all the members of our family occurred August 2, 1932. My father, busy repairing a window screen, was standing or kneeling on a windowsill on the stairway between the second and third stories of the family home. He was now sixty-seven years old, past the time for him to be engaged in such an activity. But it was the type of thing he had done all his adult life, and nothing had happened to indicate to him that he should no longer be doing it. In any event, something caused him to lose his balance and fall backward onto the cement alleyway that ran along the south side of our home, some twenty to twenty-five feet below. The head injury he sustained was mortal, causing immediate loss of consciousness. By the time the ambulance arrived at Union Memorial Hospital, about three blocks away, he was already dead. For all of us it was indeed a tragic ending, and mournful were the days and months that followed. Soon thereafter, my mother decided to sell the family home and to go to live with my sister in Washington, where they occupied a comfortable apartment in a pleasant neighborhood. There I was pleased to visit her frequently. From then on, however, her strength steadily declined. After a rather prolonged illness, during which she was cared for lovingly by my sister and with the help of a trained nurse toward the end, she died on October 12, 1939. Her death seemed to break the family circle, which had lasted so long and so happily.

Anastasia Dames Schofield Shehan and Thomas P. Shehan, the Cardinal's mother and father.

Shehan and Schofield cousins: Lawrence Shehan is at left, front row; Mary Shehan, second from right; Thomas, second from left, back row.

Shehan brothers as altar boys. Left to right: Daniel, John Brooke, Thomas, Lawrence, and William.

Lawrence J. Shehan, ordination portrait, 1922.

Walking trip through Switzerland, 1921. Lawrence Shehan is third from right.

Pastor of St. Patrick's Church, Washington, D.C., 1941-45, and Director of Washington Catholic Charities.

Pontificia Fotografia G. Felici

Pope Pius XII, Archbishop Keough, and Auxiliary Bishop Shehan at the Vatican, 1950.

Daniel, J. Brooke, Lawrence, William, Mary, and Thomas at the time of Bishop Shehan's appointment to Bridgeport, 1953.

Cardinal Cicognani and Bishop Shehan in Bridgeport, 1960.

Auxiliary Bishop T. Austin Murphy and Archbishop Shehan attend an Orioles game on Holy Name baseball night in Baltimore, 1964.

5. Pastor and Bishop, 1941-53

ON THE FEAST OF CHRISTMAS 1940 Monsignor Thomas celebrated Midnight Mass. As Protonotary Apostolic, he had the privilege to offer Pontifical Mass, wearing the mitre and accompanied by an Assistant Priest. I served as his Assistant Priest; Cowhig as Deacon; Arthur as Subdeacon; Dade preached. The church was crowded as usual on that occasion, for it was known throughout Washington that the music would be good and particularly appropriate to the feast. The weather was mild, and the church became very warm and close; the Monsignor seemed barely able to get through the Mass. He had always been almost excessively independent. It was a sign that he recognized his increasing weakness when he arranged for William Taylor, a young black man in whom he had great confidence as the driver of his automobile and member of the St. Patrick maintenance crew, to come each day to help him with his bath. Gradually he grew weaker. Early in February he developed pneumonia, and he was persuaded by his doctor to enter Georgetown Hospital. He failed to respond to treatment, gradually grew weaker, and finally died in a coma early in the morning of February 11. He was, if I remember correctly, eighty-five years old. I was privileged to be with him at the time of his death.

Archbishop Curley had gone back to visit his old Diocese of St. Augustine, Florida, to recuperate from an aggravated bronchial condition which seemed to plague him almost every winter. He was unable to come to Washington for the funeral. Archbishop Cicognani, the Apostolic Delegate, celebrated the Mass of Requiem. Monsignor Joseph Nelligan, the Chancellor, came over from Baltimore, accompanied by George Hopkins, to represent the Archbishop at the Mass and burial. John Cartwright preached a particularly appropriate and touching

93

sermon. So we laid his body to rest in the site he had chosen in the "Priests' Burial Plot" of Mount Olivet Cemetery, over whose board of trustees he had presided for twenty-four years.

After some days Nelligan telephoned informing me that the Archbishop had appointed me to the pastorate of St. Patrick's; the appointment would be announced in the next issue of *The Catholic Review* and the official document of appointment would follow as soon as the Archbishop had an opportunity to sign it after his return. Would I also accept the appointment as *Officialis* of the Tribunal, for the present at least, to see if it could fit in with my duties as pastor and Director of Charities? Having worked on the Tribunal under Monsignor Thomas so many years, the least I could do was to try. Meanwhile I had succeeded Monsignor O'Grady as Director of the Washington Catholic Charities in 1938 and would also continue in that position to the end of 1945.

I know of no appointment in my whole life that brought me so much satisfaction as that of pastor of St. Patrick's. It was now eighteen years since I had arrived as a newly ordained priest. I had come to love every part of the parish: its old fortresslike granite church with the graceful vaulted lines of its uncluttered interior; its large Gothic main altar, where I had celebrated Mass so often; its beautiful marble pulpit dedicated to the parish's most famous orator, Dr. Stafford (c. 1900); the church's fine acoustics; the rectory designed so well for both parish business and living quarters; the large granite high school for girls, efficiently conducted by the Sisters of the Holy Cross and noted throughout Washington for its business and academic training; the commodious auditorium that served not only the high school, but also as one of the best parish halls in the city; the smaller elementary school run by the Ursuline Sisters on Fourth Street, near what was left of the residential area of the parish. Finally, and more importantly, I had come to love the spirit that existed within the household and the whole parish.

Nor did I see any great difficulty in accepting, for the present at least, the responsibility of *Officialis* of the Tribunal. Within the three years before the Monsignor's death we had received two young priests who gave promise of being of great assistance, both to the parish and to the Tribunal. James Cowhig, a graduate of the North American College, had returned to Rome for a year of postgraduate work in canon law at the Gregorian University and had received the licentiate. No sooner had he arrived at St. Patrick's than he was appointed Notary in my place, and I was asked to serve as *Vice Officialis* and Judge. One of the first things that Cowhig did was to construct a large chart listing every case before the Tribunal, showing all the steps that had been taken, the exact status of the case at the time and all the steps that still remained. With this on the wall before his desk, he kept cases moving steadily ahead to their completion, the Court's decision and the then-mandatory appeal. Then, at the end the complete record of the case was filed away, ready for reference at any time.

Robert Arthur was the second of these young priests. He also was a native of St. Ann's parish in Baltimore and a product of the North American College. After he had been with us for a year, I induced him to enroll in the School of Canon Law at The Catholic University. In due time he received his licentiate and was appointed Defender of the Bond and Promoter of Justice, and proved to be a truly valuable member of the Court. I encouraged him to continue his studies for the doctorate. He did complete his class work, but one of the definite failures of my life was my endeavor to get him to complete the dissertation that would have entitled him to the doctorate. This, of course, did not detract in the least from the value of his work. At most, it might have added somewhat to the prestige of the Tribunal. Under the guidance and help of Cowhig and Arthur, it seemed to me that before long we were on our way to building up one of the most effective Tribunals in the country—after New York, Brooklyn, and Philadelphia, where in each case the diocese had an abundance of trained canonists on whom to draw. Nor should I fail to mention several excellent Judges—foremost among whom were Fathers Joseph Barron and William (Pete) Stricker—and several good Advocates, the ablest and most active of whom was Father Terence Evans.

Last but by no means least among the assistants of St. Patrick at that time was Father Thomas Dade, whose coming to the parish had actually preceded the arrival of both Cowhig and Arthur. A forthright activist, he was soon devoting the major part of his time to two fields: the instruction of converts and, after the outbreak of World War II, work with the armed service men stationed in and near Washington. In both fields he was singularly successful. Under his leadership and with the cooperation of the Knights of Columbus, their headquarters on Tenth Street near K became a beehive of activity for enlisted men for the duration of the war. His monthly meetings of Army, Navy, and Marine priests at St. Patrick's attracted a large number of chaplains of the area. His outstanding work, however, was the instruction of prospective converts and others interested in learning about the teaching and practice of the Catholic Church. Before his arrival, the number of those under instruction at St. Patrick's was always considerable from the time of Dr. Stafford. Bishop John McNamara, at one time an assistant in the parish (c. 1910-20), had left behind him an enviable reputation for such work. Monsignor John Cartwright had been particularly effective and popular (c. 1920-33). In spite of my work with the Tribunal and Catholic Charities, I was seldom without one or two under instructions. But until Dade's arrival, the method followed was individual instruction, which, in the case of Cartwright, was very time-consuming. Soon after Dade arrived, he arranged for group instructions given weekly—Tuesday evenings, I believe—in the parish school hall next to the rectory. He would conduct two such courses each year: one beginning in late September and continuing until mid-December, with preparation for Baptism or reception into the Church shortly before Christmas; the second beginning shortly after January 1 and extending to Holy Week. Soon, virtually all our prospective converts were enrolling in one of these two courses. The number continued to grow, and before the end of my pastorate the number of converts had reached about one hundred a year, which considerably surpassed the number all of us had reached in previous years, even during the times of McNamara and Cartwright. Dade prepared each lecture carefully and delivered it as an informal talk, followed by ample time for discussion.

Thus, with the support of such men as Dade, Cowhig, and Arthur, my life and work as pastor of St. Patrick's was singularly satisfying—perhaps too satisfying to last. I remember approaching the rectory one evening in the dusk with a gentle breeze rustling the ivy that clung to the walls of the church and rectory, and saying to myself: "Here I would like to live the rest of my life and die." I was now forty-five years old. During more than twenty years this had been my happy home. Here at the corner of Tenth and G Streets my roots had sunk too deeply for me ever to want to pull them up, even though great changes had taken place in the parish.

Then one day in the spring of 1945, while visiting at our rectory, Archbishop Curley asked me a question for which I was totally unprepared: "If you were to be moved from St. Patrick's, whom would you recommend as your successor?" The question caught me completely off guard, and I did not know how to answer. I had never seriously contemplated such a possibility. Seeing my embarrassment, he said: "Think about it, and write to me." I did think about it, and I wrote to him the next day. I began by saying that since he had never expressed dissatisfaction with my work at St. Patrick's (in fact, he had gone out of his way to praise me), his question to my way of thinking could only mean one thing: either my name had been placed on a *terna* of proposed candidates for the episcopate, or it was being so considered. I then went on to express the main reasons why, in my own judgment, I was not fitted to be a Bishop. I began with the most obvious—my size. I then mentioned my lack of a good memory and my absent-mindedness, which already tended to involve me in difficulties at times. Finally, I did not have the kind of systematic and orderly mind which, in my opinion, was required for the work of a Bishop. But to answer his direct question, I added: if I had to be changed, I would recommend John Cartwright, then pastor of the parish of the Immaculate Conception. I said that I knew that he considered Cartwright as the proper successor of Monsignor Buckey, who was then pastor of St. Matthew's Cathedral; but although Buckey was an old man, he seemed in good health and no one could tell how much longer he would live. Meanwhile, Cartwright himself was fifty years old, and the pulpit at St. Patrick's would be far more appropriate than that of Immaculate Conception and probably the equal of, if not superior to, that of St. Matthew's. If Cartwright were not available, then my second recommendation would be John Russell, pastor of St. Ursula's in Baltimore, whose uncle, Bishop William T. Russell, was once pastor of St. Patrick's. I believe, however, that I made it quite evident I was not looking forward to being a Bishop and that I would prefer to remain at St. Patrick's. Months passed and nothing happened. I supposed that my letter to Archbishop Curley had settled the matter.

Then, in the early part of November 1945, Archbishop Cicognani, the Apostolic Delegate, summoned me to the Delegation. He informed me that the Holy See desired to appoint me Auxiliary Bishop to the Archbishop of Baltimore and Washington, with residence in Baltimore. I told him of my letter to Archbishop Curley and the various reasons why I thought I ought not be a Bishop. He said that, in spite of that, the Holy See wished to appoint me, and "While no one is obliged to accept, my advice to you is to do so—one does not say 'no' to the Holy Father." Without further hesitation I assured him that I would accept. The announcement was made public on Thanksgiving morning, and I appeared at the Pan-American Mass that day as the Bishop-elect.

By that time, Archbishop Curley was confined to Bon Secours

Hospital, suffering from extremely high blood pressure and *herpes frontalis* (shingles of the forehead). His eyesight was also failing. Since he was unable to consecrate me, the Apostolic Delegate agreed to do so at St. Patrick's on December 12. Bishop Ireton of Richmond and Bishop McNamara, the other Auxiliary of Baltimore-Washington, were the co-consecrators. Monsignor John Cartwright delivered the sermon. The ceremony of consecration, although no rival to the simplicity of my ordination just twenty-two years before, was a very modest one. Archbishop (later Cardinal) Spellman, who was a contemporary and friend of Cartwright at the North American College and with whom I had become acquainted in the early days of my priesthood, came down to honor the occasion. He, Bishop Johannes Gunnarsson of Reykjavik, Iceland, who used to stay at St. Patrick's while on his visits to the United States, and the three ordaining bishops were, as I remember, the only prelates of episcopal rank who were present. The Mass was followed by a modest luncheon at the Mayflower Hotel. There were brief speeches by the Apostolic Delegate, Bishop McNamara, and myself. The celebration, as I recall it, was the shortest and simplest I ever attended on the occasion of the consecration of a Bishop.

Shortly after Thanksgiving Day, Monsignor Robert Achstetter, pastor of the SS. Philip and James parish in Baltimore, died unexpectedly, but after a rather prolonged illness. Archbishop Curley appointed me to succeed him. Since it was already so close to Christmas, I decided that I would end my pastorate at St. Patrick's by celebrating Pontifical Mass at midnight Christmas and take up my new residence and duties as soon as possible after the New Year. So ended twenty-three happy years at St. Patrick's. I found that my chief regret was in leaving the company of the other priests who had been so helpful during the years of my pastorate: Dade, Cowhig, and Arthur. To them I should like to pay a special tribute of affection and gratitude.

To my surprise, however, I soon found that I could be equally happy as the pastor of SS. Philip and James. This was due first to the strong parochial spirit of goodwill and cooperation that had been built up from the beginning by its first resident pastor, Father John C. Wade, together with his uniquely beloved assistant, Father Hugh Monaghan, and later by my own predecessor, Father Robert Achstetter. But it was due chiefly to the three assistants I found there— Fathers Edwin DeLawder, Francis Flanigan, and Clare O'Dwyer.

O'Dwyer I had known before, having met him at Camp St. Mary

one summer vacation. The first Sunday he arrived at SS. Philip and James he had made a hit with the congregation by beginning his first homily: "I am Father Clare O'Dwyer; I come from Brooklyn; I am twenty-six years old and I am six feet seven inches tall; my friends call me 'Slim'." He had a gracious way with all the parishioners, but he had an extraordinary rapport with youth. He had already built up probably the best Catholic Youth Organization in the archdiocese. He himself was a good athlete, especially skilled in baseball and tennis. As the youngest assistant, he was also given charge of Union Memorial Hospital, one of the principal responsibilities of the parish. It had been founded as a combination of several old Protestant hospitals, and it was thought that the key members of its board of directors and staff were unfriendly to Catholic priests and unwilling to call them except in an emergency. O'Dwyer was credited with breaking down that prejudice by first cultivating friendly relations with several members of the staff. Through them he was able to work out a system by which he was notified of the admission of all Catholic patients. With the cooperation of the other two assistants, the spiritual needs of the Catholic patients were promptly cared for.

Flanigan was in a way quite a contrast to O'Dwyer. He was calm, placid, wise beyond his years, and a good speaker—but with none of O'Dwyer's flair for oratory. He was outspoken but never offensive, meticulous in the performance of his duty, highly respected by all the members of the parish. Perhaps the best way to describe him is to say that he was the kind of assistant that every sensible pastor would wish to have.

DeLawder's outstanding characteristics were a phenomenal memory and an uncanny facility and accuracy in the handling of figures. During Achstetter's illness and after his death, as the senior assistant and later as Administrator, he had undertaken to keep the books and handle the finances of the parish. On my arrival, seeing how well he had done this, I suggested that he continue. He very readily agreed to do so. Unfortunately, a weak voice and a rather hesitant manner of speaking diminished somewhat his effectiveness as a preacher; but the substance of his talks was always good, and those who listened carefully could always profit by what he had to say.

As the Auxiliary Bishop of Baltimore, one of my main duties was to administer the Sacrament of Confirmation in the parishes of that city, in the surrounding territory, and in Western Maryland. On these occasions I was always accompanied by Father George Hopkins, who acted as master of ceremonies.

Ceremonies of ordination to the priesthood always took place at the Cathedral and, after the Archbishop had become disabled, were performed by the senior Auxiliary, Bishop John McNamara. Ordination to the subdiaconate and diaconate, however, were conferred in the seminary chapel at the early morning Mass. When I was delegated to officiate on these occasions, Father James Laubacher, Superior of the seminary, would ask me to spend the preceding evening there and address the whole body of seminarians. These talks were published in *The Voice*, the seminary newspaper, and drew some favorable comment. On the basis of some of them, Cardinal Mooney invited me to give the Detroit priests' retreat at the provincial seminary at Plymouth, Michigan, and again two years later to another group of his priests at Sacred Heart Seminary in the city of Detroit. Shortly thereafter, Bishop Francis Haas invited me to give the priests' retreat in the Diocese of Grand Rapids. Still later, Bishop Howard Carroll of the Diocese of Altoona (now Altoona-Johnstown) invited me to go there for the same purpose, as did also his brother, Bishop Coleman Carroll of Miami, Florida.

Although these duties and functions took me away from time to time, I spent as much time in the parish as possible and engaged in the ordinary activities of a parish priest. With the other priests, I heard confessions on Saturday afternoons and evenings, took my turn regularly at Sunday Mass with homily, and gave religious instruction to the eighth-grade students at our parish school. I must say, however, that my three assistant priests had so thoroughly organized the work of the parish and divided it among themselves that I found myself less busy than I had been at St. Patrick's in Washington. Only once do I remember being called upon to make an emergency sick call at Union Memorial Hospital, when all three assistants were occupied.

From the time of my arrival in Baltimore, Archbishop Curley's health had continued steadily to decline. He bore his gradual loss of sight and his continuing suffering with admirable patience and fortitude. Finally, on the evening of May 27, 1947, Monsignor Nelligan telephoned saying that Sister Helena, Administrator of Bon Secours Hospital, had informed him that the Archbishop was dying. He and I went immediately to the hospital. The Archbishop was already in a coma and did not recognize either of us. We knelt with Sister Helena and the attending Sister-nurse and said the prayers for the dying. Even as we recited the Litany, he peacefully breathed his last.

Although during the latter part of his life Archbishop Curley was burdened with ill health and steadily advancing blindness, I am convinced that he will go down in history as one of the great Archbishops of Baltimore. Long before he came to us in that capacity, he had acquired the reputation of the outstanding orator in the American hierarchy. This gift of eloquence added much to the effectiveness of his ministry here, particularly during the first ten years. The gift was built upon a quick superior intellect, a remarkable memory, a commanding presence, and a strong ringing voice. The main thrust of Curley's ministry here was in the field of education, particularly on the parochial school level. He added sixty-six parish schools to those already in existence. Nor was he oblivious to the needs of secondary education. With his encouragement and help, the Daughters of Charity established Seton High School on North Charles Street opposite SS. Philip and James Church, and the Sisters of St. Francis built and brought into operation Catholic High School in East Baltimore. That, however, had been as far as he had been able to go, for after the full effects of the Depression of 1929 were felt, all building construction ceased and could not be resumed effectively until after the end of World War II in 1945. By that time, the ravages of ill health had far advanced. Yet, during the whole of his administration Archbishop Curley had remained a commanding figure in the city of Baltimore and in the state of Maryland. Under him I had spent twenty-five years of my priestly life, two of them as his Auxiliary Bishop.

On the death of Archbishop Curley, the Consultors of the archdiocese elected Bishop John McNamara, the senior Auxiliary, to the post of Administrator. It was he, therefore, who made the arrangements for the funeral, which took place in the Basilica of the Assumption. Archbishop Cicognani, the Apostolic Delegate, celebrated the Solemn Mass of Requiem. Bishop McNamara preached. Archbishop Curley's body was buried in the crypt of the Basilica of the Assumption, the last of the Archbishops to be buried there.

Bishop McNamara held the position of Administrator for ten months. During that time, for me as for the whole of the archdiocese, life continued much as it had been before. During the last years, as his health continued to decline and his blindness increased, Archbishop Curley had come to depend almost entirely on Monsignor Nelligan, Chancellor of the archdiocese and rector of the Cathedral, for the details of archdiocesan administration. In large measure, this arrangement continued during Bishop McNamara's administration.

On November 15, 1947, the Holy See announced that Washington,

which had been established as an archdiocese on July 22, 1939, but had
remained under the administration of the Archbishop of Baltimore,
was now completely separated from Baltimore and made immediately
subject to the Holy See. On November 29, the Vatican announced that
Pope Pius XII had appointed Francis P. Keough, then Bishop of
Providence, as Archbishop of Baltimore, and that Rev. Patrick O'Boyle,
National Director of the Bishops' War Relief Organization, had been
named Archbishop of Washington.

Francis Keough, a native of New Britain, Connecticut, had begun
his studies for the priesthood at St. Thomas Seminary in Hartford. In
1911 he was sent to continue his studies at the Sulpician Seminary in
Issy, France. There he acquired remarkable facility in the use of the
French language. On the outbreak of World War I, he returned to this
country and completed his studies at St. Bernard's Seminary, Rochest-
er. He was ordained to the priesthood as a member of the Diocese of
Hartford on June 10, 1916. After filling a number of diocesan offices
with distinction, he was appointed Bishop of Providence in May 1924.
As he left the Diocese of Providence, he no doubt was best remembered
for the just but kind and pastoral way he had dealt with his priests
and people. His two outstanding specific accomplishments, however,
were: he used his knowledge of French and his gracious personality
to soften the differences between the French-speaking and English-
speaking members of his flock that had arisen under some of his
predecessors; and, through his financial ability, he had entirely wiped
out the large debt which had burdened the diocese at the time of his
arrival.

Archbishop Keough came to us with a fine reputation of a
great pastoral Bishop, much beloved by both priests and people of
Providence. He lost no time instituting in Baltimore the kind of pastoral ministry he had exercised in Providence. Within the first year,
he endeavored to visit as many of the parishes as possible, either to
administer the Sacrament of Confirmation or to conduct a special
parish visitation where this seemed required, and he created the kind
of impression one would expect in accord with his reputation. Within
the first two years, he had become familiar with every part of the
archdiocese, including the extreme western end, which lies two hundred miles from Baltimore.

From the beginning, my own relations with him were cordial. As
time progressed, I felt we had become quite close friends—close, but

never truly intimate. Recently, Brother Thomas Spalding, who is writing a long-overdue history of the archdiocese, said to me: "I get the impression that Archbishop Keough was a very private person." This, in contrast to the impression he had acquired of Archbishop Curley. The observation, I believe, is up to a point quite exact. I would draw out the contrast by adding that Curley enjoyed the spectacular and dramatically lived up to each occasion of it. Keough, on the other hand, carefully shunned anything that verged on the spectacular, almost to an excessive degree. As a consequence life under Curley tended to be more interesting, sometimes painfully so. Life under Keough was calmer and seemed less hazardous.

One thing that somewhat affected our working relationship was Archbishop Keough's apparent lack of a sense of time. During the first part of his administration, as his Auxiliary and Vicar General I adopted the habit of periodically calling on him at his office, which was then in the rectory of the Basilica of the Assumption, to report anything in my work I thought should be brought to his attention and to receive any instruction he cared to give. I always first called his secretary to inquire when it would be convenient for him to see me briefly. Invariably, on arrival I would find two or three persons waiting to see him. At the first opportunity, he would give me a very friendly greeting. Always he would say: "Père, go up to my study and wait for me. You will find plenty of reading material there. As soon as I have seen these people, I shall join you. We can then talk and have lunch together." It would be past one o'clock before he finished these seemingly indeterminate engagements. We would talk and have a very enjoyable lunch together, just the two of us. It would be well into the afternoon when I left, sometimes with nothing of importance accomplished. On the other hand, I found that I could pick up the telephone and reach him at any time; or he would call to ask me— rather apologetically, it seemed to me—to substitute for him at some particular Confirmation engagement he could not fulfill, or to undertake some task that required immediate attention. Thus, I soon came to depend on the telephone for practically all of my contacts with him. Later, when he had acquired the Lanahan estate and had taken residence in that family's former home, he never failed to invite me to dinner on the great feasts of Christmas, Easter, and Thanksgiving, as well as on some other special occasions. On the feasts, his brother Michael, Michael's wife Margaret, and their son Francis, named after the Archbishop, would be staying with him. The only other persons present were Will Galvin, the archdiocesan attorney who had also served Archbishop Curley, and Will's wife Nell. These were truly enjoyable occasions and I came to know a different and more attractive side of his personality. During that period, I drew much closer to him in friendship.

As the Archbishop moved around the archdiocese in his pastoral work, he became aware of several of its rather urgent needs. Among them was a residence for those aging individuals and couples who did not qualify for entrance into the home of the Little Sisters of the Poor by reason of utter destitution, yet needed an institution where they would find the care, safety, and a friendly and congenial religious atmosphere. He also became aware of the fact that the almost century-old children's institutions like St. Vincent's Home for Infants, St. Mary's Orphanage for Girls, and St. Vincent's Orphanage for Boys, would soon have to be replaced if the work carried on by them were to continue.

About this time, Mr. W. W. Lanahan died, leaving a magnificent estate of about one hundred fifty-three choice acres of Baltimore County rolling countryside, located about ten miles north of the city on the Dulaney Valley Road. Mr. Galvin, who by this time had become a member of the board of directors of the Safe Deposit and Trust Company, soon learned that Mrs. Lanahan was eager to sell so that she would not be burdened with the management of such a large property with its livestock, its wheat and corn fields, its farm hands, etc. Taking into consideration its potential future value, it could be purchased for a very reasonable price. The Archbishop authorized Galvin to attempt to purchase the estate, and before long, the property had been secured for the sum of $153,000. The Archbishop then engaged the architectural firm of James R. Edmunds, whose reputation had been enhanced by work recently done for the Johns Hopkins Hospital and Medical School, to draw plans for a new home for the aged. Even before that building was completed, he had another architect draw plans for a second institution to be located on the same property, ultimately to be known as Villa Maria, to replace the two orphanages of St. Vincent and St. Mary.

While Archbishop Keough kept me informed about his diocesan activities and projects, I cannot say that, except in one case of which I shall speak later, he ever really consulted me or sought my advice. There was really no reason why he should have done so. During his twelve years in Providence, he had very successfully conducted a diocese more populous than Baltimore without the assistance of an Auxiliary Bishop, and with an old and much respected pastor as his

Vicar General. I believe that I learned a great deal, however, simply by observing the Archbishop's quiet, efficient way of getting things done and from my quite general conversations with him from time to time.

After he had been here about three years, the Archbishop was obliged to undertake one project into which he did gradually draw me more closely. That was the carrying out of the provisions of the O'Neill will, which directly involved the Archbishop of Baltimore. On his death in 1929, Thomas J. O'Neill, a wealthy Catholic merchant who was the sole owner of one of the city's large department stores, left his entire fortune in trust for his wife, with the provision that on her death the corpus of the estate should be equally divided in three ways: one-third to go to the Jesuit Fathers of the Maryland Province for a specified purpose; one-third to an ecumenical board of directors, of which the Archbishop of Baltimore was to be *ex officio* chairman, for the erection and endowment of a hospital to be called "The Good Samaritan"; one-third to the Archbishop of Baltimore, Corporation Sole, for the erection of a new Cathedral. On the death of Mrs. O'Neill in 1936, the Jesuits received their part of the corpus. Since the remaining two shares of the residue were not sufficient either to erect and endow the hospital or to construct a Cathedral church, these portions were held by the Safe Deposit and Trust Company to be invested until each of the new separate corpuses would have increased sufficiently to justify undertaking the specified projects. During his tenure as a member of the board of the bank, Galvin informed the Archbishop that the Internal Revenue Service had begun to make inquiries about these two now rather large untaxed funds which had lain unused so long in the bank. Obviously, some prompt action had to be taken in reference to both projects. The Archbishop and the other members of the hospital board proceeded to buy suitable land for the hospital on Loch Raven Boulevard at the corner of Belvedere Avenue. Still, however, it was clear that the corpus was not large enough to erect and endow a modern hospital. The remainder of that corpus, therefore, was retained by the bank for further increase. But there was no sufficient reason why the Archbishop should not now take positive action for the erection of the new Cathedral.

One difficulty, however, stood in the way. In the year 1936, Archbishop Curley through William Galvin had purchased the very beautiful property on North Charles Street now occupied by the Cathedral of Mary Our Queen. On this site, he had caused to be placed a large sign stating that this was to be the site of the new Catholic Cathedral. About the same time, *The Catholic Review* published a sketch of a cathedral in the French Gothic style by the firm of Locraft and Murphy. Fred Murphy, the senior member of the firm, was reputed to be a personal friend of Archbishop Curley. But according to my memory, Locraft and Murphy had drawn the sketch on their own initiative. Curley had not ordered it and had not awarded the firm a contract, supposedly in order not to tie the hands of any successor who would be called on to build the Cathedral. Nevertheless, the sketch was published in the official archdiocesan newspaper. Did this seventeen-year-old sketch form the basis of any justifiable claim on the part of Locraft and Murphy? If it did, and if that firm advanced any claim, the whole matter was amicably settled to the satisfaction of both parties. In any event, Archbishop Keough had definitely decided that he wanted the Boston firm of Maginnis, Walsh and Kennedy to be the architects of the new Cathedral, and that firm was understandably pleased to accept the responsibility.

When preliminary sketches of the building had been prepared, the Archbishop was asked to come to Boston to examine them in the Maginnis headquarters, where members of the staff would be on hand to answer any questions. To my surprise, the Archbishop invited me to accompany himself and Galvin. He seemed truly desirous that I should come and express my opinion of what was to be offered. I naturally was glad to accept the invitation.

When we arrived, three sketches were placed before us. The first, by the elder Maginnis, was in the French Gothic style. The second, by the younger Maginnis, was completely modern. The third, by Eugene Kennedy, was what I would call a modern adaption of English Gothic. In any previous age, I am sure that I would have preferred the sketch of the elder Maginnis. But when I recalled from my Washington years the difficulty experienced by the Vestry of the Washington Episcopal Cathedral in completing their structure according to the plans and drawings of the Frohman design, I had grave doubts about the practicality of the elder Maginnis' sketch. On the other hand, my mind almost instantaneously rejected the younger Maginnis' modernistic sketch as having nothing of real beauty about it—nothing that was even reminiscent of the great cathedrals of the past. The Kennedy design, on the other hand, seemed to preserve the flavor of English Gothic. It was indeed lacking in the elaborate stonework characteristic of true Gothic, which in our times, especially since World War II, cannot be duplicated. Its windows might be described as elongated quadrangles or oblongs, but the way they were grouped and set suggested a Gothic structure. Without any doubt, it was the sketch of a cathedral and nothing else. In my opinion it had a quality of real nobility about it. I believe that in the end all three of us came to the same conclusion: that from both the aesthetic and practical points of view, the Kennedy sketch was to be preferred.

Here I may say a word about the difference between the Kennedy sketch and the actual finished structure. As I remember the original sketch, it did not show what some have criticized as the excessively long nave. That was brought about first by the large seating capacity (1500 to 1800) on which Archbishop Keough insisted as of primary importance, by his equal insistence that from every seat there be an unobstructed view of the altar, and by the long lower sanctuary with its side stalls which were meant to accommodate numbers of seminarians, garbed in cassock and surplice, who in the pre-Council days sang the chant of the Holy Week services and on the great feasts of Christmas, Easter, and Pentecost, and at other special celebrations.

In a way, it was unfortunate that the final decisions about the architecture of the Cathedral had to be made almost twenty years before the Second Vatican Council opened. As for the length of the nave, it is rather interestingly broken by the beautiful rounded baptistry and the chapel of St. Joseph on the south side and by the equally beautiful sacristy and Blessed Sacrament chapel on the north. The aesthetic quality of any building should be judged, I believe, as seen from the best angle, not the worst. To properly appreciate the new Baltimore Cathedral, one should begin by studying the two magnificent photographs made of it by A. Aubrey Bodine, one from the northeast and the other from the corresponding southeast angle, and published in *The Sun* shortly after the Cathedral was finished.

After we returned from our Boston trip, I had no subsequent opportunity to be further involved in the plans for the new Cathedral, for shortly thereafter, I received a confidential letter from the Apostolic Delegate notifying me that the Holy Father wished to appoint me Bishop of the newly founded Diocese of Bridgeport, Connecticut. I was asked to signify in writing whether or not I would accept the appointment. Although the letter was marked *sub secreto,* in order to bring the matter to the attention of the Archbishop and to seek his advice, I followed the principle that one can always consult one trustworthy person. He unhesitatingly advised me to accept the appointment. He expressed regret that the county of Litchfield had not been joined to that of Fairfield in the creation of the new diocese; but Fairfield County alone would form a good diocese, where I could advantageously exercise my espiscopal ministry. I did therefore accept, and on August 6 the Holy See announced my appointment as Bishop of Bridgeport.

6. First Bishop of Bridegport, 1953-61

WHEN I FORWARDED MY LETTER of acceptance of the Bridgeport appointment to Archbishop Cicognani, I informed him that I had planned to attend the dedication of the new North American College on October 15 in the company of Archbishop Keough. The Archbishop had also promised to preach at the ceremony of my installation if it could be conveniently postponed until after his return. Would it be proper for me to arrange a date that would meet with the Archbishop's convenience? In his response, the Apostolic Delegate assured me that he saw no difficulty in postponing the installation until after our return from Rome. After consulting Archbishop Keough, Archbishop Henry J. O'Brien of Hartford, and the acting rector of Bridgeport's newly designated Cathedral, I chose December 1, 1953, for my installation.

The dedication of the North American College turned out to be an event of solemn significance. Pope Pius XII came to bless the new college building and delivered a discourse addressed mainly to the student body. The three American Cardinals—Mooney, Stritch, and Spellman—were there, as were many American Bishops, alumni of the old college, numerous officials of the Roman Curia, heads of Roman universities and seminaries. Archbishop Keough, as Chairman of the U.S. Conference of Bishops (then the National Catholic Welfare Conference), was the celebrant of the Solemn Benediction of the Blessed Sacrament, which followed the Pope's blessing and discourse.

The day after the dedication, I left by the Rome-Paris train in order to take the S.S. *United States* back to New York. On the train, I found Cardinal Mooney and his secretary Father (now Bishop) Joseph Breitenbeck, who were scheduled to return on the same ship. The Cardinal had succeeded Bishop O'Mahoney as the spiritual director of the North American College during my last year as a student there, and his coming there had been the source of real encouragement to me at a time of unquestionable need. He had also invited me to give the priests' retreat in Detroit after reading my articles on the priesthood in *The Voice*. May I say of him that I know of no distinguished prelate in the modern Church who has been more ready to give encouragement to younger persons in whom he thought he saw signs of promise. Both on the train and on the ship he invited me to take my meals with himself and Breitenbeck. Their company made the journey home a most pleasant one.

At the New York dock I was surprised to be met by Father James McLaughlin, who introduced himself as the present administrator of St. Augustine Cathedral in Bridgeport, and Father James Murphy, Director of Bridgeport Catholic Charities, who resided at St. Augustine's and performed weekend duties in the parish. They told me that they and all the priests and people of the new diocese were delighted with its recent establishment and that I could expect from them a warm welcome and wholehearted cooperation. They then gave me a rather pressing invitation to accompany them in their automobile to Bridgeport for at least a glimpse of the church which would soon become my Cathedral, and to get an idea of the layout of offices and living quarters they were preparing for the Chancellor and myself in the rectory. I assured them that although I had an engagement that afternoon in New York which I was not free to break, the next day I would have a friend bring me by automobile to the St. Augustine rectory, where I would be happy to meet them. Meanwhile I would be pleased if they would drop me off at the Commodore Hotel, where I intended to stop during my short stay in New York.

The friend I was referring to was Father George Curtiss, who had served with me as an assistant at St. Patrick's in Washington. He had initially planned to meet me at the ship, but hearing from his friend Father Murphy that he and Father McLaughlin were already planning to meet me, Curtiss telegraphed to me that he would see me at the Commodore. That afternoon we had a long conversation in which he gave me a detailed description of my new diocese. After the year in Washington, he had spent more than fifteen years in the area that constituted the new diocese, first as assistant at St. Ann's in Bridgeport along with Father James Murphy, with whom he had developed a close friendship, and then at St. Peter's in Danbury. He was therefore familiar with the whole area and with the priestly personnel in the different parishes. He confirmed the statement of Murphy and McLaughlin that both priests and laity were greatly pleased at the establishment of the diocese in western Connecticut. He noted that the one thing most desired by the people in general was the development of Catholic education both on the elementary and, especially, on the high-school level. He gave me a good picture of the diocese as a whole, with enough details to help me to adjust to conditions I would find there. He was high in his praise of both Murphy and McLaughlin, with whom I would be associated at the Cathedral—particularly Jim Murphy. Having completed postgraduate studies in social work, Murphy had been appointed Director of Catholic Charities. He had done an excellent job and had gradually achieved a role of effective leadership in the field of welfare in the Bridgeport community. When Curtiss learned that I had promised to visit St. Augustine's the following day, he offered to stay over and drive me to Bridgeport.

Arriving at the rectory a little after eleven o'clock, I found both Murphy and McLaughlin awaiting me. After a few moments of general conversation, we proceeded to the Cathedral. It was a fairly large neo-Gothic granite structure with a high steeple rising over its main front entrance and had a seating capacity of about nine hundred. It had been erected according to the plans and under the supervision of that prolific architect Patrick Keeley at that time in the nineteenth century when Bridgeport was emerging as the main industrial center of Connecticut. In my judgment, it was no masterpiece of architecture, and it showed the dinginess and wear of many years' usage. Although its interior manifested no very striking features, it was pleasing enough in general appearance. It certainly could serve well as the Bridgeport Cathedral. It did not take long to see all that was to be seen. On returning to the rectory, we examined the offices and the living quarters that were being prepared for the Bishop and the Chancellor. All the arrangements met with my full approval. In our conversation it became clear that Archbishop O'Brien had asked McLaughlin to take responsibility for the entire ceremony of installation—the appointment and rehearsal of the officers of the Mass, selection of the proper music, preparation of the vestments, the reception of Bishops who would be attending the ceremony. He had delegated Jim Murphy to assume responsibility for all events away from the Cathedral: the reception at the railroad station of myself and the Baltimore priests and laity who would accompany me, transportation, hotel reservations, the luncheon at the Stratfield Hotel that would follow the ceremony, the invitation of guests for both the ceremony and the luncheon. It was evident that the whole affair was in capable hands and that nothing would be overlooked. I was indeed favorably impressed by the ability and the goodwill of both Murphy and McLaughlin.

At the very pleasant luncheon that followed I had an opportunity to meet the other priests of the household, Fathers Vincent Cleary and Thomas Keeney, and after luncheon, the housekeeper and the cook. To these two I remarked that apparently my coming would bring them a good deal of additional work, but they and everyone else assured me that they were pleased to have a real part in the celebration that was being prepared. Meanwhile Murphy had made a reservation for me on the early afternoon Boston-to-Washington through train and would telephone to Baltimore the time of my arrival so that someone would meet me there. I came away favorably impressed with what I had seen of the Diocese of Bridgeport—and particularly with Murphy and Mc-Laughlin. If they were representative of the priests with whom I would be working, I felt that I had good reason to believe that all would go well.

Archbishop Keough and his group returned from Europe early in November. A day or two later I learned from Monsignor Porter White the details of the trip. The group left Rome on schedule and traveled north throughout Italy by train, stopping at Florence and Venice, and then on into Switzerland. At Lucerne, which had been one of the Archbishop's favorite European cities since his student days at Issy, he suffered what seemed to be a rather mild return of the heart trouble he had experienced the previous spring. However, after resting for a day or two while the others were sightseeing, he seemed to recover enough to continue with the group. For him and Porter White, this cast a pall over the rest of the trip. The journey down the Rhine and through the Black Forest, meant to be the highlight of the trip, proved disappointing—rain and fog all the way. They saw virtually nothing of the Black Forest. Nevertheless the Archbishop pushed steadfastly on with the group until they reached LeHavre, France. There they boarded the French liner that would take them to New York. The restful voyage home seemed to infuse new strength into the Archbishop's body and to raise his spirit. He was actually able to preside over the November meeting of the Bishops' Conference.

Shortly before Thanksgiving Day, he suffered a third and massive heart seizure, which kept him confined to his bed for many days, and forced him to take the rest and treatment he should have received on the occasion of his first attack the previous spring. It was now evident that he would be unable to come to Bridgeport for my installation. Happily, Bishop Russell agreed to take his place.

Two days before my departure, a delegation of priests from the Diocese of Bridgeport arrived in Baltimore to accompany me to my new diocese. Shortly after their arrival they telephoned from the Lord Baltimore Hotel. Although it was too late to join them that evening, I arranged to meet with them in the forenoon of the following day and to have luncheon with them at the hotel. Those whom I especially remember were: Monsignor Leo Finn, pastor of St. Peter's parish, Bridgeport, and Supreme Chaplain of the Knights of Columbus; Monsignor William Kearney, pastor of Sacred Heart; Father Thomas Mooney, pastor of St. Ambrose, Bridgeport, and (lest it seem like an Irish delegation) Father Michael Carnicke, pastor of the Slovak parish of St. John Nepomucene, representing the various national (ethnic, we would say today) parishes, and finally Father Nicholas Coleman, pastor of St. John's parish in Stamford, representing, no doubt, the other important regions of the diocese outside the city of Bridgeport. They, like all others, assured me that the priests and laity of all Fairfield County were delighted to have a diocese of their own (even at the cost of having a stranger as their Bishop). They, too, stressed the warmth of the reception I would receive and the cooperation I could expect. After a pleasant luncheon and a very agreeable conversation we parted with the mutual assurance that we would meet the next morning on the train that would carry us all to Bridgeport.

Late that afternoon I paid a final visit to the Archbishop to say good-bye and to thank him for all the kindness he had shown me during the six years I had served as his Auxiliary. He was obviously still a very sick man, although he was fully alert mentally and there were signs of some physical improvement. He remarked that I would certainly be returning to Baltimore from time to time to visit my sister, my brothers and their families. He knew that it would always be more convenient to stay either at Stella Maris or at Long Crandon, where a room and bath would always be ready for me, with the chapel nearby for Mass. Moreover, transportation to wherever I wished to go would always be available. So earnest and so pressing was the invitation, and so much was it in accord with my own preference, that I most gratefully promised him that I would accept his invitation whenever I would return. This Christmas would be too soon after my installation in Bridgeport, but I did plan in future years to return each year between Christmas and the New Year to maintain contact with my family and to renew old acquaintances. I assured him that each time I would return I would first get in touch with him or with Porter White to find out whether I could accept his most generous offer without interfering with his own plans. And so I bade him a sad farewell, for in my mind I was not at all sure that I would ever see him again.

The Archbishop's powers of recovery were to prove remarkable. Perhaps most important of all, he really *wanted* to get well as soon as possible. He felt he still had important work to undertake. He wanted to build that new Cathedral. If any of the O'Neill funds were left after that, he wanted to begin the program of high school construction for which he knew his priests and people were clamoring. So, under the careful supervision of Sister Celeste, R.S.M. and his doctor, it was not long before he was able gradually to resume his work. Although from that time on, the problem of health would always be a major consideration in all that he would undertake, in the eight years that were still to be his he was able to bring nearly to completion the work to which he believed himself called.

The next morning I met the Bridgeport delegation on the train as planned. A good number of Baltimore priests and lay friends had also arranged to accompany me. Among them were Bishop Russell, who was to preach at the next day's ceremony, Joe Ells, Joe Leary, Joe Nelligan, and Jerome Sebastian, who was to succeed me as the Auxiliary Bishop of Baltimore. We were on the morning Washington-to-Boston through train.

On leaving New York, we soon crossed into the southwestern tip of Connecticut—our first sight of the Diocese of Bridgeport. Hardly had we entered my new "home state" when the train came to a sudden and unscheduled stop at Greenwich. Father Joseph Ganley, pastor of St. Catherine's Riverside, had prearranged it. On hand was a large group of his parishioners to greet me and cheer me on the way. At Stamford, a regularly scheduled stop, the scene at Greenwich was repeated with an even larger crowd participating as a result of prearrangement by Father Nicholas Coleman, who was with us, and the other local pastors. The same thing happened at Norwalk. My entrance into the diocese began to seem almost like a triumphal procession. I shall turn to Monsignor John Toomey in his brief "biography" prepared for *The Catholic Review* on the occasion of my fiftieth anniversary of ordination to the priesthood (December 23, 1972) for the description of what followed:

One of the priests of Baltimore accompanying Bishop Shehan, in describing his arrival, said, "The warmth of the reception accorded Bishop Shehan exceeded by far anything we had a right to expect or even imagine." Seven thousand people awaited the new Bishop at the rairoad station in Bridgeport. Alighting from the train the Bishop said:

"It is with deep emotion that I set foot on the soil of the Diocese of Bridgeport and the State of Connecticut. It would be untrue to say that I did not leave the Archdiocese of Baltimore, made dear by so many personal and historic associations, with real sorrow. But the spirit with which you have received me more than makes up for the sorrow of my recent parting. I am now with all my heart and soul a citizen of Connecticut, an inhabitant of Fairfield County, and a resident of Bridgeport. It is my earnest hope that I shall spend the rest of my days among you—with you I hope to live and die." [I was now fifty-five years old. In the normal course of events, I could—as I did—take for granted that this would be my last ecclesiastical assignment.]

The ceremony of Bishop Shehan's installation, held in the newly-designated Cathedral Church, St. Augustine's, was a very brilliant affair attended by Governor Lodge of Connecticut, Mayor McLevy of Bridgeport, dozens of other civic officials, twenty-seven members of the Catholic hierarchy, over four hundred priests and hundreds of religious and laity. The sermon was preached by Bishop John J. Russell of Charleston, South Carolina, classmate and friend of Bishop Shehan. He was acting in place of Archbishop Francis P. Keough of Baltimore who had fallen ill.

The Mass and ceremony of my installation were followed by a luncheon at the Stratfield Hotel. There James Murphy acted as toastmaster, and Archbishop O'Brien gave a brief talk. My own response was, I believe, something quite different from what was expected.

On the previous day when I presented to Archbishop O'Brien of Hartford the formal document of my appointment, I had taken the occasion to discuss with him and Bishop Hackett, his Auxiliary, the appointments to official posts that I would soon have to make. Before my meeting with Murphy and McLaughlin, I had known only two priests of the diocese: Bartholomew (Bert) Skelly, whom I had known at St. Charles College, and George Curtiss, who was my fellow assistant at St. Patrick's during the first year after his ordination. Skelly was already pastor of the flourishing parish of St. Teresa of Lisieux in

Trumbull and certainly could not be expected to accept willingly a position in the Chancery, where there could be no certainty of permanence. Curtiss was intelligent, hard-working, systematic, and totally reliable, qualities which I knew from long experience would be needed in a Chancellor. His one drawback was that he had no canonical training beyond that received in the ordinary seminary course, but this would have been true of anyone available for the position. When I told the Archbishop and Hackett that I thought of appointing Curtiss as Chancellor, they both expressed the opinion that he would make good in that position. I next said that I thought of making Jim Murphy rector of the Cathedral and retaining him also as Director of Charities, and that I had been favorably impressed with Jim McLaughlin and thought I could work with him with complete confidence as my secretary. They considered that I would make no mistake in either appointment. Finally I thought of appointing Monsignor John Kennedy, pastor of St. Peter's in Danbury and one of the most venerable and highly respected priests of the new diocese, whose mind was still sound and active, as the Vicar General. This, too, met with their approval.

The following day, then, in my speech at the luncheon, after thanking all the priests and people of the diocese for the warmth of their reception and paying special tribute to Murphy and McLaughlin for the preparations they had made, I went on to announce the new appointments. I then announced that the office of the Chancery would be open for business the next morning. This was possible because Murphy and McLaughlin had made all the necessary arrangements: the purchase of the proper furniture, stationery, and equipment, the installation of extra telephone lines, and the employment of a secretary who could serve in the beginning also as telephone operator. Everyone seemed genuinely pleased that we were prepared to operate as a full-fledged diocese from the very beginning.

With the exception of Monsignor Kennedy, who died within a year or two and was succeeded by Monsignor William Kearney as Vicar General, the others I have mentioned served faithfully in these or other posts throughout my entire ministry in Bridgeport. Here I should like to take time to pay tribute to them. Murphy was indeed a truly remarkable man. During his latter student days he had become rather badly crippled with arthritis of the spine, which made his stance and his movement somewhat awkward. He had a fine mind and an indomitable will which would never let his physical infirmity interfere with his priestly work. After completing the seminary course, he had attended the School of Social Work at The Catholic University of America and then was placed in charge of the Bridgeport Catholic Charities. So well had he done his work there, that long before my arrival he stood head and shoulders over every other social worker in the area.

James McLaughlin was a much younger man, friendly and intelligent, well-built, with a pleasing countenance, who during his years of service at St. Augustine's had become much loved by the parishioners. Besides serving as my secretary, he continued to fulfill many functions within the parish of St. Augustine, where he retained residence. He continued as my secretary for a period of about three years, assisting in every way possible. Then I was able to appoint him pastor of St. Mary's Church in Ridgefield, much to his satisfaction.

George Curtiss, the Chancellor of the diocese, as I have mentioned, had become a good friend when we were at St. Patrick's in Washington, and we had continued that friendship during the subsequent years. He had returned for the funeral of Monsignor Thomas and later for my ordination as Auxiliary Bishop of Baltimore and Washington. As Chancellor, he lived up to my highest expectations, and as the years went on our friendship deepened.

To remedy his lack of experience in canon law, Curtiss consulted Monsignor John J. Hayes of Stamford and two canonists on the faculty of the Holy Ghost Fathers' St. Mary Seminary in Norwalk, Fathers Charles Connors, C.S.Sp., and John Walsh of that same community. For financial matters he drew on the expertise of Mr. J. William Hope, a Catholic layman eminent in the field of accounting. With their help and under their close direction, Curtiss set up the books, records, and accounts of the Bridgeport Chancery. As a result, through his methodical care and devotion, I believe it can be said that we possessed as complete and perfect a set of records as could be found in any recently founded diocese.

Since, however, both he and I recognized the disadvantages of not having a properly trained canonist in the Chancery, we began very soon to look around for a young priest who could be so trained. With the advice of men like Kearney and Hayes, we came to the conclusion that Father John Toomey, then an assistant at St. Peter's in Bridgeport, was by far the most promising candidate to make the required studies, with the prospect of becoming Assistant Chancellor on his return. The only question was: would Toomey's health hold up under the strain of studies and three winters in Rome? Like myself as a young priest, he as a seminarian had gone through a bout with tuberculosis. In the light of my own experience, I was not inclined to look upon that as an insuperable obstacle. Moreover, he was willing to take the chance and confident that he knew sufficiently well how to safeguard his health. That the choice was a good one became evident when at the end of the first year he was signally honored for his excellence in canonical studies; it became all the more evident when at the end of his studies he returned with his doctorate. At that time he was able to take McLaughlin's place as secretary and also to assume the duties of Assistant Chancellor. If in any way I failed to measure up to the highest standards of a pastoral Bishop, it was not for the lack of guidance and support from those who surrounded me.

As I made my way around the diocese, one of the most frequent needs and desires I heard expressed by both priests and people was that for Catholic high schools. Up to that time, such high schools as existed seemed to be generally within the reach only of the wealthy or upper middle class: Fairfield College Preparatory School for boys, conducted by the Jesuit Fathers, and three high schools for girls: Sacred Heart Academy, Stamford, conducted by the Sisters of St. Joseph; and the two Academies of the Sacred Heart—one at Noroton, the other in Greenwich—conducted by the Madames of the Sacred Heart. I do not wish to imply that these schools gave no consideration to poorer students of promise, but in the nature of things the kind of education they offered was in general beyond the reach of those families on the lower income scale. I should mention that Monsignor Michael Guerin of St. Mary's, Greenwich, had received permission to start a parish high school for boys and girls in that city. One of my earlier decisions was that I would try to overcome the imbalance of Catholic high school education in the diocese. Bridgeport itself, without any Catholic high school facilities, seemed the proper place to begin. If we were successful there, then we could proceed to other areas—Stamford, Norwalk, and Danbury, in particular.

At the time, one of the most prominent fund-raising firms which seemed to specialize in working for Catholic institutions was the Community Counselling Service, with headquarters in New York City. Accordingly, I invited that organization to conduct a survey of the city of Bridgeport and the surrounding area in an effort to see if a financial campaign for the erection of a high school might be feasible. The survey showed that not only did such a campaign seem feasible, but that it was much desired by both priests and people as the only way of acquiring a Catholic high school. Accordingly, the Community Counselling Service was retained to conduct the campaign. Such endeavors have become so common since then that there is no need here to describe it in any detail. Suffice it to say that the effort was highly successful, producing far more than the anticipated amount. As a result, we were able to erect the truly beautiful high school of Notre Dame for both boys and girls, one of the first co-educational Catholic high schools in Connecticut, with a total capacity of almost two thousand students. The Holy Cross Fathers, Eastern Province, undertook to staff the boys' division. The Notre Dame de Namur Sisters provided the staff for that of the girls. From the beginning, the school flourished and proved effective encouragement to go on to the erection of Stamford Catholic High and later Central Catholic High in Norwalk. When those three were finished and in successful operation, we purchased suitable property in the Danbury region, but before plans were even started my Bridgeport ministry had ended.

To provide some picture of my life and activity during the Bridgeport years, I turn again to Monsignor John Toomey, as one who seemed to me to have the ability to state well what came under his personal observation. Let me assure the reader that I had no knowledge of Toomey's piece until I saw it in print. I hasten to add that I was pleased that he had written it; moreover, I am pleased to use it in this chapter. The reader must remember, however, that the account has been written by a friend who himself played an important part in what we accomplished, by his constant help and encouragement, about which he remains completely silent.

Here I give part of the Toomey narrative:

Bishop Shehan ordained 151 priests in Bridgeport. He introduced into the diocese six new religious communities of women and three new communities of men. At his invitation four communities of sisters established new provincial houses; one community of men located its provincial house here. Under religious auspices a new seminary and new novitiate were set up.

A major accomplishment was the erection by Bishop Shehan of St. Joseph's Manor, a beautiful multi-million dollar home for the aged in Trumbull, Connecticut, set in rolling hills. It was dedicated in 1960 by Archbishop Henry J. O'Brien of Hartford. Accommodating 300 guests, it is administered by the Carmelite

Sisters for the Sick and Aged. For its beauty, its up-to-date services and care given to the elderly, it remains a show-piece for the practice of geriatrics. . . .

In June 1961 he celebrated the first Diocesan Synod, to enact and promulgate legislation for the spiritual and temporal welfare of the diocese. This climaxed a year's work by synodal commissions and officials with whom he worked closely and intensely.

Just before leaving in 1961 he launched the project of a diocesan youth recreation center located in the heart of the City of Bridgeport. When completed a year later, it was named the Archbishop Shehan Center.

I should pause to pay tribute to those whose help was essential to me in carrying out these various projects. The layman on whom I placed the greatest reliance and from whom I received most help was Mr. Philip Epifano, head of the E & F (Epifano and Frasinnelli) Construction Company. Not only was he a generous contributor to the diocese, but on every possible occasion he was of the most valuable help and undertook for me the greatest part of the construction work. In all of it, I placed complete confidence in him, and never did I have reason to regret it. Hardly less do I owe to Mr. J. William Hope. To his advice and guidance the diocese in large measure owed the soundness of its financial operation from the beginning. Again, one of the leading and most helpful laymen was Mr. Gerald Phelan, head of a prominent architectural firm of Bridgeport, and designer of two of our finest high schools as well as St. Joseph Manor for the Aged. Richard Joyce Smith, distinguished attorney, I held as a valuable advisor and still hold as a true friend. In this group must of course be included Mr. James O'Connell. Almost from the beginning, with the exception of the first few months, he served as our diocesan attorney. He was always at our service and always most helpful. Alphonsus J. Donahue, Jr., of Stamford was not only one of the leading citizens of that city, but also most helpful to the Church, and a true friend of myself and John Toomey, through whom I first came to know him. Last but by no means least, John Doran of Danbury, a close friend also of George Curtiss, who accompanied me to Rome in 1965, when I received the Red Hat, and again in 1977 to celebrate the 300th anniversary of the Irish Dominicans at San Clemente, my titular church. Finally, I must express my deep gratitude to Miss Margaret Gruce for her devoted service as secretary.

The small circle of priest-advisors and friends I have already mentioned on several occasions: John Toomey, George Curtiss, James

Murphy, and James McLaughlin. When Murphy died, his place was taken by John Barney, both as pastor of the Cathedral parish and as good friend and adviser. To that circle was later added William Genuario, who shortly after my arrival was ordained by me, went to Rome for studies in canon law, and returned to make himself indispensable in so many ways. To many others I shall always owe a deep debt of gratitude: Bert Skelly, pastor of St. Teresa's parish in Trumbull; Thomas Henehan of the parish of the Assumption in Fairfield; Henry Callahan of St. Mary's in Norwalk, who unfortunately died about the middle of my administration; Harry Flanagan of St. Thomas Church, Norwalk; David Bannon of St. Peter's in Bridgeport; Michael Carnicke, pastor of St. John Nepomucene Slovak parish in Bridgeport and later Holy Name Slovak parish in Stamford, famous for his knowledge of and readiness to discuss the history of the Chornok Schism that had occurred many years before my arrival; William Fox, grand old man of St. Aloysius in New Canaan, and Francis McGuire, who succeeded him on his death; Martin O'Connor, rough and ready chaplain of World War II who returned to carry out his own unique ministry in the diocese; Michael Guerin, already mentioned, who was able to combine a ministry to both rich and poor of that unique town of Greenwich.

In the city of Stamford there were two prelatial characters who deserve very special mention. John Hayes, as pastor of St. Mary's parish, was thought by many to preside over the most beautiful church in the diocese. He was a colorful speaker with a good literary style, widely read in English literature, and fond of quoting Shakespeare and Browning. He became the first *Officialis* of the diocese, but I am afraid he gave the Tribunal only the broadest supervision; most of the work was done by the hard-working and very efficient secretary, Father Patrick Donnelly, later named Monsignor. Finally, there was Monsignor Nicholas P. Coleman, pastor of St. John's in Stamford, efficient, lovable, but also crotchety. One of the priests who had known him from boyhood described him as "notorious for evaluating his parishioners according to their standing in the envelope collection list, and for collecting long-overdue cemetery bills for past annual care, with interest." Nick, as all his friends called him, was in Rome in 1959 for the centennial of the North American College at the time I was there for the only *ad limina* visit of my Bridgeport career. At my invitation, he joined those who accompanied me to the Vatican for my private audience. When Pope John XXIII emerged with me from his study to meet those who had come with me, Nick took him by the elbow and engaged him in friendly conversation in surprisingly fluent Italian. Pope John, however, brought the conversation to a rather sudden end by good-humoredly referring to "us old men." Nick, of course, was delighted to be put in the same class with the Pope.

In the middle of my Bridgeport administration one incident which may be worthy of notice was occasioned by an attempt to introduce into this rather conservative area an example of what I would call ultra-modern church architecture. The region of the little village of Georgetown had begun to develop rapidly. The still-young pastor rightly decided that a new church was needed in the neighboring town of Weston. Without previous consultation with me, he interested an architect who had received acclaim for some modern commercial structures to produce preliminary drawings for a new church. Together they agreed that it must be modern in style. The special virtue of his design was that all lines of the church would converge on the altar. This meant that the lines of the ceiling would be slanted to lead the eye to the altar; there would be within the church no visible supports for the ceiling and roof. The architect, however, claimed that he could guarantee the projected church would be structurally sound. He and the pastor elicited enthusiastic support from some very prominent persons. To make a long story short, as soon as I received the drawings together with a description of the proposed structure and had gone over them hastily, I handed them over to Philip Epifano for his judgment. After a few days he returned them to me and assured me that he had studied them carefully. He said that he would not build such a structure under any conditions. He had two main criticisms: the type of roof that was proposed, besides presenting obvious difficulties of drainage, could not be trusted to sustain the weight of the accumulated snow that had to be expected in that area; second, even supposing that these difficulties could be resolved, the construction costs of such a project would be completely out of line with that of other parish churches throughout the diocese. On the basis of Epifano's report, I decided that I would have to bring to an end the dream of the pastor, the architect, and their supporters. The decision, I am confident, won me the reputation of being no friend of modern church architecture, but such is the cost one must pay for having to make final decisions. I considered myself then, as I do now, reasonably open on such matters.

When I had arrived in Bridgeport, I had taken up residence in the rectory of St. Augustine's, as had George Curtiss. We both had our offices and our bedrooms there, and a small additional room had been set aside on the first floor for the two lay secretaries who were needed for answering the telephone, bookkeeping, correspondence, and other typing required in the conduct of the diocese. The fact that all this was in addition to the regular parish staff of pastor and three assistants made the rectory crowded—or, I should rather say, overcrowded. The person most deeply sensitive to the inconveniences of the existing arrangement was Jim Murphy, who, as pastor, was ultimately responsible for the running of the household. At the end of the first year, he became firmly convinced that the Bishop should have a residence of his own. He discussed the problem with me, and with my approval began to make inquiry among his knowledgeable friends about a suitable home that might be purchased. One day, with visible enthusiasm, he gave me some information. The Walker home on Algonquin Road, Fairfield, one of the finest in the whole area, could be purchased at a reasonable price. On the death of the widow of the builder and only occupant, it had remained vacant for more than two years. I must come out immediately to see it and go through it. So, with Murphy and Curtiss, I went. It really was a beautiful house and had been designed by a distinguished Boston firm of architects and built just after World War I. Set back about twenty-five feet from the street, it was a lovely red brick house designed in what seemed to me pure Georgian style. On completion the home had been given a high award by a distinguished society of New England architects. It was ample for all our needs, yet by no means palatial in size or appearance.

Again, the first person we consulted was Philip Epifano. Having gone over the whole house carefully, he assured us of the soundness and high quality of the structure and stated that the house itself could not be reproduced at that time (1955) for less than $100,000. He advised us to purchase it immediately. Bill Hope, who was one of the best judges of property values in the area and was familiar with the financial condition of the diocese, gave me the same advice. I was still somewhat hesitant about spending that amount of money ($50,000) for a home. The son, Webster Walker, was so anxious to make the sale promptly that he lowered the price to $45,000, but stated he could go no lower without appearing to be a fool in the eyes of friends and associates.

Besides its attractiveness and its solid structure, the Walker house had other attributes: it was conveniently located within fifteen minutes walk from the Cathedral. It would serve our purpose admirably. There was no possibility that I could obtain anything similar for a comparable price. Without further delay I decided to go ahead with the purchase. The reason why Walker was anxious to get it off his hands was, no doubt, that his wife and children for some reason did not wish to live there. He was unable to put it on the open market because the Brookland Association, which had developed the whole area had bound his father by covenant not to sell to a person or persons not approved by the association. Meanwhile, he was paying taxes; he had to keep the place heated, at least minimally, all winter; he had also to hire someone to keep the grounds. The Brookland Association was willing that he sell the place to the new Bishop of Bridgeport, who perhaps would not damage the reputation of the area controlled by the association (he might possibly add a little prestige?). I must say, however, that those who ruled the Brookland Country Club and the association never so much as gave Curtiss and myself a nod of welcome.

But the area in which our home was located was not so exclusive as to make it objectionable from our point of view either. It was in the lower part of Brookland, where an elderly Jewish couple already lived next door and a prominent doctor with an Irish name and his large family lived just across the street. Our houses were in the lowlands while the Yankee aristocrats lived in the hills above. Even the seven acres did not present a serious problem. At least five were in the form of an open field which had been leveled and made into an expansive lawn. We acquired a power mower with revolving blades, cutting a swath of lawn at least six feet in width. In the late spring and summer evenings, Curtiss and I would take turns in mowing the lawn. The flower beds and shrubbery around the house were cared for at first by an elderly Italian gardener, working part-time, and later by Frieda Althoff, our cook, who loved flowers and was endowed with the proverbial "green thumb."

During the first three or four years, Curtiss lived in the Algonquin Road house with me. Mrs. Althoff and Mrs. Mary Holland, who had been cook and housekeeper at SS. Philip and James Rectory, came up from Baltimore to serve us in those capacities. When the pastor of St. Charles Church in Bridgeport died, Curtiss, to my surprise, asked that he be appointed to that post. No doubt, now that he had been ordained a priest for twenty-five years, he was looking for a position with some permanence—and there is no guaranteed permanence in the position of Chancellor. I acceded to his request, and he left 91 Algonquin Road. John Toomey came to take his place. I must say that I spent seven happy years at that residence in the company of Curtiss and Toomey, with Mrs. Althoff and Mrs. Holland supplying most efficient and agreeable service.

During those eight years while I was Bishop of Bridgeport I used to visit Baltimore each year from the day after Christmas to the Sunday after New Year's Day. Always this gave me an opportunity to renew not only my friendship with Archbishop Keough, but also my family bonds with my sister Mary and my three brothers, Dan, Brooke, and Will, and their families, including a now-growing number of grand-nephews and grand-nieces. During the last days of 1960, I went down and stayed with the Archbishop at Stella Maris Hospice, to which he had removed his residence after his severe heart attack in the fall of 1953. Shortly before my visit, Bishop Jerome Sebastian, who had succeeded me as Auxiliary Bishop in 1954, had died October 11, 1960. During my stay with the Archbishop, he told me that instead of asking for an Auxiliary, he was thinking of seeking from the Holy See the appointment of a Co-adjutor with the right of succession. Would I accept the position if he were to ask for me and the Holy See were to offer it to me? I told him that I had been very happy as bishop of Bridgeport and that I had never given thought to such a possibility—particularly since at that time it seemed to be the policy of the Holy See not to transfer a Bishop back to the see of his origin. Moreover, since I was only two or three years younger than Bishop Sebastian, his recently deceased Auxiliary, I felt confident that the Holy See would not appoint a man of my age to become the Archbishop's Coadjutor. I promised, however, to give the matter thought and to write to him after my return.

On January 5, 1961, I did write to him from Bridgeport and these are the words of my response:

> I have given considerable thought to your suggestion about the future. I have always tried to make it my practice to seek nothing, but to accept what is assigned to me and then to do the best I can. I do not want it thought that I am asking for a change. Nor would I want it thought that I have been unhappy up here. On the contrary, I have been very happy, particularly in the things I have been able to accomplish with the cooperation of the priests and people. I am confident that I would go on being happy, for there is still plenty to be done. The point is that I shall be content with whatever the Holy See wants me to do.

Many months passed and I heard nothing further from Archbishop Keough. I took for granted that the tone of my letter had discouraged him from asking for my appointment. How far my thoughts were from a return to Baltimore can be judged, I believe, from the fact that during those months we were pushing forward to the end of the year-long consultations on new statutes to be enacted in the First Synod of the Diocese of Bridgeport. The Synod was actually held, with all proper solemnities, in the Cathedral of St. Augustine on June 14, 1961. Looking back over the synodal statutes, they present, thanks chiefly to John Toomey, J.C.D., and William Genuario, J.C.D., a good example of what such statutes at that time should have been. The chief criticism that would be made now is that they show no indication that any of the laity of the diocese had been consulted. But that was a condition common to the Church before the Second Vatican Council.

Then, sometime after the middle of July 1961, I received a message from Archbishop Vagnozzi, Apostolic Delegate to the United States at that time, informing me that the Holy Father, Pope John XXIII, had appointed me Coadjutor to the Archbishop of Baltimore with the right to succeed to that see. The official apostolic letter for the appointment arrived with a covering letter from the Apostolic Delegate dated September 11. It was then finally arranged that I should leave Bridgeport on the morning of September 27, should present my letter of appointment to Archbishop Keough that evening, and that the public ceremony for my installation should be held on September 28. Thus, with a sense of genuine regret, came to an end what I had anticipated would be my last period of priestly and episcopal ministry. The new one that was now to open would prove even more exciting and eventful, but also more replete with periods of distress and even discouragement.

To bring this account of my Bridgeport days to an end, I resort once more to the Toomey "biography":

When his appointment as Coadjutor Archbishop of Baltimore was announced, he [Bishop Shehan] gave this statement:

"I am profoundly grateful to our Holy Father, Pope John XXIII, for the great honor he has conferred upon me in appointing me Coadjutor Archbishop of Baltimore. To him I pledge my complete and undying devotion and loyalty.

"It will be the source of understandable satisfaction for me to return to my beloved native diocese and See of Baltimore, and particularly to take up my work once more under Archbishop Keough, with whom I served as Auxiliary Bishop for so many years.

"It is, however, with deepest regret that I leave the Diocese of Bridgeport. From its priests and people I have received the greatest kindness and most loyal and helpful cooperation. Among them I spent more than seven of the happiest years of my life. It is my sincere hope that they will continue to keep me in their prayers."

Archbishop Shehan left Bridgeport September 27, 1961. As on

the day of his arrival in 1953, thousands of Bridgeporters were gathered at the railroad station to see him. While civic and church leaders bade him farewell, the crowds waved and shouted a tumultuous good-bye. Some one hundred members of the Bridgeport Diocese, clerical and lay, in specially reserved railroad cars accompanied the prelate to Baltimore. The next day they took part in the festive Reception Ceremony in the Cathedral of Mary Our Queen with which the new Coadjutor Archbishop was welcomed back to his home diocese. Priests and laity in Bridgeport experienced a deep sense of loss at the departure of one who was for them truly a father and friend.

I cannot close this chapter on Bridgeport without expressing my deepest gratitude to and affection for both Curtiss and Toomey. Curtiss served as my Chancellor most of the time I was Bishop of Bridgeport; he was most prompt and meticulous in the performance of his duties and displayed a genuine devotion to the diocese, and on all occasions sought its highest good. The same thing must be said about Toomey; in his case I must add: his keen intelligence, his wide and precise knowledge of canon law, his great skill in the use of the English language, and the remarkable facility he possessed in composition gave him a very special value in my eyes. The highest personal tribute that I can pay to both of them is that today, nearly 20 years after I was transferred back to Baltimore, I count them both among my closest friends.

7. Twelfth Archbishop of Baltimore

ON MY ARRIVAL IN BALTIMORE in the late afternoon of September 17, 1961, I was met by Archbishop Keough, his secretary, Porter White, his Chancellor, George Hopkins (who was also rector of the old Cathedral), and Thomas Whelan, rector of the new Cathedral of Mary Our Queen. All three bore the title of Monsignor. The Archbishop seemed genuinely pleased at my return, as did those who accompanied him. Tom Whelan had arranged for transportation of the Bridgeport priests to the Lord Baltimore Hotel, where I would later join them and some thirty visiting Bishops who would be attending the next day's ceremony. An informal dinner had been arranged at the hotel that evening for both groups. Meanwhile, the Archbishop and Tom Whelan accompanied me to the new Cathedral rectory, where the Archbishop indicated he wished me to reside in the quarters that had been designed for his own use. There I presented to the Archbishop and his consultors the apostolic letter by which the Holy Father appointed me Coadjutor Archbishop of Baltimore. By that action, I officially became Archbishop Keough's Coadjutor. Then the Archbishop went on to Stella Maris Hospice, where he would continue to reside, having assured us that he would return in the morning to preside at the public ceremony of installation.

The ceremony of my installation took place the next morning at 11 A.M. in the new Cathedral. As planned under the direction of the Archbishop, I was the celebrant. After the Gospel, Porter White read a translation of the apostolic letter of my appointment, and I delivered the homily. The music of the Mass was beautifully rendered by the seminary choir and that of the new Cathedral under Mr. Robert Twynham. Perhaps my thoughts and sentiments on the occasion may be best expressed by excerpts from my sermon:

In coming back to Baltimore, I am deeply conscious of returning to the main source of the great traditions of the American Church. Those traditions center in the person of John Carroll, our first Bishop and Archbishop. Not only did Carroll firmly establish the ecclesiastical structure which has served so well the Church in this country; he also more than any other person gave origin to those noble traditions which have given to the American Church its special character. Those traditions were strengthened and developed by the first Seven Provincial Councils and by the Three Plenary Councils which stretched out over a great part of the nineteenth century. All these Councils held in the old Cathedral of the Assumption were presided over by Carroll's successors. They still exercise their salutary influence on the life of the American Church.

The tradition which comes most vividly to mind at the present time when Catholics are figuring so prominently in national life and in public controversies is the Church-State relationship which sprang chiefly from John Carroll and has become for us a sort of sacred heritage. Shortly after George Washington had been elected our First President, Carroll, himself recently consecrated Bishop, joined four of the most prominent lay Catholics of this country, two of them his close relatives bearing the same family name, in addressing to the President a letter of congratulations on his unanimous election to the highest honor within the giving of his fellow citizens. They expressed not only their satisfaction at the state of affairs which had come into existence under his leadership but also their confidence that as long as this country continued to preserve her independence they and their fellow Catholics would have every title to claim from her justice, the equal right of citizenship as the price of their blood and of their common exertion for their country's defense. To this letter Washington replied that he hoped that America would ever appear foremost among the nations of the world in examples of justice and liberality and that Americans would never forget the important part Catholics have taken in the accomplishment of their revolution and in the establishment of their government. Thus it was that Carroll helped to establish that spirit of devoted loyalty on the part of American Catholics and that spirit of justice, confidence and friendliness on the part of the Federal Government which has characterized the history of the Church in the United States. . . .

The traditions of Carroll have nowhere been more carefully preserved and strengthened than in the See of Baltimore by the long line of Carroll's successors—Kendrick, Spalding and Gibbons, to mention only a few. Within those traditions the Church of the United States and the See of Baltimore have continued to flourish. They have been fittingly enshrined in this magnificent new Cathedral which will ever stand as a monument to Archbishop Keough. It is with a deep sense of these noble traditions that I take up my work in the See of Baltimore pledging to you, Archbishop Keough, to your priests and your people my every effort to carry our treasured traditions forward into the future.

That evening at a dinner given in my honor and attended by the priests, religious and laity of the archdiocese, I spoke in a lighter vein:

After listening to the many kind remarks which really have exceeded the requirements of even such an occasion as this, all will agree that at this point protocol calls for me to disclaim most if not all the credit for the things praised. Instead of following such a traditional course, I am going to take the occasion to announce two newly discovered laws. The first in the fabulous era of 1984 will probably be found in all the sociology text books under the impressive title of Shehan's "Law of Increasing Returns." All of us are familiar with the "Law of Diminishing Returns," the essence of which is that, after passing a certain point, the multiplication of material conveniences gives rise to constantly lessening returns. Telephones multiplied become not only a convenience, but also increasingly a nuisance, a source of annoyance, of distraction, of wasted time. Rapid proliferation has caused automobiles to serve not only as apt means of rapid transportation, but increasingly as instruments for stalling us for long hours on overcrowded roads on unbearably hot days. Now Shehan's law of increasing returns, complementing the older and bettter-known law, presents its obverse. In simplest terms, it runs: "the smaller the resources the greater the returns—at least up to a certain point." It has two main applications to the events of today. The first deals with reputation—the smaller and weaker the individual the greater the reputation he acquires for the things he does. What would seem ordinary in a man of height, breadth and physical power, becomes extraordinary in the measure the individual approaches what someone has unkindly called the diminutive. But the law has a second and deeper meaning which can be summed up thus: "The smaller the individual the more abundant the help available to him for his work." The law can be stated in the homely phrase: "Everybody likes to help the little fellow." People are so convinced that he does not measure up to the greater tasks that they cannot resist the temptation to pitch in and help him. I need not comment on the way this remarkable law has worked to my advantage.

Now I pass on to a discussion of the second recently discovered law, one suggested by the phrase contained in the apostolic letters "cum jure successionis"—a law favoring not me but our Most Reverend Archbishop. Judging from early accounts of my appointment in the newspapers, I would say that the laity in general and the press in particular do not seem to realize how conditional this right is. They fail to realize that the Holy See can supply to an Ordinary no more effective aid to health and longevity than the naming of a coadjutor. Clerical sociologists have established the existence of this second indisputable law: An Ordinary has a five-to-one chance to bury his Coadjutor. I am sure that all of us hope and pray for the full operation of this law in Baltimore. Certainly, I know of no more honorable end that could come to my career than to have Archbishop Keough preside at my obsequies. I hope, however, that such an event will come only after I have had an opportunity to serve him long, faithfully, and to his full satisfaction.

It is only left to me to express once more to Our Holy Father my profound gratitude for the honor he has conferred upon me and my sincere thanks to Archbishop Keough for having received me with such graciousness and warmth as his Coadjutor.

The rest of my speech was devoted to expressing my gratitude to the Archbishops and Bishops who had come to Baltimore for the ceremony of my installation, particularly to Archbishop Alter, Chairman of the Administrative Board of the National Catholic Welfare Conference, for naming me Episcopal Chairman of the Department of Education of that organization, and others present to whom I owed a special debt of gratitude.

After my installation as Coadjutor Archbishop, I found that I fitted very easily into my duties within the archdiocese. I offered my regular daily Mass in the beautiful little chapel of the Cathedral rectory. On Sunday mornings I began the practice of offering the eight o'clock

Mass of the Cathedral parish and preaching the homily. I asked that the rector have my name placed over one of the unused confessionals, and took my place in it every Saturday afternoon—evening, too, when the number of penitents was great enough to justify it. I found myself involved almost immediately in the fall schedule of Confirmations in the various parishes of the archdiocese. During this period, I kept in as close touch with the Archbishop as possible, but once again, mindful of my experience while still his Auxiliary, I relied chiefly on the telephone to do so.

On only one occasion did we have even a short-lived difference. One morning three priests called upon me at the new Cathedral. Two of them I knew well as men of mature judgment. With them was a younger man who had a serious complaint to make against an older priest, whose periodic condition due to alcoholism was well known among his fellow priests. They urgently requested that I come with them to observe for myself this priest's condition, and I felt that the matter was of sufficient importance to comply. I found conditions as they reported them, and judged that immediate action was required. Using my authority as Vicar General, I withdrew the faculties of the archdiocese until he would have gotten himself straightened out physically, made a retreat, and reported back to me or to the Archbishop. After a rather long talk with him, he agreed to follow my directions. The two older priests offered to take him to the hospital, where I had arranged by telephone with the Sister Superior that he be accepted and receive immediate attention. The person involved had remarkable recuperative powers. By Wednesday, one of the priests took him to a local monastery for a brief retreat. The following Saturday, the deeply repentant priest came to see me. I restored his faculties in order that he might appear in his parish for duty over the weekend. Naturally, as soon as possible after I had taken the initial action, I called on the Archbishop personally and acquainted him with what I had done, before he would receive anyone else's story. He was visibly perturbed, and thought I had acted hastily and too severely. I did not deny that it might have been so, but said that I had done what had seemed necessary under the unusual conditions. In the future I would make no such decisions until I had been able to consult him first.

My regular diocesan duties were interrupted several times that fall by out-of-town engagements. Thus, on October 8-9 I went to St. Paul for the funeral of Archbishop Brady, whom I had known since college days at St. Charles; on November 4, I was at the Apostolic Delegation in Washington for the celebration of the anniversary of the Pope's coronation; again, I was in Washington for a meeting of the Board of

Trustees of The Catholic University; on November 6-7, I was in New Orleans for the installation of Archbishop Cody; on November 8-9, I was in Buffalo for the National Conference of Catholic Youth, where I preached at the opening Mass, and again in Washington, November 13-17, for the Bishops' Meeting, Catholic University Board of Trustees, and the Administrative Board of the National Catholic Welfare Conference; in Bridgeport, November 20-21, for the installation of Bishop Curtis as my successor. Thus the fall months of 1961 were a very busy time for me.

That year Thanksgiving fell on November 23. The Archbishop decided to celebrate it as in the old days. His brother Michael and family came down from New Britain the day before and would stay at Long Crandon over the weekend. Porter White, who had now been the Archbishop's secretary for seven or eight years, living close to him at Stella Maris, would be with us, as had become his custom. Will Galvin had died some three or four years previously, so he and Nell would be missing. The Archbishop himself appeared to be in excellent spirits. He had spent a great part of the afternoon in one of his favorite pastimes: watching one of the professional football games on television. It was indeed a joyous celebration. We all hoped there would be many more. However, it was the last one over which Archbishop Keough would preside.

Among the things that the Archbishop, Porter, and I discussed was the trip we planned to New York to be present the next Monday evening at the reception for Cardinal Cicognani. He had been Apostolic Delegate in the United States for twenty-five years. The newly elected Pope John XXIII evidently decided that this was long enough, for he summoned him back to Rome and named him Cardinal in the first consistory, held December 15, 1958. There had not been time then to arrange the kind of reception the U.S. hierarchy had wished to hold for him. However, they had elicited the promise that he would return for such a reception. Now, at last, the reception had been arranged in the Starlight Ballroom of the Waldorf Astoria Hotel for November 27, 1961. Archbishop Keough had been among the first U.S. Bishops consecrated by Cardinal Cicognani in the year 1934. I, too, had received episcopal consecration at his hands on December 12, 1945. Both of us felt that we must be present at the reception.

The Archbishop, Porter, and I took the train to New York on Monday in time to claim our rooms at the Waldorf and to prepare for the evening celebration. Virtually the whole hierarchy was there, and also a large number of priests and laymen, for there was a widespread appreciation of the contribution that Cardinal Cicognani had made to the Church of this country during the record-breaking span of his service as Apostolic Delegate. Few, if any, foreigners, and not many Americans have had a wider knowledge of the American Church or a keener appreciation of its strengths. The evening was a memorable one: Before the traditional speeches, appropriate musical selections were sung by a star of the Metropolitan Opera; Archbishop Alter was the main speaker of the evening and presented to the Cardinal an appropriate gift from the U.S. Bishops. Cicognani responded by paying tribute to the Church in the United States.

Archbishop Keough and Porter had planned to stay over an extra day in New York—probably to enable the Archbishop to do some Christmas shopping for gifts to his brother's family and the immediate members of his household. I, however, had promised, while still Bishop of Bridgeport, to go to Dallas and to participate in the program of the National Convention of the Confraternity of Christian Doctrine. Therefore, on Tuesday morning I took a plane for Dallas where I was scheduled to stay until the convention's end on Friday.

According to his plans, the Archbishop, with Porter, was back at Stella Maris late Wednesday afternoon. On Thursday he and Porter went to his office at 408 North Charles Street. There he kept a rather large number of appointments—a backlog after his three-day absence. He and Porter had lunch together and then the Archbishop retired to the bedroom that he still maintained in the old Archbishop's House. When at 3:30 P.M. Porter heard no sound of movement in the apartment or even in the bedroom, he entered. The Archbishop had fallen next to the washbasin in the bathroom and lay motionless, crowded against the marble wall of the shower. The right side of his face had sagged badly, and he was able to murmur only a few almost indistinguishable words. Porter quickly summoned George Hopkins and with considerable difficulty they got him back on his bed. Porter immediately called Sister Celeste at Stella Maris, told her what had happened, and asked her to come as soon as she could. He then called Dr. George Schreiner at Georgetown Hospital in Washington, whom the Archbishop had chosen as his personal physician shortly after his 1953 heart attack. Schreiner promised to come as soon as he could change from his hospital garb and get to his automobile.

In view of the distance of Stella Maris from the Archbishop's House, Sister Celeste arrived in a remarkably short time. As soon as she had taken charge of the patient, Porter telephoned me in Dallas and gave me an account of what had happened. I promised to take the first plane I could get back to Baltimore. However, I soon found that it was already too late to get a flight that day, and I had to settle for an early plane Friday morning.

George Hopkins met me at the airport and drove me immediately to Georgetown Hospital. We were admitted to see the Archbishop briefly, but were warned that his condition was critical and we should not attempt to carry on any conversation with him. He had a tube in his nostrils and there was an oxygen tank nearby. He was being fed intravenously. Nearby there was equipment that monitored his breathing, heartbeat, and body temperature. A nurse was in constant attention. I took his hand in my own and pressed it gently while the nurse murmured my name in his ear. He slowly opened his eyes, pressed my hand ever so slightly as if in recognition; that was all. It was the same with George Hopkins. Almost immediately, he seemed to sink into a gentle sleep. There was nothing we could do or say, so George and I quietly left.

We found Porter in the nearby room that had been assigned to him. It was then that he gave me the full details of what had happened, and why it was that the Archbishop came to Georgetown Hospital. As soon as Dr. Schreiner had arrived at the Archbishop's House and had given him as thorough an examination as circumstances permitted, he recommended immediate hospitalization and suggested nearby Mercy Hospital. The Archbishop knew that Schreiner would not be able to supervise his case there, so he inquired about the possibility of Georgetown, where Schreiner held a position of great influence. That was a possibility, but it would entail the additional risk of the rather long ambulance drive of at least one hour to get there. The Archbishop indicated that he preferred to take that risk, if Schreiner were willing to make the arrangements and continue to supervise his case. So determined did he seem that the doctor concluded that the risk of the ambulance ride was less than the risk of insistence on hospitalization in any Baltimore hospital.

George Hopkins and I returned to the hospital on Saturday and found the Archbishop in relatively the same condition. It was the same on Sunday. Then, however, I did meet with Dr. Schreiner. All he could say was that the patient's condition was stabilized. He could give no definite prognosis. Thus things went on day after day. On the one hand, there was no sign of positive response to treatment; on the other, there was no telling how long life could be prolonged by modern medicine. On the morning of December 8, however, the nurse noticed a worsening of his condition and she quickly summoned the doctor on duty. Both agreed that the end seemed to be approaching. They notified Porter; he, in turn, notified Sister Celeste. Together they began the prayers for the dying. Even as they said these, the Archbishop gasped several times and then became perfectly still. He had breathed his last. It seemed eminently appropriate that he, who had retained throughout his life a profound devotion to Mary should have died on this, her greatest feast day—that of the Immaculate Conception.

When Porter called, I had gone over to the new Cathedral to celebrate the 8 A.M. Mass. Tom Whelan took the call. By the time he reached the sacristy, I had already begun the Mass. He came into the sanctuary and briefly interrupted me to give me Porter's message. I thereupon notified the congregation that the Archbishop had just died and that this Mass was being offered for the repose of his soul. His great devotion to Mary as an example to us was the subject of that morning's homily.

My first duty as Archbishop of Baltimore was to arrange for the funeral. All of us immediately concerned decided that the time, if possible, would be Thursday, December 14, at 11 A.M The Apostolic Delegate should be asked to offer the Pontifical Funeral Mass. As for the preacher, those who had been closest to him were dead: Bishop Matthew Brady, boyhood friend, whom he had chosen to preach at his installation; Cardinals Mooney and Stritch, who, after Matt Brady, had been his closest friends in the American hierarchy; Bishop Howard Carroll, with whom he had worked so closely during the period when he was closely associated with the National Catholic Welfare Conference. Those to whom I now had to look for advice—White, Hopkins, Mardaga, Whelan—all urged that I was the logical person to deliver what, in those pre-conciliar days, was everywhere called the eulogy of the funeral Mass. So it was decided that it should be.

On Sunday afternoon at 5 P.M., the body of Archbishop Keough was brought to the Cathedral of Mary Our Queen. I, with the rectors and priests of both the Cathedral and the Basilica, met the body at the door and conducted the brief ceremony provided by the Ritual for such an occasion. Then on the following three days Mass was offered in the presence of particular groups. That on Monday was celebrated by Monsignor Whelan for the members of the Cathedral parish; that on Tuesday, by Monsignor Porter White for the Holy Name Society, Sodality of the Blessed Virgin Mary, the Catholic Daughters of America, Knights of Columbus, etc.; that on Wednesday, for the school children of the archdiocese I myself offered.

The funeral Mass on Thursday was a solemn and impressive event. The Most Reverend Egidio Vagnozzi, Apostolic Delegate in the United States was celebrant. Cardinal Spellman presided. The officers of the Mass were Monsignor Joseph Leary, Monsignor Stanislaus Wachowiak, Monsignor Louis Vaeth, Rev. F. Joseph Gossman. Five Archbishops attended: O'Boyle of Washington, Krol of Philadelphia, Hurley of St. Augustine, Swint of Wheeling, Toolen of Mobile-Birmingham. They and the thirty-three Bishops with their attendants filled the great sanctuary of the Cathedral; the correspondingly great nave was crowded to capacity. The music of the Mass was majestically rendered under the direction of Robert Twynham, who still trains and leads the Cathedral choir. As I have already indicated, I myself delivered the funeral sermon. Whether it measured up to the occasion I must leave to the judgment of others.

This I do remember: as I set about the task of writing it, I had a deep sense of sorrow and personal loss at the death of one who in so many ways—but always in his own unique way—had shown me so many signs of friendship. My sorrow was all the more poignant because on my return to Baltimore, I had looked forward to working with him for some—hopefully, many—years and to a growing personal friendship. Nor did I feel any sense of exhilaration at the thought that I was now the twelfth Archbishop of Baltimore, successor to that truly great line of my predecessors that stretched back so far into the past: Carroll, Maréchal, Kendrick, Spalding, Bayley, Gibbons, Curley, and Keough. There was in my heart a sinking feeling that I had no consciousness of the power to live up to that role. My chief consolation was my knowledge that I had not wanted to be a Bishop in the first place and had in no way sought appointment to Bridgeport or to any other diocese. Yet, these honors and responsibilities had come to me, and somehow, in spite of the consciousness of my limitations, with the help of God, I had been able to live up to them. Now, once more I would simply have to trust to the goodness of God and His grace.

That mood pervaded the days right up to Christmas. Meanwhile, with the funeral past, I was plunged straight into the full responsibility of being Ordinary of a large archdiocese, with the necessity of becoming involved in the details of those archdiocesan projects Archbishop Keough had already undertaken, and those parochial projects which he had authorized. In becoming adjusted to my new responsibilities, three persons were of great help: Monsignor Porter White, who as the

Archbishop's secretary had been closest to him during the last years of his life; Francis X. Gallagher, the archdiocesan attorney, on whom he had so completely relied in launching and expediting his projects; and Monsignor Joseph Leary, who under the direction of the Archbishop, supervised his construction program of Catholic high schools and the central archdiocesan office building.

That Christmas, at midnight I celebrated my first Pontifical Mass as Archbishop of Baltimore. Again, the Cathedral was crowded to capacity, with a number of people standing in the aisles. After our period of mourning, the Christmas music seemed to ring out with a new joy. During the lull in activity which always seems to come between Christmas and the New Year, I had an opportunity to renew and strengthen my family ties. I took Christmas dinner with my brother Dan and his family. From the beginning of his professional career, he had been very successful in the practice of dentistry. He had married in his mid-twenties and with his devoted wife he had raised a family of five children. After the birth of his youngest, he and his wife had purchased a beautiful but one of the less pretentious houses in Homeland, the residential area just east of the new Cathedral.

On New Year's evening, I took dinner with my other surviving brother, John Brooke, and his family. He, too, had married in his mid-twenties and raised a family of five. Although his wife was non-Catholic and remained so throughout her life, no one could have been more faithful to the promises made at the time of marriage. All of their children had a complete Catholic education. I maintained a close relationship with the family, particularly because Peg, my sister-in-law, had always manifested a special concern for and devotion to my sister, Mary. Midway in the week, I had dinner with Mary, who had also been present at Dan's and Brooke's. She had made it the occasion of a family gathering by inviting both our brothers and their wives.

With the dawn of the new year 1962, my calendar shows how quickly and how completely I had become immersed in the affairs of the archdiocese. My days were filled with appointments with individual priests, with meetings of boards and various committees, and often my evenings were occupied with Confirmations. These had been scheduled late in the previous fall, under the supposition that both Archbishop Keough and I would be available. Now it became evident that it was impossible for me to cover them all alone. Fortunately, Bishop Michael Hyle, who had succeeded to the See of Wilmington the previous year, found it possible to fill ten of these appointments during the month of May.

Even before that, it had become clear that I very badly needed the assistance of an Auxiliary Bishop without delay. Fortunately, at the previous meeting of the Bishops of the Province, a list of priests who were deemed qualified to be raised to the episcopate had been drawn up and sent to the Apostolic Delegate to be forwarded to the Sacred Consistorial Congregation. Three Baltimore priests were on the list. I now drew up a petition, arranged the names of these three in the order of my preference, and signified why I thought that one of these was best suited for the position. I sent my petition to the Sacred Congregation through the Apostolic Delegate. Meanwhile, I also sent a personal letter to Cardinal Cicognani, who now, besides being Secretary of State was a member of the Consistorial Congregation. On May 18, 1962, much to my satisfaction, the Holy See announced that Rev. T. Austin Murphy, pastor of the parish of St. Rose of Lima, had been appointed the Auxiliary Bishop of Baltimore. Needless to say, there was great rejoicing throughout the archdiocese. So far as I could judge, the universal opinion among the priests was that the choice was a good one.

Austin soon chose the date of July 3 for his consecration. He first asked me to consecrate him. I, in turn, suggested that he write the Apostolic Delegate, since it was my understanding that he enjoyed officiating on such occasions, and it seemed particularly appropriate since Baltimore was so near to Washington. The Delegate did very promptly and willingly accept the invitation. Thereupon, Austin asked me to preach. Arrangements were made accordingly, and we proceeded to get out the invitations to the Bishops of the country.

Meanwhile, my own busy schedule went on almost without a break, culminating in the ordination of our own new priests on Saturday, May 26; ordination to minor orders and subdiaconate at Mount St. Mary's on June 2; tonsure at St. Mary's Seminary on June 4; first minor orders June 5; second minors June 6, and subdiaconate June 7. In addition, there were ordinations to subdiaconate at Woodstock June 15, diaconate June 16, and priesthood June 17. Meanwhile, I had administered Confirmation during Pontifical Mass at the new Cathedral June 10, made my annual retreat June 11-15 with the priests of the archdiocese, and administered Confirmation to the adults the evening of Sunday, June 17. In addition to these appointments, it was necessary to carry on the regular business that fell to the Archbishop of Baltimore. Thus it appears that I rather desperately needed the help of an Auxiliary, all the more so in view of the fact that the Second Vatican Council was scheduled to open October 11. The consecration of Bishop Murphy, carried out with due solemnity in the new Cathedral, filled to capacity with his many friends and admirers, formed a fitting climax to one of the busiest periods of my life that I remember.

At the time of Bishop Murphy's consecration, a number of us discussed plans for traveling to Rome for the Council. Seven of us decided that we would rather go by ship on the most convenient vessel of the Italian Line: Bishops Russell and Unterkoefler of Richmond, Hodges of Wheeling, Hyle of Wilmington, Murphy, Monsignor White, and I from Baltimore. Russell and Unterkoefler had already decided that they would prefer to try a new hotel, the "Residenza." The remaining five had decided to stay at the Grand Hotel, which at that time had not undergone the extensive renovations which have made it one of the most expensive hostelries of Rome. Then it was simply known as one of the fine old hotels, conveniently located, which had preserved its good reputation and was offering satisfactory accommodations at reasonable rates. Since Porter White would be accompanying me as my secretary during the Council, we entrusted to him the task of making our reservations.

After Bishop Murphy's consecration, my time again became fully occupied, in spite of the help he was now able to give me. Most of my appointments were with individuals who for particular reasons requested to see me personally. This continued right up to the day of our departure. On September 20, we took the train to New York, and the following day Bishop Austin Murphy, Porter White and I boarded the Italian liner *Rex* headed for Naples, whence we intended to go directly to Rome by train. This would enable us to arrive in plenty of time to get settled in our hotel and make preparations for the opening of the Council.

We were to find the Grand Hotel very conveniently located for practically all our needs. It was a few hundred feet from the Church of Santa Susanna, which was staffed by the Paulist Fathers and frequented by many Americans visiting or residing in Rome. I went there each morning about seven o'clock to offer Mass. Soon Father Cunningham, the very efficient and affable pastor, invited me to offer the regular parish Mass scheduled for that time and attended by a small but devout congregation. This I continued to do all during the Council. About fifteen Bishops and consultants (periti) were staying at the Grand. A bus would call for us every morning to take us to St. Peter's for the daily General Congregation and bring us back after the meeting was over. So convenient was the Grand that soon Bishop Russell and Unter-koefler came to join us there.

All during his prolonged stay in Washington, Cardinal Cicognani had come to St. Patrick's on Thanksgiving Day for the Pan-American Mass and had showed an interest in my work in the parish, at Catholic Charities, and later when I was Auxiliary Bishop of the Archdiocese of Baltimore-Washington and first Bishop of Bridgeport. I therefore called upon him at his residence in the Vatican during the days before the solemn opening of the Council. From then on, from time to time, he would invite me to have luncheon or to go for a walk with him in the Vatican Gardens during the late afternoon. This continued all during Vatican II.

Since our Baltimore Commission on Christian Unity was the first such commission to receive Vatican approval, Porter White and I called upon Cardinal Bea during the days before the Council. I was pleased to tell the Cardinal of the interest of our archdiocese in the ecumenical movement since the days of Cardinal Gibbons. As a consequence of this, no doubt, I was later invited to become a member of the Secretariat for Christian Unity, and Porter White was appointed one of its consultants. This gave him the privilege of attending each of the daily general congregations of the Council Fathers, as well as those of the Unity Secretariat. Thus, Porter and I put to good use those days between our arrival in Rome and the Solemn Opening of the Council.

Before launching into my memories of the Second Vatican Council, I want to say a few words about the terminology I shall use. Generally when persons speak of that Council, they speak of the four sessions that took place between October 11, 1962, and December 8, 1965; that is, one session in each of those four years. However, in the official volume published by the Vatican Press, entitled *Sacrosanctum Oecumenicum Concilium Vaticanum II, Constitutiones Decreta Declarationes*, we are told: "The *Sessions*, which were held in the *four periods*, are *ten* in *number*." I gather from the text of the book itself that the word "period" is used to denote the four periods of time in which the 168 general congregations (daily meetings of the Council Fathers) were held. The word "sessions" is reserved to those solemn meetings of the Council Fathers over which the Pope presided in order to open or close the periods, or to sign and promulgate the different Council documents. Thus, in my narrative I will speak of the four *periods* of the Council, in order to be in accord with the usage of the council itself through its General Secretariat.

8. The Second Vatican Council: Periods I and II

THE SECOND VATICAN COUNCIL opened in the Basilica of St. Peter on October 11, 1962, with the singing of the traditional hymn *Veni Creator Spiritus*. Pope John XXIII presided from the modest throne erected according to his direction to replace the more elaborate one originally provided, before the towering *baldachino* of Bernini that rises above the tomb of St. Peter. Cardinal Tisserant, Dean of the Sacred College, then celebrated the Mass of the Holy Spirit. Finally the eighty-year-old Pope delivered his first discourse of the Council to 2,540 Bishops robed in their white copes and miters, seated in rising tiers of bench-seats on either side of the great nave of St. Peter's.

In his discourse, the Pope gave what must always remain the authentic account of the origin of Vatican II:

> As regards the initiative for the great event which gathers us here, it will suffice to repeat as historical documentation our personal account of the first sudden bringing up in our hearts and lips the simple words "Ecumenical Council." We uttered these words in the presence of the Sacred College of Cardinals on that memorable January 25, 1959, the feast of the Conversion of St. Paul, in the Basilica dedicated to him. It was utterly unexpected, like a flash of heavenly light, shedding sweetness in the eyes and heart. And at the same time, it gave rise to great fervor.

The Pope then went on to speak of the preparations made for the Council:

> There have elapsed three years of laborious preparation, during which a wide and profound examination was made regarding

modern conditions of faith and religious practice, and of Christian and especially of Catholic vitality. These years have seemed to us an initial gift of heavenly grace.

Here I would add that in order to carry on this work of preparation the Pope had established ten commissions: (1) the Theological Commission, or Commission on Faith and Doctrine, (2) the Commission on Bishops and Diocesan Government, (3) the Discipline of the Clergy, (4) the Religious, (5) the Sacraments, (6) the Sacred Liturgy, (7) Christian Education, (8) the Eastern Churches, (9) the Missions, (10) the Lay Apostolate. Besides these, there were two secretariats: Social Communication and Christian Unity. Finally, there was set up a central commission to follow the course of labors of the individual commissions and, where necessary, to coordinate them.

The Pope, however, was not silent about the difficulties and frustrations he had experienced in preparing for the Council:

> In the daily exercise of our pastoral office, we sometimes have to listen, much to our regret, to voices of persons who, though burning with zeal, are not endowed with too much sense of discretion or measure. In these modern times they can see nothing but prevarication and ruin. They say that our era, in comparison with past eras, is getting worse, and they behave as though they have learned nothing from history, which is, none the less, the teacher of life. They behave as though at the time of former Councils, everything was a full triumph for the Christian idea and life and for proper religious liberty. We feel that we must disagree with these prophets of doom who are always forecasting disaster as though the end of the world were at hand. In the present order of things, Divine Providence is leading us to a new order of human relations which, by men's own efforts and even beyond their expectations, are directed towards the fulfillment of God's superior and inscrutable designs. And everything, even human differences, leads to the greater good of the Church.

Concerning his hopes for the benefits to be derived from the Council, he said:

> Illuminated by the light of this Council, the Church—we confidently trust—will become greater in spiritual riches and, gaining the strength of new energies therefrom, she will look to the future without fear. In fact, by bringing herself up to date,

where required, and by a wise organization of mutual cooperation, the Church will make men, families, and peoples really turn their minds to heavenly things. (See NCWC *Council Daybook*, Session I, pp. 25-29.)

The Pope concluded by emphasizing the pastoral purpose and character he intended this Council to have in comparison with previous General Councils. It was indeed a most noteworthy discourse, delivered in clear, resonant tones that could be heard throughout the great Basilica. All of us, I believe, were conscious that it had opened up a new era in the history of the Church.

On Saturday, October 13, two days after the opening, the first general congregation of the Council was held in St. Peter's for the purpose of electing the 160 members of the ten commissions that would be responsible for the presentation and discussion of the schemata and for the formulation of the final conciliar documents. Each of us was given three pamphlets: one contained a full list of the members of the Council, the second was a list of those who had served as members or consultants of the preparatory commissions, and the third contained ballots to be used in voting for members of the various commissions. After the Mass, with which every general congregation began, the Council turned to the business of the day. Cardinal Leinart, Bishop of Lille, set off what, with evident exaggeration, was often called the first bombshell of the Council. In reality, it was nothing more than a dictate of common sense. He moved that before voting the Council should adjourn to give the members time for the consultation that would be necessary to vote intelligently. Cardinal Frings, Archbishop of Cologne, immediately seconded the motion. It was evident that the Fathers generally were in full accord. The first general congregation was therefore immediately adjourned with the understanding that the members would next meet on Tuesday, October 16, to proceed with the election.

Over the weekend and until Monday evening, there was intense activity among the various national or regional groups in anticipation of the Tuesday election. Lists of recommended candidates from each group were prepared, but with the understanding that not more than two names from each national or regional group be submitted for any one of the ten commissions. On Tuesday we met according to schedule and cast our votes. Because of the great number of ballots to be counted it was decided that the next general congregation would not be held until October 20. The final result was that the commissions elected were far more representative of the Council as a whole than would otherwise have been possible.

When the results were published, I found myself a member of the Commission on the Discipline of the Clergy. I had, however, as a result of my ecumenical activity in the Archdiocese of Baltimore, already been invited to become a member of the Secretariat for the Promotion of Christian Unity and had accepted that invitation. To show the importance he attached to the cause of unity, the Pope later raised the secretariat to the rank of a commission. A little later, in order to spread the work of the Council as far as posssible among the members, the Pope ruled that no member could serve on more than one commission. Since the chairman of the Commission on Discipline was a French Archbishop who always spoke in his native tongue, and since most of the discussion was in French, which I could generally follow but could not speak fluently enough to engage in active discussion, I relinquished my membership on the Commission on Discipline in order to continue to serve on the secretariat, where I felt I could make a more significant contribution.

On October 20, with the elections behind us, we met for the third general congregation. The Presidency (the ten Cardinals who presided over the general congregation—later increased to twelve) had decided that the first schema to be discussed was that on the Sacred Liturgy. Two reasons led to this decision: first, the obvious practical importance of the subject; second, the Preparatory Liturgical Commission had done its work very carefully and hence the schema was not likely to run into serious difficulty. This schema was accepted for discussion with no significant opposition. But the discussion was surprisingly prolonged, chiefly on the subject of the use of the vernacular in the Mass. There were some who insisted that there be no tampering with the Mass at all, that the so-called Tridentine Mass must be preserved without change. Others recognized the advisability of some changes in the rite, but wished Latin to be retained for the entire Mass. In this group, if I remember correctly, were both Cardinals Spellman and McIntyre, and, strange to say, some African Bishops. I later talked to one native African seated close to me who said that there were dozens of dialects spoken in his diocese; a change from Latin would cause him serious difficulties. Finally, there were others who wished that a great part, if not all, of the Mass should be permitted in the vernacular.

The Council continued to discuss the Schema on the Liturgy, including every important aspect of the Church's liturgical life, down to

November 13. The final document, entitled The Constitution on the Sacred Liturgy, was not completed for presentation to the whole Council until the next year and signed by Pope Paul VI on December 4, 1963, almost at the end of the Second Period.

The next schema presented to the Fathers in the First Period was that on Divine Revelation, which had been produced by the Preparatory Commission on Faith and Doctrine. From the beginning, it was evident that there were wide differences of opinion. It was staunchly defended by those members of the Commission on Doctrine who had been chiefly responsible for producing it. But it was far more vigorously attacked by others who claimed that it gave an inadequate and sometimes misleading concept of revelation; that it assumed that nothing new could be added to what the Council of Trent had said four centuries ago; it was totally lacking in the spirit of ecumenism, named by John XXIII as one of the important aims of the Council. Such were the main criticisms leveled against the schema. It was during this debate that Bishop DeSmedt, of Bruges, Belgium, speaking for the Secretariat for Christian Unity, delivered the first of his eloquent speeches, and it was in criticism of the schema presented. The speech received loud and prolonged applause. It may be said to have sounded the death-knell of the Schema on Revelation as presented by the preparatory commission.

On November 20, Archbishop Felici, Secretary General of the Council, announced that by decision of the Council Presidents, a vote would be taken on whether debate should be halted or continued. A clear majority indicated they wished the discussion discontinued at that point (1386 to 822), but not the two-thirds required by the Council rules for total rejection of a schema. After a brief discussion with the Board of Presidents, Archbishop Felici announced that the discussion would continue. And continue it did in a desultory fashion for the rest of the morning. But was a vote to discontinue discussion equivalent to a vote to reject? Or did it mean that the majority simply wished the discussion stopped at that point in order that the schema might be revised and brought back for future discussion? A great deal of confusion ensued. The following day the Pope ordered that the schema be withdrawn. He then appointed an new commission with Cardinal Bea and Cardinal Ottaviani as co-chairmen to draw up a new or revised schema to be presented to the Council during the next period.

Here I would say that Bishop Austin Murphy, who had been with us at the Grand Hotel, had contracted a severe cold from which he seemed unable to get relief, due possibly to November weather in Rome. He decided that he would return to Baltimore. Later, since Auxiliary Bishops were not required to be present, he decided that he would not return to the Council, but would remain in Baltimore to be available for any duties that would be required of him there. In a word, in my absence he headed the archdiocesan organization. While he regretted that he would miss the experience of the Council, nevertheless it was a source of satisfaction to me that he was in charge of affairs in Baltimore.

Following the withdrawal of the Schema on Revelation, the Council considered two proposals, one drawn up by a special commission headed by Archbishop Martin J. O'Connor for a Decree on the Instruments of Social Communication and another drawn up by the Secretariat for Christian Unity for a Decree on Ecumenism. Both of these were favorably received, but in the discussion a considerable amount of criticism was aired. They were taken back for revision by their respective commissions. They, too, were to be brought back for further discussion and final amendments and submitted for a final approval only in the following period.

We were now at December 2, just six days away from the announced closing of the First Period. Next on the agenda was the schema treating the nature of the Church, which, like the Schema on Revelation, was the work of the Commission on Faith and Doctrine headed by Cardinal Ottaviani. When the presiding officer of the day announced that this was the next subject on the agenda, Cardinal Ottaviani rose and objected that there would not be enough time left in the First Period for the proper discussion of a subject so important and asked that the debate on this schema be postponed to the following period. After a brief conference of the Presidents, the presiding officer replied that the request would not be granted and called upon the commission to proceed with their presentation of the schema. Thereupon Ottaviani himself presented some introductory remarks, *ex tempore*, which were not very helpful, since they seemed to imply that this document should be immune to serious criticism. He told how the schema was the work of seventy learned theologians over many months and that it had the approval of the Holy Father himself. He said that the document was both pastoral and biblical in its approach and that special effort had been made to avoid even the appearance of Scholastic formulations, for that, he said, seemed to be the main objection to all the Theological Commission's projects. He concluded on a humorous note, asking forbearance for the relator, Bishop Franic of Split, Yugoslavia, who, he said, would be very conscious of the need for brevity, since he must feel, even before facing the Fathers, that the lions were breathing down his neck: *"Tolle, tolle; subicite eum."* "Take him away, take him away! Down with him!" These concluding remarks brought laughter and applause. He left the microphone beaming.

After Ottaviani had finished his remarks, Bishop Franic delivered his *relatio,* outlining as succinctly as he could the chapters contained in the Schema on the Church. At once the debate began. Immediately, Cardinal Lienart took the microphone, and after paying tribute to the work that had gone into the schema and its treatment of the Church as Christ's Mystical Body, called attention to some of its main defects— particularly its juridical tone. Cardinal Ruffini, the conservative Arch- bishop of Palermo, then defended the schema in its entirety, acknow- ledging, however, that here and there it could be improved. Cardinal Koenig of Vienna called for an abbreviation of the schema and emphasis on the duties of the Church to preach the Gospel and to serve, rather than to stand on its rights.

Among the most effective pieces of criticism presented during these final days of the First Period were those of Cardinal Montini, the Arch- bishop of Milan, soon to be Pope; Cardinal Suenens, Archbishop of Malines-Brussels; and Cardinal Lercaro, Archbishop of Bologna.

As in the case of the Schema on Revelation, it was the voice of Bishop DeSmedt that seemed to deal the death-blow to the preliminary Schema on the Church. In what was, in my opinion, by far the most eloquent and memorable speech of the whole Council, DeSmedt criti- cized the document on three main grounds: its *triumphalism*—it repre- sents the Church militant drawn up in battle array, not as the humble flock of Christ; its *clericalism*—the Church is not just priests, Bishops, and Pope, as the schema seem to imply, but all the people of God; its *juridicism*—in place of its juridical concept, the Church ought to be placed before the world as the Mother of Mankind. "Reread pages 15 and 16 of this document," he said, "and see to what misconception this legalistic spirit can give rise. No mother ever spoke thus."

In all the Council there was no period of debate that I found so interesting and so enlightening as that which lasted from December 1 to December 7, the last days of the First Period. No formal action was taken on the Schema on the Church; none was needed. Had there been a vote, it was evident that the majority of the Fathers would have reject- ed the schema as presented. No such action was taken, probably out of deference to Cardinal Ottaviani. The rejection of both of his schemas, covering perhaps the most important matters to come before the Coun-

cil, Revelation and the Church, would have been a humiliation greater
than the old Cardinal deserved. The whole matter was tactfully settled
by the Pope himself. On the morning of December 6, the Secretary General of the Council read a message from the Pope: In the nine months
between the adjournment of the First Period of Vatican II and its
Second Period, to be opened September of 1963, *all* the schemas, particularly those already discussed, were to be reworked by mixed commissions and sent to the Bishops for their comments and recommendations. We were instructed to return our observations and criticisms as
soon as possible. To coordinate the work of the collaborating commissions, the Holy Father had decided to create a new Coordinating
Commission under the presidency of Cardinal Cicognani.

During the last two weeks of November, there seemed to be evidence of the Pope's failing health. He had to cancel one public audience,
and there were widespread rumors that his condition was daily de-
teriorating. Then in early December he seemed to rally. On Tuesday
evening, December 4, it was announced that the Pope would bless the
pilgrims at midday on Wednesday. Desiring to take advantage of the
occasion, the Fathers of the Council decided to end that day's general
congregation early. We left the Basilica shortly before noon and joined
the immense throng of priests, Sisters, and laypeople who were waiting
for the Holy Father to appear. Precisely at noon the window of the
papal apartment opened and the Pope began to recite the Angelus. As
he finished, the crowd broke into a thunderous burst of applause.
Signaling for silence, the Pope said:

> My sons, Divine Providence is with us. As you see, from one day
> to the next there is progress, not going down, but coming up,
> *piano, piano.* Sickness, then convalescence. Now we are convales-
> cing. The satisfaction afforded me by this gathering is a reason for
> rejoicing. It is an augury of the strength and robustness which are
> coming back to us. What a spectacle we see here today—the
> Church grouped here today in full representation: Behold its bish-
> ops! Behold its priests! Behold its Christian people! A whole family
> here present, the family of Christ!

The Pope presided at the final Mass celebrated by Cardinal Marella, Archpriest of the Vatican Basilica of St. Peter, and then delivered
the discourse by which he closed the First Period. It was the last appearance of Pope John XXIII at the Second Vatican Council.

In his closing discourse, John XXIII had expressed the hope that the Council would be able to complete its work before the following Christmas. He reminded us that the Council of Trent had closed its work in the year 1563. What better way to celebrate the fourth centenary year of Trent than by bringing this Council to a happy end by Christmas 1963. On January 3, the Pope sent a letter to all the Bishops of the world giving directives concerning the work to be done during the interval before the Second Period. He particularly recommended collaboration between the members of national or regional groups of Bishops. In spite of his recent illness, he manifested the hope that he would live to see the Council through to a happy ending.

Late in May, however, he suffered a recurrence of gastric cancer, from which he had been suffering during the preceding year. He died June 3, 1963. Although his papacy had lasted but a brief five years, it seems certain that he will go down in history as one of the truly great Popes. I can think of no Pope who has left a deeper imprint on the Church, with the possible exception of Pope (St.) Leo I (the Great).

After the death of John XXIII, certain "prophets of doom" were quick to foretell that it would be found that with him died the Second Vatican Council. The conclave of Cardinals, which met following his funeral Mass and burial, on June 21 elected Giovanni Battista Montini, Cardinal Archbishop of Milan, who chose the name Pope Paul VI. The day after his election, he announced that the Bishops would meet for the Second Period of the Council on Sunday, September 29, and would resume their work promptly.

During the First Period of the Council I had come to the conclusion that I could profit greatly and would be able to participate more effectively if I had the advice of a professional theologian. It is true that at the end of my course of theology at the University of Propaganda I had received the doctorate of theology, but that certainly did not guarantee that I was a true theologian in the scholarly sense of the word. All of my life as priest and Bishop I had been engaged in an extremely active ministry, which left me little time to pursue systematic study of theology. Monsignor Porter White, my secretary during the Council, had a wide knowledge of theology and was very helpful, but he was primarily a canonist. The theologian I knew best and in whom I had the greatest confidence was Father James Laubacher, S.S., who had taught theology for many years. While I was Auxiliary at Baltimore, he had been rector of St. Mary's Seminary, Roland Park. During that period he was kind enough to serve as my confessor and spiritual director. After my appointment as Bishop of Bridgeport, his term at St. Mary's ended and he became rector of St. Patrick's Seminary in Menlo Park, California. During the interval between the First and Second Periods, I wrote to him and invited him to accompany me to the following periods of the Council if he were free and if he cared to do so. He answered that he would be pleased to have the opportunity to attend the Council. Through Monsignor White I arranged for him to stay with our group at the Grand Hotel, and by virtue of his knowledge and experience he was readily designated a *peritus* of the Council. Here I would like to pay tribute to Father Laubacher for the great help he gave to me and to the other Bishops of the Province.

Here, too, I should like to express my gratitude to Monsignor Porter J. White for his invaluable assistance during all four periods of the Council. His expertise in the use of Latin was really indispensable in preparing my interventions for presentation in the Council hall. Ordinarily, these interventions, to be truly relevant to the subject under discussion, had to be prepared quickly. They could hardly be prepared far in advance. In many other ways he was most helpful: in checking and paying my bills and those of the other Bishops of the Province, and in taking care of innumerable small practical problems that arose during the four years the Council lasted.

At the opening of the Second Period, Pope Paul VI presided at the Solemn Mass of the Holy Spirit celebrated by Cardinal Tisserant. Then the Pope gave his opening discourse. He paid a glowing and touching tribute to Pope John XXIII, apostrophizing him as if he were there in our midst. He reminded us of the main objectives that John had placed before the Council at the beginning and expressed his own determination to pursue them until they had been accomplished.

The following day we got down to the business before us in the discussion of the revised Schema on the Church. It was a very different document from that which we had rejected in the last days of the First Period. Gone was the first chapter on the Church Militant. In its place was an opening chapter on the Mystery of the Church. Gone, too, were those qualities that Bishop DeSmedt had criticized so severely—the triumphalism, the clericalism, the juridicism or legalism. In it, however, were certain statements concerning the character of all believers in Christ which ultimately was to give rise to Chapter 2 on the People of God in the final version of the schema. Two full days were given to the general character of the revised text. The comments generally were favorable, and at the end of the second day the Fathers voted overwhelmingly to accept this new schema on the Church as a basis for further discussion. Then on the following day we began the detailed discussion of the four chapters that then constituted the revised schema. One of the severest pieces of criticism of this revised text came from Cardinal Bea. In a speech he delivered on October 3, he urged that the schema's quotations from Scripture and its arguments from Tradition should be carefully reexamined. "Some of them do not prove what they attempt to prove." Later, when we consider the further revision discussed in the Third Period and the final text of the constitution, we shall see what was done about the Bea criticism. The discussion of the entire document was to go on up to October 30.

It was during this discussion that I made my first two speeches in the Council. The first related to the second chapter of the schema: "On the Hierarchical Nature of the Church." Following the repetition of Vatican I's definition on papal infallibility, there were four footnotes containing a whole page from Bishop Gasser's explanation of infallibility, showing its limits and the conditions that must accompany its exercise. Bishop Gasser had been perhaps the outstanding theologian of Vatican I and the relator there of the Constitution *Pastor Aeternus,* which contained the definition on papal infallibility. Since infallibilty remained one of the main sources of difficulty for Protestants relative to the Church's teachings, in my intervention I recommended that the substance of Gasser footnotes be incorporated into Vatican II's text covering the subject. A comparison between that part of the schema then under consideration and the corresponding part of the final schema shows how much it was amended. The further fact that in the final schema the passages from Gasser have been dropped and only footnote references have been retained seems to indicate that the substance of Gasser passages have been incorporated there and hence into Vatican II's Dogmatic Constitution on the Church.

My second intervention was made when the chapter "On the Laity" was being discussed. There it was said that the *"infausta separatio* (the ominous separation) of Church and State" is to be avoided. The average American, and particularly the American Catholic, was bound to interpret this as a sort of condemnation of that separation of Church and State guaranteed by the First Amendment to the United States Constitution, always considered as the foundation of religious liberty, which from the beginning has been the boast of our country and under which the Catholic Church in America has flourished. In this intervention I recommended that the phrase *"infausta separatio"* be eliminated. In fact, I suggested that that whole part of the text be dropped, since the relation between Church and State was too delicate and too important to be treated casually, as if in passing, as was the case in the article under discussion. I also pointed out that in the same section the word *"mundus"* (world) was used ambiguously. I suggested a short amendment by which I believed the ambiguity would be eliminated.

In the previous weekly meeting of American Bishops, I had explained the subject of my intervention and the way I intended to treat it. They considered it important enough to authorize me to speak in their name. Accordingly, I began my intervention by saying that I spoke in the name of all the American Bishops. I had presented the first part of my prepared speech and had launched into the second part, where I offered an amendment that, I hoped, would eliminate the ambiguity of the word *"mundus,"* and was giving my reasons for it, my mind intent on my script and on finishing within the allotted time, when in the midst of a sentence the voice of the moderator, Cardinal Lercaro, suddenly interrupted me. I was naturally startled into silence. In the confusion of the moment, I missed the meaning of his first few words, but soon realized that he was addressing all the Fathers in order to correct a mistake in an amendment on which we were all supposed to vote.

At the end of his remarks he referred to the fact that the corrected amendment had already been read by the General Secretary. Since he made no sign for me to resume, I presumed that he was referring to the Secretary for further explanation. I had made all my main points and had little to add, so I took the occasion of the pause to say over the amplifier, "dixi" (I have finished speaking), and proceeded to my Council seat. When the Cardinal saw the effect of the interruption, he seemed to become upset, or at least apologetic. "Please excuse me, Father! Continue your speech! Go on speaking!" he said. By that time, however, it was too late to mend the broken thread of my discourse and, since I had no microphone nearby, I simply gestured from my seat that I had indeed finished speaking and had no wish to continue. So he went on to the next item on the agenda.

The conciliar record of the meeting shows the precise point at which the interruption occurred and what was said. Then the record takes up my manuscript at that exact point, completes the broken sentence and goes on to the end. I do not remember any subsequent speaker having been interrupted in such a sudden and startling way. So my embarrassing experience at least may have had that good effect.

In my original draft of this chapter, it had not even occurred to me to include that intervention. I suppose it was one of those unpleasant experiences one likes to forget. When, however, I asked Porter White to read the draft, he not only recalled the incident but also thought it important enough to be included. He furthermore produced a copy of the conciliar record of the intervention, showing the strange ending of the oral part of the intervention and the typewritten conclusion. As a matter of fact, the final draft and Chapter 3 of the Constitution show that the phrase *"infausta separatio"* has been eliminated, as has also the ambiguous use of the word "world."

The importance attached to the intervention, at least by the American Bishops' press panel, is shown by the fact that on that afternoon I was invited to be the speaker at the first of the series of weekly press conferences which were continued to the end of the Council.

In addition to a summary of these events, the NCWC *Council Daybook* notes: "The day's work began with the celebration of the Mass of the Holy Spirit by Archbishop Shehan, the first American Council Father to celebrate the opening Mass of a council meeting since the Council's opening in October, 1962."

In the discussion of the Second Period on the Church and on the Pastoral Office of the Bishops, it became evident that the Council Fathers were rather seriously divided on two subjects: the use of the word "college" or "collegiality" in connection with the Bishops of the Church, and the revival of the permanent diaconate. So sharp and so vocal was this division that at the end of the discussion of the schema, Bishop John Wright, in behalf of the Commission on Doctrine, of which he was a member, presented a series of five questions meant to show clearly the mind of the majority of the Fathers on these subjects. Because of the importance of these two matters, particularly collegiality, I include the five questions with their respective answers: as they are given in the *Council Daybook* (Session I, p. 225):

1. Whether episcopal consecration is the highest grade of the Sacrament of Holy Orders: yes, 2,123; no, 34.
2. Whether every bishop, who is in union with all the bishops and

the pope, belongs to the body or college of bishops: yes, 2,049; no, 104.

3. Whether the college of bishops succeeds the college of Apostles and, together with the pope, has full and supreme power over the whole Church: yes 1,808; no, 336.
4. Whether the college of bishops, in union with the pope, has this power by divine right: yes, 1,717; no, 408.
5. Whether the diaconate should be restored as a distinct and permanent rank in the sacred ministry: yes, 1,588; no, 525.

Because of the overwhelming number of favorable answers it seemed that the questions both of collegiality and the permanent diaconate were settled once and for all. That this was not so in the case of collegiality was soon to be evident.

As the discussion of the revised Schema on the Church proceeded, a number of the speakers had expressed the opinion that the proposed statement on the Virgin Mary should be included as one of the chapters of the schema. Others, however, held steadfastly to the opinion that Mary, because of her importance and special relationship to the Church, merited a special document, as had been contemplated by the preparatory commission. In fact, early in the Second Period, when the Secretary General had announced the agenda for that period, he had informed us that after completion of the discussion of the Schema on the Church, the next item on the calendar was a discussion of the separate statement that had been prepared on the Blessed Virgin Mary. Evidently the question had to be settled before the debate on the Church was completed. A good deal of emotion had entered into the controversy, particularly on the part of some who held out for a separate document. Finally, Cardinal Ottaviani announced that before a vote was to be taken, two members of the Doctrinal Commission would present the two sides of the question.

As the time approached, one of the weekly meetings of the U.S. Bishops was devoted to the subject. Two American *periti*, both Scripture scholars (Father Barnabas Ahern, C.P., and Monsignor Eugene Maly of the Archdiocese of Cincinnati) were invited to address us. Both presented strong arguments in favor of including the statement in the Constitution. As a result of their talks and the discussion that followed, most of us were firmly convinced that it should be included. On the day of the vote, Cardinal Santos of Manila spoke strongly in favor of a separate statement. Cardinal Koenig spoke in favor of inclusion.

The ensuing vote was the closest of the whole Council: 1,114 for in-
clusion; 1,074 for a separate document—a margin of only forty votes.
So the statement on Mary would appear as the last chapter of the final
Schema on the Church. Meanwhile, it had also been decided that the
seventh chapter would be on the "Eschatological Nature of the
Church."

After completion of the discussion on the Schema on the Church,
the next item of business was "The Bishops' Pastoral Office in the
Church," a subject that was closely related to the chapter on the
hierarchical nature of the Church. Cardinal Marella, President of the
Commission on Bishops, opened the discussion with a few brief remarks
and then turned the meeting over to Bishop Carli of Segni, an Italian,
who had been chosen as the spokesman or *relator* of the commission.
As soon as Carli had finished his speech and called for the discussion to
begin, the revised schema was subjected to a number of severe criticisms. The revision, it was said, was the work, not of the commission
as a whole, but of a group of bishops living near Rome. It had been
unduly shortened; the whole first chapter had been eliminated, with
nothing to take its place. The document was too juridical in tone. The
words "college" and "collegial," and the very concept of collegiality,
had been eliminated. Some speakers, of course, came to the defense of
the schema. Cardinal Ruffini of Palermo was the first to speak in its
favor. He considered the document a good one, although he admitted
that it could be improved in some places. He pointed out that the answer to Bishop Wright's question on collegiality was indicative and not
prescriptive. Cardinal Browne, Vice President of the Commission on
Doctrine as well as Vice Prefect of the Holy Office, agreed with Cardinal Ruffini in favoring the schema and with his contention that the
vote of the Bishops in answer to Bishop Wright's question on collegiality was merely indicative. He seemed to speak in a critical tone of
the concept as well as the phrase "college of bishops." He was definitely
critical of the way the subject had been placed before the Council.
Since there was a matter of doctrine involved, the subject should have
been placed before the Commission on Doctrine and its opinion—one
might say, its decision—should have been sought and obtained before
the subject was placed before the Council.

These remarks of Cardinal Browne brought to the microphone
Cardinal Frings, Archbishop of Cologne, and a member of the Coun-

cil's Presidency, at the next general meeting on Friday, November 8. Frings began:

> Remarks recently made in the council to the effect that the Fathers must wait for a definitive response from the Theological Commission are indeed amazing. They seem to insinuate that this commission has at its disposal sources of truth unknown to the other council Fathers. Such observations also appear to lose sight of the fact that the commissions are to function only as tools of the general congregation [council meetings] and are to execute the will of the council Fathers.
>
> The distinction between administrative and judicial procedures in the Roman curia should be extended to all areas, including the Supreme Sacred Congregation of the Holy Office. Its procedures are out of harmony with modern times, are a source of harm to the faithful and of scandal to those outside the Church. No Roman congregation should have authority to accuse, judge and condemn an individual who has had no opportunity to defend himself. With all due reverence and gratitude for the devoted individuals who spend their lives in the difficult work of the Holy Office, we feel that its methods should be basically revised.
>
> It would be advisable to diminish substantially the number of bishops working in curial offices. No one should be consecrated a bishop just in order to honor him or the office he holds. If a man is consecrated a bishop, then he should be a bishop and nothing else. No one is ever ordained to the priesthood as a mark of honor or gratitude.
>
> Not a few of the tasks of the Roman curia could be performed by laymen. Consequently, efforts should be made to use fewer bishops, fewer priests, and more laymen. (*Council Daybook*, Session 1, p. 247)

Loud spontaneous applause immediately following his remarks indicated that there was a considerable amount of agreement with Cardinal Frings in his dissatisfaction over methods attributed to the Holy Office and over the rather widespread reputation that Sacred Congregation had acquired. It was not surprising, therefore, that at the next general meeting Ottaviani was immediately on his feet ready to deliver his response to the criticism that had been made of the

Holy Office. In a voice that was obviously filled with intense emotion, he began:

> The opportunity must be taken to protest most vigorously against the condemnation of the Holy Office voiced in this council hall. It should not be forgotten that the prefect of the Holy Office is none other than the sovereign pontiff himself. The criticism formulated proceeds from a lack of knowledge, not to use a stronger term, of the procedures of this sacred congregation.
>
> No one is ever accused, judged and condemned without a thorough previous investigation carried on with the help of competent consultors and experienced specialists. Besides, all decisions of the Holy Office are approved by the Pope personally, and thus such criticisms are a reflection on the Vicar of Christ.
>
> The five points recently submitted for the approval of the council Fathers were drawn up by the council moderators. They should have been submitted to the Theological Commission for careful study, and the commission would have been able to perfect certain expression and eliminate certain obscurities.
>
> Those who propose the collegiality of the bishops proceed in a vicious circle since they presume that the Apostles existed and acted as a collegial body. From the collegial character of the Apostolic College they deduce the collegial character of the body of the bishops. But even learned and experienced professors of Sacred Scripture will admit that this thesis has no solid foundations in the sacred books. Defending collegiality entails some limitation of at least the exercise of the universal primacy of the Roman pontiff. The fact is that Peter only has responsibility for the whole flock of Christ. It is not the sheep who lead Peter, but it is Peter who leads the sheep. (Idem, p. 247-248)

It seems to me that in his response Ottaviani made three fatal errors. First, he had so identified the Holy Office with the Pope that any criticism of it would have to be regarded as criticism of the Pope himself, as its Prefect. Second, he had attacked Frings personally by attributing to him a lack of knowledge, "not to use a stronger term" (ignorance? ill will? malice of some sort?). Third, he placed the Theological Commission, of which he was President and evidently spokesman, above the Council itself. I believe it is safe to say that it was the criticism of Cardinal Frings, and above all the response of Ottaviani, that began the movement which led Pope Paul to issue his *motu proprio, Integrae Servandae,* changing the name of the Congregation of the Holy Office to Congregation for the Doctrine of the Faith and also altering the organization, purpose, and method of operation, on the last working day of the Council—December 7, 1965.

Actually, the Pope, probably out of deference to the feelings of Ottaviani, seems to have retained his title of Prefect until the time when Cardinal Seper replaced Ottaviani as head of the Congregation on June 8, 1968. From that date on, Cardinal Seper is listed as the Prefect of the Congregation in the *Annuario Pontificio.* This, no doubt, is the reason why in the *New Catholic Encyclopedia* (published in 1966) in the article on the Congregation for the Doctrine of the Faith, the Pope is still called the Prefect. I am not implying that the Congregation lost its importance. In the *Annuario,* it is still placed first among the Sacred Congregations. Its decisions are still subject to the scrutiny and approval of the Pope.

What made the dramatic confrontation all the more remarkable was the age and the physical condition of the two participants. Both were old men, and both were fast approaching the state of blindness where neither could use a manuscript. Frings was then seventy-six; Ottaviani seventy-three. Both had retained great mental alertness, and both displayed a remarkable command of the Latin language. In addition to their age, the eminence of the positions these two men still occupied and the end result of their emotionally charged exchange before the two thousand or more members of the Council—all made it an unforgettable event of the Second Period. Until two years ago, I suppose it would have been indelicate to speak so freely about this confrontation. But now these two noble old men have passed away, and in the words of the old Stephen Foster song, "We'll never see their likes again."

The discussion of the Schema on the Bishops' Pastoral Office continued until Friday, November 15, without achieving notable positive results. It was then decided that the schema which had thus far been discussed, together with some four hundred suggested amendments, should be turned over to a Commission on Bishops for revision. The revision was not presented to the Council until the following period (1964).

On Monday, November 18, the Schema on Ecumenism was finally brought before the Council after a long delay. The secretariat had been working on it almost since the beginning of the Council and it had gone through a number of revisions. It now consisted of five chapters; three on ecumenism itself, but now included in it were also the Statement on the Jews which formed Chapter 4, and the Declaration on Religious Liberty which formed Chapter 5. Joseph-Marie Martin, Archbishop of Rouen and prominent member of the secretariat, was chosen to introduce the first three chapters on ecumenism proper. His introductory speech received vigorous applause, indicating that the great majority of the Fathers were in favor of ecumenism as he described it in the three chapters that would be considered.

Martin was followed by Cardinal Bea, who introduced the Statement on the Jews (Chapter 4). He told how Pope John, who had dealt with the suffering of Jewish refugees in Bulgaria, had asked him personally to prepare a statement on what the Church's relationship to the Jews should be in our present age. The result was the secretariat's present statement. He, too, received long and vigorous applause. Bishop DeSmedt introduced the Declaration on Religious Liberty. It was a subject in which he had a deep personal interest, and he was introducing a document on which he had put many long hours of work. His speech was an example of his best oratory. It, too, received the acclaim it merited. All things seemed favorable for the schema. There was no doubt where the minds and hearts of the vast majority of the Fathers lay. All seemed to bode well for the way the Council would deal with the whole schema—ecumenism proper, relations with the Jews in harmony with the views of John XXIII and Bea, and with an outright declaration in favor of religious freedom.

At the end of two days of general discussion, the moderators announced that they would proceed to vote on whether the first three chapters were acceptable as a basis of discussion. The Secretary General added that voting on Chapters 4 and 5 would take place later. The vote in favor of accepting the first three chapters as a basis of discussion was overwhelming (1,996 to 86). At that point, things seemed most promising. The three chapters were discussed in detail, and a number of amendments to improve the text were proposed. The secretariat took back the three chapters with the proposed amendments in order to prepare the final text.

But still the Statement on the Jews and the Declaration on Religious Liberty were not presented for a vote. The Bishops of the Oriental rites were, as was abundantly clear, opposed to any Council statement on the Jews, and it was known that a number of Spanish and Italian Bishops were far from enthusiastic about the Declaration on Religious Liberty. Both groups no doubt felt justified in delaying the vote on these two documents as long as possible. In any event, the Second Period came to an end without any vote on them having been taken.

As we reached the end of the Second Period, the Council still had very little to show in the way of accomplishment. It is true the Constitution on the Sacred Liturgy had been completed, voted, signed, and promulgated, as had also the shorter document on Social Communication. But this seemed almost insignificant compared to the vast task that lay before us. Besides this, the Schema of the Constitution on the Church had been revised and discussed at length, and had been made ready for a final revision. This had also been the case with the Schema of the Decree on Ecumenism. But what of the Declaration on Religious Liberty, without which no real advance in ecumenism could be expected? Most of us at the end of the Second Period felt a sense of discouragement over the prospect. At this rate, how long would the Council go on? In the end, would the results really be worth the time, the expense, the effort? However, there was nothing to be done except to go on, determined somehow, with the help of the Holy Spirit, that the Council would be brought to some satisfactory conclusion.

While we were still in the midst of our discussion of the document on Ecumenism, a most tragic event took place in the United States—the assassination of President John F. Kennedy. In Rome it was about eight o'clock in the evening. The Bishops of our Province, together with Porter White and James Laubacher, were seated at dinner in the Grand Hotel. Suddenly our waiter came to the table, visibly disturbed, and said simply, "Il vostro Presidente è stato colpito" (your President has been shot). We sat stunned for a moment. Then Porter went out into the lobby to make inquiries about the report. Before his return, the waiter was back and said: "È morto" (he is dead). Almost immediately Porter returned: "Yes, it is true President Kennedy has been shot and killed." That one so young, so vigorous, and so able and still so full of promise should thus be brought to such a sudden and violent end was indeed a tragedy that struck deep in every sensitive mind and heart throughout the world. No body of men could have been more profoundly moved than the American Bishops gathered for this Council of peace and unity. When the Council met the following Monday, many Bishops from all parts of the world approached the American Bishops to express their sorrow and sympathy, showing in a concrete way how the whole world had been touched by the tragedy.

Before the ending of the Second Period, the Secretary General announced that the Pope had decided that the opening of the Third Period would take place on September 14, 1964, and would end November 21, in order to give those Fathers who wished to do so an opportunity to attend the International Eucharistic Congress in Bombay, which would take place immediately after the ending of the Third Period. Since I was still a member of the Permanent Committee for the Promotion of International Eucharistic Congresses, I would have to make arrangements for Porter White and myself to be present for the Congress. It was now clear that there would almost certainly be a Fourth Period of the Council, because, with all the work still to be done, it would be practically impossible to bring the Council to an end between September 14 and November 21. The necessity of a Fourth Period seemed all the more certain, for since the publication of the encyclical of Pope John XXIII, *Pacem in Terris,* April 11, 1963, a totally new kind of document was developing and taking shape in the Council, a document such as never had been produced in any previous Council. This document was to view the Church as it stood in relationship to the modern world, with its problems of poverty, starvation, and strife, with its scientific and technological developments, with the presence of nuclear power and arms, and the threat of nuclear warfare. There were voices within the Council that were raising insistent pleas that these great problems of the modern world be addressed, voices that could be neither ignored nor stilled.

Shortly after our return to Baltimore from the Second Period, Father Gustave Weigel, S.J., who from the beginning had been the most influential American on the Secretariat for Christian Unity, lectured in the parish hall of the new Cathedral under the auspices of our Commission on Christian Unity. The hall that December 10 was filled to capacity. Having served during the first two periods as translator and consultant to the English-speaking Protestant observers, he was his wittiest and best, filled with interesting observations about the Council and the prospects of the movement of ecumenism. There was no reason to believe that he would not be with us for many years to lead the movement forward, as he had done. That was the last time I saw Gus Weigel. He died suddenly in New York City the following January 3. It was the greatest loss our Secretariat on Christian Unity suffered during the period of the Council. His body was brought back to Woodstock and buried on January 8. I was privileged to preside at the funeral Mass. A most gifted and learned man of great intelligence, wide sympathy and understanding, his death created a much mourned gap in the Woodstock faculty, an irreplaceable loss to the Roman Secretariat of Christian Unity, and to our own local commission. He has rightly been called not only a Catholic pioneer in the ecumenical movement in the United States, but also "the most significant active and respected Catholic ecumenist in America."

In February 1964 I was once more summoned to Rome to take part in a week-long plenary session of the Secretariat for Unity held at Gesu Divin Maestro, the retreat house at Ariccia in the Alban Hills. The main purpose of the meeting was to draft what we hoped would be the final version of the Declaration on Religious Liberty. By the end of the Second Period, it had become evident that such a declaration would not become a chapter in the Schema on Ecumenism as had been planned; it would have to stand, as it were, on its own feet. It had to be the work of the full secretariat; it had to anticipate all the significant objections we knew would be raised against any conciliar statement of the right of all individuals and all religious groups to true religious freedom. Yet, in order to be presented effectively, it had to be fairly short.

Rome itself can be uncomfortably cold in the month of February, as I and those who would be with me would experience the following year. But February in the Alban Hills can be bitterly cold, as it was this February 1964. I remember the week as one of constant discomfort. The retreat house was advertised as heated during the winter season. Even Porter White, who can stand the cold better than any other man I know, called it "psychological heat." However, once we clothed ourselves as warmly as we could and made up our minds to endure the chill, we had a rather pleasant week of uninterrupted work under the leadership of Cardinal Bea, Bishop Willebrands, Bishop DeSmedt, and Father John Courtney Murray. The last named, having been allegedly excluded from the First Period as a *peritus* by Cardinal Ottaviani, and having subsequently been invited by Cardinal Spellman to accompany him as a theological consultant to the Second and following periods, had been welcomed into the ranks of the secretariat. It was, I think it safe to say, Bishop DeSmedt and Father Murray who —with many suggestions and assists from the rest—hammered out the statement that emerged toward the end of our meeting. Having come safely through this week, Porter and I gladly departed for Baltimore.

After my return from the meeting at Gesu Divin Maestro, I became directly involved in the settlement of the controversy between the Dioceses of Miami and St. Augustine. When Bishop Joseph P. Hurley was appointed Ordinary of St. Augustine in 1940, that diocese included the entire state of Florida, with the exception of the north-western panhandle of Pensacola. Following World War I, the popula-tion of Florida experienced a period of remarkably fast growth, as it did again after World War II. In 1958, the Holy See decided to divide the state of Florida into two dioceses and established the new Diocese of Miami, which included the seventeen southern counties as its territory. Bishop Coleman Carroll, former Auxiliary Bishop of Pitts-burgh, was appointed first Bishop of Miami. The dispute between Bishop Carroll and the (then) Archbishop Hurley arose over the fact that at the time of the division the Diocese of St. Augustine was in possession of more than three hundred tracts of property spread throughout Florida.

Conscious of the steadily increasing value of property in Florida and of the growing difficulty of acquiring good sites, Archbishop Hurley had adopted a policy of extensive land purchase. To obtain funds to carry out these projects, he had assessed each parish 80 percent of its gross income during the year 1952. This sum each pastor could raise in one of three ways: he could take the entire sum from the reserves of the parish, where this was possible; or he could negotiate a loan, endorsed by the Bishop, from the bank with which the parish dealt, or he could spread the payment over three, but not more than four, years. Here it should be said that soon Archbishop Hurley acquired the reputation of being a remarkably shrewd judge of land values. No one since then, so far as I know, has ever ques-tioned his judgment in this respect. But the question was how were these many properties to be divided between the two dioceses?

When it became clear that the two Bishops could not agree either on the distribution of seminary students or on the division of the properties, this was brought to the attention of the Apostolic Delegate and through him to the Holy See. Bishop James Griffith, Auxiliary Bishop to the Cardinal Archbishop of New York, was appointed to work with the two Bishops in an attempt to bring about a just and amicable solution. The question of the seminarians was soon settled, but Bishop Griffith had to report failure to bring about an agreement on property division. Thereupon the Holy See, through a decree signed by Cardinal Confalonieri, Prefect of the Sacred Consistorial Congre-gation, appointed a committee of three to make a definitive decision concerning the matter: Archbishop Egidio Vagnozzi, Apostolic Dele-gate; Archbishop Francis P. Keough, Metropolitan of the Province

of Baltimore to which the two Dioceses of Miami and St. Augustine at
that time belonged; Bishop James Griffith, who was already familiar
with the problem. The decision was not subject to appeal until after
the two Bishops had fulfilled its terms. This commission met with
Bishops Hurley and Carroll on November 3, 1961. To Bishop Griffith
was assigned the task of collecting all the necessary information
concerning the properties and drafting a tentative decision. Archbishop Keough died December 8, 1961. I, as his successor, took his
place on the commission.

Bishop Griffith spent a great deal of time collecting reams of
documentary evidence concerning all of the 315 properties: the exact
location and a description of each property; date of purchase and the
price paid; the purpose for which each property was designated,
where there was such designation, etc. He had begun to draw up his
suggested decision for the commission, but before he had completed
the task, he died suddenly, February 24, 1964. As he had gone about
his work on the decision, he had scattered the numerous documents he
had been using, singly or in piles throughout his study, in an order
that could have been known only to himself. The authorities of the
Archdiocese of New York had gathered up these papers and transferred them to the Apostolic Delegate. Shortly thereafter, the Delegate entrusted the whole package to me, with the request that I
attempt to draw up the final decision. My first question was: who
could help me with such a formidable task? The obvious answer was
Porter White, the only person I knew who had the patience and the
meticulous care needed first to put the documents in order and then
the knowledge of canon law needed to work out a satisfactory decision. Porter very willingly undertook the job. In an incredibly short
time, he had put order into all the documents, and had then gone on
to draft a proposed decision. Meanwhile, Francis Gallagher, our
archdiocesan attorney, at my request had offered to give Porter
whatever help he could.

After Porter and Francis had completed their work, I met with
them to discuss the document in detail. They both assured me that the
proposed decision met every requirement of canon law and civil law.
I could see no way of improving upon the decision as formulated and
I asked Porter to have copies prepared for both the Delegate and
Bishop John Maguire, who had replaced Bishop Griffith on the commission. The three of us met at the Apostolic Delegation on July 2,
1964, and signed the twenty-seven page decision, which gave a detailed statement of the canon law and civil law as they applied to

the case, all the pertinent facts, and the mandates imposed on both Bishops; this was to be sent to the Sacred Consistorial Congregation. We also signed the Summary Decision, a copy of which was then sent to the two Florida Bishops with a covering letter, by certified mail, return receipt requested. The postal receipt showed that each copy was delivered July 10. This meant that they had until August 10 to carry out the mandate. The Bishop of Miami acknowledged receipt of the decision on July 13; the Bishop of St. Augustine on July 20. Both promised to do their best to carry out the terms of the decision within the time specified.

The Bishop of Miami informed me that, on the receipt of the decision, he made out a check in the amount specified by the decision and gave it to his lawyers to be turned over to the Bishop of St. Augustine upon his fulfillment of the terms of the decision. In a telegram dated August 7, the Bishop of St. Augustine sent the following message:

> I AM UNABLE TO COMPLY WITH THE DIRECTION OF THE EPISCOPAL COMMISSION DATED JULY 2ND STOP LEGAL COUNSEL ADVISES ME THAT THE EXECUTION OF PROPOSED CONVEYANCE IS IN VIOLATION OF FLORIDA LAW STOP WE HAVE ADVISED THE ORDINARY OF THE DIOCESE OF MIAMI OF OUR POSITION STOP I RESPECTFULLY ASK YOUR INDULGENCE IN GRANTING AT LEAST THREE MONTHS FOR CLARIFICATION OF DECISION STOP DETAILED LETTER FOLLOWS
>
> JOSEPH P. HURLEY

Without waiting for the detailed letter, that day I consulted Francis X. Gallagher and was assured by him that Archbishop Hurley's interpretation of the civil law of the state of Florida was without solid foundation. Porter White also advised me that Hurley was forbidden by canon law to appeal to civil authority against any decision of the Holy See or its representative, under the severest possible penalty, automatically incurred. I then telephoned the Apostolic Delegate and Archbishop Maguire and received their approval of the following letter, which I sent off immediately:

August 8, 1964

My dear Archbishop Hurley:

In your letter of July 20, 1964, you seemed to imply that no appeal to the Holy See was provided for in the July 2 Decision of the Episcopal Commission in the case of Miami–St. Augustine. While it is true that an *appellatio in suspensivo* is expressly ruled out, an *appellatio in devolutivo* is not. The formula preceding the Decision sets forth the mandate of the Sacred Consistorial Congregation (Prot. N. 818/59) dated February 15, 1962, over the signature of his Eminence Cardinal Confalonieri. By this mandate, the Commission was instructed to render its decision in the case "*quacumque appellatione postposita.*" In obedience to it, the Commission gave the Decision which Your Excellency received on July 10, setting forth in its final sentence the exact words of the mandate in the Rescript from the Sacred Congregation.

After the terms of the Decision have been fully carried out, then, either party to this dispute may, of course, appeal to the Holy See. Since Your Excellency received the Decision on July 10, and the time for fully carrying out its terms is 30 calendar days from the date of its receipt, the provisions of the Decision must be carried into effect on or before August 10.

In your more recent telegram, Your Excellency asks for a three-month delay in the fulfillment of the provisions of the Decision of the Commission. This delay the members of the Commission are unable to grant.

After consultation with legal counsel, the Commission is convinced that Florida law presents no insuperable obstacle to the fulfillment of the provisions of this Decision. To avoid scandal, the Commission is of the opinion that a separate deed for each piece of property affected by the Decision is preferable.

We call your attention, moreover, to the provisions of Canon 2333 and 2334, 2°, which clearly indicate the mind of the Church regarding recourse to lay power to impede the execution of acts of the Holy See or its representative.

Assuring Your Excellency of my sentiments of esteem, I am

Sincerely yours in Christ,
+ Lawrence J. Shehan
Archbishop of Baltimore

The two canons referred to in the last sentence state quite clearly that any Catholic who attempts to impede the actions of the Holy See or its representative, by appealing to the civil law or otherwise, incurs excommunication, reserved to the Holy See.

In a letter dated September 2, 1964, Archbishop Hurley informed me that he had carried out the mandates of the decision of July 2, but also notified me that he intended to appeal the sentence to the Holy See. He did make his appeal shortly thereafter, and in January 1965 the Sacred Consistorial Congregation sent a copy of the appeal to the Apostolic Delegate. He in turn sent a copy to me, together with a letter suggesting that I study it and prepare for a meeting with the other members of the Commission somewhat later. Porter White and Frank Gallagher immediately began composing a rebuttal of every complaint and erroneous allegation contained in the appeal. With a covering letter dated May 7, 1965, I sent two copies of this sixty-four page document to the Apostolic Delegate, one for himself and one for Archbishop Maguire. The Delegate forwarded a copy of the rebuttal to the Sacred Congregation as our response to and comment on the appeal.

While the Apostolic Delegate, Archbishop Maguire, Monsignor White, and I were in Rome attending the Fourth Period of the Council, the Sacred Congregation in a letter dated November 18, 1965, informed the Delegate that, after carefully studying every aspect of the case, the Congregation had come to the conclusion that the complaints submitted by Archbishop Hurley against the decision of July 2, 1964, were unfounded. The Sacred Congregation had presented its conclusion to the Holy Father, who in turn decided that the case was now definitely settled, and that the parties involved should carry out the terms of the decision. Thus, more than seven years after the separation of the Dioceses of Miami and St. Augustine and the origin of the dispute, the controversy was settled once and for all.

My final comment on the case would be this: the justice of the decision was confirmed not only by the action of the Sacred Congregation and the Holy Father, but also by the fact that, according to reports given to me by third parties who were in a position to know, the final reactions of both Archbishop Hurley and Bishop Carroll, were favorable. While neither got all that he had originally claimed, each apparently got more than he expected from such a long and complicated controversy. While I never subsequently discussed the decision with either party, I never received the slightest indication that Archbishop Hurley was in any way dissatisfied, which, given his disposition, certainly otherwise would not have been the case. On the other hand, Bishop Carroll never missed the opportunity of expressing his gratitude for the part Porter and I played in resolving the controversy, which once seemed almost interminable.

Although a good deal of my time after my return from the meeting of the Secretariat on Christian Unity held at Ariccia was occupied with the controversy between the Dioceses of St. Augustine and Miami, most of the time-consuming work was actually done by Porter White with the help of Francis Gallagher, while Bishop Murphy and I carried on the ordinary activities of the archdiocese.

The last two appointments listed on my calendar of September 8, 1964, are: 9:30 Mr. Jacob Blaustein; 10:30 Clergy Conference. Mr. Blaustein was the most prominent Jewish leader in Baltimore. From the time it became known that the Secretariat for Christian Unity, at the request of Pope John XXIII, was preparing a statement on the Jews—or, rather, on the relationship of the Catholic Church to Jews— Mr. Blaustein had displayed an intense interest in the projected statement. He was particularly concerned that the Church, through the Council, should reprobate the use by Catholics of the infamous term "deicide" as applied to Jews and of other such terms as "a people rejected by God" and "a nation accursed by God." Such terms he and other Jewish leaders considered one of the main causes of the anti-Semitism that caused so much suffering to the Jewish people of Germany during the years of the Nazi ascendancy. I assured him that not only I, but also the Secretariat on Unity as a whole, was firmly convinced that such terms should be reprobated and that we were working toward that end. I reminded him, however, that the situation in the Council was complicated by the fact that many Bishops of the Council came from the Arab countries of the Near East where the people for whom they were responsible resided. He was well aware of the problem that arose from the confused situation of the Near East, and neither of us was anxious to get into a discussion of that matter. However, he expressed the hope that a statement along the lines he had suggested, which corresponded to the statement proposed by Cardinal Bea, could be forthcoming.

The Clergy Conference, which was the second item on my calendar of that day, consisted of a meeting of all the priests of the archdiocese to discuss the Constitution on the Sacred Liturgy promulgated at the end of the Second Period, December 4, 1963, and the Pope's letter (*motu proprio*) January 26, 1964. I had asked Bishop Murphy to serve as chairman of our own Liturgical Commission and to appoint to it those priests he considered most familiar with the Constitution and most interested in the implementation of the chapter dealing with the Sacrifice of the Mass. The purpose of the conference was to discuss the conclusions of the Liturgical Commission concerning changes that could be put into effect at the present time. The complete new rite would have to await the publication of the New Roman Missal of Pope Paul VI and the authorized translation of that Missal.

The day following the conference, Porter White and I left for Rome to prepare for the opening of the Third Period of the Second Vatican Council.

9. The Second Vatican Council:
Periods III and IV

THE THIRD PERIOD OPENED September 14, 1964, with a concelebrated Mass offered by Pope Paul VI together with twenty-four Council Fathers, among whom were Archbishop Krol and myself. The ancient custom of concelebration had fallen into disuse in the Latin rite except for the Mass of Ordination of Priests and Bishops. The Constitution on the Sacred Liturgy, signed and promulgated by Pope Paul VI on December 4, 1963, had undertaken to revive it on certain occasions and under certain circumstances. This was the first concelebrated Mass in the Latin rite within the Second Vatican Council. In view of the principal item on the agenda, it was not surprising that the Pope's introductory discourse dealt with the role of the Bishops and the mutual relationship between the Pope and the Episcopate. "The integrity of Catholic truth now calls for a clarification consonant with the doctrine of the Papacy which will place in its splendid light the role and mandate of the Episcopate."

The first item on the agenda the following day was a discussion of the revised Schema on the Church which had been sent to all of us after its completion during the summer of 1964. This was a rather bulky volume of 214 pages, in which the new schema (1964) was printed side by side with the previous schema (1963) in parallel columns. In making the revision, the Doctrinal Commission, to which such scholars as Joseph Ratzinger, Karl Rahner, Charles Moeller, Gerard Philips (who had become the General Secretary of the commission) and G. Thils had been added, had divided the material found in the four chapters of the 1963 revision into six chapters. To these had been added two completely new chapters, one on the eschatological nature of the Church, and the other on Mary's role in the Mystery

171

of Christ and His Church. The new schema, therefore, consisted of these eight chapters: 1. The Mystery of the Church, 2. The People of God, 3. The Hierarchical Nature of the Church, 4. The Laity, 5. The Call of All Members of the Church to Holiness, 6. The Religious, 7. The Eschatological Nature of the Church and the Union of the Pilgrim Church with the Heavenly Church, 8. The Role of the Blessed Virgin Mary, Mother of God, in the Mystery of Christ and of His Church.

Since the material of the first six chapters had been discussed at length during the Second Period of the Council, only the last two chapters were now discussed in detail. The debate on these chapters came to an end on the fifth day of the Third Period, September 18. Meanwhile, voting on the individual chapters, broken down into suitable sections, had already begun and was to continue throughout a great part of the Third Period, while discussion on other schemas was proceeding at convenient intervals. The final revision of the schema was not ready for a vote until November 18, two days before the end of the period.

It seems proper to ask what had happened as a result of Cardinal Bea's criticism of the poor use of Scripture in the 1963 version and his suggestion that the texts should be re-examined since some of them did not prove what they attempted to prove. One of the places to which Bea's criticism certainly applied was Article 13 of the 1963 schema, "On the Bishops as Successors of the Apostles." This article is printed side by side in parallel columns with Article 20 of the 1964 volume, both bearing the identical title. They are found on pages 60-62 in the volume to which I have already referred. It is therefore a very simple matter to compare them.

The first thing that strikes us about the text in the new schema is that virtually the whole of Article 20 has been revised. Forty-five out of the forty-nine lines of the text appear in italics, indicating that they are new; only four lines of the previous text have been retained. The second thing that strikes us is the changed use of Scripture in the new text. In the old text, all the scriptural references are imbedded in the text as if to indicate that they are given as proof of the statements to which they are attached. In the new text, only three scriptural references are found in the text: Matthew 28:20; Acts 20:28; and Luke 10:16. Some of the references in the old text have been eliminated in the new. The rest, together with some additional references and all the references to ancient tradition (e.g., St. Clement to the Corinthians, c. A.D. 96; St. Ignatius of Antioch to various churches, c. A.D. 110) are consigned to footnotes, indicating that they are given, not as strict logical *proof,* but as historically relevant texts from Scripture and Tradition. If one reads carefully Article 20 one sees that all of these, taken together, form a suitable basis for the Church's teaching on apostolic succession presented in that article.

In the complete record of Vatican II, found in the library of The Catholic University of America and in other Catholic libraries of similar rank, there is no indication that Cardinal Bea submitted any criticism, written or oral, of the use of scripture in the 1964 Schema on the Church. Finally, I observe that one of the prominent signatures attached to the Constitution on the Church, based on the 1964 schema, is that of Augustin Cardinal Bea.

Does all this mean that Bea was satisfied that at least the essential points of his criticism had been met in Article 20 of the final version of the schema? To me it seems to say that. If it were not so, I believe that Cardinal Bea would still have been under moral obligation, which a man of his integrity would certainly have fulfilled, to make his judgment known during that interval between the completion of the revision and its enactment into the final Dogmatic Constitution on the Church, November 21, 1964.

In his introduction to the commentary on that section, Gerard Philips, General Secretary of the commission, tells us that among the commission members who dealt with that whole section (Articles 18-29) were Cardinal Koenig and Cardinal Florit, both Scripture scholars, and such *periti* as Charles Moeller, Karl Rahner, Joseph Ratzinger, and G. Thils.

I make no pretense at being a Scripture scholar, yet given the actual teaching of Article 20 and those for whom the teaching was primarily meant, I would venture the opinion that, in this particular case at least, the Council has made a very proper use of Scripture *and* Tradition, taken always together and never apart—as Rahner insists in his comments on Article 20 in the *Herder and Herder* (*Vorgrimler*) *Commentary* (vol. I, pp. 190-191).

Following the discussion of the Schema on the Church, the next order of business was a brief discussion of the revised Schema on the Pastoral Office of Bishops. Then came a consideration of the revised Statement on Religious Liberty. Bishop DeSmedt introduced the Declaration on Religious Liberty with an excellent detailed statement. Cardinal Ruffini was the first to speak, and he was highly critical of the declaration: the title should be "Religious Toleration," not "Religious Liberty," that was in accord with the tradition of the Church; that was what Leo XIII, Pius XI, and Pius XII had taught; error has no rights, etc. He was followed by the Spanish Cardinal Archbishop of Seville who took a similar line of attack. Then came Cardinal Léger of Montreal and three American Cardinals: Cushing, Ritter, and Meyer. Particularly strong was Meyer's speech. He ended by saying that unless the Council Fathers approved this or a similar statement on religious freedom, anything else that the Council did would have little or no effect. In spite of certain adverse voices, the discussion showed that the great majority of the Fathers strongly favored the declaration.

On September 25, three days after Bishop DeSmedt had introduced the Declaration on Religious Liberty, Cardinal Bea rose to give his detailed introduction on the revised Statement on the Jews. In it he pointed out the reasons why such a statement had to be made by the Council, and he anticipated and answered the objections that almost certainly would be raised against it. Although Bea's introduction was long, it was clear, interesting, and eloquent, and was applauded vigorously. It had been announced that only two full days would be devoted to discussion. Personally, and as a member of the Secretariat for Christian Unity from the beginning of the Council, I had been deeply interested in the Schema on Ecumenism and in the statements both on Religious Liberty and the Church's relations to the Jews and planned to speak on both of the latter. I was listed to speak on the Jews among those of the second day of discussion, for after Bea's introduction of the statement, there had been time for only seven speakers, mostly Cardinals, on the first day. Anyone who has sat through twenty-one consecutive speakers in one session will understand the opening comment on the *Council Daybook* narrative for September 28: "Among the speakers on the closing day of discussion of the Jewish declaration were three Americans, one of whom won applause when he declared that he was yielding his right to speak because his points had been adequately covered by other speeches. He was Archbishop Lawrence J. Shehan of Baltimore." Never was applause more easily won!

The Statement on the Jews was quite short—eighty lines. There were just so many things that could be said, and what I had intended to say had already been said over and over again. Under the circumstances, perhaps the written statement which I submitted and which became part of the permanent record may have had more effect than if it had been spoken. In any event, for the sake of those who may be interested, particularly my Jewish friends of Baltimore, I here give a translation of my intended intervention:

I am pleased for the most part with what we find said concerning the Jews in article 32 of the Schema on Ecumenism [the statement on the relation of the Church to the Jews was then still chapter 5 of the Schema on Ecumenism]. In six lines of this article, however, I wish to propose a few amendments which seem to me to be of no little importance.

1. In line 30 after the words, "refer to them as a rejected nation," the clause "or accuse them [the Jews] of deicide," should be reinserted. My reasons are these: (a) This calumny—that the Jewish people are guilty of deicide—is considered by the Jews of the present day the primary and root source of the anti-Semitism of many Christians. . . . Unlesss these very words, whose renunciation many Jews (and, indeed, those well disposed toward the Church) have confidently [liberenti animo] sought, are repeated among many, both Jews and non-Jews, there will arise not only displeasure, but also doubt, not to say disgust, concerning the good will and motives of the Fathers of the Council. (b) In addition, to omit the disavowal of this calumny from the declaration, or to be silent concerning it, seems to be imprudent, or at least most inopportune, when the Church itself is being vilified by calumnies concerning her alleged part in the persecution of the Jews during World War II (1939-45).

2. In line 31, the clause "to seem to be in hatred or contempt of the Jews" should be restored, in place of the clause "to alienate minds from the Jews." The reason: the clause "to alienate minds from the Jews" inadequately expresses the depravity of men who through the centuries, and particularly in this century, have perpetrated inhuman crimes against Jews.

3. Finally, in order to produce a better order in this passage, I propose that the last sentence, i.e., "Let them take care not to impute to the Jews of our times the things that were done in the Passion of Christ," be transposed so that it becomes part of the first sentence; and the clause "and let them not do or say anything else" become the last and the summary sentence of the passage. The reason: thus the ideas expressed in the clauses seem to have a better logical order.

In summary: the passage should be so amended that it reads thus: "Therefore let all take care lest, in teaching catechism, or in preaching the Word of God, or in daily conversation, they refer to the Jewish people as a rejected nation, or accuse them of deicide,

or impute to the Jews of our times those things which were done in
the Passion of Christ, and let them do nothing else which could
seem to generate hatred or contempt of Jews in their minds.

The whole purpose of my intervention was to restore to the statement the strength that the Secretariat for Christian Unity had originally given it.

When the discussion of the Declaration on Religious Liberty and
that on the Jews and other non-Christian religions came to an end, the
Secretariat for Christian Unity took back both with all the proposed
amendments to work on what we hoped would be final revisions. All
of us who were particularly interested in these documents were confident at that point that they would be brought back for a final vote
before the end of the Third Period.

Discussion on the next matter of business, the revised Schema on
Revelation, went on from September 30 to October 6. The debate
lacked some of the intensity of the First Period, when the original
schema was so vigorously attacked and virtually rejected by a substantial majority of the Fathers; yet there was still a spirited exchange
between those who might be called the champions of the old concept of
revelation, with its twin sources of Scripture and Tradition, and those
who favored a new and more exact concept, which had sprung largely from the influence of Pius XII's encyclical *Divino Afflante Spiritu*
and the modern Catholic Scripture study to which it gave birth. The
latter viewpoint was championed in the Council by such leaders as Bea,
Koenig, Meyer, Léger, and Landazuri Ricketts (of Lima, Peru).

In his intervention on Chapter 3, On "The Divine Inspiration and
the Interpretation of Sacred Scripture," Cardinal Meyer may be said to
have spoken for the American Bishops. He began by saying that, while
the document contained some excellent points, it failed to state clearly
or properly the nature of divine inspiration. It seemed to consider
inspiration to be confined to the establishment of logical truth and to
the formulation of a series of propositions leading to the conclusion that
its whole value consists in the quality of inerrancy. The proper consideration of inspiration should begin and end with the fact that it is a
personal communication to men of the Word of God that goes beyond
merely manifesting concepts. The very idea of the Word of God means
that something was being communicated by a Person speaking and
looking for a response or reaction. It was the heart of God that was

revealed, not propositions; what was guaranteed was not so much inerrancy but the means for educating and impelling to every good work, as St. Paul insists. Finally, the reconciliation of inerrancy and inspiration must take into consideration human deficiencies and limitations, as Cardinal Koenig had already pointed out.

In line with this was my own contribution to the discussion of this document on October 1, 1964. After stating that in general I approved of the schema, I noted that the document seemed defective in one respect. It did not make sufficiently clear and emphasize the role man played in the process of revelation. To this end, I offered an amendment to the text.

The *Council Daybook*, after noting that Archbishop Lorenz Jaeger of Paderborn called for a fuller concept of Revelation which he described as a colloquy of God with man through Christ, says:

> The same stress on this point was given by Archbishop Shehan, who said he thought that the text is not complete enough and not sufficiently explicit because there is a certain task left to the subject of Revelation, which is the human mind.
>
> Supernatural Revelation is really the communication of God to men by which God manifests himself to men, he said. There should be inserted into the text, he stated, both parts of the process of Revelation—one, that action of God which is broader than the mere presentation of certain propositions to be believed, and, two, that reception of this action and its interpretation by men. This interpretation depends on objective deeds in history and therefore is not completely subjective. The role that man played in the reception of Revelation should not be ignored, he concluded (*Council Daybook*, Session 3, p. 90).

It was the leadership of such men as I have mentioned (Bea, Koenig, Meyer, etc.) that produced, as an example, the opening text of Chapter 3 on "The Divine Inspiration and the Interpretation of Sacred Scripture":

> Those divinely revealed realities which are contained and presented in sacred Scripture have been committed to writing under the inspiration of the Holy Spirit. Holy Mother Church, relying on the belief of the apostles, holds that the books of both the Old and New Testament in their entirety, with all their

parts, are sacred and canonical because, having been written under the inspiration of the Holy Spirit (cf. John 20:31; 2 Tim. 3:16; 2 Pet. 1:19-21; 3:15-16) they have God as their author and have been handed on as such to the Church herself. In composing the sacred books, God chose men and while employed by Him they made use of their powers and abilities, so that with Him acting in them and through them, they, as true authors, consigned to writing everything and only those things which He wanted.

Therefore, since everything asserted by the insired authors or sacred writers must be held to be asserted by the Holy Spirit, it follows that the books of Scripture must be acknowledged as teaching firmly, faithfully, and without error that truth which God wanted to put into the sacred writings for the sake of our salvation. Therefore "all Scripture is inspired by God and useful for teaching, for reproving, for correcting, for instruction in justice; that the man of God may be perfect, equipped for every good work" (2 Tim. 3:16-17, Greek text).

However, since God speaks in sacred Scripture through men in human fashion, the interpreter of sacred Scripture, in order to see clearly what God wanted to communicate to us, should carefully investigate what meaning the sacred writers really intended, and what God wanted to manifest by means of their words.

Those who search out the intention of the sacred writers must, among other things, have regard for "literary forms." For truth is proposed and expressed in a variety of ways, depending on whether a text is history of one kind or another, or whether its form is that of prophecy, poetry, or some other type of speech. The interpreter must investigate what meaning the sacred writer intended to express and actually expressed in particular circumstances as he used contemporary literary forms in accordance with the situation of his own time and culture. (*The Documents of Vatican II*, ed., Walter M. Abbott, S.J., pp. 188-120).

Discussion of the revised Schema on Revelation continued until October 6. Then conciliar discussion centered on two shorter but important schemas, Apostolate of the Laity (October 7-12) and Priestly Ministry and Life (October 12-15). The latter was followed by the discussion of the Decree on Eastern Catholic Churches (October 15-20). All three schemas were severely criticized and were sent back to their respective commissions, with many proposed amendments, to be revised.

October 20, 1964, was a red-letter day for the many Bishops and *periti* who were deeply interested in the development of the totally new kind of conciliar document represented by the Schema on the Church in the Modern World and had eagerly awaited its presentation on the Council floor. The quality of the reception it received can in a measure be judged by the number of important Council members who welcomed it with praise. Cardinal Lienart spoke first; later came the three American Cardinals, Spellman, Ritter, and Meyer; Léger of Montreal; Suenens of Malines-Brussels; Doepfner of Munich; Lercaro of Bologna; Silva Henriquez of Santiago, Chile; Bea for the Christian Unity Secretariat; Wojtyla of Cracow (now Pope John Paul II); Landazuri Ricketts of Lima, Peru; followed by a number of Archbishops and Bishops. Needless to say, none found the schema perfect and there were many suggestions for improvement, but for three days the comments were generally very favorable.

Then suddenly the picture changed. On the morning of October 2, Archbishop Heenan made a slashing attack on the schema as a whole. The *Council Daybook* called his speech "a violent attack couched in some of the strongest language the Council has heard." After praising the subcommission that was responsible for producing the schema for its hard work, he then went on to denounce the schema itself as "a dangerous set of platitudes—unworthy of a council." He said:

> I must speak plainly. This document is going to dash the hopes of everyone who has been awaiting it. Its authors do not seem to realize even to whom the message should be directed . . . . The whole treatise reads more like a sermon than a document of a council.
>
> We have been given the schema itself, together with certain supplements. The fact is that the schema, even read with the supplements, remains obscure and misleading; read on its own it is dangerous and could prove harmful. I would like the Fathers of the Council to consider this question very seriously. We have been told to debate the schema and to pass over the rest without comment. But if we fail to scrutinize both documents with care, the mind of the council will have to be interpreted to the world by the specialists. God forbid that this should happen! [Then parodying a famous line from Vergil's *Aeneid*] *Timeo peritos adnexa ferentes.* I fear specialists when they are left to explain what the bishops meant. Between sessions of the Council, the Church of God has

suffered a great deal from the writings and speeches of some of
the specialists.

The Archbishop then went on to pay his respects to the specialists
(*periti*).

They are few in number, but their sound has gone forth to the
end of the earth. These few specialists care nothing for the ordinary
teaching authority of the bishops—nor, I regret to say, for that of
the pope . . . . Perhaps the commission (members) responsible for
this document had no chance of success from the outset. They were,
in fact, denied the help of experts who really knew their subjects.
. . . *It is useless to seek advice only from those who since their
youth have spent their lives in monasteries, seminaries, or universities.* [Emphasis added]. These eminent men may hardly know the
world as it really is. The world can be unpleasant and cruel. These
scholars often have a childlike trust in the opinions of men in the
world. Certainly they are simple as doves but they are not always
wise as serpents. (*Council Daybook*, Session 3, pp. 175-176).

Undoubtedly in the course of his broadside Heenan hit upon some
valid points of criticism, but all these points had already been treated
more reasonably and more helpfully in the speeches of the three previous days. One can only wonder why he let go such an ill-timed blast
in view of the fact that so many of his distinguished peers saw in the
schema reasons for praise and grounds for hope. One might opine that
the speech says more about Heenan the popular orator of Hyde Park
than it does about the schema itself.

In any event, the almost perfect answer to Heenan's attack so far
as the *periti* were concerned came from the Abbot Reetz, Superior of
the Benedictine Monastery of Beuron in Germany, without so much as
a mention of Heenan's name. The Archbishop had given his talk on
Friday, October 22. The Abbot rose to respond at the next general
meeting of the Council, Monday, October 25. He began:

It is with fear and trepidation I speak to the Fathers, because
we heard yesterday that it is useless for the Council to call upon
men from religious houses, seminaries, and universities. I, a monk
and Abbot, who hardly knows the world, am now addressing the
assembly, speaking with the simplicity of the dove rather than with
the asperity of the serpent. Perhaps the forty monks once sent

to make *angels* of the *Angles* did not know much about the world. But it was a monk who was the first Primate of England, Saint Augustine of Canterbury; and it is a monk, St. Benedict, whom the Pope will proclaim as the patron of all Europe tomorrow at Monte Cassino.

In its own kind, the exchange of the Third Period was worthy to rank with the DeSmedt attacks on the two schemas, on Revelation and on the Church, of the First Session and the Frings-Ottaviani confrontation of the Second. Far different, however, was the outcome. Even Heenan apparently was delighted that his blunderbuss had been so completely and wittily silenced by the skillfully chosen words of the trembling Abbot. In any event, the incident served to restore balance to the discussion as it continued.

On the very day of Heenan's broadside, I was called upon to deliver my previously prepared and scheduled intervention. I began by saying that, in general, I was pleased with the schema, but that in my judgment it ought to be changed in many places. I was mainly concerned about specific changes which I believed would bring about marked improvement in the revision of the text:

> In our schema, I propose that the encyclical letter of the Holy Father, *Ecclesiam Suam*, be referred to. In certain parts of our schema, the ideas are too generally and obscurely expressed, and those ideas are described by means of very lofty and pompous language. In the encyclical, however, we have a document whose suitable riches, precisely because of its depth, are still not fully valued. Since in the encyclical are found not a few sketches of the problems of our times, which are directly and deeply treated, these are most apt for the revision of the schema. Next it is necessary that the schema specifically refer to those things which were written in the encyclical and which concern the matter at hand, and especially those things which concern the origin of the Church in regard to doctrines and institutions.
>
> Indeed, the Church cannot change the deposit of Faith in which its main treasure resides, nor, at the same time, can it change its fundamental structure which was given to it by Christ the Lord. Nor are those doctrines changeable which have been defined under the influence of the Holy Spirit. Nevertheless, the Church has progressed and has to continue to progress in regard to its doctrine and its structure, so that it may respond to the prob-

lems of the world by adapting itself, especially to those problems which arise from the relationships between those things and men who are always becoming their originators.

More than one hundred years ago, John Henry Newman, who afterwards was named a cardinal of the holy Roman Church, wrote a great work, *Essay on the Development of Christian Doctrine,* in which is found the sentence, repeated in various ways: "a power of development is a proof of life." The same truth, which is of great importance for our schema, is sketched, I believe, in various places and in diverse ways, if not openly expressed, in the encyclical *Ecclesiam Suam* of Pope Paul VI— especially on page 12 of the copy of that encyclical distributed in this hall—where it states: "The Church . . . advances more and more in the awareness of its duty, of the nature of its mysteries, of its doctrines. . . ."

In my humble opinion, this sentence should be explained in detail so that it might constitute a part of the schema that we are now talking about.

The discussion of the Schema on the Church in the Modern World went on down almost to the middle of November, when finally the Bishops voted to end the discussion and accepted the schema with the many proposed amendments as the basis for a revised text. Meanwhile the debate had been interrupted here and there to discuss and vote on some of the shorter schemas in order that they might undergo the final revision. This was true of the Decrees on the Pastoral Office of Bishops, Priestly Formation (Seminaries), Ministry and Life of Priests, The Missions. During this period, two things stand out in my memory. On the day when the Schema on the Missions was scheduled to be discussed, Cardinal Agagianian, Prefect of the Congregation of Propaganda, was in the moderator's chair. Supposedly at his invitation and perhaps due to his urging, the Pope came into the Council hall in time to preside at the opening Mass and then gave a short exhortation in behalf of the schema. He indicated that the Fathers should have little difficulty in accepting and passing the document with some little revision. It was said later that Agagianian had failed, unwittingly perhaps, to advise the Pope concerning the mood of many Bishops relative to the schema. Generally, missionary Bishops were not at all pleased with its contents and form.

Fortunately, the Pope left the hall immediately after delivering his speech. Three Cardinals spoke in criticism of the schema, but it was the Carmelite missionary Bishop, Donal Lamont of Umtali in Rhodesia, who gave fullest and strongest expression to the missionary Bishops' dissatisfaction with the schema in a burst of oratory that was long remembered. He likened the bare propositions, to which the original schema had been reduced, to the bare bones scattered over the valley in the vision of Ezekiel:

> May I ask of you what the Lord asked of Ezekiel? "Son of man, can these bones live? And I answered, O Lord, thou knowest." Dry bones without flesh, without nerves—only God knows if they will ever live. With all reverence, may I say that this schema should be completely overhauled. Something better is wanted. We need something alive, something worthy of the Second Pentecost.

It was an eloquent speech and in large measure I believe it was effective. Whether the full Declaration on the Missions that was finally adopted by the Council met the expectation of Lamont and the other missionary Bishops, I cannot say, but it was a very different document from those bare bones of propositions that were first discussed.

The second incident worthy of comment was the hour or more of real drama that occurred as we drew near the end of the Third Period. Many had confidently expected that the two relatively short schemas on Religious Liberty and on the Attitude of the Church toward the Jews would be placed before the Council for a final vote. Instead of that, Cardinal Tisserant, the Dean of the Presidency, announced that many Fathers (the number 200 had been used) had expressed the desire to submit additional comments on the Declaration on Religious Liberty; therefore, it had been decided that no vote would be taken on the subject during the present period.

Widespread consternation was the immediate reaction. Cardinal Meyer hastened to Cardinal Tisserant's chair and was seen expostulating with him; he was joined by Cardinal Ritter. The word was passed around that Tisserant was adamant; the Moderators had made their decision and it would stand. Soon, some of the Fathers drew up a petition to the Holy Father asking him to reverse the Tisserant decision. Their short but urgent message read: "We ask you, Holy Father, urgently, very urgently, most urgently (*instanter! instantius! instantissime!*) to reverse this decision, lest from it the Church and the Council suffer irreparable harm." The Fathers were seen hastening from their Council seats to places where copies of the petition were to be found awaiting signatures.

Over four hundred had been collected before Cardinals Meyer, Ritter, and Léger left the Council hall for the Pope's Vatican quarters. They were immediately admitted into the presence of the Pope, who supposedly had witnessed the whole scene in St. Peter's on closed-circuit television. By the time they arrived, the Pope had consulted the Council rules and had decided that, strictly speaking, the delay on the vote decreed by the Moderators fell within their right. He therefore felt that he should not reverse the decision. He promised, however, that the vote on Religious Liberty would be the first item on the agenda in 1965. Under the circumstances, this was gratifying, for without such assurance we would have been left wondering whether the shrewd and seemingly determined opposing group would devise ways of preventing the vote from ever being taken.

We were now at the end of the Third Period. A good deal had been accomplished. The all-important Dogmatic Constitution on the Church had been signed and promulgated. The revised Schema on Revelation had been discussed, received further amendments and had been accepted; it certainly would be promulgated during the next period. The Pastoral Constitution on the Church in the Modern World was at a point where there was no turning back. The Constitution on the Liturgy, as we have seen, had been promulgated in the Second Period. These four greatest of the Council Documents were in themselves assurance of the Council's overall success. The Decree on Ecumenism, so important to the ecumenical purpose of the Council, had also been signed and promulgated. All the shorter decrees had been discussed and made ready for final revision.

The Secretariat on Christian Unity had been disappointed that the Declaration on the Jews would not achieve the status of an independent document. The joint commission to which it had been referred had joined it to a statement on the Church's relation to the Muslims, the Hindus, and the Buddhists, under the title: Declaration on the Relationship of the Church to Non-Catholic Peoples. The Secretariat would have preferred that it form the fourth chapter of the Decree on Ecumenism or that it stand as a separate statement, even if another statement would need to be made on the Church's relationship to other non-Christian religions. Given the ancestral relationship of the Church to the Jews and St. Paul's statement concerning the Jews in Romans 9:1-32, the members of the Secretariat felt that a separate document devoted solely to the Jews would have been appropriate.

Although there seemed to be ample reason now confidently to expect a fitting conclusion to the Council, still the success of the determined minority in blocking immediate action on the Declaration on Religious Liberty left a certain sense of apprehension in the minds of many Council Fathers.

With the end of the Third Period, Father Laubacher made ready to return to his post at the seminary in Menlo Park, while Porter and I prepared to depart for Bombay.

The Thirty-Eighth International Eucharistic Congress opened in Bombay, India, November 28, 1964. Monsignor Porter White and I took the plane from Rome on Wednesday, November 25, and arrived in Bombay in the forenoon of the following day. There we found ourselves assigned to very pleasant quarters in the Taj Mahal Hotel, within a short walking distance to the Oval Meridian, the Cooperage Football Grounds (sites of events of the Congress), the Holy Name Cathedral, and the headquarters of the Congress.

The Oval, center of the Congress, is a large downtown park about two-fifths of a mile long and one-fifth of a mile wide, with its two ends rounded. At the center of the Oval was constructed a very large three-tiered platform, which held the altar, twenty-five feet square. Here, in a low tabernacle, the Eucharist would be reserved throughout the Congress. A striking feature of the altar were two wooden flares, each rising about thirty feet, with the inner edges slanted so as to meet and slightly overlap above the tabernacle. From their meeting point was suspended a large wooden crucifix. The whole structure, with the exception of the natural wood crucifix, was painted a gleaming white. A broad, gently rising stairway, carpeted in red, ascended to the front of the altar. The two flares, seeming to symbolize shafts of light, gave a pleasing oriental aspect. All the main Eucharistic ceremonies of the Congress were to take place here. The altar with its two nearby platforms, one for the choir, the other for prelates and distinguished guests, divided the oval into two equal parts, each of which provided seating space for 40,000, and standing room for another 40,000, or a total congregation of 160,000. The whole arrangement indicated the immense amount of planning and work on the part of Cardinal Gracias, Archbishop of Bombay, together with his clergy and laity, with the cooperation of their Hindu fellow citizens.

The solemn opening ceremony on Saturday afternoon began with the enthronement of the Papal Legate, Cardinal Agagianian, who was to preside over the Congress, pending the arrival of Pope Paul VI. Cardinal Gracias delivered his discourse of welcome; then came speeches from the Vice-president of India and the Governor of the state of Maharashtra, of which Bombay is the capital and largest city. To these speeches of welcome, the Legate made a very fitting response. The eloquent Archbishop (soon to be named Cardinal) Heenan of Westminister delivered the main address on the theme of the Congress, "The Eucharist and the New Man." The program ended with Solemn Benediction of the Blessed Sacrament celebrated by the Most Reverend J. Attipetty, Archbishop of Verapoly, India.

The most important Eucharistic Liturgy of the Congress, the *Statio Orbis* (Station of the World) took place the following day, again at five o'clock in the afternoon. This Liturgy, common to all such Eucharistic Congresses, is so named because all the dioceses of the world are invited to join in a like Liturgy to honor the Holy Eucharist and to pray for the peace of the world. Cardinal Agagianian celebrated Mass in the Oval and gave the homily. The Oval was now crowded to capacity. There is no need here to describe the Liturgy itself except to comment on the dignity, the precision, and the solemnity with which it was carried out, the excellence with which the music of the Mass was chanted and the incidental motets were sung by the great choir. What merits special notice, however, was the great reverence manifested by the huge congregation made up of Hindus as well as Christians—and it was the same at all the great Liturgies.

After the celebration of the *Statio Orbis*, the high-light of the week proved to be the arrival of the Pope by plane on Wednesday afternoon. I joined the other members of the committee in the trip to the airport to meet His Holiness' plane. As we neared our destination, it was surprising to see the number of native Indians who were making their way on foot to the same place, and still more surprising to find the great crowd of spectators already waiting at the airport. When the Pope's plane arrived and the Pope himself appeared, a great roar of welcome rose from the crowd. He was indeed a striking and friendly figure, clothed in his white robes and skullcap, his long red cape draped from his shoulders and his arms extended in an all-embracing gesture. After a brief pause, he descended the steps followed by Cardinal Gracias. The road back to Bombay was thronged with people so that progress had to be very slow. It was estimated that more than a million people turned out to glimpse the Pope, to shout their greeting, and to receive his blessing. It was to be that way wherever he appeared during his entire stay.

The chief Eucharistic Liturgy celebrated by Pope Paul was that of late Thursday afternoon at which four native sons of India, recently chosen to become Bishops, were ordained by him to the episcopate. The crowd that attended the Pope's Solemn Liturgy of Consecration was even greater than that of the previous Sunday. Many failed to find accommodation within the Oval and had to stand in the path that surrounded the park and even the property beyond, from which there was an unobstructed view of the altar and the entire ceremony. Again, there was always and everywhere that same manifestation of reverence.

The activities of these days may be said to have been pervaded by the Pope's presence. The last Eucharistic Liturgy he attended and over which he presided was the Syro-Malenkan Rite Mass and the blessing of the sick on Friday evening. The Pope gave his own general blessing of the sick and then joined the Cardinals and Bishops in ministering to them individually. Late that evening he departed for Rome.

One of the effects of the Pope's departure, however, was that during the last two days of the Congress there seemed to be a general letdown from the enthusiasm that thus far had marked the events. This was particularly noticeable at the solemn Mass of closing: the procession of the Blessed Sacrament from the Oval to the Gateway to India, and the Solemn Benediction there, with which the Congress came to an end. All this, evidently planned to be one of the great events of the Congress seemed a sort of anticlimax. Much the same thing happened, as I recall it, at the Eucharistic Congress in Bogota, Columbia, four years later. This may very well have been the reason that Paul VI decided not to go to the Congress in Melbourne in 1973 and to Philadelphia in 1976.

On the way home, Porter White and I decided to stop briefly at New Delhi. The brevity of our visit permitted us only to glimpse the gleaming newness and seeming luxury of the new Delhi in contrast to the intense and extensive poverty that surrounds so many relics of past architectural beauty and splendor of the old city. While in Delhi, we seized the opportunity to join a party of travelers in a one-day automobile trip to Agra to see the Taj Mahal, that uniquely beautiful monument, and then to Jodh-Puhr to visit the fifteenth-century architectural monuments. The following day we set off on our almost unbroken journey by air to Beirut, to Rome, to Paris, to New York—half-way around the world in so few hours. We were already well into the month of December when Porter White and I arrived back in Baltimore.

On my return from Bombay after the three-month absence, I found conditions much as I had expected. Bishop Murphy had conducted the affairs of the archdiocese with his usual dispatch and much to the satisfaction of both priests and people; no unusual problems awaited me. Both Porter White and I slipped easily back into the routine of our daily duties. I celebrated the Christmas Midnight Mass at the new Cathedral. The new year dawned without hint that any significant change awaited either me or the archdiocese.

Then, on the morning of Friday, January 15, I received a telephone call from Archbishop Vagnozzi, the Apostolic Delegate, asking if it would be possible for me to receive him if he were to drive over to Baltimore in the afternoon. I replied that I would be very happy to receive him. But could I not go over to Washington to save him the time and trouble of the trip to Baltimore? No, he had a duty to perform for the Holy Father which required him to call on me personally.

When he arrived that afternoon I brought him to my study. Before we were seated, he handed me a sealed envelope addressed to me. He said that he had been instructed by the Holy Father to deliver this letter in person. On opening the envelope, I saw that the letter it contained was a short one, written in Latin and bearing the Pope's own signature. After the customary greeting, it read:

Dearly Beloved Son:

Through this letter I notify you that in the next Consistory we shall elect you to [or enroll you in: *esse te cooptaturos*] the Sacred College of the Cardinals of the Holy Roman Church in order that we may be able to repay your goodness to the Church by the reward of the insignia of this high dignity.

Meanwhile, you must know that the contents of this letter must be held in strict secrecy until they have been made public. From our heart we impart to you our Apostolic Blessing.

From the Vatican Palace the 10th day of January, the second year of our pontificate.

Paul VI

My immediate reaction was stunned silence and utter amazement. I could not understand why this honor was being bestowed upon me. Here I was, already sixty-seven years old. It is true I was not conscious of any diminution of such powers as had been given me; but I had, in the judgment of men generally, passed the prime of my life. I could only be filled with wonder at what was happening to me. At the same time I felt a deep emotion of gratitude—gratitude to the Pope for his goodness and kindness in conferring on me this sign of his favor; gratitude, above all, to God. All during the course of my life I had occasion to thank God for His protection and guidance, for having safeguarded me from many pitfalls into which I could have stumbled so easily, and for having opened the way, as it were, before me. This latest happening seemed a culmination of His special goodness to me. I must add that, mingled with my other emotions, was a certain sense of fear that I should not prove able to live up to what would be expected of me.

Ten days after the Delegate's visit, the Vatican released the news of the forthcoming consistory, to take place February 22. Twenty-three were to receive the title of Cardinal. Among them were a number who had become known to me in the Council: Heenan of Westminster; Conway of Armagh, Martin of Rouen, Roy of Quebec, Colombo of Milan, Zoungrana of Africa, Cooray of India, McCann of South Africa, Rossi of Brazil, Duval of Algeria, etc. I was the only American in the number; my sense of wonder and awe was deepened.

Immediately, messages of congratulation began to pour in from all sides—from the four already existing American Cardinals (Spellman, Cushing, McIntyre, and Ritter); from Bishops throughout the country, the President of the United States, the Governor of Maryland, the Mayor of Baltimore, the President of the City Council, and countless friends and well-wishers. That day the General Assembly in Annapolis passed a special resolution in commemoration of the event and of congratulations to me. Last but not least, the congratulations of my sister and my two surviving brothers and their families.

From such exaltation of spirit as I experienced by reason of the honor itself and the abundance of congratulations, I was soon brought down to earth by the many practical details that demanded immediate attention.

Late that morning, I received an urgent call from William McCarthy of the McCarthy brothers of New York, managers of the Catholic Travel League, known to us from the fact that their organization had been used by Archbishop Keough to plan all his trips to Europe. Bill McCarthy assured me that his firm had planned the trip of Cardinal

Spellman and later that of Cardinal Cushing when each of them received the Red Hat. Members of his firm were therefore familiar with all the requirements of such an event. He and his brother were convinced from previous experience that two planes would be needed to take those from Baltimore and Bridgeport who would wish to go to Rome for the occasion. They were in a position to guarantee two Alitalia airliners from Baltimore to Rome and back on the proper dates as well as hotel reservations for the group for the entire period of two weeks. One flight would leave Baltimore in the morning, one in the evening. The cost per person seemed reasonable. The guarantees for the reservations both of planes and hotel could not be extended beyond forty-eight hours. In arranging Archbishop Keough's trips, they had dealt with either Monsignor White or Monsignor Hopkins. These two could relieve me of all details.

I consulted Porter and George without delay, and they were convinced of the advantage of the McCarthy offer and were willing to take on responsibility for the entire detailed plans. We decided to give no final word until the following day. However, since no Baltimore agency made an inquiry or suggestion about our plans, and since the time before departure would be so short, the following day we decided to accept the McCarthy offer. Later I came to regret that we did not delay our decision longer, particularly since one of the local agents made some troublesome complaints. Under the circumstances, however, I believe we were completely justified in making our decision when we did. In any event, from that point on, I was happily freed from the worry of the details of the proposed trip.

McCarthy himself made contacts with the Diocese of Bridgeport and proved correct in his assumption that from the two dioceses more than enough people would be interested in making the journey to justify chartering two planes. Besides Bishop Murphy and five other Bishops who joined our party, there were thirty-five priests of the Baltimore Archdiocese, nineteen of Bridgeport, two from Washington, D.C. The two hundred twenty-three people from Baltimore and Bridgeport were in the same proportion, two-thirds to one-third—all of them truly representative of the two dioceses.

Shortly after the public announcement by the Vatican, Bishop Reh, rector of the North American College, called to invite me to stay with their community during the period I would remain in Rome. I was happy to accept his invitation, for the college seemed an appropriate environment to prepare for the coming events. Porter White and George Hopkins both decided to stay at the Grand, where they could be helpful to the travelers as occasions should arise. Father P. Francis Murphy, a Baltimore priest who was an assistant rector of the college, would undertake to serve as my secretary during the period.

On Monday, February 22, the ancient rite of the secret consistory was held. All the Cardinals who were present in Rome met with the Pope. The rite is a simple one: the Pope presents to the Cardinals the names of those whom he, after careful thought, has considered worthy to be raised to the rank of Cardinal. Although each Cardinal is called upon individually to cast his vote, it would seem almost a matter of form, since a very thorough investigation must have been made before the public announcement; yet, it most certainly would not have been mere routine during certain medieval or renaissance periods, and I suppose need not be so even today. While the consistory was in session, seven of us waited at the North American College: Cardinal Conway, Heenan, McCann, Rossi, Duval, and Zoungrana. Immediately after the consistory, a Vatican messenger came bringing to each his *biglietto,* the document announcing the fact that his nomination and election had formally taken place. Not long thereafter, individual Cardinals, members of the Vatican diplomatic corps, heads of colleges, members of our Baltimore and Bridgeport groups, and others began to make formal calls of greetings and congratulations.

The public ceremony took place with the concelebration of Mass by Pope Paul VI on Friday forenoon, during which the red biretta was conferred and the Red Hat, the large round *galero,* was presented. This last has become simply symbolical in modern times and is supposed to be placed before the catafalque of the recipient at his funeral and thereafter hung in the church over which he had presided. The remains of Cardinal Gibbons' *galero* still hang in the Basilica, the old Cathedral of Baltimore. Ours was the last group of Cardinals to receive the *galero.* It now seems to have been abandoned completely.

One part of the ceremony which has left a special imprint on my mind was that in which the Pope presented each of the Cardinals with a ring commemorative of the occasion. Mine, in my judgment and in that of the many people who have commented on its appearance, is a rather plain but very handsome ring. Its main feature is a dull dark green chrysolite oval stone, a little less than an inch in length. Surmounting the curved surface is a slender plain gold cross delicately attached to the setting. In a small depressed circle in the metal back of the stone is the coat of arms of Paul VI in red enamel and gold. A crown of thorns is embossed on the gold band. The plain cross and the crown of thorns are, of course, meant to remind one of the sufferings and death of Christ, and are reminiscent of the words the Pope repeats to each Cardinal indicating that he must be ready to suffer for Christ and His Church—even martyrdom, should that be called for. During the more than seventeen years I have constantly worn the ring, it has been the most precious of the things I own. Its chief value consists in the fact that it is a personal gift of Pope Paul VI, to whom I owe so much. Its special added value comes from the fact that it symbolizes for me the trials and disappointments of these years, but also the faith and the hope that have sustained me during this time.

One of the most cherished memories of that week was my installation in my titular church of San Clemente by Cardinal Cicognani. It had been his titular church before it became mine. He had relinquished it when, becoming Cardinal Secretary of State, he had been given the rank of Cardinal Bishop of Frascati. He, I felt confident, had suggested that it be conferred upon me. Since his arrival in Washington as Apostolic Delegate in 1933, he had taken an interest in me and my work as Director of Catholic Charities of Washington, as pastor of St. Patrick's, as Auxiliary Bishop of Baltimore, and Ordinary of the Diocese of Bridgeport. He could have given me no more treasured sign of the bond between us than the inheritance of this, his titular church.

San Clemente is probably the most interesting of such churches in Rome. The ruins of the Temple of Mithras, and of the supposed ancient palazzo of St. Clement form its lowest level. At the second level is the fifth-century church with its memory of Cyril and Methodius, missionary apostles to the Slavic people, and its tomb of St. Methodius. The present church, dating from the middle ages and containing one of Rome's most handsome medieval mosaics, forms the highest level. The year following my installation, the old sacristy caved in, becoming unusable, as was evident at the time of my next visit. Following the good example of my predecessor, who had from time to time made generous benefactions to the ancient church while he was its titular head, I undertook to restore it as a mark of respect to him and of gratitude to the Irish Dominican monks who for the past three centuries had cared for it with such reverence and zeal. They, in turn, had an impressive stone plaque placed upon its wall as a sort of permanent memorial of the past seventeen years of my incumbency—to the special interest of many Baltimore visitors to Rome who have found their way to the ancient church.

During our stay in Rome, Count Thomas Pangborn gave a dinner in my honor for the Baltimore group at the Grand Hotel, where a profusion of beautiful red roses lined the tables. Not to be outdone, the Bridgeport group held a dinner in my honor at the Excelsior that was equally memorable. I had enjoyed a very pleasant evening reviving happy memories with close friends of my Bridgeport days. After the last course had been served, Jim O'Connell, who had served as attorney for the diocese and was still fulfilling that position under Bishop Curtis, arose to act as toastmaster. There were to be only two speeches: that of Bishop Curtis and my own response.

After a proper introduction, Bishop Curtis made a short and gracious speech. Then Jim rose to introduce me. It was the time when the Otto Preminger film *The Cardinal*, based on the Henry Morton Robinson novel of the same title, was at the height of its popularity. The career of the hero was said to have been suggested by the life of Cardinal Spellman, with elements of pure fiction added to give spice and pathos—e.g., a romantic episode for the hero and the waywardness of a younger sister, both of which, it was rumored, had infuriated Spellman, but left him nothing to do but to be silent. The general theme of both book and picture, insofar as they can be said to have had one, was the steady rise of the clerical hero from obscurity to cardinalatial heights. This theme was symbolized in the picture through the device of a series of flashbacks, showing the cleric climbing! climbing! climbing!—climbing until he had reached the summit symbolized by the title.

In his introduction of me, which proved to be the longest speech of the evening, Jim chose to compare my career to the career of the picture's hero—my rise from the very humble circumstances of my beginnings until I had achieved the present exalted moment. The thing I remember best about the speech was the way I winced as I was pictured rising! rising! rising!—or was it, as the film portrayed, climbing! climbing! climbing? When, at last, Jim turned to me to speak, I remember that my first words were: "Jim, you are a wonderful lawyer as both Bishop Curtis and I can testify, but you are a terrible toastmaster thus to introduce me as a clerical climber!" There was a burst of laughter, showing that there was no need to elaborate. Later I can remember saying to myself: never act as if you are at the top; there will not be lacking those who will say that you climbed there.

The following Monday both parties departed for home, leaving Porter and myself to stay for the plenary session of the Sacred Consistorial Congregation to which I had been appointed after receiving the Red Hat.

After returning from Rome, I found myself faced with a number of receptions which I suppose are almost inevitable under such circumstances. The people of Baltimore—Catholic, Protestant, and Jew—seemed particularly impressed by the fact that I was the only American named Cardinal in the recent consistory and were anxious to show their appreciation of the honor that had come to their city. The chief occasion was the Mass held in the great auditorium of the Fifth Regiment Armory on Laetare Sunday afternoon. Also the Association of Commerce, to which all the leading businessmen of the community seemed to belong, held a large dinner in my honor at one of the leading hotels. The Churchmen's Club of the Episcopal Diocese of Maryland gave another dinner at the Belvedere at which they asked me to be the guest of honor. Nor were my Jewish friends to be outdone. I must say I never felt completely comfortable amid this sort of celebration. I trust, however, that I accepted it with good grace—at least I saw no reason to suspect that I was failing to do so.

Of all the celebrations, however, the one I remember best was that at St. Mary's Seminary in Roland Park. I had felt extremely close to the seminary in my student days and during the period when I was Auxiliary Bishop of Baltimore and Father Laubacher was the rector. Now Father John Sullivan, S.S., was rector. I had complete confidence in him, as I have today, and felt very close to him. The celebration he had arranged was a very simple one—hardly more than a regular evening meal, save that there was enough of the special to show that it was a celebration. The whole faculty was there, as well as the entire student body. It was a good meal, prepared by the Sisters, and it was well served. There were no set speeches. Father Sullivan's words of introduction were informal and came from the heart. My response was equally informal and came also from my heart. After dinner I mingled with friendly students for a short time, and then retired to the Faculty Common Room where I spent a very pleasant evening. I suppose that simple celebration stays so clearly in my mind because it was one of the last of my completely happy memories of the seminary for what seemed a long time. But of this I shall treat later when I speak of the problems of the post-conciliar years.

These celebrations actually occupied but little of my time. Meanwhile, I had become immediately engrossed in my regular duties, the administration of the archdiocese, in which I was greatly helped by those who surrounded me: Bishop Murphy, Monsignor Thomas Mardaga, who then had residence at the Basilica rectory and was in charge of the annual Charity Campaign, Porter White, and Joseph Gossman.

Besides these duties, there was my sacramental ministry of Sunday Mass with homily and weekday morning Mass at the Basilica, Confirmations, and Ordinations. My calendar for 1965 shows that considerable time was being devoted to the special appeal that would enable me to help provide for the badly needed new home for the Little Sisters of the Poor, the House of the Good Shepherd, the St. Elizabeth School of Special Education (for subnormal and retarded youth), and for completion of the Catholic high school building program.

During the summer months I had several visits from Mr. Jacob Blaustein, of the Jewish community, one visit from Dr. Jacob Lichten of the national office of B'nai B'rith, and another from Rabbi Marc Tannenbaum, prominent national Jewish leader. These visits indicated the concern of the local Jewish community and the national Jewish organizations over the delay in the publication of the Declaration on the Jews and the reports that, in the revised schema, the original strong statement had been considerably watered down by eliminating specific condemnation of the hated term "deicide," and at the reported joining of the declaration with a statement on the Muslims, Hindus, and Buddhists. These visits gave me an opportunity first to call the attention of these leaders to what the Secretariat on Christian Unity had done and was still endeavoring to do, but also to the problems the Council faced, since many of our Eastern rite churches existed in Arab lands. I am afraid that Mr. Blaustein, Dr. Lichten, and Rabbi Tannenbaum overestimated the strength of my influence now that I was both a Cardinal and a member of the secretariat. Still, basically I had only one vote in the more than two thousand ballots cast, and when the count was made the vote of a Cardinal was worth no more than that of the latest ordained Bishop.

With my time occupied by many concerns, the summer months of 1965 seemed to roll up rapidly. Before its end, both Porter and I had departed for Rome for the opening of the fourth and last period of the Council on September 14.

In his discourse which followed the Mass opening the Fourth Period, Pope Paul VI announced his intention of establishing the Synod of Bishops, which had been provided for in each version of the Schema on the Pastoral Office of Bishops. The Synod was actually called into being by the *motu proprio* which the Pope signed and promulgated the following day. The wording of this document is very clear and specific: "On our initiative and by our own authority, we erect and constitute in this city of Rome a body for the Universal Church, directly and immediately subject to our authority, to which we give the special name of Synod of Bishops." It would be formed, for the most part, of Bishops elected by the national or regional conferences of Bishops throughout the world; some (not more than 15 percent) the Pope himself would name. It would meet at the Pope's call as he judged the need of the advice and help it could give him. Here I may note that the first Synod was to meet September 29, 1967. Archbishop (now Cardinal) John Dearden and I were elected by the National Conference of Catholic Bishops (then still called the National Catholic Welfare Conference) to serve as members of that Synod. Since then, there has been created a General Secretariat of the Synod of Bishops with a permanent General Secretary; the Synod now meets every third year. Thus, at the beginning of the Fourth Period, we saw the birth of what seems to be a genuine development in the permanent structure of the Church.

In conformity with the promise the Pope had given, the first item of business of the Fourth Period was the Declaration on Religious Liberty. Once again, Bishop DeSmedt, in behalf of the Secretariat for Christian Unity, was called upon to present a detailed introduction to this latest amended version of the declaration. As was to be expected, the document received strong support from Cardinal Lienart of Lille; the American Cardinals Spellman, Cushing, and Ritter; Frings of Munich, and Alfrink of Utrecht. Of special interest was the support of Cardinal Urbani of Venice, who spoke in the name of thirty-two Italian Bishops. Once again, however, the document met with strong criticism and even opposition: Cardinals Ruffini, Siri, but especially deArriba of Tarragona, Spain, who asked that the document be rejected and the whole subject be left to the national conferences of Bishops.

While it is not likely that the Declaration on Religious Liberty will ever be rated in the same class with the Dogmatic Constitution on the Church or the Pastoral Constitution of the Church in the Modern World, yet it is, in the words of Pope Paul VI, "one of the major texts of the Council." From the point of view of ecumenism and the relation of the Church to the whole modern world, it would be difficult to exaggerate its importance. The press of Europe and of North and South America followed the fortunes of this document with an intense interest and close scrutiny accorded to no other. Cardinal Meyer, in an intervention presented during the Third Period, made the startling statement that unless the Council enacted this or a similar declaration, nothing else it did would make much difference. Those well acquainted with Meyer's retiring disposition and his distaste for mere rhetoric realized that he would have been the last person in the world to have used such words except as a result of long reflection and deep conviction of its great importance in the world today.

Looking back from the present with the knowledge of the overwhelming support it ultimately received in the Council and its universal acceptance by the Church as a whole, it is difficult for one to realize how many serious obstacles the declaration had to overcome in its course through three sessions of the Council. Father John Courtney Murray, the American Jesuit scholar, has received well-deserved acclaim for his work in the formation of the document. Antecedent in time, and probably equally valuable in effect, was the work of Bishop Emile DeSmedt of Bruges, one of the original members of the secretariat, whose voice was the great advocate of the Doctrine of Religious Liberty in the Council; and constant was the strong support of Cardinal Bea. Invaluable also was the work of a number of expert consultors, like Monsignor Pietro Pavan, Father Barnabas Ahern, C.P., and my own secretary Monsignor Porter J. White. Revisions had gone through five separate printings; more than two thousand *modi* (suggestions for amendment) had been received; some of these were, of course, almost identical, but each had to be examined, and suggestions of value had to be noted and considered. Now, during the Fourth Period, the subject of the declaration was being publicly debated in the Council for the third time. From the beginning, as a member of the secretariat, I had been deeply interested in the declaration. My opportunity to speak on the subject came September 20.

One of the main arguments used by the opponents of the proposed declaration was that the doctrine of religious freedom was nowhere found in the traditional doctrine of the Church. Religious toleration, not religious freedom, they claimed, was the doctrine found in the writings of Pope Leo XIII, and in this he was followed by both Pius XI and Pius XII. In answer to this argument, I began by stating that the right to religious freedom was based solidly on the dignity of the human persons, and it was a dictate of human reason; it was confirmed, moreover, by Scripture, from the way God dealt with man and from the work and action of Christ and His Apostles. I intended to show that the doctrine found in our schema is a development of the doctrine as found in the writings of the modern Popes.

The first stages of this development, I pointed out, are found in many of the writings of Pope Leo XIII. No one holds that this doctrine is explicitly stated in his writings, but the teachings of Leo are already a development over the doctrine commonly held in the Middle Ages and in the Post-Reformation period. Leo XIII took the first steps along that path of development followed by subsequent Popes, particularly Pius XI, Pius XII, John XXIII, and finally Paul VI.

Contrary to what the declaration's opponents maintained, I said it would be a mistake to see Leo XIII's doctrine on toleration as the central point of his teaching, or as the final and unchangeable teaching of the Church on religious liberty. His doctrine in no way prevents us from going on, in the light of experience and the deeper understanding of the dignity of the human person, to find religious liberty properly understood as a universal human right. It would be a mistake to say that Leo's master idea was the exclusive right of truth and the denial of all right to error. He insists that truth and error, right and wrong, do not enter the juridical order on an equal title—contrary to the sophism of the rationalists. What is true and good may receive positive juridical authorization; what is false or evil may receive, for grave and sufficient reasons, only juridical toleration. This is the only concrete juridical sense that can attach to the otherwise unhelpful abstraction that error has no rights; and no sensible person would quarrel with this concrete sense. Strictly speaking, rights inhere in persons; they cannot inhere in abstractions.

There are, I noted, two central ideas in the writings of Leo: (1) the clear distinction between the authority of the Church and the authority of the State; and (2) the freedom of the Church. I then went on to develop further Leo's teaching on the freedom of the Church and, by implication, the religious freedom of the individual as a juridical institution correlative with constitutional government.

Thus Leo opened the way to the teaching of Pope Pius XI in his famous letter of 1932 against Italian fascism and his two equally famous letters against German national socialism (the Nazis) in March 1937 and against atheistic communism in December 1937. Pope Pius XII, in his radio message of 1942, brought this development a step further, as did Pope John XXIII in his encyclical *Pacem in Terris*. To bring the teaching of modern Popes to a climax, I quoted the words of Pope Paul VI in an address to the United Nations the previous year:

The Church also is busy with a problem that is not without affinity with the present object of your research. It is the problem of religious freedom. The importance and the amplitude of the question are so great that it has claimed the attention of the

Ecumenical Council. It is legitimate to expect the promulgation of a text on this subject that will be of great import not only for the Church, but also for all those—countless in number—who feel that an authoritative declaration on the subject is a matter of concern to them.

I concluded my intervention:

It is obvious that the whole world expects of this Council a declaration on religious liberty. The world needs such a declaration, for without the recognition of the right to religious liberty there can be no true and lasting peace among men. The Church, too, needs such a declaration, for only through the recognition of religious liberty can the Church be revived in those countries where her life has been virtually stamped out; only through the recognition of religious liberty can the Church be free in those countries where she is in shackles; only in an atmosphere of religious freedom can the Church flourish in those new and developing nations which hold out so much promise for the future. The doctrine of religious freedom in our schema is a sound doctrine, in full harmony with the body of the Church's traditional teaching. It is to be hoped therefore, that this schema will receive overwhelming approval from the Fathers.

In his book *American Participation in the Second Vatican Council*, Vincent Yzermans comments that these concluding words "summarized the whole body of arguments that the Americans—and the Unity Secretariat itself—had proposed throughout the two past years." (p. 634).

My intervention took place on the final day of the discussion. The following morning the General Secretary put before the Fathers the question whether or not they were pleased to accept the amended schema that had just been discussed as the basis of the definitive text of the Council's Declaration on Religious Liberty. The vote was: yes, 1,997; no, 224. Thereupon the Secretariat for Christian Unity took the text once more, together with the additional proposed amendments, to prepare the final version.

The Council then began its final debate on the schema, The Church in the Modern World. This document had been discussed at some length in the Third Period and on October 22, 1964, I had noted in particular the relevance of Newman's concept of the development of Christian doctrine to the document and had recommended that specific reference be made to Pope Paul VI's encyclical *Ecclesiam Suam*. Now again on September 24 of the Fourth Period I spoke of the revised version and noted that I considered an unduly wide separation appearing between the two orders: the material and natural on the one hand, and the spiritual and supernatural on the other. I noted three passages in particular where this widespread division appeared: where the document spoke of the influence of Satan in the world, where it spoke of man's knowledge of God on the one hand and the problem of atheism on the other, where it dealt with conjugal love and its relation to the institution of matrimony. What was needed, it seemed to me, was a kind of synthesis—a synthesis not in the sense of a compromise; the two orders are indeed distinct and must remain so, yet they are not opposed; rather, they are complementary. The three passages should be perfected in this respect.

While we were still discussing the document on the Church in the Modern World, the Pope left to address the United Nations on October 4. In his discourse he not only endorsed the concept of the U.N., but also praised the organization and spoke of its work in behalf of universal peace. The following day he returned to Rome and entered the main door, walking the length of the church amid the enthusiastic and continued applause of the entire assembly of Bishops. Previous to his arrival, we had been discussing the final chapter, "Lasting Peace and the Establishment of a Community of Nations." It was almost as if we were reaping the first fruits of the text which we had just been discussing.

Two days after the Pope's return, the Council concluded its discussion of the schema. One of the final discourses was a rather brief one delivered by Cardinal Ottaviani. In it he first outlined what he considered the necessary steps to be taken for the avoidance of war and then went on to appeal to the Council and the Church to lead the way in the search for universal peace. He ended with these words: "The Council should therefore give its all to the creation of one world republic composed of all the nations of the world in which no longer would there be strife among various nations, but an entire world living in peace: the peace of Christ in the reign of Christ." The long and vigorous applause which was accorded him on that occasion must have done much to wipe out the painful memories that he had of the rejection of the two documents he had championed in the First Period, and his own ill-timed and ill-judged attack on Cardinal Frings and his defense of the Holy Office in the Second Period. Since that time, many of the Council Fathers had regarded him as opposed to the development and progress for which the Council had stood. Now this was largely offset by the events of the Fourth Period.

After concluding the debate on the Church in the Modern World the Council, in its last public debate on the documents, turned to the schema on the Decree on the Ministry and Life of the Priest. It was on this subject that I delivered my last speech in the Council on October 16, 1965. In it I said:

(1) Although the pastoral orientation of the schema is very laudable and emphasis is placed on the priest's ministry to the people of God and all men, there is a lack of balance in the schema's treatment of the full ministry of the priest, who after the image of the One Mediator, is a mediator between God and men. This mediation has a twofold direction: toward God and toward men. In my opinion the Godward movement is too sparsely treated in the schema, which results in it being excessively anthropocentric. . . .
(2) In my opinion the revised text, in its general tone and in some particular numbers, labors under a certain impression regarding the fundamental basis of the relationship between bishops and priests. As a result the schema may defeat its very purpose of putting an end to the unfortunate separation of priests from their bishops and of fostering a true union between them. This lack of clarity should be remedied for two reasons: (1) The same theology of the priesthood which is so beautifully taught in *Lumen Gentium* should be faithfully adhered to in the schema; (2) For the sake of a renewal of the union in this mission, work and life of bishops and priests, anything smacking of episcopalism should be avoided so that priests do not look upon bishops as authoritarian employers rather than fellow priests. . . . (For the full text see Yzermans, *American Participation in the Second Vatican Council*, pp. 493-495.)

A careful reading of the Decree on Priestly Life and Ministry of Vatican II will, I believe, show that both of these defects have been remedied.

The actual value of my interventions will have to be judged by others. I do not present them as great contributions to the Second Vatican Council but rather as some concrete examples of my active participation in the Council. Nor do I present them as my personal contributions. They were actually the joint product of three of us: Father James Laubacher, S.S., Monsignor Porter White, and myself. Their main value, I would not hesitate to say, derives from Father Laubacher. After he had arrived at the beginning of the Second Period, the Bishops of our Province began to have regular conferences with him, when we would discuss significant conciliar activities of the preceding week as well as the documents that would be considered during the following week. Practically every evening, he joined us at a social gathering and was with us at dinner.

Not infrequently, other Bishops and priests joined us. Among those I recall were Bishop (later Archbishop) Hallinan, an important and influential member of the Commission on the Sacred Liturgy; Bishop DeSmedt, one of the most active and important members of the Secretariat for Christian Unity; Father Gustave Weigel, S.J., one of the earliest American priests to promote the ecumenical movement and also a member of the Secretariat for Christian Unity; Father John Courtney Murray, S.J., who, with Bishop DeSmedt, must be regarded as an architect of the Declaration on Religious Liberty; Father Barnabas Ahern, C.P., a *peritus* of the Commission on Christian Doctrine and advisor to many American Bishops. Living in the charged atmosphere of the Council and its stirring events, these meetings greatly enhanced my participation in the Council.

But, I repeat it was to Father Laubacher and Porter White that I owe most of the value of my own interventions. Generally when we had decided on the subject of an intervention it was Father Laubacher who hammered out the English text—that would fit within the ten minutes allowed for each intervention—and it was Porter White who put it into acceptable Latin.

Formal debate in the Council hall ended October 16, the day I made my last intervention. From that point on most of the time was given to the finishing of the yet-unfinished Council documents. Five of these were submitted to the Council's final vote October 28, when they were approved, signed, and promulgated: Decree on the Pastoral Office of Bishops, Decree on the Renewal of Religious Life, Decree on the Formation of Priests (Seminaries), Declaration on Christian Education, Declaration on the Relation of the Church to Non-Christian Religions. This still left six to be completed and to receive final action; among these the most important were the Dogmatic Constitution on

Divine Revelation, the Pastoral Constitution on the Church in the Modern World, and the Declaration on Religious Liberty. The Constitution on Divine Revelation was to receive final vote in the next public session, set for November 18; the Pastoral Constitution on the Church in the Modern World and the Declaration on Religious Freedom were to receive their final action only at the last session, December 7, the day before the Council's solemn closing.

As we drew close to the ending of the Council, it became known that the Pope, with the help of the Secretariat for Christian Unity, was planning two ecumenical services of great significance: a prayer service in which members of the Council and Protestant and Greek Orthodox observers would participate and over which the Pope would preside, and later two simultaneous liturgies, over one of which the Pope would preside in Rome, while the Patriarch would preside over the other in Constantinople (Istanbul). The first service took place Saturday, December 4, in the Basilica of St. Paul, where Pope John XXIII had first announced his intention of holding the Second Vatican Council. It took the form of the Liturgy of the Word; prayers, psalms, and Scriptural readings in English by Dr. Robert C. Outh, the American Protestant Observer; in Greek, by a Greek Orthodox Priest-Observer; and in French by a French Catholic priest. The Pope gave a moving speech appropriate to such an occasion. The service ended with the singing of the hymn, "Now Thank We All Our God," composed by a Lutheran of the seventeenth century.

Some days before the interdenominational service in St. Paul's, Bishop Willebrands inquired whether I would be willing to serve as a member of a delegation which, it was hoped, Pope Paul would send to Istanbul for the simultaneous ceremony planned by the Pope and the Greek Orthodox Patriarch of Constantinople, Athenagoras I, for December 7. Naturally, I assured him of my willingness, although I did feel some regret at the likelihood that this would prevent me from being present for the solemn closing of the Council, set for the following day. Immediately after the December 4 ceremony in St. Paul's, Bishop Willebrands sought me out, and informed me that the Pope had given his approval of the delegation to Istanbul. As the only Cardinal in the group, I would serve as the head of the delegation and Porter White would accompany me as my secretary. Father John Long, S.J., the bi-ritual member of the Secretariat staff, would make all the necessary arrangements for traveling. Other members would be Archbishop Nicodemo of Bari, and Father Pierre Duprey, P.A.

We left by airplane on Monday morning, December 6, and arrived in Istanbul that afternoon. After we were settled in our hotel, we went as a group to visit the Patriarch Athenagoras at his modest residence in the Phanar district of the city, where the Orthodox Cathedral of St. George was also located. The Patriarch greeted us as we entered his home, garbed in his usual flowing black robe and the black headpiece which I believe is an almost inseparable part of the Greek Orthodox clerical garb. Then and on the following day, he was the essence of gracious but unostentatious hospitality.

The Patriarch was an impressive figure of a man, somewhat over six feet tall, well-built, pleasant of countenance, with distinctive features and a long flowing gray beard. A native of Epirus in northwestern Greece, he was educated there and later at the Patriarchal Theological School on the Island of Halki near Istanbul. After ordination, his rise within the Greek Orthodox Church was rapid, and at the age of thirty-six he was named Archbishop of Corfu and Paxos. In 1931 he had become Archbishop of the Greek Orthodox Archdiocese of North and South America and in 1938 became a citizen of the United States. When Maximos V retired, the Holy Synod of Constantinople elected Athenagoras to the position of spiritual leader of world Orthodoxy with the joint title of "Archbishop of Constantinople and Ecumenical Patriarch." He had become a close friend of Pope John XXIII, whose pectoral cross, a personal gift from the Pope, he was wearing at the time he greeted and entertained us in his home. On the wall behind his desk hung the portrait of Pope John. He had first met Pope Paul VI on the occasion of Paul's historic pilgrimage to the Holy Land after the Second Period of the Council in January 1964, and had later been a guest at the Vatican. It was undoubtedly then that he and the Pope had decided on the historic ceremony to which we had come, and had drawn up the joint statement to be read at the next day's ceremony. We had a most pleasant conversation with him that afternoon, during which we were served a simple unpretentious "tea."

The following morning at the Cathedral of St. George, we prepared for the solemn Eucharistic Liturgy with which the occasion was being celebrated. The Patriarch, accompanied by the Metropolitans of the Synod, presided from his regular throne. I, as the head of the papal delegation, presided from a temporary throne placed on the opposite side of the Cathedral. At the end of the Liturgy the joint statement of the Pope and the Patriarch was read to all of us present with a solemnity proper to the occasion. After the ceremony we were again guests of the Patriarch and his suffragans at luncheon, which brought our celebration to a pleasant ending.

That afternoon I had an opportunity to visit the Agia Sophia, the great Byzantine Church erected by the Emperor Justinian in the sixth century, a thousand years before the Basilica of St. Peter's was built. It is still standing intact and now used by the Turkish government as a museum. Later we visited the Golden Horn, the beautiful waterfront at the juncture of the Strait of Bosphorus and the Sea of Marmara, the site chosen by Constantine in the fourth century for the New Rome, and other places of historic and scenic interest.

· Our schedule called for us to leave Istanbul the next morning (December 8) by the earliest plane bound for Rome. At Athens we were met by the Greek government's Minister of Religion. Since we had a layover of an hour, the Minister had arranged for a brief but interesting visit to the Acropolis. It was past noon when we arrived at the Roman airport. Porter and I arranged for transportation directly to St. Peter's.

After changing into my choir robes in the sacristy of the Basilica, I emerged into the piazza by the extreme northern exit and found myself at the edge of the great number of Bishops who were in attendance, garbed in white copes and miters. I could see that we had arrived none too soon, for it was evident that the long ceremony was drawing to a close. Fortunately, the very helpful master of ceremonies, who had taken charge of me at the ceremony of my reception of the Red Hat and at each of the subsequent papal ceremonies I had since attended, recognized me in my red robes and came and placed me in a convenient location. At a suitable pause in the ceremony he accompanied me to the Pope, to whom I was able to report that our mission to Istanbul had been successfully accomplished.

Not long after that came the final prayers of the Liturgy and the solemn papal blessing. Then Cardinal Felici read the official document signed by the Pope which brought the Council to an end. As I looked back over the years that had elapsed since Pope John XXIII had announced the opening of the Council, down to this, its solemn closing, I was deeply conscious of the fact that I had not only lived through, but also had been a part—a very small part—of the four most significant years of the Church's modern history.

10. A Time of Hope and Accomplishment, 1965-68

WHEN I ARRIVED BACK IN BALTIMORE in the early evening of December 9, 1965, I was met by Bishop T. Austin Murphy, Monsignor Thomas J. Mardaga, then rector of the Basilica (the old Baltimore Cathedral), Monsignor P. Francis Murphy, who had become my secretary after his return from the North American College where he had been a vice rector, and Monsignor F. Joseph Gossman, Vice Chancellor. This was the group on whom, with Monsignor Porter J. White, who was still in Rome, and Francis X. Gallagher, archdiocesan attorney, I chiefly depended for advice in archdiocesan affairs. After retrieving my luggage, we set off for the Basilica rectory, which had remained my residence since the outbreak of the racial trouble in 1963. The Sisters, who were then still in domestic service at the Basilica rectory, had prepared a special supper to celebrate my return. Immediately thereafter, I went down to the basement kitchen to greet and thank them.

Meanwhile, the rest of the group had gathered in my second-story study, where I joined them to continue the conversation we had begun at supper. Virtually all our talk centered on the implementation of the Council within the archdiocese. Through our regular correspondence, Bishop Murphy knew of my desire to get such implementation under way as soon as possible after the beginning of the new year and also some of my general thoughts on the subject. Starting with that, this group of advisors had gone on to form a suggested plan that they considered feasible and effective. The plan covered a two-year period. The first year would be devoted to a series of pastoral visits in which I would be accompanied by Frank Murphy, who would make all the arrangements, and Father Charles Riepe as master of ceremonies, who would plan and supervise the Liturgy that would be an important part of each visitation. Charles was chosen for this part because of his intense interest in the Liturgy. As a student at the Seminary of Innsbruck in Austria, he had come under the influence of the well-known liturgist Father Joseph A. Jungmann, S.J. He had followed with great interest the activity of the Commission on the Sacred Liturgy, particularly that part devoted to the changes in the Liturgy of the Mass. Hence, he was happy to be chosen to take responsibility for this part of the visitation. Each visit would begin with the Mass, which I was to celebrate. I naturally gave the homily, which in this case would be a discourse on the Council, its relation to the archdiocese and to every parish, and the changes that had been brought about in the Liturgy.

The Mass would be followed by a break and then an open meeting, preferably in the parish hall, if there were one; otherwise, in the church. Discussion at the meeting would be open and free. Along with myself, Murphy, Riepe, and the regional moderator would preside and we would undertake to answer all questions and carry on such discussion as seemed necessary or advisable.

Since it would be impossible for me in a single year to make an individual visitation to each of the 129 parishes, our committee had divided the archdiocese into thirty separate regions, each consisting of four to six neighboring parishes according to the density of the Catholic population. The main church in each region was named the "stational church," and the pastor of that church would be "regional moderator." Murphy and Riepe would consult with him about the general plan and the Liturgy. He in turn would see to it that all the parishes of the region were kept properly informed and involved.

The plan for the second year provided for a visitation of every parish of the archdiocese which would be carried out by Bishop Murphy, a second Auxiliary Bishop whose appointment I intended to seek, and myself. These visitations would be somewhat after the manner of those made famous by St. Charles Borromeo after he had been appointed Archbishop of Milan. They were intended to do the real work of implementing the Council, and would be far more important than the introductory regional visitations of the first year. The plan as a whole seemed a good one, and we decided that evening to adopt it. If it were to start at the beginning of the new year, some immediate steps had to be taken. Through our weekly correspondence Bishop Murphy knew that I approved the general plan being formed and proceeded accordingly. In my name he had already chosen the regional moderators and had selected Thursday morning, December 16, as the time for my meeting with them at the Belvedere Hotel. Since some moderators would be coming from a distance, luncheon at the hotel following the meeting had been tentatively arranged.

The days between my return and Christmas were busy ones: getting back into my regular duties of office after a three-month absence, answering accumulated correspondence that required my personal reply, visiting, in the company of Monsignor Joseph Leary, each of the construction projects.

On Tuesday, December 14, the National Conference of Christians and Jews held a dinner at which they conferred upon me their highest award in recognition of my work in behalf of the Council's statement on the relationship of the Church with the Jews. They, like most of the Jewish leaders, had been disappointed that the Council had not adopted the strong original statement proposed by our Secretariat for the Promotion of Christian Unity. But they had come to understand that the special circumstances of the Council had made the adoption of that particular separate statement impossible. The one that finally appeared as part of the Declaration on the Relationship of the Church to Non-Christian Religions, however, was in general conformity to the original statement, although somewhat shorter and lacking explicit condemnation of the word "deicide." Instead, the Council had decided to reprobate the use of *all* such opprobrious expressions in reference to the Jews. In any event, the National Conference had decided to recognize my own efforts by this national award, and for it I was sincerely appreciative.

Christmas of that year is etched on my memory as a time of inner peace and contentment, of joy and hope. Its observance began with the usual Christmas Eve carol service which was traditional at the new Cathedral. To me, the service that year seemed beautiful and touching. The music of the Mass that followed was magnificent. Into my brief homily I tried to introduce some of my own sense of peace and hope. As was usual on Christmas Eve, the great edifice was crowded to capacity. It was the first time I had celebrated the Christmas Midnight Mass as the Cardinal Archbishop. On my way back to the rectory with Frank Murphy, the lovely lines and simple melody of the Philip Brooks carol kept running through my mind:

O little town of Bethlehem, how still I see thee lie,
Above thy deep and dreamless sleep the silent stars go by,
Yet in thy dark streets shineth the Everlasting Light,
The hopes and fears of all the years are met in thee tonight.

That stanza seemed to symbolize the peace and hope that filled my heart that season.

We held our meeting of the regional moderators on Thursday, December 16, and at that time made our first public announcement of the 1966 program of visitations. By that time Frank Murphy and Charlie Riepe had formed a time-schedule for the visitations. They would begin on Tuesday, February 1, at St. Mark's in Catonsville, followed by St. Matthew's, Little Flower, and other large parishes within the Baltimore metropolitan area. This would continue until the beginning of June. We would resume again in September and then go on until December 1. By that time we would have covered every region of the archdiocese.

St. Mark's was chosen first, because of its size and location, and because we knew that Monsignor Joseph Leary and his staff could be counted on to give their full cooperation. Furthermore, many of its people had the reputation of being ultra-conservative and in general not too sympathetic to the changes proposed by Vatican II. They were so devoted to their pastor, however, that we expected that they would cooperate fully with him. If we could be successful there, it was likely that we would be successful everywhere else.

And we were successful! With St. Mark's were joined St. Joseph Monastery parish, St. Paul's in Ellicott City, and St. Mary's in Ilchester. Under the leadership of Monsignor Leary, all of the priests of the region had carefully prepared their people. The Liturgy of the Mass was beautifully carried out, with good participation on the part of the people. The homily was well received. The discussion period which followed was free and lively. At the end of our visit to St. Mark's, we judged that the program was a good one and that it had been carried out as well as we could have expected. The program of this visit became the pattern we would follow in virtually all those that would come later. Everywhere we went, we were met with visible signs of welcome on the part of both priests and people, and with the spirit of cooperation.

In the midst of our program, not long before we were due to arrive at our summer break, I underwent a period of the longest and most severe physical pain I have experienced during my life. During the Fourth Period of the Council, I had developed a small ulcer on the in-

side of my right cheek. This I was convinced was caused by the rubbing
of the jagged surface of a tooth I had broken while in Rome. Since that
period was already far advanced, and since in my student days I had
experienced difficulty in dealing with Roman dentists, I decided to
wait until I returned home to have the tooth repaired. I felt sure that,
once that was done, nature—aided, perhaps, by medication—would
take care of the healing process. The days after my return were busy
ones and I was experiencing no real pain, so I put off until after
Christmas my visit to the dentist.

On Christmas Day, however, I had dinner with the family of my
brother Dan, who had established an excellent reputation within his
profession as a dentist. In his younger days when he was building up
his practice from scratch, he had accepted an offer of a part-time
teaching position at the University of Maryland Dental School, a position he had retained through the years, even after he had a large and
flourishing practice, because it kept him abreast of the latest developments in his profession and afforded him some excellent contacts he
was anxious to preserve. After dinner on Christmas, I told him about
the trouble I had developed. With the aid of a small flashlight, Dan
took a look at the faulty tooth and the ulcerated membrane and told
me to see him at his office in the Medical Arts Building on Monday.

It did not take him long to repair the tooth. He gave me samples of
the most effective mouthwash he knew of, and told me to use it
regularly and return to see him in two weeks' time. If, however, I
should experience any pain or notice any further deterioration in the
ulcerated area, I was to come to his office immediately. In his judgment I had already allowed the matter to run on too long.

Actually, I suffered no pain, and there appeared to be no further
deterioration, but neither was there any sign of healing. So after three
weeks I did return. This time he arranged to have his friend, Dr.
Calvin J. Gaver, recently retired professor of oral surgery at the
dental school, come in and take a look at the affected area. After conferring for a few moments, they decided that I should go to Dr. Myron
S. Aisenberg, head of the Department of Pathology of the University of
Maryland School of Medicine, who subsequently took a biopsy. The
final verdict was that, although there were no positive signs of cancer,
yet the whole affected area of mucous membrane looked suspicious
enough to warrant elimination of it through the process of irradiation.
Dr. Aisenberg in turn referred me to Dr. Fernando Bloedorn, professor
of radiology and head of radiation therapy at the University of Maryland School of Medicine. My 1966 calendar shows that my first visit to

Dr. Bloedorn was on March 8. I saw him again on March 17, when he informed me he had concluded that the best way to treat the affected area was through the use of radon seeds. Radon, he explained, is a radioactive gas given off by radium as it disintegrates, and it is entrapped in small capsules. These he intended to implant in a circle around the affected area. At first I would feel little or no effect from their presence. Then, as the radon did its work, I would experience increasing discomfort until the activity of the radon reached its peak; then, after a period of rather intense discomfort, the activity of the radon would gradually decrease and finally come to an end. My experience actually corresponded quite closely with Dr. Bloedorn's prediction, except that my reaction was somewhat slower than I anticipated. In any event, I had entered into the period of what Dr. Bloedorn had described as one of severe discomfort, but turned out to be one of intense pain, during the early part of May. At that time my friend Eddie Jones, a lawyer who had undergone similar treatment, wrote me the following letter which describes more exactly than I would care to do the condition under which I was to live for the next month or so. He wrote:

Your Eminence
or, more appropriately at the moment,
Hi, fellow-sufferer—

I read in the paper yesterday of your entrance into Bon Secours for a rest. Having gone through a similar treatment, I know you must be enduring constant and unrelenting pain. This, in itself, saps your strength, and even a little physical effort makes you feel that you've been digging ditches all day.

Unfortunately, I doubt that other than the rest, the doctors and good nuns at Bon Secours can do much at the moment to change this condition except to give you a peck of assorted pills. I must have taken a jillion!

I don't recall exactly, but I think it was about three weeks after I had the needle implant before I felt the full effects of the radiation reaction. I do remember distinctly that right after the implant the doctor informed me: "There is nothing you will or can do that will aggravate the reaction, nor is there much, if anything, we can do to mitigate it. The fact is, it must complete its cycle." As I recall, this was ten to twelve weeks (it seemed an eternity at the time).

Thanks be to God, that ordeal is now behind me, as I am sure your present ordeal will be over shortly. As soon as the radiant energy is dissipated, the radiation reaction will cease. It will probably stop even more quickly than it started.

In my case, during the cycle I was convinced the doctors were giving me the run-around, because no guy could hurt so much and be so tired all the time and still live. I did, though, and now realize the doctors were right all along.

Sure wish I could do something to alleviate that constant gnawing, unrelenting pain, but only God's time will do the trick. We will continue to keep you in our prayers, and I am certain that in a very, very short time all of this will be forgotten and you will be your old vivacious self.

Sincerely yours,
Eddie Jones

Although the pain caused by the radon implants was undoubtedly severe, yet it never completely immobilized me. In fact, I soon found out that the best way to control it was to concentrate on the work that required my presence and action. The effects of the radon implants never prevented me from offering daily Mass and never, to any noticeable extent, interfered with my speech. I found, therefore, that with the help of Frank Murphy and Charlie Riepe I was able to carry out our original plan of archdiocesan regional visitation. Besides this, there were other important engagements that had to be met during this period. Here I recall that Francis X. Gallagher was able to control the pain of his periodic migraine headaches, which some claim is the worst suffering man can endure, throughout the whole of his adult life by intense concentration on his work and the needs of his family. I may say that something similar seemed to happen to me during this much shorter period of 1966.

In any event, we completed successfully our spring program of regional visitations, and I went into the summer carrying my pain with me. However, I officiated at the Rite of Ordination to the Priesthood at the new Cathedral on Saturday, May 21, and at Woodstock on June 16. Meanwhile, my 1966 calendar shows that I presided at the commencement exercises of four colleges, one junior college, five high schools, St. Charles College, St. Mary's Seminary; and on Sunday, May 22, I had the happiness of dedicating John Carroll High School at Bel Air. So in spite of Eddie Jones's grim predictions, perhaps with the help of his prayers and sympathy, my calendar seems to say that I was bearing up quite well.

In September, we resumed our regional visitations. Whereas those of the late winter and early spring had kept us pretty well within the area of metropolitan Baltimore, where the great concentration of Catholics was located, those of the fall took us to the outlying districts of central and western Maryland: St. John's in Westminister, St. John's in Frederick, St. Mary's in Hagerstown, St. Peter's in Westernport, St. Patrick's and St. Mary's in Cumberland. Everywhere we were well received and quite satisfied with the results—everywhere except in Frank Murphy's native town of Cumberland and, of all places, his native parish of St. Mary's. There we ran into our only serious difficulty of the whole program. I suspect that, because of his familiarity with the parish, Frank chose it with the knowledge that we would probably run into trouble there and from the trouble the parish might derive some benefit.

Father John Lyness had recently become the pastor of St. Patrick's in Cumberland and from him we received the same kind of welcome and cooperation we had received from Monsignor Leary at St. Mark's in Catonsville. When we moved over to St. Mary's the next day, the atmosphere was very different. It was rumored that the pastor thought all the changes brought about by Vatican II were nonsense. It was with reluctance that he allowed himself to be persuaded by Frank Murphy to arrange an altar facing the people. But he had drawn the line at having the people ask their own questions during the discussion period in his church. He had provided that in his parish the laity would write out their questions or their comments and present them to him or to his senior assistant, who would be at the one stationary microphone placed in the middle of the church. From there, he or his assistant would relay them (properly censored?) to me and the others presiding.

Shortly before the ceremony was to begin, Murphy and Riepe learned that the pastor had made this change in the program. Murphy immediately brought me this information. I sent word back with him that we would follow the same plan here that we had followed elsewhere, and that the laity would be invited to come to the microphone and ask their own questions. I added that the pastor and his assistant were invited to take their places with the other priests who were present; that Riepe would be in entire charge of the Liturgy, and that Murphy would have charge of the microphone; he was placed under strict obedience to follow my ruling in this matter. Meanwhile, I had gone to the sacristy to be near the scene of altercation, if altercation there were to be. When this word was given to him, overlooking the fact he was near a sensitive microphone, in anger he uttered an expletive that is generally considered inadmissable in polite society. A little later, learning that I had overheard his remark, he came to me in what seemed to be a humble and repentant mood, begged pardon for both his burst of temper and his crudity, and promised from then on that he would do everything possible to cooperate. And so he did. In the end, this turned out to be one of our most pleasant and fruitful visitations.

By the beginning of December we had completed all our visitations. Left to stand alone, I would have to say that effect of these visits would have proved superficial. Their value resided in the fact that they laid the foundation for the far more serious work of the next year in which we were to undertake the parish-by-parish visitation of the whole archdiocese.

Before we could undertake the second phase, another important event had to take place: the appointment of a second Auxiliary Bishop who would share this work with Bishop Murphy and myself. When we had first planned our program, I already had in mind the priest whom I wished to have as my second Auxiliary. He was Monsignor Thomas Mardaga, then rector of the Basilica of the Assumption. He had first come into special prominence in the archdiocese after Archbishop Keough appointed him Director of the Annual Appeal for the Associated Catholic Charities. In this position he had done an outstanding job. After the regular meeting of the Bishops of the Province, the week after Easter, I asked Rome to appoint him as Auxiliary Bishop of Baltimore, placing his name first on the *terna* of approved priests. I imagine that my request did not actually come before the Sacred Congregation until the fall. In any event, it was only on December 10, 1966, that the Vatican announced that Thomas Mardaga had been named Bishop to the Titular See of Mutugenna and Auxiliary Bishop of Baltimore.

Bishop Mardaga was consecrated on Tuesday, January 25, 1967, and soon thereafter joined Bishop Murphy and myself in the series of parish visitations. As far as possible these were carried out over weekends. We would arrive late Saturday afternoon, speak at the Saturday evening Masses, and afterwards would hold individual interviews with each of the priests of the parish. On Sunday we would again preach at each of the Masses, and at the principal parish Mass would administer the Sacrament of Confirmation. That afternoon we would hold an open meeting for all members of the parish and later meet with individuals or groups who had made an appointment to see us. These interviews continued through a good part of Sunday evening. On Monday morning we would visit the parish school, wherever one existed, and then continue our interviews Monday afternoon and evening, staying on through Tuesday in some of the larger parishes, or even longer, whenever it was deemed necessary or desirable. It was in these parish visitations that the real work of implementation of the Council was effected. So we went on up to Christmas, 1967.

The following year I endeavored to establish an Archdiocesan Pastoral Council by appointing highly recommended representatives of the various parts of the archdiocese. I soon found, however, that such a body could not function properly until Area Councils were established which could elect their own representatives and until a constitution and by-laws had been drawn up and formally adopted. Therefore, I appointed a committee to draw up a constitution and allowed the members to choose their own chairman. One considerable difficulty developed; the chairman and a group of his followers wished the Council to be called "deliberative," to distinguish it clearly from a body that would be merely advisory. I proposed that the word "consultative" be used. The chairman of the committee considered this to be open to the interpretation that it was merely advisory. I was determined that, owing to the overtones of the word "deliberative" in this country, that word would not be used. We finally decided on the phrase "highest collegial body," which the chairman proposed as a compromise. Since this term had been applied to the Synod of Bishops without in the least diminishing the authority of the Pope, I accepted it. The committee was concerned that the Council should have two particular rights: that of receiving the archdiocesan annual budget before it be made final, and that it have the right to be consulted on the establishment of new parishes. I found no objection to either of these provisions.

By the time the committee produced a document that was satisfactory to all concerned, the end of my administration was drawing near. For a time I had serious doubts concerning the propriety of my signing the document and establishing such a Council at the very end of my administration. When I reflected on the time and effort the committee had devoted to the document, however, and that they had yielded on every point which I considered important, it seemed to me that it would appear petty of me if I were to refuse. Besides, the new Archbishop, who would soon be appointed, would certainly know that he had the power to change anything he found objectionable, and in fact could abolish the organization and start over with a new set of advisers if he wished. So I signed the document and thus established the Archdiocesan Pastoral Council as the final important act in my effort to implement the Second Vatican Council. As a matter of fact, Archbishop Borders was to find in the Council strong support, one might even say unceasing insistence on the balancing of the archdiocesan budget, which by that time had become particularly important.

While the program for implementing Vatican II was proceeding during 1966 and 1967, at the same time, my mind was much occupied with the Cardinal's Campaign which had already started before I left for the Fourth Period of the Council. It had its origin in my first visit to the Home of the Little Sisters of the Poor on their patronal feast of St. Joseph, March 19, 1962, soon after I had become Archbishop of Baltimore. It was an old custom that the Archbishop should visit their home on that day and help to serve the special dinner provided for the old people on that occasion. Custom also called for me to visit the sick in the various dormitories and in the infirmary of the home. Everywhere there was evidence of the spotless condition in which the whole building was kept and of the excellent care given to the old people. Everywhere it was also evident that the place was a tinderbox. On remarking about this, I was informed by the Sister Superior who accompanied me that because of the danger this condition presented, the capacity of the home had been reduced from 276, during the days of Depression, to 170. Later I learned from her and the Provincial, when they visited me, that they had been warned that it was only a question of time before the whole building, which was now almost a century old, would be condemned as an institution for aged people.

Later I visited the House of Good Shepherd and found that much the same condition existed there. Part of this building was even older than that of the Little Sisters. The Sisters of Good Shepherd were faced with a special problem, which from another point of view was an opportunity. The city authorities wanted to acquire the Mount Street property for a new public school to replace several old and small schools of that area. Since the building itself was useless, the city could pay only the value of the ground, which would undoubtedly cover the cost of a new site but contribute nothing toward the cost of a new building. Temporarily, the Sisters could combine their whole operation in their Calverton Road building, which had been acquired for their work with young Black women in the days when the strictest segregation was still the policy everywhere below the Mason-Dixon Line. That building also would soon have to be replaced or abandoned. Evidently, if the archdiocese were going to retain the invaluable services of these two groups of Sisters and continue their two essential programs of charity, it would have to come to their help in the near future.

Early in 1963 I consulted Bishop Murphy; Monsignor David Dorsch, Director of the Associated Catholic Charities; Monsignor Thomas Mardaga; and Monsignor George Hopkins, then Chancellor and rector of the old Cathedral. We all agreed that the archdiocese would have to undertake to help both groups of Sisters acquire new homes and that this could be done only through a special appeal to the Catholics of the whole archdiocese such as had never been attempted before. As a result of our conference, I suggested to the two communities of Sisters that they look for suitable properties and engage architects who could submit reliable estimates of cost. I then asked Mr. Henry J. Knott whether he would be willing to take a leading part in the financial campaign we were contemplating. He willingly consented to become Chairman of the Advance Gifts Unit. I asked Bishop Murphy to be Chairman of the general phase of the campaign that would seek gifts from all the Catholics of the archdiocese through parish organizations. He, too, willingly consented.

By the time the Sisters had acquired their properties, had their plans drawn and estimates made, we were already well into 1964. It was found that it would require about $3 million to build the new home for the Little Sisters of the Poor, to be located on Maiden Choice Lane next to the St. Charles College property, and about $2 million for the new Good Shepherd Center, which would be located on Maple Avenue in Halethorpe. Meanwhile, the Sisters of Good Shepherd had sold the Mount Street property. The proceeds, together with some funds the Sisters had put aside against the day when they would be able to erect a new home, had reduced the amount they required for their new institution. It was now decided that the Archdiocesan Campaign for Charity should open some time in the latter part of June 1965, after the annual appeal for the Associated Catholic Charities would have been completed.

Meanwhile, Mr. James Anderson, retired comptroller for the Standard Oil Company of New Jersey, came to me to inquire whether the St. Elizabeth School for Special Education could be included in our campaign. The Sisters of St. Francis (Mill Hill) had for many years conducted a school for handicapped young people of elementary-school

age on Maryland Avenue. They had found out that an educational institution for youths past the age of elementary school was urgently needed
and they had begun such a project in unused space in their Ellerslie
Avenue motherhouse. The project had proved successful beyond all
expectation, and now in order to continue and expand it they needed a
new building adapted to their program. They had acquired adjoining
property on Argonne Drive and had plans drawn. Mr. Thomas McNulty,
a well-known singer and owner of a radio station, had for some years
shown a special interest in their project. He had attempted to raise the
$500,000 needed for the new building, but soon found that alone he
could not get very far and had persuaded Jim Anderson, on his retirement, to help him out. Between them they had succeeded in raising
some $50,000.

That the project was a worthy and a much-needed one was clear
beyond doubt. We all decided it was to everybody's advantage to have it
included. Our campaign goal now became $5,500,000. It was decided
that no publicity would be given to the projected campaign until completion of the annual appeal for the Associated Catholic Charities.
Meanwhile, as we have already seen, the title of Cardinal was unexpectedly conferred upon me on February 22, 1965, with little more
than one month's notice that the Holy Father intended to raise me
to that rank.

In preparation for our campaign I had written to Mr. Frank Zimmermann, President of the Community Counselling Service, Inc., of
New York, the organization I had used successfully in my three Bridgeport diocesan campaigns. On the basis of a survey his organization
made, he agreed to assign one of his staff to act as our campaign
director. Zimmermann later wrote to me urging that the title of our
campaign be simply "The Cardinal's Campaign." At first I strongly
demurred; it seemed to me almost as if this would be commercializa-
tion of my title, and, to tell the truth, I feared it might be so interpreted
in Rome. However Henry Knott, Bishop Murphy, and all others involved strongly approved of Zimmermann's suggestion. As was not
unusual in such circumstances, Henry Knott put an end to all hesitation
by the simple and blunt question: "Look, Cardinal, what good is your
title to the archdiocese if it can't be put to good use for the benefit of
these three worthy institutions?" From that point on, our project became known as "The Cardinal's Campaign."

After the question of the title had been settled, Frank Zimmermann
informed me that his company had assigned Mr. Robert Valente to become Director of the campaign and that he would arrive the Tuesday

after Easter, April 20, 1965, to take up temporary residence in Baltimore. After conferring with Henry Knott and Bishop Murphy, and after
visiting the three institutions which would be the beneficiaries, Mr.
Valente prepared the publicity for the announcement to be released
in *The Catholic Review* and the secular newspapers about the middle of
June. Meanwhile, Henry Knott, as Chairman of the Advance Gifts Unit,
decided that the campaign would open with a dinner on Tuseday evening, June 28, at Long Crandon, the one-time home of the W. W.
Lanahan family, which later had become the residence of Archbishop
Keough and which Porter White and I had used as a summer residence
during the past two years. With its large handsome dining room, its
equally large and properly furnished living room, its spacious front
lawn, overlooking the blue waters of Loch Raven in the distance and
the wooded watershed in between, it now proved the perfect setting for
the opening of the campaign. The invited guests were the Catholic
businessmen, bankers, doctors, lawyers, and other professional men
on whose generous support and help Henry felt we could count.

At Henry's suggestion Sister Mary Celeste, then Superior of the
nearby Stella Maris Hospice, had prepared the dining room and supervised the preparation and service of the excellent dinner that was
placed before us. It was indeed a very enjoyable repast. When we had
finished eating, we all moved to the front lawn, where Henry Knott
opened the meeting: "Gentlemen, we all know why we have come to
this meeting; it is to begin a campaign meant to raise sufficient money
to meet some very urgent needs that are facing this archdiocese. The
best way to begin is to have Cardinal Shehan describe for us those needs
just as he found them."

I began my very informal talk by telling about my first visit to the
Little Sisters of the Poor on the Feast of St. Joseph, as I have already
mentioned. I spoke of the condition in which I found the buildings; of
the constant fire hazard it presented not only to the old people, but
also to the Sisters, particularly those whose sleeping quarters were
located at the top of the building; of the increasing need of their work
with the relative number of old people in our society constantly increasing; of the steps the Sisters had already taken, and at the way
we had arrived at the figure of $3 million as their basic need. I then
went on to outline the equally important needs of the Sisters of Good
Shepherd and how we arrived at the figure of $2 million for them, and
finally why we were led to include in our plans St. Elizabeth School for
Special Education. In any event the archdiocese was faced with the
necessity of raising the sum of $5,500,000 by appealing to the charity of

our Catholic people. This evening I was making an earnest appeal to those present to help me in this greatest charitable appeal the archdiocese had ever undertaken. I must say that I have never spoken to a more interested and attentive audience.

At the end of my talk, Henry asked if there were any questions. Since there were none, he began his own typically brief speech, direct and to the point: "Gentlemen, we know the need. We, the members of the Advance Gifts Unit, have to set the example if the Cardinal's Campaign is going to be a success, as I have no doubt it will be. We are obviously looking for money—big money. We are asking you, in making your own contribution, not merely to give out of your current surplus income, but, if necessary in order to make a representative gift, to dip into capital. This is not an annual appeal, it is a once-in-a-lifetime drive. The Cardinal has assured me that during the rest of his lifetime he will never make an attempt to organize another financial campaign like this one. To get this one off to a proper start, my wife Marion and I are pledging $346,000 over the next three years." Then, after a brief pause: "Who is going to follow suit?"

There was a moment of silence. Then Henry turned to his friend, Ralph DeChiaro. "Ralph, what are you and Dorothy willing to do?" Ralph hemmed and hawed for a moment or so, and then laughingly said: "Henry, you're putting the bite on me." "Of course," said Henry, with a laugh, "That's what I intend to do." "Well," said Ralph, "Dorothy and I can't meet your generous gift, but I think we can pledge $150,000; if we can give more, we will." (Their final gift was $164,000.) Next Henry turned to John Curley. In the name of Eastern Stainless Steel, of which he was President, he pledged $100,000, and $25,000 for himself and his wife Jean. Jim Keelty spoke up next, pledging $100,000 for himself and his wife, Louise. Henry's three brothers (John, Martin, and Charles) were not present. I suppose Henry allotted the limited number of places at table to prospects, eliminating those who were already committed. Henry announced in the name of all three a total pledge of $134,000. We were off to a good start—more than $650,000 pledged in less than a half hour.

Other large gifts that were pledged either that evening or came in later were: Associated Italian Charities, $25,000; Jacob Blaustein, $25,000; Emmett Bradley, $25,000; Florence Cahill, $35,000; William P. Carton, $51,000; Chesapeake and Potomac Telephone Company, $53,000; Equitable Trust Company $40,000; Fidelity and Deposit Company of Maryland, $35,000; P. Flanigan & Sons, Inc., $30,000; Lucien Gaudreau, $20,000; Henry and Katherine Irr, $35,000; Maryland

National Bank (Nicholas Mueller) $40,000; William Rogers, Sr., $20,000; Dr. and Mrs. F. Frederick Ruzika, $50,000; Savings Bank of Baltimore, $18,000; Union Trust Company of Maryland, $40,000; James J. Ward on behalf of Green Spring Dairy, $30,000. Other substantial gifts of $15,000 and less, too numerous to mention here, were also received through Henry Knott's Advance Gifts Unit. On May 26, 1966, Henry Knott submitted the complete report of the Advance Gifts Unit. The total pledges received amounted to $1,959,671.

The summer of 1965 was the last time Porter White and I used Long Crandon as a summer residence. It was just too large for that purpose and the upkeep was too expensive. That fall I was happy to turn it over to the Sisters of Mercy to be used as a home for their aged and retired Sisters until such time as they acquired a retirement home of their own. When Mercy Villa had been erected, I then had Long Crandon fitted out as a home for retired priests, and since then it seems to serve that purpose admirably. But in the summer of 1965 it had proved a useful asset to the beginning of the Cardinal's Campaign.

The favorable report of Henry Knott's Advance Gifts Unit proved to be an encouraging incentive to Bishop Murphy and Bob Valente and the other members of the General Campaign Committee in perfecting their organization and making final plans for the opening of their phase of the campaign in September of that year. It may be well to mention that in the fall of 1965 we received the largest gift of the whole campaign. On Thanksgiving Day of that year, while I was in Rome for the last period of the Second Vatican Council, Francis Gallagher received a rather urgent telephone call from the nurse of Mrs. Florence Cahill, who had already presented her gift of $35,000 to the Advance Gifts Unit. Mrs. Cahill requested that Francis visit her as soon as was possible. He went that afternoon and found that during the previous night she had become seriously ill and was scheduled to enter Mercy Hospital the next day. Before doing so she wished to change her will in which she had already made various bequests to relatives and friends. Now she wished to add a codicil providing that the residue of her rather large estate be divided so that one half of it should go to Mercy Hospital, to which she had formed a strong attachment. The other half she wished to go to the Cardinal's Campaign, to be used in the erection of the new home for the Little Sisters of the Poor. Francis then and there added the codicil to her satisfaction; she signed it and Francis had it attested by the two required witnesses. A few days later she died. The will was promptly probated, but was executed only one year later. It was then learned that the Cardinal's Campaign had received the sum of over $400,000. Since the final report of the Advance Gifts Unit had already been submitted, that sum was added to the results of the general phase of the campaign, much to the satisfaction of the committee in charge. Here I might add that I had come to know Mrs. Cahill when I became pastor of the parish of SS. Philip and James in January of 1946. She remained a devoted and generous parishioner and personal friend all during my pastorate and down to her death.

Once the general phase of the campaign got started it went forward with the same kind of enthusiastic response given to the Advance Gifts Unit. Early in February 1968, Bob Valente sent Henry Knott, Frank Zimmermann of the Community Counselling Service, and myself a message on telegram forms, notifying us that at that time, with the January reports still incomplete, the Campaign had passed the $8 million mark. By the time we had brought the campaign operations to a close, the pledges amounted to more than $13 million. When we closed the books, they showed that a total of $11, 787,329 had been received in cash. It was said that this was the largest amount ever raised in the Baltimore area by any such financial campaign. While a few who had pledged died before their promises were completely fulfilled and some, through unforeseen difficulties, were unable to live up to their commitment, small amounts continued to come in for over a year after the campaign had ended.

When it had become evident that the results would exceed the original goal of $5,500,000, the heads of the three institutions named as the main beneficiaries of the campaign were authorized to go ahead with the construction of their buildings. Even before the campaign had ended, St. Elizabeth School of Special Education had been completed and was serving its purpose. Not long after the campaign, St. Martin Home for the Aged (of the Little Sisters of the Poor) was in full operation. About a year later the same thing could be said of the new Good Shepherd Center, as a fully integrated operation. Nothing in my administration of the archdiocese brought me greater satisfaction than the blessing and dedication of St. Martin Home. Much the same thing must be said of the St. Elizabeth School of Special Education and the Good Shepherd Center. The Cardinal's Campaign, however, had also enabled me to bring to completion the high school construction program. It was also to bring me an unforeseen satisfaction, in that it encouraged me to go ahead with the erection of the badly needed medical wing for Stella Maris Hospice. With the recently opened residence known as St. Elizabeth Hall and the rest of the Stella Maris complex, through the kind thoughtfulness of Archbishop Borders and Sister Louis Mary, R.S.M., it now forms the Cardinal Shehan Center for the Aging.

There had never been any question about the ability of the archdiocese to raise enough funds for the replacement of the old Home of the Little Sisters of the Poor. So well known and admired had been their work, and so beloved had the Sisters become, that the Catholic people of Baltimore would have rallied to their side to provide whatever was necessary for continuation of their work for the destitute aged. Henry Knott, Bishop Austin Murphy, and Bob Valente of the Community Counselling Services knew well how to use the popularity of their appeal as the central thrust of the Cardinal's Campaign. Nor would there have been any great difficulty in providing for the work of the Franciscan Sisters of Baltimore at St. Elizabeth School of Special Education and Rehabilitation Center, once that was established. The case of the Good Shepherd Center was somewhat different. The one thing necessary for carrying on the difficult and delicate work of rehabilitation of wayward young women was, ironically, lack of publicity. Then, too, earlier in the century the theory of professional social work had a positive prejudice against the use of institutions for that particular kind of work. Instead the theory called for the use of foster homes, supplemented by case work. So vigorously was the theory preached that at one time (c. 1940-50) there seemed to be danger that the Sisters of the Good Shepherd would be eliminated from their traditional field. In Baltimore, however, two stalwart and very influential champions of the Sisters and their work appeared on the scene: Judge Michael Manley (whom I have heard referred to as the "lawyers' lawyer") and Judge Joseph Byrnes. They were aided by Miss Dorothy Sanford, Chief Probation Officer of the Juvenile Court. I believe it is true that the newer professionals found it practically impossible to find suitable foster homes willing to accommodate wayward young women. In any event, after a decade or so of trial, applications for placement in the House of the Good Shepherd came flooding back in such volume as to strain its capacity.

As the two Catholic judges advanced in years (both have long since died), they interested a younger, able lawyer, George Constable, who became a champion of the Sisters and helped with their work wherever it impinged on the field of law. He has worked devotedly with the Sisters for many years. Then, too, a surprising thing happened. When the President of Goucher College (long noted as a bastion of Methodism) retired, an able and staunch Catholic woman educator from the North

was chosen as the new President of the college. Eyebrows were raised:
What kind of Catholic? Then a little later, something else equally surprising happened. Dr. Rhoda Dorsey, the new President of Goucher,
had offered her free-time service to the Sisters of the Good Shepherd to
help them deal with young women at the opposite end of the social arm
from those with whom she had been accustomed to deal. That was ten
years ago. Dr. Dorsey has been serving for five years on the Executive
Committee of the Good Shepherd Center. This may all be traceable to
the spirit of Vatican II.

One of the results of the success of the Cardinal's Campaign, as I
have already mentioned, was that it made possible the completion of
the program of Catholic high school construction. To understand the
pressure that during the fifties and sixties was being brought on Church
authorities by parents to provide Catholic education for their children,
one must recall the decision of the Supreme Court in the McCollum case
(1948), by which all religious instruction was excluded from the public
schools. This exclusion was widened and strengthened by that Court's
decision in the Madalyn Murray case in the early sixties.

During that same period, intense pressure was being successfully
brought to bear on public school authorities to add sex education to the
public school curriculum, including the presentation of facts related to
the process of procreation and such subjects as contraception, abortion,
and venereal disease. Many Catholics and others feared that such education, without appropriate moral instruction based on a solid foundation of religious truth, would be an incentive to sex experimentation and
premarital sex by students. Hence, the strong reluctance of Catholic
parents to send their children to public schools, particularly to public
high schools, so evident during the fifties and sixties. Hence also, the
pressure on Catholic Bishops to increase the number of Catholic high
schools in their dioceses. I had felt that pressure in Bridgeport almost
immediately after my arrival there in 1953, and I had subsequently
experienced the favorable response from the people of that diocese in
the series of financial appeals made in favor of Catholic high schools.

Archbishop Keough had experienced the same sort of pressure in
Baltimore following his arrival. After he had completed the construction of the Cathedral of Mary Our Queen, he had decided to launch into
a program of high school construction, using the remainder of the
O'Neill bequest. Before I arrived here as his Coadjutor in September,
1961, he had presided at the opening of Archbishop Curley High School

in East Baltimore, staffed by the Capitular Franciscan priests and brothers. He had also seen well on its way to completion Cardinal Gibbons High School, located on the property of the old St. Mary's Industrial School, owned by the archdiocese. Mr. Howard Hall, the architect of Gibbons High, had the difficult task of incorporating into his design a part of the old Industrial School. He had fulfilled his contract to the complete satisfaction of the Archbishop, and as a favor to the Archbishop, he had supervised the completion of Curley High, after the Archbishop and the architect of that project had developed serious misunderstandings. During the summer after Archbishop Keough's death, when Hall's firm was completing its work on Cardinal Gibbons High, he told me that he would like to start work on the girls' high school which was to be located next to Gibbons. This project had been promised to him by the Archbishop.

About the same time Mr. John Eyring, a prominent Catholic architect of this city, informed me that he was nearing the completion of plans for the archdiocesan central office building, which Archbishop Keough had engaged him to design. The Archbishop had discussed neither of these projects with me, probably because no suitable opportunity had offered itself during the brief period between my arrival and the Archbishop's death. I told both Eyring and Hall that I did not in the least doubt their word, but they would have to give me some days to consider these projects, since I would have to assume the ultimate responsibility in both cases.

As soon as possible, I consulted those who had been close to the Archbishop during the latter years of his life: Monsignor White, Francis Gallagher, Monsignor Hopkins, Monsignor Joseph Leary, who worked closely with him in building projects, and Monsignor James Donohue, Director of Education. All of them were aware that the Archbishop had engaged Eyring to design the archdiocesan office building, which came to be called the Catholic Center, and that he had promised Howard Hall the privilege of designing the girls' high school. I raised some question about the advisability of locating the Catholic Center on the old Calvert Hall property because of the serious parking problem. Both Gallagher and White, however, said that Archbishop Keough had given this and other problems very serious consideration and nevertheless reached a firm decision on the location. Moreover, the downtown community and the whole city, particularly those interested in the renewal of downtown Baltimore, were so delighted that the Archbishop had decided to build on that site, at the corner of Cathedral and Mulberry Streets, that they thought it would be most unwise for me to raise any question about the

location. By the end of our conference I had decided that I would authorize both architects to go ahead.

Shortly before completion of the plans for the Catholic Center, John Eyring died quite suddenly. In his death, the Archdiocese lost
one of its most eminent men of his profession and a most loyal and devoted son of the Church. As head of the firm, Eyring was succeeded by
his nephew, Charles Novak. It was he, accompanied by his partner,
who brought me the complete plans and specifications just before I
was scheduled to leave for Rome, for the opening of the Second Vatican Council. Bishop Murphy would also be in Rome for the same purpose. Who, then, would see to it that the Eyring plans were properly
executed? After giving the plans the attention I could, I called on Monsignor Joseph Leary, who had worked most effectively with Archbishop Keough on a number of construction projects, and asked him to
take charge of this one in my absence. Later, while I was still in Rome,
Leary informed me that the low bidder was the firm of Kirby and Maguire. The bid was quite satisfactory. I asked him to get the project
under way as soon as he could. Here I might add that the whole
project went ahead without any serious hitch. The building was completed and ready for occupancy during the Fourth Period of the Council in 1965.

During 1963, Leary and I agreed that there should be a permanent
Archdiocesan Building Committee. Leary agreed to serve as Chairman.
After consultation with him, I appointed as Vice Chairman Monsignor
Joseph Nelligan, for many years Chancellor of the archdiocese. The
other members were Monsignor Joseph Ells, who had done an outstanding job in the difficult task of enlarging and renovating the once
tiny church of St. Dominic in order to accommodate his now very
large parish, and Father Charles Dausch, then pastor of St. Joseph's
Church, Hagerstown, in whom Leary had great confidence. Leary was
particularly anxious to have Mr. John Russell, a retired but still very
active engineer who had been of so much help to him in the erection
of his own parish church of St. Mark in Catonsville, as consultant to
the committee for all projects. This appointment I gladly made. It was
understood that Francis Gallagher would serve as legal consultant.
The committee served me most effectively down to the end of my term
of office.

In the spring of 1963, Howard Hall brought me the plans for the
new girls' high school. After examining them carefully, I turned them
over to Monsignor Leary and his committee for the supervision of the
project, for again that year I would be in Rome during the entire fall

for the Second Period of the Council. Again, this project was carried out to my entire satisfaction. The building was completed and occupied in 1965. To it we gave the name Archbishop Keough High School in honor of my beloved predecessor.

Meanwhile, Leary and Gallagher called to my attention the fact that Archbishop Keough had intended to erect two other high schools— one at Bel Air and the other in Cumberland. To both, the Archbishop attached great importance, in order to make it manifest that the arch- diocese was concerned about areas other than the metropolitan district of Baltimore. I authorized Francis Gallagher to see if suitable proper- ties were available in or near these two towns. Through his lawyer friends, Freeborn Brown of Bel Air and William Walsh of Cumberland, we were able to acquire very desirable pieces of property that would serve for high school sites, against the time when the archdiocese would have the resources necessary to undertake construction.

Not long afterward, we engaged the firm of Gaudreau to design both these schools, since it was thought that simultaneous planning and erection of the two would make possible notable economies. Actually, John Carroll in Bel Air was completed and brought into operation first, in 1964; Bishop Walsh in Cumberland was delayed somewhat due to the rocky nature of the soil on top of the so-called "Haystack Moun- tain." It opened its doors in 1966. The Catholics of two other areas made strong pleas for Catholic high schools: the extreme northwest area of metropolitan Baltimore toward Pikesville, and Dundalk in the southeastern area. To both, for the time being at least, I had to turn a deaf ear because it seemed that archdiocesan resouces were fully committed. But then a third additional claim arose in the fast-growing northern area of Anne Arundel County, which seemed impossible to ignore or even postpone.

For many years, Glen Burnie had been a typical small Maryland country town. Then in the fifties it, together with the whole area, began to develop rapidly and with it grew the parish of Holy Trinity. Father Arthur Slade, the pastor, with commendable foresight had erected a large parochial school with a correspondingly large convent for the Sisters of Notre Dame de Namur, who had undertaken to staff it. While a portion of the school was still unoccupied, Father Slade and the Sisters decided to start a high school for girls, using the still vacant classrooms. By 1965 the elementary school students numbered 1,705 with fifteen teaching sisters and sixteen lay teachers; and the high school students numbered 275 with eight teaching sisters. That spring Father Slade came to me with his problem. He had to make additional classrooms available for the elementary school, but he simply could not face the sudden termination of the high school. The only solution was to build a parish high school of moderate size. I promised to visit his parish the next afternoon and discuss the situation.

It was a sunny spring afternoon. We were standing on the very spot where Father Slade proposed to erect the high school. Suddenly there zoomed over our heads a twin engine airplane, seemingly less than 200 feet above. The noise brought our conversation to a sudden halt. It turned out that we were standing directly in the path of one of the main runways of Friendship Airport, hidden to view by the intervening woodland. When the plane had passed, we looked at each other for a moment in silence. Then he said: "I suppose that there go my hopes for the high school." "Yes," I replied, "there go your hopes. I could never authorize the erection of any school building on this site, but let's give some further thought to the problem."

The next day I called a meeting of my regular advisors. All were aware of the rapid growth of the area in question and of Holy Trinity parish, although like myself they had not been aware of Father Slade's pressing problem which had suddenly become our own. Were we, while in the process of constructing new high schools, to permit this flourishing and badly needed one simply to be closed, and the young women students to turn to the existing public schools of the area? What about the other young women who had not been able to gain admittance to Holy Trinity High because of lack of classroom space? What about the many young men of the area who needed Catholic education just as much as did the young women? And what about the eight teaching Sisters? Were we simply to turn them away, to be assigned to other projects, perhaps not nearly so urgently needed? All of us agreed that we would have to stretch the resources of the archdiocese to include a high school in northern Anne Arundel County. Francis Gallagher was again commissioned to see if a tract of suitable land was available, one that could serve Glen Burnie and the rest of the northern part of the county. Soon such a property was found. The firm of Border and Donaldson was commissioned as architect. During all of the Council years, the four high school projects went forward smoothly under the careful supervision of Monsignor Leary and his Building Commission, with considerable help from Francis X. Gallagher. Unfortunately, and much to my sorrow, Monsignor Leary died in March of 1967, but his place was taken and his work completed by Monsignor Nelligan.

When, in 1968, Martin Spalding High opened its doors in Severn, Anne Arundel County, with fifteen Sisters of Notre Dame de Namur and ten lay teachers, taking the place of Holy Trinity High in Glen Burnie, the future of all six of our archdiocesan high schools seemed very bright. It is true the cost of construction had put a strain on the unrestricted reserves of the archdiocese and also that the steadily increasing costs of Catholic education, particularly at the high school level, were causing me some rather serious concern; but of this I shall speak in my next chapter.

Some, no doubt, will question my judgment in going ahead with these expensive building projects. There have been times when, looking back, I have questioned that judgment myself. I must say, however, I acted only in answer to a deeply felt and urgently expressed need of our people and priests, and after consultation with the best advisors I had. I can only say of my efforts to meet the Catholic educational needs both of Bridgeport and Baltimore: "More I could not do; less I dared not."

I should add that one thing has occurred recently which seems to indicate that there was a certain wisdom in building those high schools at that time. I refer to the recent establishment by Henry Knott, for the benefit of the Archdiocese of Baltimore, of the Marion Burk Knott Scholarship Fund, so named in honor of his wife. At maturity the fund will total approximately $20 million. It is, in my eyes, singularly appropriate that Henry Knott, whose leadership was so largely responsible for the success of the financial campaign that made possible completion of the high school construction program, should now complement that work by giving these high schools along with our elementary schools and the three specified Catholic colleges a certain stability and an incentive to excellence they would otherwise lack. The thought that particularly strikes me is that those six archdiocesan high schools, which all stand well-designed and sound of structure, would probably cost today four or five times what they cost in the decade between 1958 and 1968, perhaps more. Further, the question arises in my mind: would Henry Knott have considered making the archdiocese the beneficiary of such a gift if it were not in possession of those high schools which he so generously helped us to build? So even today, fifteen to twenty years after their completion, the construction of those schools is to me a source of considerable satisfaction.

One aspect of my ministry as Archbishop of Baltimore which brought me special satisfaction was the establishment of new parishes. There were fourteen in all—the first in 1963, the second full year of my ministry here, and the last in 1974, the year of my retirement. I have decided to treat the subject here because in 1968—my banner year for foundation of parishes—five were established and three of these were to prove of particular significance as successful post-conciliar parishes in the sense that they were meant to meet the special conditions that marked that difficult period.

The first of the fourteen was the parish of the Holy Spirit, located in Joppa, a small town near the Bush River about fifteen miles northeast of Baltimore, and within the boundary of the parish of St. Stephen, Bradshaw, whose pastor was Father Austin Healy. An aggressive real estate operator seemed to have gained control of most, if not all, of the valuable land in and around Joppa and had succeeded in bringing about an early rapid growth in population. Observing what was happening, Father Healy purchased a choice plot of ground in the heart of the new development. In the early part of 1963 he informed me that in his judgment the number of Catholic families was large enough to call for the establishment of a new parish. Father Charles Dausch was appointed the first pastor. He found a newly built home adjacent to the rear of that property that could serve as a rectory. Setting aside the front part of the property for the erection of a parish church, in the rear he immediately began construction of a multipurpose red brick structure which would provide a temporary church and also serve as a hall for large meetings, space for schoolrooms for religious instruction, parish offices, storage, and other necessary facilities.

The early growth of the parish appeared promising. Soon however the developer seemed "to run out of steam." From that point on the growth of the town was slow, sometimes hardly perceptible. Much the same thing happened to the parish. Now after nearly twenty years the parish still does not possess its much-desired church, although a respectable sum has been set aside toward its construction, if inflation and rising building costs are ever halted. Recently I had the occasion to go there to administer the Sacrament of Confirmation. There is every evidence that Father Dausch is as devoted to his work and to his parishioners as ever, and that he is universally loved. Externally however the parish appears much as it did at the time the multipurpose building was completed.

Similar in origin but very different in early history was the second parish I established in 1964—that of St. Philip Neri in Linthicum Heights, Anne Arundel County. Here, too, the origin was due to the foresight and care of the pastor of the mother parish. Father Arthur Slade, of Holy Trinity Parish in Glen Burnie. Linthicum Heights may be said to have been in a class by itself; it seems to have attracted to itself much, if not all, of the affluence of the northern part of the county. The first pastor was Father Joseph Healy, Austin Healy's older brother, who after graduating from college had a remarkably successful business career before he decided, ten years later, to follow his younger brother into the priesthood. Besides a truly pastoral spirit, he brought from his business experience two valuable qualities: the ability to inspire confidence in those with whom he worked and to win their wholehearted cooperation. Accurately assessing the financial resources on which he could count, he persuaded his people to undertake with him the erection of an entire parish plant: church, school, and rectory. He had already persuaded the Sisters of Notre Dame de Namur to staff the school. Since they would continue to reside in the large convent of Holy Trinity, there was fortunately no need to build a convent. Within a surprisingly short time the parish plant had been erected and the entire debt was paid off before the end of ten years. Within a few years, however, the Sisters of Notre Dame de Namur, because of the decrease of their number, were withdrawn from the school. They were replaced by Catholic lay teachers and principal. Thus St. Philip Neri stands out as the last parish to build a parochial school, the first parish to have an entire lay staff of teachers, and the first to demonstrate what was to be the increased cost of Catholic education in the post-conciliar Church.

Two other parishes established during those early years deserve special mention. St. Ann's in Hagerstown (1966), built with the help of a generous gift of Thomas Pangborn, benefactor of the archdiocese in many ways, was, I believe, aesthetically our most impressive parish church erected during modern times. Our Lady of Hope parish (1967), formed by combining two smaller parishes, was the first to erect a parish church designed specifically with the liturgical changes of Vatican II in mind. As construction was going forward, many questions about the style of architecture were raised. Once it was completed, there was soon very vocal criticism of the church's appearance. Such criticism was almost entirely muted when the Liturgical Arts Guild of the prestigious American Institute of Architects conferred its highest award on Our Lady of Hope Church, Baltimore, Mr. William Gaudreau, architect.

Three of the five parishes established in 1968 call for a somewhat more detailed consideration because of their special significance: St. Mark's in Fallston, Nativity of Our Lord Jesus Christ in Timonium, and Annunciation in Baltimore County just north of the city boundary in the McCormack Road area. St. Mark's in Fallston had been established back in 1888 as a small country mission to serve the Catholic farming families of that area. Then, in the late 1960s, it began to develop very rapidly, with the increased movement of people from the city of Baltimore into the suburbs and county. Father John McCall was appointed pastor and, from the beginning, under his direction the parish proved to be an outstanding success. So well did he do his job that after ten years he was transferred to St. Mark's in Catonsville, one of the largest and most complex parishes of the archdiocese, which was then beset by some serious problems.

But it is to the other two parishes that I wish to call particular attention: Annunciation and Nativity. In the early movement of Baltimoreans from the city north into the suburbs and county, most Catholic families seemed to settle in or near the already established parishes of Immaculate Conception, Towson; St. Joseph's, Texas; St. Joseph's, Fullerton; St. Michael's, Overlea; and St. John's, Long Green. Only later did the territory between these parishes and the northern part of the city become inhabited by a large number of Catholic families. In this area these two new parishes were established. Father Charles Meisel was appointed pastor of Nativity; Father August Abendschoen, that of the Annunciation. They were contemporaries and friends; both had fine records as assistants and were facing their first pastoral assignments. Since it was already evident that there would be no Sisters available for a parish school, no provision would be made for one in their plans. On the tract of land purchased by the archdiocese for Father Abendschoen's parish of the Annunciation, there was an old residence that could be renovated and used as a rectory; on that of the Nativity, there was nothing. Father Meisel took up temporary residence in Stella Maris Hospice, which was located within the boundaries of his parish, until he could find a house to serve as his rectory. Both these men brought to their tasks a fine pastoral spirit, which won them wholehearted support from the beginning.

Since the problems these two priests faced were similar, they decided to choose the same architect, Mr. Edward Rogers, with whom they were acquainted and in whom they had confidence. They began with the assumption that they needed a building which would provide, first of all, suitable space for Saturday evening and Sunday Masses and large parish meetings, a smaller chapel that would serve for reservation of the Blessed Sacrament and weekday Masses, a convenient sacristy, classroom spaces for religious instruction, parish offices, storage space, and other necessary facilities. With their needs determined, Rogers went ahead with the drawing of the plans. The two multipurpose buildings, which would form the parish plant for the foreseeable future, were brought to completion within a comparatively short period of time.

Inevitably, there was a certain similarity between the two buildings, and I suppose it can be said that neither was in the class of an architectural masterpiece. They were not, however, mere replicas of one another. Aesthetics were never a prime consideration, although never lost to sight. Each had its own individuality by reason of the lay of the ground, the material chosen for construction, requirements of neighborhood and landscape. The exterior design gave to each its own pleasing religious or ecclesiastical appearance, and I believe it can be said that both groups of parishioners were pleased with and proud of the results.

In both parishes, a religious sister of the Mission Helpers of the Sacred Heart was engaged to take charge of the religious instructions, with the title of Coordinator of the Confraternity of Christian Doctrine. Just how far the Confraternity can take the place of a parochial school, which for so long was considered the key to the success and strength of the Church in the United States, I am not prepared to say, but it seems to me that these two are already among the truly great parishes of the archdiocese and that they serve as examples of the best in post-conciliar parishes. Henceforth, no new parishes could come into existence within the archdiocese without reference to Annunciation and Nativity.

Not all the parishes for whose beginning I was responsible had the smooth sailing of Annunciation and Nativity. Three definitely had a difficult time. In all three cases, the fundamental trouble was the inability of parishioners and pastor to get along. In all these cases, however, the right pastor was eventually found, even for the parish whose key parishioners turned out to be a little obstreperous.

A special word should be said concerning the last two parishes, established in the year 1974. The Church of the Resurrection in Ellicott City had come into existence as a mission church of the mother parish, St. Paul's. Before long the mission had outgrown the mother parish. The old parochial school had to be replaced, and it was found advisable to transfer it to the rapidly developing mission, where it has flourished. The parish of the Resurrection in Ellicott City, under the capable direction of Father Brian Rafferty, may well become one of the great parishes of the archdiocese.

The very last, Our Lady of Grace, with Father Edward Lynch as pastor, seems not less promising. It was located at a little place, hardly a village, in Baltimore County called Hereford. Two days before the establishment was to be announced, a Baltimore newspaper carried a screaming front-page headline: "Crime wave sweeps Hereford!" What had happened was that in this peaceful rural setting three tough individuals had settled. For some time, they were suspects of questionable activities throughout the county, but they had been protected from prosecution by a clever lawyer. Now, both arson and threats of violence were found directly traceable to them, and under the glare of the publicity their immunity came to a sudden end. Our announcement went forward as planned by the notice reading: "Parish of Our Lady of Grace established in Parkton." Parkton is the post office that covers that area.

At the present, Our Lady of Grace is still a rather small though gradually growing parish. Father Lynch seems content with its progress and happy over its promise of future growth and development. In the end, all fourteen parishes which I established turned out to be real assets to the archdiocese.

11. The Years of Crisis, 1968-74

Traditionally, Baltimore had not been a place of acute racial tension. The city had its origin and early development as a center of commerce, banking and shipping with a population that was predominantly White. After the Civil War a great number of Blacks passed through Baltimore, which had long been known as the "Gateway to the South." Some remained here, but most passed on to the northern centers of industry where opportunities for employment were more numerous. Even in 1900, in the regular U.S. decennial census, only 14 percent of the city's population was Black. After the Great Fire of 1904, Baltimore's attention was turned more and more to the development of industry, and the number of Blacks increased with the need of labor to develop and carry it on. During World War I, however, the industries located around its port rapidly expanded, since Baltimore was the sheltered deep-water port most accessible by way of the Caribbean to the ore mines and oil fields of Central and South America, and also by railroad to the coal mines of Pennsylvania, Western Maryland, and West Virginia, as well as the great wheat fields of the Midwest. During that time the Black population of the city increased greatly, and a certain tension began to develop between Whites and Blacks, largely because suffcient decent housing for the newcomers was not available.

However, it was during and after World War II, with the further rapid expansion of the city's industries and the large in-pouring of Blacks, that the tension in Baltimore became truly acute. The condition, of course, was not peculiar to Baltimore but was common to other large cities.

In 1958 the Bishops of the country issued a statement entitled "Discrimination and the Christian Conscience." It was signed by Archbishop Keough as Chairman of the National Catholic Welfare Conference. In spite of that statement, however, conditions continued to deteriorate within the Archdiocese of Baltimore and throughout the state of Maryland. I believe I can best describe those conditions by quoting several passages of the Pastoral Letter I issued early in 1963, shortly after our country had celebrated the centennial of the publication of President Lincoln's Emancipation Proclamation (January 1, 1863). By the centennial year this city was experiencing acute racial tension. I began the letter by referring to the Bishops' statement. I went on to note that the state of Maryland lacked legislation giving Blacks equal rights with Whites and that only the previous year such an ordinance had failed to pass the Baltimore City Council. I said:

> In this, the oldest and most venerable See in the United States, it should be particularly disconcerting to all of us to know that last year an equal accommodations ordinance then before the Baltimore City Council failed to receive the support of some Catholic legislators who represented districts heavily Catholic in population. Does this mean that many of our own people have failed to recognize the serious duty of justice which flows from the basic equality of men of all races and all social conditions?
>
> Such a failure is all the more regrettable since our Christian faith imposes upon us all a special duty of both justice and charity toward all men, no matter what may be their racial and social origin. By the very terms of Christian teaching, we believe that all men are God's special creatures, made to His image and likeness. We believe that the Son of God, Jesus Christ, the God-man, came into the world to save all men; that on the Cross of Calvary He shed His Blood to redeem all of us from our iniquity—all, without any exception . . . .
>
> Within the time and space available to me in this letter, it is impossible to set forth in detail the extent and the nobility of the duty of justice and charity incumbent upon us as members of Christ's Mystical Body. Under the circumstances of today, however, it may be useful if I attempt to state briefly the minimum that is required of us as members of Christ's Church in this Archdiocese.
>
> There is, I hope, no need to say that in our churches and in our parochial life generally there must be not only no racial

segregation, but also no distinction of rank or place or treatment based upon racial difference: "... because we are members one of another ... Do not grieve the Holy Spirit of God in whom you were sealed for the day of redemption" (Ephesians 4:25, 30). "For now the justice of God has been made manifest ... through faith in Jesus Christ *upon all who believe. For there is no distinction*: as *all* have sinned and need the glory of God" (Romans 3:21-23).

In our schools, both elementary and secondary, the same general policy holds. As Catholic schools, they are meant primarily, although not exclusively, for Catholic students—for all Catholic students insofar as facilities can be made available—without racial or any other discrimination. This means that in the registration of students a common policy, approved by our Catholic School Board, must be followed in the case of all Catholic children living within the boundaries of every parish fortunate enough to have its own school. The same policy must govern all transfers from one school to another. Within the school, identical academic standards must apply to all students, and all must be treated with equal justice and charity.

In our diocesan organizations and institutions of charity, a sincere effort has been made over a period of years to eliminate discrimination and to effect true integration. Longstanding social and cultural patterns have at times made this process difficult. With the opening of the new St. Vincent's Home, we believe that the last traces of discrimination in this field will disappear.

It is some months now since all our Catholic hospitals gave formal approval and acceptance to the policies of non-discrimination I specifically proposed to them. This means that they have agreed to admit and treat applicants for medical and surgical service without distinction in their out-patient departments; to follow the same procedure in admitting patients into the hospital, and in assigning beds to them; that there shall be no discrimination practiced in handling applications for membership on medical, surgical, and nursing staffs; that advancement within each staff will be governed only by ability, training, experience, and character; that a policy of integration and non-discrimination is to be effective for all employees of the hospital ....

The duty of justice and charity applies not only to our churches, our schools, our charitable organizations and institutions, and our hospitals, but also to all of us as individuals. It must guide us in our personal relationships—within our block, our neighborhood, our community; in our social and fraternal organizations; in the business we may conduct; in the labor unions to which we may belong; at work and at play; in all the circumstances of everyday life.

Particularly lamentable, I said, was the unreasonable and automatic panic too often fanned by unscrupulous and disreputable real estate brokers and speculators, which accompanied the arrival of a Black family in an area previously occupied by White families only. The flight of the Whites from such a neighborhood not only unfairly prejudged the new neighbors, but it worked economic hardship on the departing property owners, destroyed the community, undermined church life, and hit hard at substantial investments made in schools, rectories, convents, recreational facilities, and in churches themselves. In order to forestall such panic and flight, I said, all should bear in mind what was sought by the average Black family which, having improved its economic condition, desired to find a home in a stable neighborhood. The head of such a family was seeking a place where he and his family could live in peace, freedom, and dignity; where he and his wife could raise their children in moral and physical safety; where they could give them good education and training; where the whole family could function as good citizens and useful, respected and valued neighbors. "These are the things that ought to be expected of such a family. Their neighbors ought to help them to do what should be expected of them. They should welcome them into associations dedicated to neighborhood stability and betterment. If such were to become the general attitude and policy of the community, the unscrupulous speculator would soon find his speculations unprofitable, and the disreputable broker would shortly be driven from business."

The pastoral letter received widespread publicity in the press and was warmly welcomed by responsible community leaders who were striving earnestly to have outlawed all policies and practices of discrimination in Baltimore, as the cause of tensions that continued to flourish. I believe it can be safely said that within a reasonable time the last traces of discrimination disappeared from the parishes and institutions of the archdiocese. That of course does not mean racial antipathy ceased to exist among all Catholic people of the area.

In keeping with my concern for racial justice, I decided at this time to change my residence from the new Cathedral rectory, located in a neighborhood that was then highly restricted, to the old Archbishop's House, which was in a downtown area free from any such discrimination. This change of residence offered me the additional advantage of being only one block from my office, which was the center of my whole archiepiscopal program.

One consequence of the pastoral was that in January 1966, when a bill, popularly known as the "Open Housing Bill," had been introduced in the City Council, I was invited by the young Catholic President of the Council, Thomas D'Alesandro III, to testify at the public hearing on January 13, 1966. So great was the interest in the bill that the hearing had to be transferred from the City Hall to the larger auditorium of the nearby War Memorial Building. Early in the evening of the hearing, my brother Dan received an anonymous telephone call informing him that if I were to appear to testify in favor of the bill, I would be shot. Knowing that I was determined to give my testimony, he telephoned, not to me, but to the police and to Francis Gallagher.

The latter, without mentioning the threat, accompanied me to the auditorium; we arrived and I took my place without incident. I was the first witness to be called. Hardly had I read the first sentence from my carefully prepared statement, when loud jeering broke out from one segment of the audience and continued, as if the group was determined not to permit me to proceed. I stood silent at the podium waiting for the noise to cease. Finally, the President had to call on the police to expel the noise makers. When silence was regained I proceeded with my testimony. After me came other religious leaders and the rest of the witnesses. The next day the newspapers featured the "jeering of the Cardinal" in their accounts of the hearing. Again, so strong was the opposition, that the bill failed to pass the Council. Shortly thereafter, however, the United States Congress enacted legislation forbidding discrimination in all public places throughout the country.

Racial tensions, needless to say, continued to exist and were to flourish in many places other than Baltimore. It all came to a head with the senseless murder of Dr. Martin Luther King, the most eminent and eloquent Black leader of that time, April 4, 1968. The following week, which happened to be Holy Week, the full fury of Black people broke out throughout the land wherever there was a large concentration of Black population. Rioting, looting, arson, and all forms of property damage ensued, aimed chiefly against places of business conducted by Whites. Countless millions worth of damage was done. When finally the anger and violence had spent themselves it was found that most of the damage had occurred within or nearby areas inhabited by Blacks. When it was all over it was evident that the Blacks themselves were the chief victims.

One beneficial result of this national tragic episode was that responsible Black and White leaders everywhere came to the conclusion that it was necessary for them to form joint plans of action to remove, as fas as was possible, the roots of the evil of such bitter racial antipathy. For the most part it can be said that such efforts have been to some degree successful. In Baltimore, however, one further episode seemed to indicate how far such efforts have failed to achieve full success. In February 1978, the Baltimore area experienced the heaviest snowstorm within its recorded history. So deep lay the snow in the streets of the city that all vehicular traffic became practically impossible for two days. Under the cover of such unprecedented conditions rioting broke out in the vicinity of two of the most densely populated Black neighborhoods. As in 1968 there was extensive arson, looting, various forms of property damage. Before police forces and properly equipped and manned fire trucks could get through to the scene, it was estimated that $30 million in damage had taken place. Where police and fire equipment had failed, persons equipped with television cameras had succeeded. The pictures that were taken showed a number of adults were involved, but the great number consisted of Black youths, some of them hardly more than children. Many of the adults turned out to be men with criminal records or with shady reputations.

The early reaction of the community was one of great disappointment and pessimism. Black and White communities however were equally prompt in denouncing the spree of destruction occasioned by such an unheard-of condition of weather. The damage was soon repaired, and the spirit of helpful cooperation resumed its course.

The response of both priests and people to the founding of the six archdiocesan high schools had been most encouraging. Encouraging, too, was the spirit of the religious communities which had accepted responsibility for staffing and directing these institutions. Each of the schools had been planned to accommodate about 1,000 students. That number seemed desirable in order that they be able to operate economically with a sufficiently sound and varied program to assure both their excellence and their accreditation. To go much beyond that number, it was thought, would be to invite the development of problems that we wished to avoid.

By 1968, Archbishop Curley High, under the Conventual Franciscan Fathers and Brothers, could boast a student body of 1,080. By 1970, Cardinal Gibbons High, first under the leadership of Brother Matthew Betz and later Brother William Abel of the Society of Mary, reached a total of 1,040 students. Archbishop Keough High School, under the School Sisters of Notre Dame, with Sister Mary Virginia as principal, passed the 1,000 mark in 1971, Both John Carroll in Bel Air and Bishop Walsh in Cumberland had a somewhat slower growth, but each of them, within a few short years, was reputed to be the best high school, public or private, in its respective area; and in the seventies John Carroll's student enrollment was to come close to the 1,000 mark. Martin Spalding in north Anne Arundel County was the last of the six to be brought into operation, but in 1971, with a teaching staff which included seventeen Sisters of Notre Dame de Namur and a student body of 670, it seemed to be coming along satisfactorily and to give good promise for the future. Meanwhile, however, the subsidies required of the archdiocese to maintain and operate these institutions had reached alarming proportions.

Any understanding of the financial problem arising from our archdiocesan high schools should begin with an understanding of the policy established by Archbishop Keough, with Monsignor James Donohue as Superintendent of Schools. As Monsignor William Newman expressed it in a memorandum submitted to me when he had become Superintendent of Education (1968), Keough's policy was "to give education of a high quality to Catholic young men and women at reasonable tuition rates (1961-1965: $150.00)." The policy was indeed a highly idealistic and praiseworthy one; but, needless to say, even at that time (1961) it fell far short of the cost-per-student of high school education. At the end of the five-year policy, tuition rates were raised to $300 yearly for the period 1965-70. Even that fell short of basic costs, but I and the advisors on whom I depended felt it would be unwise, and in fact self-defeating, at that time to increase the rate further.

In 1967, when the subsidies for the high schools and the inner-city parishes for the first time went beyond the sum of $1 million, I decided I needed expert advice and guidance and I appointed an Archdiocesan Finance Committee. On this I asked to serve: Henry J. Knott, generally acknowledged as the leading Catholic financial figure in Baltimore; William McGuirk, then Chairman of the Board of Mercantile-Safe Deposit & Trust Company; J. Early Hardesty, retired treasurer of Black & Decker Company; William Phelan, Vice President of United States Fidelity & Guaranty Company; Francis X. Gallagher, archdiocesan attorney; and Monsignor Porter White, Chancellor. Later, at the suggestion of the committee members I added Monsignor Thomas Mardaga, known to all as the successful Director of the Catholic Charities Annual Appeal, and Monsignor Joseph M. Nelligan, long-time Chancellor of the Archdiocese under Archbishop Curley. The committee elected Monsignor Mardaga as its Chairman on December 6, 1967. By a remarkable coincidence, the Holy See announced his appointment as Auxiliary Bishop of Baltimore on December 9, 1967. The following year, subsidies were reduced to a point where they probably could have been covered from the earnings of the unrestricted reserves and the annual ordinary revenues of the archdiocese, if they had remained at that level. At the end of one year, however, Bishop Mardaga was appointed to the Diocese of Wilmington. Monsignor Nelligan was elected Chairman of the Finance Committee. Whether the committee was unable to maintain the hard line taken under the leadership of Bishop Mardaga, or whether the needs had become so urgent that they could not be ignored, the subsidies began to increase once more to a point where I again became greatly concerned over the situation.

This concern seems to be reflected in a confidential memorandum on the archdiocesan financial picture from Francis X. Gallagher to me, October 13, 1969, from which I quote:

> An examination of the Consolidated Fund of the Roman Catholic Archbishop of Baltimore indicates that in the interval between September 30, 1968, and October 2, 1969, there has been an increase in the market value of securities held in the amount of $1,301,947. This increase has occurred despite a drop of 6.8 in the stock market. Had this drop not occurred, the value of the increase in the thirteen months would have been $1,569,800.
>
> The low point in the value of the Consolidated Fund was 1966, when the assets had a market value of $8,121,037. In the three year interval, the market value of the Consolidated Fund has increased $3,559,588. (That is, to $11,680,625).
>
> In the intervening three years, withdrawals amounted to $993,000. During that same period of time, the additions from income alone amounted to aproximately $720,000. Additions from other sources, bequests and sale of real property, etc., during

the same period of time from 1966, amounted to approximately $3,400,000.

During the year 1968-69, the Consolidated Fund income on unrestricted investments amounted to $386,893. Of this amount, however, $309,000 was reinvested, so that only $77,000 was actually forwarded to the Archdiocese from that particular income.

In all, therefore, during the last fiscal year total reinvestment of the income amounted to $334,000. . . .

The obvious purpose of the memorandum was to encourage me, and this it undoubtedly did, at the time. At the end of that fiscal year, however, the subsidies approved by the Finance Committee as necessary for high schools, for inner-city parishes, for the care of retired and infirm priests, and for other purposes, reached the unprecedented total of $1,636,000. If this were to continue, the unrestricted reserves would disappear before many years. The fiscal year 1971-72 was indeed an exceptional year, but, in spite of my best effort and dedicated work of the Finance Committee, large unforeseen deficits in the high school operations continued and immense subsidies were required to keep the schools in operation. Why did this take place? Why was it that these institutions which were so earnestly desired during the fifties and early sixties were so difficult to maintain during the late sixties and early seventies?

A number of reasons might be given. Here I shall mention only the more important. First, I should say that central to it all was the great change that took place within the Church itself, or perhaps it would be better to say within many people of the Church, including priests, religious and the laity. More than once this was called a "crisis of faith." In this country, this rapidly made itself felt after the tragic year of 1968, although it had begun to manifest itself some two or three years earlier. So far as Catholic education is concerned it was seen in the rapid decline in the number of teaching Sisters, priests, and Brothers. The numbers I give are taken from the *Official Catholic Directory* published by P. J. Kenedy & Sons for the years 1965 and 1980. These statistics, I believe, can be accepted as accurate. In 1965, the teaching Sisters numbered 104,436; in 1980, 41,135. Much the same thing happened in the case of teaching priests and Brothers. In 1965, teaching priests numbered 12,346; in 1980, 5,444. In the case of teaching Brothers: in 1965, 5,868; in 1980, 3,271. Since most of the vacancies had to be filled by lay teachers, and since the salaries of qualified lay teachers have to bear some relation to the salaries of public and private high school teachers of the area, the cost of Catholic high school education has been enormously affected. The rise in the cost of the teaching staff has been accompanied by the increase of costs all along the line: in teaching materials such as books and paper, in building maintenance, in transportation, etc. Again an important element affecting costs are the changes, often adversely considered by Catholic parents and by Catholic people generally, that have taken place within many Catholic high schools.

I give one example from our own archdiocese. One of our high schools, which had a student body of over a thousand by 1968, within two or three years had experienced a decline to around 650. This was an extreme case but, it was by no means exceptional. After two rather conservative principals, a young man was appointed by his community to take the position. Besides being young and attractive, he had all the necessary academic qualifications. He seemed imbued with the "progressive" ideals of modern high school education. Old ideas of discipline were out. What one of his fellow principals in a prestigious private Catholic high school called "reasonable permissiveness" was the guiding principle in his own and his faculty's dealing with students. But many parents also did not like what they saw. Why should they support what they did not approve and did not like? So came the rapid decline from about 1,000 to 650. It was the financial squeeze, no doubt, that brought about his resignation. A more traditional-minded principal replaced him. But in the case of high schools and other institutions, as in the case of individuals, a reputation once lost is lost, and slow to be regained. Nor is what happened in parochial grade schools, traditionally the main feeder of Catholic high schools, totally unrelated to what happened in Catholic high schools. In 1965 the number of students in parochial schools in the United States was 4,446,881; those in 1980, 2,251,000—barely one-half.

The second major source of financial difficulty was the increasing subsidies required to keep the impoverished inner-city parishes and their schools in operation. To provide help and guidance for these parishes I had appointed an Urban Commission, with the very able and zealous Father Henry Offer, a member of the Community of Josephite Fathers and pastor of one of our largest Black parishes, as Director. The members of the commission were a group of dedicated priests and lay persons, both Black and White, who were convinced, as were Father Offer and I, that the role of the parishes and schools in the inner-city is essential to the mission of the Church of Baltimore. When in 1968 Bishop Gossman succeeded Bishop Mardaga as an Auxiliary Bishop of

Baltimore, I asked him if he would undertake the supervision of the impoverished parishes of the inner-city and of the Urban Commission. He became our first Urban Vicar, although that title was not used widely until the appointment of his successor, Bishop Stafford. Bishop Gossman took residence in the rectory of St. Peter's parish in the heart of the inner-city. He threw himself wholeheartedly into the work, and steadfastly stuck to it to the end. One of his early undertakings was to plan, with the help of the Urban Commission, the clustering of schools in the hope of bringing about greater economy in the use of personnel. It must be said, however, that the harder he worked, the deeper became his conviction of the great needs of the inner-city churches and schools.

In the late spring of 1972, after he had received word of the subsidy of the Urban Commission for the fiscal year 1972-73, he wrote to Monsignor Nelligan, Chairman of the Finance Committee, asking for a definite statement of the amount of money the committee would allot to the commission for the years 1974, 1975, and 1976. To this Monsignor Nelligan replied in a letter dated July 24, 1972. I give the letter here in part, because it presents the clearest and most succinct statement of the financial problem of the archdiocese that I can offer. The letter reads:

Dear Bishop Gossman,

I write in further reference to your request that there be provided a projection of the amount of Archdiocesan funds which will be definitely committed for fiscal '74, '75 and '76 to assist in supporting inner city parishes and institutions.

The other members of the Executive Committee of the Finance Committee and myself have given very careful thought to the matter which you have proposed. All are agreed that, under existing circumstances, it is well-nigh impossible to give a realistic estimate for 1975 and 1976 of the amount of money which could be allotted to the Urban Commission in terms of a firm commitment. To a lesser degree this applies also to fiscal 1974. The reasons for this are numerous but basically they stem from the uncertainties existing in the present state of Archdiocesan Finances.

First of all there is the proposal, supported by both the Committee of Secretaries and the Finance Committee and approved by His Eminence, the Cardinal, that the Archdiocesan operating deficit be reduced by $600,000 in each of the three fiscal years, namely 1973, 1974 and 1975. With generous cooperation of all concerned, and I may say particularly of the Urban Commission, this objective has been accomplished for the current accounting period.

If the plan is to succeed in the next fiscal year (F.Y. 1974) further reductions will have to be made in subsidies unless it is found possible to generate additional income. While serious studies are being made of such possibilities they are by no means finalized. This is one of the uncertainties.

Another grey area is the question of continuing large grants of money to Martin Spalding and Bishop Walsh High Schools. With regard to the latter, all recognize that the situation is unique because of the economically depressed area in which the School is located. Some financial assistance will have to be provided for this institution. Some months ago, however, we were given assurance by the School administration and a committee of laymen that they had plans to increase income and secure greater community involvement and support—plans which were quite convincing. But when their fiscal '73 budget was received the Department of Education was shocked. Increased costs completely offset additional revenue. Monsignor Newman returned the request and succeeded in obtaining a reduction of $20,000.

Martin Spalding High School is operating under a tentative arrangement which calls for a reevaluation to determine what prospects there are for a greatly increased enrollment. Should indications prove favorable this will involve an additional two year period of subsidy support. If, on the other hand, there appears to be no hope of improvement in pupil census it is proposed that steps be taken to dispose of the facility.

To make a prudent judgment for fiscal '75 and '76 we shall need more definite information from the Department of Education regarding these two High Schools. . . .

If this presentation falls short of your expectations, be assured that the circumstance is due to no lack of willingness or of a desire to be helpful and cooperative in the work of the Urban Commission. Our position is dictated solely by a sense of responsibility to strive for fiscal stability for the Archdiocese as a complete entity.

With all good wishes, I am

Sincerely,
Joseph M. Nelligan

Nothing it seems to me could bring out more clearly the gravity of the financial problems that faced the archdiocese just eight months before the date of my anticipated retirement, which would be March 18, 1973. It was then with a heavy heart that I foresaw passing on to my successor such a difficult burden.

Here, however, let me say that one aspect of the financial problem met with a happier solution than did the problem of the subsidies required by the high schools and the urban churches and schools, that is, those required to meet the pensions of retired and disabled priests.

The Second Vatican Council, in speaking of the care that Bishops should provide for the priests of their dioceses, urges that each priest when he reaches his seventy-fifth year should voluntarily submit his resignation to his Bishop, who is free to accept it, if he judges that there are sufficient reasons to do so, or to reject it if he judges that the individual can render further valuable work to the diocese or the parish. In 1965, the last year of the Council, only three names were carried on the list of retired pastors of the Archdiocese of Baltimore, although others were being cared for out of the unrestricted reserves of the archdiocese. Now, however, it became necessary to establish some definite policy. We decided we would set seventy-five years as the age of obligatory retirement, seventy that of optional retirement, and sixty-five for special cases in which the advisability of retirement seemed clearly evident. By 1970, in addition to the three I have already mentioned, thirty-seven had joined the list of retired priests. In view of the diminishing unrestricted reserves of the archdiocese, this became a not inconsiderable item on the list of subsidies. What would happen should these reserves diminish to the vanishing point, as seemed not unlikely at the rate subsidies were being demanded, both for the needs of the inner-city and for the operation of the high schools? The Finance Committee at that point came up with what seemed like a happy solution of the problem. They were aware that at the time when I was made a Cardinal I had received gifts of about $500,000. These I had never considered personal, but had invested them in the name of the archdiocese, though in such a way that they remained under my personal control as long as I was Archbishop. The Finance Committee now suggested that I use this money to create the nucleus of a Priests' Retirement Trust Fund. To this, they suggested there be added a bequest of an estate of $1,200,000 that came to the archdiocese at that time, plus other uncommitted resources amounting to $3,100,000, all of which would be sufficient to establish a Priests' Retirement Trust Fund, whose earnings would take care of the retirement of priests. I authorized this plan on July 1, 1972, and the following November I wrote to the priests of the archdiocese informing them that a Priests' Retirement Trust Fund had been established in the amount of $4,800,000. Whether in these days of inflation and financial uncertainty this offers a permanent solution to the financial problem arising from the retirement of priests, I cannot say. It does seem to me to have been a step in the right direction. This, however, did not touch the larger problem of high school and inner-city subsidies which I would have to pass on to my successor.

The darkest aspects of the years following upon 1968 were caused not by the racial tensions and conflicts, nor by the growing financial burdens of the archdiocese, nor by the grave social problems that marked that period, but by the phenomenon that came to be called "crisis of the faith." The main roots of that crisis went back far beyond the beginning of this century, as I shall mention later. But the crisis came to the surface in the lives of many Catholic people shortly after the appearance of the Statement of Dissent issued by the ten theologians of The Catholic University of America, accompanied by almost a hundred signatures of other American "theologians." Let us begin, therefore, by considering the appearance of that document.

Pope Paul VI signed his encyclical letter *Humanae Vitae* on the Feast of St. James, July 25, 1968. The following Monday morning, July 29, the Vatican released to the press the original Latin text, and English, Italian, German, French, Spanish, and Portuguese translations, together with a general statement on the nature and the contents of the encyclical. Within the shortest time possible, the news concerning the publication of the Pope's letter and its general character was flashed around the world by the Associated Press and other such international news services with bureaus in Rome. Shortly thereafter, the Associated Press began to transmit to the United States the English translation of the more than five-thousand-word letter. How long it took to transmit the complete document I have no way of telling, but late that afternoon the text of the encyclical was still rolling from the presses of the *Washington Post*, in preparation for its publication the following morning, July 30.

According to a subsequent account of events given by the *Post*, after receiving the first news of the publication of the encyclical, the Rev. Charles E. Curran, instructor in moral theology of The Catholic University of America, flew back to Washington from the West where he had been staying. Late that afternoon, he and nine other professors of theology of The Catholic University met, by evident prearrangement, in Caldwell Hall to receive, again by prearrangement with the *Washington Post*, the encyclical, part by part, as it came from the press. The story further indicated that by nine o'clock that night, they had received the whole encyclical, had read it, had analyzed it, criticized it, and had composed their six-hundred-word "Statement of Dissent." Then they began that long series of telephone calls to "theologians" throughout the East, which went on, according to the *Post*, until 3:30 A.M., seeking authorization to attach their names as endorsers ("signers" was the term used) of the statement, although those to whom they had telephoned could not have had an opportunity to see either the encyclical or their statement. Meanwhile, they had arranged through one of the television stations to have the statement broadcast that night.

The first thing that we have to note about the whole performance is this: so far as I have been able to discern, never in the recorded history of the Church, has a solemn proclamation of a Pope been received by any group of Catholic people with so much disrespect and contempt. What made this statement all the more noteworthy is the fact that these ten theologians were all members of a pontifical university—one owing a special loyalty to the Supreme Pontiff. The very rapidity with which the action was taken seemed to me to mark it as an act of emotional rebellion rather than a true, carefully considered act of intellectual dissent. As for the statement itself, it began with a seemingly pious acknowledgment that the encyclical contained many statements of positive value concerning marriage and the family. Then immediately it went into its expression of dissent:

> We take exception to the ecclesiology implied and the methodology used by Paul VI . . . they are incompatible with the . . . Second Vatican Council. The encyclical assumes that the Church is identical with the hierarchical office . . . the encyclical betrays a narrow positivistic notion of papal authority . . . . We take exception to some of the specific ethical conclusions contained in the encyclical. They are based on an inadequate concept of natural law. The multiple forms of natural law theory are ignored, and the fact that competent philosophers come to different conclusions on this very question is disregarded. . . .

Concerning this document, I shall make only the following remarks:

1. To the statement, "We take exception to the ecclesiology im-

plied: the encyclical assumes that the Church is identical with the hierarchical office," I would reply that, to speak exactly, the encyclical itself makes no assumptions, but expresses the assumption of its author, the Pope, who, with the Bishops, is author also of the Constitution on the Church, where in Article 2 it is stated explicitly that the Church is the People of God, the whole people, from the Pope to the humblest member of the faithful. To say that the Pope in the encyclical assumes that the Church is identical with the hierarchical office is far-fetched indeed.

2. To the statement that some of the ethical conclusions of the encyclical "are based on an inadequate concept of natural law... the multiple forms of natural law theory are ignored," etc., I would say that the ethical conclusions contained in the encyclical are based not on modern theories of natural law, but on "natural law enriched by Christian Revelation," i.e., natural law as found in St. Paul's Letter to the Romans 2:12-17, and in the constant teaching of the Church, found in the ancient Fathers of the Church, the great medieval theologians, the modern Popes (Pius XI, Pius XII, John XXIII), and the Second Vatican Council. Their own conclusion, contradicting the ethical conclusion of the Pope, that married couples may, and on some occasions must, use artificial contraception is expressed in the very words of the Lambeth Conference of 1930, which was the first Protestant group to break with the constant Christian teachings since the time of St. Paul.

The ten dissenting theologians arranged a press conference for the afternoon of Tuesday, July 30, at the Mayflower Hotel in Washington. Father John Corrigan, a Washington priest who held a teaching position at The Catholic University, acted as chairman. Father Charles Curran was the main speaker, presenting the Statement of Dissent and the names of some seventy-two "signing" theologians. Kenneth Dole, the reporter who covered the press conference for the *Washington Post*, evidently had some questions about the gathering of the names of so many theologians in so short a time, at an hour when even in the case of the *Post* the encyclical was being prepared for distribution in the issue of the following morning, before those theologians had an opportunity even to see the encyclical. In his article published the next day, Dole said that many of them had been reached by telephone. They gave statements supporting the Statement of Dissent. He quoted three as being typical: those of Father Christopher Mooney of Fordham University in New York, of Father Francis Keating of St. Peter's College in Jersey City, and Father Frank Coreen of Canisius College in Buffalo.

Particularly worthy of comment is that of Father Mooney: "The ideal is to take time to study, but we feel an obligation at the present time. . . . We acted out of loyalty to the Church in helping Church members to decide how to handle problems raised by the encyclical." Here indeed was a totally new concept in Catholic ecclesiology: Catholic theologians, priests, and people acting against and in contradiction to the supreme teaching authority of that Church, one of whose main notes is "unity."

The news conference, with the presentation of the Statement of Dissent and the seventy-two signers, received ample coverage on television and radio that evening and in the press the following day.

What made the Statement of Dissent particularly disturbing to me was the fact that among the "signers" were five professors of St. Mary's Seminary in Baltimore. As Archbishop of Baltimore and as the Chancellor of the seminary, to which the status of a pontifical university had been granted by the Holy See as far back as Archbishop Ambrose Maréchal, the third Archbishop of Baltimore (1817-28), I had a very definite responsibility for the teaching of the Catholic religion throughout the archdiocese, but particularly in the seminary. My calendar for 1968 indicates that on the day the Statement of Dissent with the names of its many "signers" was published, I telephoned to Father John Dede, rector of the seminary and President of the seminary and university, and that I had a meeting with him the following morning in my office to discuss the seriousness of the problem at the seminary. Since the five professors in question were on vacation, he promised to have them get in touch with me as soon as possible. When at the end of the week I had not heard from them, I telephoned to Father Paul Purta, S.S., Provincial Superior of all Sulpician Fathers in this country, on the afternoon of August 6 and met with him and Bishops T. Austin Murphy and F. Joseph Gossman on the morning of August 7. Shortly thereafter, I received a letter signed by all five seminary professors in which they undertook to defend their action of authorizing the use of their names as signers of the Statement of Dissent. Meanwhile, before I could get the seminary problem settled, as we shall see a little later, I suddenly found myself confronted by an even more urgent problem within the Archdiocese of Baltimore, which required my immediate full-time attention. It was therefore only on August 9 that I was able to write to Father Dede informing him that I had heard from the five professors, and that their letter and the explanation of their action were not satisfactory.

I set forth four questions which required from each of them a positive answer if they were to continue to occupy their teaching positions in the Archdiocese of Baltimore:

1. Do you accept the teaching of the Catholic Church that the Pope is the supreme teaching authority in the Roman Catholic Church as defined in the First Vatican Council?

2. Do you promise that you will neither speak nor preach contrary to the teaching contained in the encyclical *Humanae Vitae?*

3. Do you promise that in administering the Sacrament of Penance you will be guided by the teaching of the encyclical *Humanae Vitae?*

4. Do you promise that in teaching in the Seminary you will present the teaching of *Humanae Vitae* as the sole authentic doctrine of the Church on the regulation of birth and family, and on the use of contraception?

These four questions had been decided upon in a meeting between myself and my two Auxiliary Bishops, who were also my Vicars General. The implication of my letter was clear. If they, the five professors, could not answer all four questions affirmatively, the faculties of the archdiocese would be withdrawn from them and they would lose all right and privilege of teaching within the archdiocese.

Meanwhile, as I have noted, something more distressful had happened within the archdiocese, causing a delay in getting the seminary problem settled. On Monday morning, August 5, I was startled to read in the *Baltimore Sun* that seventy-two priests of the Baltimore area had signed the Statement of Dissent: two additional Sulpicians, fifteen Jesuit Fathers, and fifty-five priests of the archdiocese. So quietly had this gathering of names taken place that neither I, nor my two Auxiliaries, nor the Chancellor had received the slightest indication that this was taking place. How it actually did take place became definitely known to me only in April of the following year when I received a copy of the testimony given by Father John Thirlkel, S.S., Dean of the Seminary's School of Theology, before the Board of Inquiry of the faculty of The Catholic University.

No matter what its origin, it became evident that, besides the seminary problem, I was now faced with a serious and even more urgent problem involving fifty-five of our own archdiocesan priests who were placed in our parishes and whose status had to be settled promptly if priestly ministry in the archdiocese were to be carried on without serious interruption. In consultation with my Vicars, I decided that I would issue no public statements and would hold no meetings with groups of signers of dissent, but would deal with each of our priests individually, using the first three of the four questions I have already given when treating the seminary problem. Having made this decision, I telephoned Father Hugh J. Kennedy, S.J., the ever-cooperative Socius of the Maryland Province of the Jesuit Fathers, explaining to him the way I had decided to deal with our own priests and asking him to conduct similar interviews with the fifteen Jesuit priests whose names had appeared in the *Sun* article of that day. This Father Kennedy promised to do, assuring me that he was grateful for being allowed to settle their problem within their own Society. The problem of the two additional Sulpician Fathers would be dealt with in the handling of the overall problem of the seminary.

Meanwhile, shortly after breakfast on Monday, August 5, I began to receive telephone calls from some priests whose names had been published that morning, assuring me that they had not authorized the publication of their names; they had simply given permission for the use of their names in what they understood was to be a private communication to me informing me how a number of the priests of the archdiocese regarded the encyclical *Humanae Vitae*. In any event, it now appeared that my problem was not nearly as extensive as the original newspaper article had led me to believe.

As soon as possible, I set about the task of conducting individual interviews with our own priests. This proved to be a time-consuming procedure involving as it now did from forty to forty-five individuals. However, I must say that I ran into no serious difficulties. Many expressed their gratitude that I had decided to deal with the problem this way rather than with public statements and meetings with groups subject to newspaper reports. Everywhere I seemed to meet with a spirit of good will and cooperation.

While I was in the midst of this work, a group of American Cardinals decided to go to Rome to assure the Pope of their own loyal support and that of the U.S. Church, in spite of the notoriety that had attended the Statement of Dissent. They invited me and I would have liked to go to show my own solidarity with them, but it seemed to me that my own problem was too pressing to permit me to leave the archdiocese at that time. Fearing that my absence would be misunderstood, I wrote to Cardinal Cicognani, who was still Secretary of State, explaining my own problem and the way I was trying to solve it. To this, the Cardinal replied under the date of September 7. Since the

letter is not marked secret or confidential, and since the events referred to are so far past and the Cardinal himself is long dead, I give
the full text of his letter:

Your Eminence,

    I was very glad to receive your letter of August 9, in which
Your Eminence explained why you were unable to come to Rome
with the other American Cardinals. Your action was most wise, and
I think your way of dealing with the situation is that most suited to
present circumstances. I hope your efforts were fully successful.

    I brought Your Eminence's letter to the notice of the Holy
Father, and I can assure you that the sentiments you expressed
were truly appreciated.

    Naturally your visit to Bogotá gave you a happy occasion to see
the Holy Father and to exchange a few words with him.

    Let us hope that by the timely and wise directives of the United
States Episcopacy, a speedy advance may be made to the solution
of the present problems so that America may carry on her great
tradition of devotion and loyalty to the Church and to the Church's
visible head.

    Looking forward to see Your Eminence in the near future, and
renewing the assurance of my high esteem and regard, I remain

Devotedly yours in Christ,
A. G. Cicognani

    The visit to Bogotá to which the Cardinal refers was on the occa-
sion of the International Eucharistic Congress held August 18 to August
25, 1968. Since the International Eucharistic Congress at Munich, in
1960, I had been a member of the Commission for the Promotion of
International Eucharistic Congresses, and after that at Bombay in
1964 had been named one of the Vice Presidents of the commission. In
that capacity I had promised to be present at the 1968 Congress in
Bogotá, Columbia. On August 17, I therefore left for Bogotá via Miami.
I attended the opening Liturgy the following day, was on hand with the
other members of the commission to greet Pope Paul VI on his arrival
about the middle of the week, and stayed for the solemn closing
Liturgy on August 25. By the time of my return to Baltimore, the
month of August was almost ended. Still, I was very mindful that the
seminary problem had still to be settled finally.

On my return from Bogotá, I found awaiting me a letter signed by all five of the seminary professors assuring me that they had no difficulty accepting all four conditions that I had laid down in my letter of August 9 to Father Dede. They, however, wished to add one condition of their own: namely, that if in teaching they expressed an opinion contrary to *Humanae Vitae*, they would make it clear that it was their own private opinion and not the official doctrine of the Church. As soon as possible, I telephoned the rector, advising him that the condition expressed by the professors was not acceptable to me and that the four points I had set forth in my letter of August 9 would have to stand without further condition. He thereupon asked me to arrange to meet with the five professors and make clear to them personally my decision on the matter. This I promised to do. Meanwhile, I had every reason to believe that the rector told them that I would not and could not accept their fifth condition, and I felt confident that there would be no difficulty in their acceptance of this refusal. However, Bishop Gossman's episcopal consecration was planned for Wednesday, September 11; he would be absent some days before that, making his preparatory retreat, and had planned to be out of town several days thereafter. Owing to that and some other unavoidable complications, it was not possible for me to arrange our meeting with the seminary professors until the morning of Wednesday, September 25.

That meeting of September 25, in my judgment at the time, was a successful one. Supported by Bishops Murphy and Gossman, I had little difficulty in getting the now eight professors to recognize that, as Archbishop of Baltimore, I could not permit any doctrine contrary to the encyclical *Humanae Vitae* to be taught in the seminary or anywhere else in the archdiocese. Father John Cronin raised the question: What were the professors to do if a student made an inquiry about the Statement of Dissent? I freely admitted that he could not ignore either the existence or the content of the Statement of Dissent. But the doctrine of the encyclical was the only doctrine on the regulation of birth and contraception that I could permit to be taught within the archdiocese. The meeting was a long one and there was much lively discussion, but at the end I was convinced that with the backing of the two Bishops, I had made my points.

After that meeting, I felt certain that I had settled my problem arising from the Statement of Dissent in both the seminary and the archdiocese as well as could be under the circumstances. How mistaken I was in regard to the seminary was to become clear to me only the following spring. Meanwhile I must say that I have never heard that there was voiced in the seminary any criticism of the encyclical or that any doctrine contrary to that of the encyclical was ever taught in the seminary. It is my fervent hope that, under its present leadership, the seminary will regain the position that it once held from the beginning down to the 1968 episode.

Although the appearance of the crisis of faith was occasioned by the Statement of Dissent, issued so speedily and so offensively after the publication of *Humanae Vitae*, yet the roots of the crisis go far back in history, far beyond the beginning of this century. It had its deeper cause in the supposed conflict between science and religion that so many people of the modern world take for granted, in the not uncommon view that all the phenomena of the world can be explained only by science and reason, in the excessive attachment to material wealth and to the conveniences, the comforts, the pleasures that wealth can buy. Here, however, I am concerned not so much with the origins of the crisis as with some of the harmful consequences that soon began to appear.

To me the most painful consequence was the experience, unprecedented, I believe, in the whole history of the Church, of seeing or learning of so many priests leaving their priestly life and ministry. When one considers the pains taken to make sure the candidate for the priesthood understands the permanent and serious nature of the obligation he assumes with his reception of the Order of Priesthood and the reluctance of the Church to dispense from that obligation, one can only conclude that this phenomenon, which became relatively common in the decade 1968-78, had its origin in a real crisis of faith in many of the individuals involved. Although all of us must have become aware of the phenomenon, yet it is one whose size it is virtually impossible to measure with accuracy.

In contrast, a related phenomenon of equal importance is subject to almost exact measurement—that of the decline of the number of priestly vocations as measured by the decline in the number of candidates for the priesthood in the seminary. In order to judge the size and rapidity of the decline, it will be helpful to present and compare the figures submitted by their respective Bishops for the major diocesan seminaries in this country. The figures given in the following chart are taken from the statistics presented in the 1968 and 1978 editions of the *Official Catholic Directory.*

Archdiocese	Seminary	Student Body 1968	1978
Baltimore	St. Mary's, Roland Park	294	176
Boston	St. John's, Brighton	317	142
New York	St. Joseph's, Dunwoodie°	195 (179)	72 (64)
Philadelphia	St. Charles, Overbrook°	474 (359)	171 (120)
Chicago	St. Mary of the Lake, Mundelein	395	122
Detroit	St. John's, Plymouth	170	85

° The first figure represents the total student body; the second, the students of the respective archdioceses.

It should be noted that St. Mary's Seminary (Paca Street), which had become the House of Philosophy, had been abandoned because of the unsafe conditions of the ancient building, and had been demolished. It had formerly been the most popular of all the houses of the seminary.

Another phenomenon of great importance which can hardly be explained adequately without taking into consideration a crisis of faith is the rapid decline in the Catholic birth rate in this country as measured by the number of infant Catholic baptisms. Again, the extent of this phenomenon may be gauged by taking the figures of infant baptisms from the *Official Catholic Directory* of the years 1968 and 1978. In the chart which follows, I have placed first the Archdiocese of Washington where the Statement of Dissent originated, and the nearby Archdiocese of Baltimore, to which the effect of the Statement so rapidly spread; then I give the figures for the larger centers of Catholic population.

Archdiocese	Catholic Baptisms 1968	Catholic Population 1968	Catholic Baptisms 1978	Catholic Population 1978
Washington	11,302	384,400	6,350	397,103
Baltimore°	11,130	475,745	6,969	390,320
Boston	44,114	1,871,000	27,110	2,026,247
New York	49,400	1,870,000	31,892	1,825,062
Philadelphia	30,504	1,353,024	20,348	1,377,333
Chicago	47,174	2,342,000	34,834	2,430,180
Detroit	30,092	1,548,594	17,321	1,515,450
Los Angeles	57,052	1,602,242	60,504	1,950,000

° Sharp decline in Catholic population probably due to insistence on greater accuracy in parish annual reports.

Here it should be noted that the only archdiocese of the country to show an actual increase in the number of infant baptisms was Los Angeles; that increase was a comparatively small 3 percent; the growth of the Catholic population was about 9 percent, so that the overall picture of the effect of the Statement of Dissent and its aftermath was not notably different there from the picture of the other archdioceses of the country.

The final figure that needs to be considered here as giving evidence of what was happening to the Church in this country is the decline in the number of parochial school students. In 1968, the year when the parochial school seems to have reached the peak of its development in terms of enrollment, the number stood at 4,804,826; in 1978 that number had declined to 2,339,665; in 1981 there was a still further decline to 2,232,911. I have already commented on the increasing costs of Catholic education, both at the high school and the elementary school level. How much the decline in numbers of parochial school students has been affected by increasing costs and how much it has been the result of a crisis of faith among Catholic parents is difficult, perhaps impossible, accurately to estimate. Nevertheless, so great and rapid a decline would seem to give evidence of such a crisis.

By way of summary, I would conclude that all of the phenomena considered: the number of priests departing from priestly life and ministry, the decline in vocations to the priesthood, the decline of the number of teaching Sisters, the decline of the number of Catholic elementary school children, the decline in the number of Catholic births (baptisms)—all of these taken together present a picture that cannot be explained adequately, apart from what we have called a "crisis of faith" during the decade that followed upon 1968.

One of the most difficult and time-consuming tasks I was asked to undertake during this period was that of serving as Chairman of a committee formed to present to the Board of Trustees of The Catholic University a body of by-laws which would conform more closely to the by-laws of other universities of the United States. To understand the special difficulty of this task, one has to know something of the previous history of that university.

The Catholic University of America had its origin in a request presented to Pope Leo XIII by the U.S. Bishops, meeting in the Third Baltimore Plenary Council (1884), for permission to establish a graduate school of theology in Washington, D.C., then a part of the Archdiocese of Baltimore. In due time the Pope issued an apostolic letter authorizing the establishment of such a school for priests qualified to pursue higher studies in theology and with the letter he included a body of statutes. The school or university was to be owned by the Bishops of the United States; it was to be governed by a Board of Trustees, twenty-five in number, who would consist of all of the Archbishops Ordinary, then ten in number, and such Bishops, priests, and laymen whom they would choose. The Archbishop of Baltimore (then James Cardinal Gibbons) would be *ex officio* Chairman; the Rector of the University, who would preside over the school's operation and would be a member of the Board of Trustees, would be appointed by the Pope. The university was incorporated under the civil laws of the District of Columbia in 1887 and began to operate November 13 of that same year. The number of staff members was ten; the number of students was forty-eight. In 1895 the Schools of Canon Law and of History were established, and qualified laymen were declared eligible to become students; some years later, qualified female students, both religious and lay, were admitted.

The early growth of the university was slow. After World War II, growth became very rapid; in 1964 the number of students had increased to 4,115 full-time students and 1,935 part-time; the faculty had increased to 437 full-time professors, 128 lecturers, and 106 graduate assistants. Meanwhile, the number of Archbishops Ordinary of this country had increased to twenty-seven. To make room for these, the Board of Trustees was increased to fifty, making it somewhat cumbersome. Meanwhile, in 1900, The Catholic University of America had become a charter member of the American Association of Universities, and shortly thereafter was admitted into membership of the Middle States Association of Colleges and Secondary Schools, the regional accrediting agency.

While the university had remained small, it seems to have experienced no major internal difficulties. During the period of rapid growth, however, many such difficulties began to manifest themselves. When the Middle States Association conducted its regular quadrennial review of The Catholic University in 1966, it received so many complaints that it warned the Board of Trustees that unless its by-laws were changed to provide means of properly handling the complaints of faculty and students, accreditation of The Catholic University would be withdrawn at the time of the next review in 1970. That would mean that its academic degrees would become valueless and would inevitably result in wholesale withdrawal of both students and faculty members, to be followed by the bankruptcy and closing of the university.

To avoid such a catastrophe, the board requested Dr. Carroll Hochwalt, an eminent Catholic layman whose academic standing was above question, to accept the chairmanship of a Committee on Survey and Review, which would submit recommendations for changes in the by-laws. Dr. Hochwalt agreed, formed his committee, and set about studying the situation. Much to my surprise, in the latter part of December 1966 I received a letter from him asking me to be Chairman of the Subcommittee on Revision of the By-Laws. Other members of the subcommittee, who apparently had already agreed to serve, were: Father Lawrence McGinley, S.J., President of Fordham University; Dr. John Budd, President of the University of Connecticut; Dr. Stephen Kuttner, Professor of Yale University; Francis X. Gallagher, Attorney for the Archdiocese of Baltimore, and John Cardinal Cody, Archbishop of Chicago. With all of these, except Dr. Budd, I was acquainted. My only difficulty in relationship to such a position was that my sole connection with the higher academic field was my service over a number of years on the board of The Catholic University. However, both Francis Gallagher and Monsignor White urged me to accept and promised their wholehearted cooperation.

The subcommittee got to work as soon as possible. Our task was a rather difficult and delicate one, for we would have to produce a document that would meet the requirements of the MSA but would also meet the conditions necessary to preserve the pontifical status of The Catholic University of America. In fact, the document we would produce, after receiving approval of the Board of Trustees, would have to be approved by the Sacred Congregation for Catholic Education before it could become final.

Here I shall give simply a summary of the most pertinent by-laws and statutes which our subcommittee produced. The by-laws begin with the statement: "The membership of this corporation shall consist of the members of the Board of Trustees." The board would consist of thirty members, of whom fifteen would be clerics and fifteen laymen. All Cardinals who are Ordinaries of dioceses in the United States are *ex officio* members of the Board of Trustees unless they decline or resign from membership. Vacancies on the board are filled by the board. On behalf of the corporation, the board holds title to all property and has power to dispose of this property, in accordance with the board's charter and amendments, etc. All such action requires at least a three-fourths vote of the Board of Trustees.

In the section devoted to the Board of Trustees, provision is also made for an Academic Senate which shall share with the President responsibility for the academic governing of the university by establishing and maintaining the academic policies, without, however, infringing on the ultimate responsibilities of the Board of Trustees. The Academic Senate shall make its own rules and regulations which shall have the same force as the by-laws, if approved by the Board of Trustees. Its decisions in academic matters are final, unless overturned by the board. In view of the complaints of students which helped to bring about the ongoing change or reform, it is important that "the Academic Senate shall give due consideration to students' welfare and representation" in appropriate matters.

Of highest importance is Article 8: "The Board of Trustees shall authorize the existence and operation of the Ecclesiastical Schools of the University. These schools shall adopt statutes subject to the Board of Trustees *and in accordance with the directives of appropriate ecclesiastical authorities,* after consultation with the Academic Senate."

Next in importance after the section on the Board of Trustees is that on the President of the university, for he takes the place of the Rector of the former order of things as the highest administrative officer. The main difference between the President and the Rector is that, whereas the Rector, under the former statutes, was appointed by the Pope, now under the proposed new by-laws, the President is to be elected by the Board of Trustees. Of him, the proposed by-laws (Section VII) say: "He shall exercise and possess all customary powers and duties usually possessed and exercised by the President of a University." There is no reason here to add other details.

I should note that the bulk of the work of formulating the by-laws fell on the shoulders of Francis X. Gallagher, who, however, had the full cooperation of the other members of the subcommittee and of Father John Whalen, who at that time was the Acting-Rector of the university. As for the statutes of the ecclesiastical schools, Monsignor Porter White may be said to have been chiefly responsible for them, with the cooperation of Dr. Stephen Kuttner, Father Frederick McManus, J.C.D., Dean of the School of Canon Law, and Father Walter Schmitz, S.S., S.T.D., Dean of the School of Sacred Theology.

About the statutes I shall here make only two remarks: In Statute VII, our subcommittee originally provided that the Chancellor of the university, and particularly of the ecclesiastical schools, should be not the Archbishop of Washington, but the President of the National Conference of Bishops, because it seemed to us that the Apostolic Constitution *Deus Scientiarum Dominus* implied that the Chancellor of a Pontifical University should not be the Bishop Ordinary of the place where the university is located, but some other Bishop, and that the logical other person would be the President of the Conference of Bishops. When Statute VII came to the attention of Cardinal O'Boyle, he very properly objected that according to the Code of Canon Law he, as Archbishop of Washington, was responsible for the teaching of the Catholic faith throughout his archdiocese. If Statute VII were to stand as we had formulated it, two persons would exercise the same authority; hence the likelihood of confusion and even of conflict. Soon thereafter I received a letter from Cardinal Garrone stating that it was the mind and wish of the Holy See that the Archbishop of Washington should be *de iure* Chancellor of The Catholic University of America. Second, in proper statutes it is stated that the ecclesiastical schools are subject to the Sacred Congregation for Catholic Education. It was by this means especially that our subcommittee hoped to preserve the pontifical status of The Catholic University of America.

Our subcommittee had finished its work by the beginning of 1969. I sent two copies of our completed document to Dr. Hochwalt, one for the Chairman of the Board of Trustees, notifying him that we expected to present the proposed by-laws and statutes to the board at the spring meeting, which was to be held at Houston, Texas, in connection with the annual meeting of the National Conference of Bishops. Shortly before that meeting I was notified that the Academic Senate, through its President, had requested that consideration of the by-laws be postponed until the fall meeting of the Board of Trustees, because some members of the Senate wished to propose certain changes in our revised by-laws. This delay seemed unfortunate because of the urgent need to have the by-laws approved by both the board and the Congregation for Catholic Education before the crucial MSA review, due in the early part of 1970.

The fall meeting of the Board of Trustees was held on September 13. There was a long discussion of both the by-laws and the statutes. Various changes were discussed and voted on, some of them small, but a few of them rather important. At the end of the discussion, I was asked to take the by-laws and statutes back to our subcommittee for what was hoped would be the final revision.

This I did, and after the revision had been made, I sent one copy to the Chairman of the Board of Trustees and a second copy to Cardinal Garrone, the Prefect of the Sacred Congregation for Catholic Education, together with a letter setting forth the history of the document and informing him that I intended to be in Rome from November 23 until the early part of December for a plenary session of the Sacred Congregation for the Teaching of the Faith and a meeting of the Secretariat of

Christian Unity. In case he or the other members of his Congregation had any questions or instructions for me, I would call at his office then. Meanwhile, I had been informed that the meeting of the Board of Trustees of The Catholic University would be held December 3.

On the day after my arrival in Rome, I called on the Cardinal and was informed by him that a meeting of the Congregation was planned for Thursday, November 27, to review the proposed amended statutes and by-laws of The Catholic University of America and he wished me to be present for the meeting. I arranged with him to bring with me Francis Gallagher and Monsignor Porter White, since both of them had worked closely with me in the formulation of the document.

That afternoon I put in an international telephone call to Francis Gallagher, informing him of what had happened and asking him to bring Monsignor White with him to Rome to be present at the meeting. He promised me that they would be there. I then made arrangements for my customary and obligatory private audience with the Pope for the morning of Friday, November 28. I also requested Bishop Marcinkus to act as my interpreter at the audience, and asked if I might bring Francis Gallagher with me, so that at the end of my audience I might present Francis to the Pope and perhaps have the official photographer take a picture for Francis' family back home.

Our meeting with the Congregation for Catholic Education went off very well. Father James Naughton, S.J., for many years American Assistant to the General of the Society of Jesus, acted as our interpreter. We left the meeting with the feeling that all would be smooth sailing for the revised statutes and by-laws of The Catholic University of America.

My audience with Pope Paul VI was indeed a very pleasant one. So, too, was Francis Gallagher's meeting with him. I am certain that, since Francis Gallagher's untimely death, his picture with the Pope is one of his family's prized possessions. On the day after our audience, Porter, Francis, and I took the plane back to Baltimore to prepare for our meeting with the Board of Trustees. This took place as scheduled on Saturday, December 6. As the Chairman of the responsible sub-committee, I again had the duty of making the presentation, and again Francis Gallagher and Monsignor Porter White accompanied me to lend their help in answering questions and meeting objections. Since the members of the board had all received copies of the proposed by-laws, after a few introductory remarks, I read a carefully prepared detailed statement making five major points:

    1. In answer to the criticism that the Statement of Objectives was

not adequate, I pointed out that this Statement of Objectives was not part of the by-laws, but a part of the preliminary statement which had been drawn up by the Committee on Survey and Objectives, in consultation with the officers of the Academic Senate of the Faculty. It had been adopted by an overwhelming majority of the Board of Trustees; hence it was not within the purview of our subcommittee to make changes in it.

2. To the objection that the draft submitted did not adequately protect the orthodox teaching of the Magisterium of the Church, I responded by saying that, according to the final version of the revision, the Archbishop of Washington would always be Chancellor; he would have the same jurisdiction over matters pertaining to Catholic doctrine as he had always exercised in the archdiocese. If he, as Chancellor and as Archbishop, particularly when backed by a Board of Trustees, half of whose members were Catholic clerics, could not safeguard orthodox teaching in the university, I would not know how it could be safeguarded.

3. I stated that we were writing basic documents and not detailed legislative povisions. The by-laws, in the view of the subcommittee, is not the place for that sort of thing. Resolutions of the board, handbooks, faculty contracts, and administrative decisions must be relied on to conduct the day-to-day operation of the university. By-laws and statutes are written from the policy point of view to provide the skeletal outline of the framework of the university. These basic documents are not meant to anticipate every possible eventuality, but for the normal, the routine, and the expected. However, we provide the general mechanism for adjustment to meet the critical and unexpected.

4. I noted the urgency of final action on the part of the Trustees. We had what virtually amounted to an ultimatum from the Middle States Association of Colleges and Secondary Schools. The fact that we did not like it, or took exception to it, did not remove the power which that organization had to remove our accreditation.

5. I emphasized that two basic concerns expressed by some members of the board had been given careful consideration: (a) Disposal of any property of the university would require a three-fourths vote of the entire board; (b) no reduction of the number of clerics on the Board of Trustees could be made without a three-fourths vote. Neither the existing nor the previous by-laws contained such stringent requirements; these by-laws, therefore, represented a tightening of the reins.

At the end of my presentation, I moved that the by-laws as presented be adopted without change in substance. The motion was seconded by Cardinal Cody. A lengthy discussion then ensued concerning the main matters covered in my introductory statement. At length a vote was called for. The written ballots showed fifteen votes for the motion and seven against. The motion was therefore carried by one vote more than the required two-thirds majority.

Immediately, another motion was proposed: that the Chairman be empowered to appoint a Permanent Committee on Revision of the By-Laws and Statutes. The motion was seconded and carried unanimously. The Chairman thereupon appointed Cardinal Krol to chair the permanent committee.

The final revision of the by-laws then had to be presented to the Holy See. Cardinal Cody was due to depart for Rome shortly after the meeting, and offered to present them personally to the Sacred Congregation for Catholic Education. As soon as these, together with an account of the meeting of the Board of Trustees and the results of the voting, could be prepared, I dispatched them registered mail, special delivery, to his New York hotel. To my painful surprise, they were returned to me ten days later, marked "undelivered." Ten precious days had been lost. I immediately telephoned to the Apostolic Delegate in Washington, asking him if my packet could be included in the diplomatic pouch which I knew was sent weekly to the Vatican. He assured me that he would be pleased to see that this would be done. I enclosed in my packet a covering letter addressed to Cardinal Garrone, informing him what had happened and explaining the importance of having the revised statutes and by-laws approved and in effect before the expected visit and review of The Catholic University of America by the Middle States Association of Colleges and Secondary Schools.

Early in January 1970, Dr. Clarence Walton, who had become President of The Catholic University, was informed by the Middle States Association that the review of The Catholic University which had been expected in the spring had been advanced to the month of February. Thereupon, Walton sent this information to Cardinal Garrone by cable, again emphasizing the importance of having the by-laws approved and in effect by the time of the MSA committee's visit. On January 22 Cardinal Garrone cabled the Apostolic Delegate that the by-laws had been approved on a five-year experimental basis, and asked him to transmit this information to Walton. In a letter dated January 23, signed by himself as Prefect of the Congregation, Cardinal Garrone sent me the official confirmation of the by-laws. With a certain sense of satisfaction, I quote one of the final paragraphs of Cardinal Garrone's letter:

Now, Your Eminence, that you have come to the end of your term of office as the Chairman of the Committee on Revision of the Statutes, a difficult labor indeed, it is our pleasant duty to sincerely and cordially thank you for the faith, the intelligence, and the perseverance with which you have executed this office and completed happily this delicate task. This Sacred Congregation believes that, as they are now formulated, the Statutes will constitute a great help in the development of the University and in the efficacious accomplishment of its Catholic purposes, so that it can be an effective and secure leader in the area of higher studies and scientific endeavor in America.

Later, Dr. Walton informed me that on their arrival early in February, the first thing the examining committee asked for was a copy of the by-laws then in effect. These they found satisfactory, and from that point on the review of The Catholic University went forward without difficulty. There were no further threats of discontinuing accreditation. Now it seemed that The Catholic University of America would be able to take and retain its proper place among the universities of this country and still remain a Pontifical University.

The organization of Catholic Charities of the Archdiocese of Baltimore was founded back in the early twenties by Monsignor Edwin Leonard, under whom it had become firmly established and had developed valuable programs of family welfare, child placement, and service to unmarried mothers and their children. After his retirement the organization ran into some difficult times. But with the appointment of Monsignor John Daly as Director it resumed its course of development and in 1952 was incorporated under the laws of Maryland under the name of Associated Catholic Charities. It was governed by a Board of Directors of which the Archbishop was Chairman, and the Director appointed by him was an *ex officio* member. Other members of the Board were prominent Catholic laymen of the archdiocese. Monsignor Daly was succeeded by Monsignor David Dorsch, and under both of them the Associated Catholic Charities enjoyed an enviable reputation. Such was the organization when I returned to Baltimore in 1961, to become its Archbishop.

When Monsignor Dorsch was appointed pastor of St. Mary's Church, Cumberland, in 1965, Monsignor J. Francis Stafford, who had previously completed his course in professional social work at The Catholic University and then had become assistant to Monsignor Dorsch, succeeded as Director. Stafford was a man of high intelligence, not only sympathetic to the needs of the poor, but also endowed with qualities of exceptional leadership. In my mind there is no doubt that the Associated Catholic Charities could have gone on indefinitely into the future.

In 1968, however, I came under increasing pressure to have the Associated Catholic Charities unite with the Community Fund and the Associated Jewish Charities in one annual community-wide campaign. The pressure originated, I believe, in the Greater Baltimore Committee, a powerful group representing most of the prominent business people of the city, but also came from some of our Catholic lay leaders.

As I have already mentioned, as far back as 1929 Archbishop Curley had approved the membership of the Catholic Charities of Washington in the Community Chest of that city. For sixteen years, first as Assistant Director and later as Director of the Washington Catholic Charities, I had experienced no serious difficulties while participating in the Community Chest of that city. Later, when I was appointed Bishop of Bridgeport, I found that the Catholic Charities of that city was already a member of the Community Chest, and my experience there practically paralleled that in Washington. In both places, I had observed the practical advantages of one community-wide charity appeal. My mind, then, was open, to say the least, to the idea of a united appeal in Baltimore.

To make a long story short, in the latter part of 1968, or the early part of 1969, the Associated Catholic Charities joined with the Associated Jewish Charities, the American Red Cross, and the Community Chest agencies to form a new organization known as the "United Fund" in order to conduct one community-wide campaign for charitable purposes. For the five succeeding years this organization operated to the satisfaction of the four founding members and their subsidiary agencies. Then a serious difficulty arose which, in the light of subsequent events, made me question the wisdom of having given up the independence and security of the ACC annual appeal for the advantages of a common campaign. However, given the circumstances of that time, it would have been practically impossible to foresee all the consequences of that decision. Furthermore, the atmosphere of ecumenism, friendliness, and cooperation toward the non-Catholic community that followed upon the Second Vatican Council made the decision all the more understandable.

The difficulty arose from the fact that in 1974 the Commerce and

Industry Combined Health Appeal (CICHA) applied for membership in the United Fund. The application had the enthusiastic backing of the Greater Baltimore Committee and was favored by the Chairman and majority of the board of United Fund. One of the member agencies of CICHA, however, was Planned Parenthood, which, after the sweeping 1973 Supreme Court decision legalizing abortion throughout the United States, had undertaken a program of abortion counseling in addition to its already objectionable program. As soon as this application became known, the board of ACC decided to oppose the admission of CICHA to the United Fund and instructed its four representatives to vote against the admission of CICHA so long as Planned Parenthood remained a member.

On February 4, 1974, Mr. Wallace Lanahan, United Fund Chairman called to inform me that he was certain that the majority of the board of United Fund would vote for the admission of CICHA and to express the hope that ACC would remain a member of the United Fund and participate in the campaign. On March 1, I wrote to Mr. Lanahan calling his attention to the fact that the Catholic Church finds the propram of Planned Parenthood highly objectionable on moral grounds and that Catholics would find it difficult to support the United Fund with Planned Parenthood as a member agency. I concluded my letter by saying: "It is my sincere hope that the leaders of the United Fund will rethink their decision to admit Planned Parenthood into the United Fund." On March 18, the day scheduled for my retirement as Archbishop of Baltimore, Mr. Lanahan again wrote, saying: Planned Parenthood Association has stated that it has no hesitation in giving assurances that none of the money it would receive from CICHA will be used for abortion counseling." He concluded his letter: I sincerely trust that this letter will relieve Your Eminence of the concern expressed in your letter of March 1 to me, and that not only Your Eminence as Archbishop of Baltimore, but also the Associated Catholic Charities, Inc., and all other Catholic organizations and agencies will endorse and strongly support the projected joint fund raising campaign of United Fund and CICHA, and that you will advise me to this effect."

It was obvious that Mr. Lanahan was asking of me more than I had the power to grant. As Archbishop of Baltimore, I never had the authority or the power to assure him that Associated Catholic Charities and all other Catholic organizations and agencies (e.g., the Knights of Columbus, the Catholic Daughters of America, the Ancient Order of Hibernians, etc.) would endorse and strongly support the projected financial campaign of United Fund and CICHA. His letter, however, brought me face-to-face with a very difficult dilemma. As a founding member of the United Fund, ACC had a right to its just share of funds raised in a community-wide drive; the presence, against our will and over our adverse vote, of one objectionable agency did not destroy that right. If the assurance that none of the money raised in the next and following campaigns would be used for abortion or any abortion-related activities were to be made binding, I would have to give some word indicating at least the possibility—and even the probability—of ACC participation. On the one hand, the Associated Catholic Charities would have to have assurance of funds sufficient to carry on its important programs. On the other hand, in the very brief time that was left to me as Archbishop I could not cause ACC to organize a separate campaign of its own. Nor could I expect the new Archbishop after his appointment and installation immediately to cause such a campaign to be organized. I was still pondering my difficulty and wondering what answer I would give Mr. Lanahan, when on April 2, 1974, the Holy See announced the appointment of Most Reverend William D. Borders, hitherto Bishop of Orlando, Florida, as the new Archbishop of Baltimore. Until his installation, I would hold the title of Apostolic Administrator. Archbishop Borders chose June 26 as the day for his installation.

The appointment of Archbishop Borders partially solved my difficulty, but I was still faced with the problem of seeing that ACC had sufficient funds to carry on its programs until Archbishop Borders had time to size up the whole situation in Baltimore and to decide what course of action he would take. It seemed to me that on the basis of the assurances given that no funds raised in the joint campaign would be used for abortion-related activities, I could assure Mr. Lanahan that ACC would participate in the 1974 campaign (I could see no viable alternative), and that I myself would endorse and support the campaign; that I hoped that Archbishop Borders would also do so. But further than that I could not go. If I were to give no assurance that ACC would participate, I was convinced that the United Fund, CICHA, and Planned Parenthood could consider themselves as not bound by the agreement that no funds of the campaign would be used for abortions, since that agreement had been made on the basis of ACC participation. As of April 2, 1974, I could no longer promise anything or sign anything as Archbishop of Baltimore. Accordingly, on April 16 I wrote to Mr. Lanahan of my decision and signed the letter simply as Apostolic Administrator.

On August 2, 1974, *The Catholic Review* carried on its front page a prominently displayed and headlined article by Monsignor Stafford entitled "Merger Causes Deep Concern." After reviewing the strong opposition of the board of ACC to the merger of the United Fund and CICHA, and its failure to prevent the merger, Monsignor Stafford went on to say: "I believe that this union presents serious pastoral problems to the Catholic community. However, the alternative—Catholic withdrawal from the United Fund—would divide the Baltimore Metropolitan Community so profoundly that its ability to meet the serious social injustices among us would be further diminished. . . . All their ecumenical and interfaith efforts would be jeopardized if we should withdraw from the fund. In my judgment this is not a viable moral alternative . . . . I believe we must live with this moral and pastoral ambiguity which the United Fund Board has presented to us."

The *Sun* carried a four-column article on August 23 under the prominent headline "Abortion Funding Rift is Resolved in CICHA-UF Merger Agreement." The article stated: "Funds now contributed to the joint fund-raising campaign of the Commerce and Industry Combined Health Appeal (CICHA) and the United Fund of Central Maryland, which includes both Catholic Charities and Planned Parenthood, will not be used to finance abortions or abortion-related services, *according to the CICHA-United Fund merger agreement.*" Later, Mr. Lanahan was quoted as saying: "*The agreement* states that Planned Parenthood will not become a member of the United Fund but will remain a part of the CICHA organization. . . . Planned Parenthood has *agreed* that no donated funds will be used for any abortion-related activities." (Emphasis added.) In my eyes, the important thing was that, what in Mr. Lanahan's letter of March 1 was simply an assurance on the part of Planned Parenthood, had now become incorporated into an agreement which involved, as the main parties, United Fund and CICHA. The article ended: "With the signing of the agreement last month, a joint campaign kick-off date has been set for September 24 in the main ballroom of the Hilton Hotel." This solution was indeed far from perfect. However, in the light of all the pertinent circumstances, it was perhaps as satisfactory a solution of the difficult problem as could be expected.

The combined campaign of that fall went forward under the leadership of a new organization called the "United Way," a combination of the United Fund and CICHA, without any untoward incident. The same was true in the four subsequent campaigns. Then early in October 1980, when the United Way opened its campaign, a group of local Pro-Life Association members picketed the headquarters of United Way in protest of the fact that the campagin included Planned Parenthood.

Later, at noon of that day the same group, or some of their fellow members, appeared outside the Catholic Center, where the headquarters of Associated Catholic Charities and the office of the Archbishop are located, to carry on their picketing there. The following day, in an article in the *Sun*, Frank Somerville, Religion Editor, went into some detail concerning his interview of Mr. Philip Schneiderman, Executive Secretary of the United Way of Central Maryland, concerning a meeting of the latter with the leaders of the picketing group. The article says that Schneiderman met the protest with the flat statement: "None of the money raised by us is used for abortion or abortion-related activity." Later in the article, Mr. Schneiderman is quoted as saying that such tactics as were used by the group in question are self-defeating, since their effect up to the present time has been to increase the number of donors who have designated Planned Parenthood as the agency of their choice.

Here, however, I am mainly concerned with the actions of the pro-life group in picketing the Associated Catholic Charities headquarters and the Archbishop's office. If their tactics have been self-defeating in reference to the United Way Campaign, they must be said to have been doubly self-defeating in their activity outside the Catholic Center. In the first place, they gave the impression to those outside the Church that Catholics are divided in their opposition to abortion at this time when it is all-important for Catholics to present a united front against this great and growing evil. No one could have been stronger and clearer in his condemnation of abortion than Archbishop Borders. I believe that my own condemnation had been equally clear and strong. My public statements on the subject go back as at least as far as 1968, when I published the first edition of *Guidelines for the Teaching of Religion in the Archdiocese of Baltimore,* and the second edition soon after the publication of *Humanae Vitae,* July 29, 1968—long before the pro-life Associations came into existence. Their tactics are self-defeating also because they tend to throw doubt in the minds of thoughtful and influential people about the judgment of the pro-life leaders, who are held responsible for—or at least approving of—such actions, and because they were aimed at the one agency, Associated Catholic Charities, which has an effective anti-abortion and pro-life program in the Baltimore area. If their tactics were successful and carried to their logical conclusion, they not only would harm that program, but also Catholic Charities' other important programs of family service and child care.

Every thoughtful person who is familiar with local conditions knows that, so long as the United Fund gives assurance that none of its money is used for abortion or abortion-counseling, it would be almost impossible successfully to organize and conduct a separate Associated Catholic Charities campaign in the Central Maryland area. Against this widely recognized fact, some of the pro-life group cite the example of Cardinal Emmett Carter of Toronto, who withdrew from the Toronto United Way on the abortion issue and successfully organized a campaign for the Toronto Catholic Charities. During the meeting of all the Cardinals in Rome (November 5-9, 1979), I had an opportunity to discuss with Cardinal Carter the situation in Toronto. He assured me that unless he had *proof* that money from the Toronto United Way was being used directly for abortions, he would not have been able to successfully organize his own separate campaign in Toronto. I repeat: no one has ever proved that any of the money from the United Way campaign here has been used for abortion or abortion-related activities. If such proof should ever come to light I have no doubt that the Catholics of Baltimore would rally to Archbishop Borders in a successful separate Catholic campaign.

Most archdiocesan difficulties which in any way involved the law fell first into the hands of Francis X. Gallagher, the archdiocesan attorney. Early one evening in January 1966, he telephoned to me that two of our young priests, Joseph Wenderoth and Neil McLaughlin, had been arrested with Father Philip Berrigan and a group of his followers and were being held in the Baltimore City Jail awaiting transfer to the Federal Court in Harrisburg, where they would face charges of having violated the federal law. Both were apparently good young priests, still somewhat boyish in appearance and idealistic in their frame of mind. Both had fallen under the influence of the two Fathers Berrigan, one of whom, Philip, a Josephite priest, had been assigned to St. Peter Claver's parish in Baltimore. They had been impressed particularly by the Berrigans' open protest against war, and they had joined Father Philip's followers in and near Baltimore.

Before long, this group, under the leadership of Philip Berrigan, had gone from vocal opposition to acts of violence, meant to impede the U.S. prosecution of the war in Vietnam. Some of them had forcibly entered three recruiting stations in the vicinity of Baltimore and in southern Pennsylvania, had destroyed some records, and had defaced others by pouring blood over them. Now, however, they were accused of a far more serious violation of federal law. They were to be transferred to the Harrisburg Federal Court the following day. From the information he had been able to gather, Francis Gallagher was convinced that the forecast for the future of the two priests and their companions was not bright. I asked him to try to arrange permission for me to visit the two and talk to them that night. Not only did he arrange for the visit, he actually accompanied me and made further arrangements for a room where he and I could converse with the two priests in complete privacy.

When we first met them, they still seemed buoyed up with the excitement of their arrest and the prospect of becoming "martyrs for peace." Soon, however, Francis Gallagher brought them face-to-face with the reality of their situation: the probability that they would be convicted and sentenced to prison, the harrowing experience they might well be subjected to in prison with hardened criminals, the necessity of their having proper legal advice and defense. As we had suspected, they had not the slightest notion as to how they should go about obtaining proper legal counsel and defense. They knew no one they could turn to for help—except now to the archdiocese and to Francis Gallagher himself. Philip Berrigan would have the legal counsel and help that would be supplied to him by Father George O'Dea, the Superior General of the Josephite Fathers, but neither he nor his community had any responsibility for Wenderoth or McLaughlin. They would have to depend upon what help could be supplied to them through our own archdiocesan attorney, Francis X. Gallagher. Realizing their own helplessness, they both very earnestly asked Francis to help them in whatever way he could. He promised them he would be present in the Federal Court in Harrisburg at the time of their arraignment and that he would give or obtain for them the best legal counsel and defense he could. Needless to say, by the time our conversation was brought to an end by the necessity for Gallagher and me to leave the jail, their imagined "martyr's halo" had already considerably tarnished.

Understandably my own visit to the jail and my prolonged conference with the two priest-prisoners did not go unnoticed by the reporters who knew that this group, including the three priests, had been consigned to the jail on the charge of serious violation of federal law. The next day the newspapers headlined my speedily undertaken visit to my two "law-breaking" young priests. I believe I can take for granted that practically all the priests of the archdiocese and most of the laity understood and approved my concern, and the reason for my visit. But this was certainly not true of all. Some thought my speedy reaction was precipitate and uncalled for; law-breakers, particularly priest-lawbreakers, ought to be left to face the consequences of their actions; it was not the business of the Cardinal Archbishop to interfere in a case like this, etc. As always seems to happen, the critical ones were the vocal ones and commanded the attention of the press and other media. To all of them, of course, I had as my guide and as the explanation of my action the words of Christ in his great discourse on the Last Judgment: "I was in prison and you came to me." When were you in prison and we came to you?" "As often as you did it to one of these my least brethren you did it also to me." (Matt. 25:35-40)

Francis Gallagher was in the Harrisburg Federal Court on the day the accused were arraigned. The two serious charges made against them were: (1) that they had conspired to enter the underground tunnel system of the city of Washington and to detonate explosives that would render inoperative the heating system of the government buildings; (2) that they had conspired to abduct the presidential advisor, Henry Kissinger. On both charges all members of the group were indicted and held for trial. Without further consultation with me, as if he were anxious to keep the archdiocese out of the picture as far as possible, Francis Gallagher assumed full responsibility for arranging for the defense of Wenderoth and McLaughlin through lawyer-friends and acquaintances in the Harrisburg area. However, unknown to me at the time, he commuted to and from Harrisburg during the entire time of the trial, in addition to bearing the already heavy burdens he was carrying. As he had foreseen, the entire group was found guilty and all were sentenced to prison terms. Through the efforts of Francis, however, both Wenderoth and McLaughlin were released on parole. Both of them remained deeply grateful to Francis Gallagher for all that he had done for them.

The Wenderoth-McLaughlin affair was followed by a sad—I might say tragic—event for both the archdiocese and for myself personally. Shortly after their release on parole, Francis X. Gallagher was stricken suddenly with very serious heart failure and after only two days·in the intensive care unit of the Johns Hopkins Hospital died on Friday, February 11, 1972, at the age of forty-two. It must have been noted by the reader that I have always referred to him by the name "Francis X." There was another lawyer of this city, prominent in political life, with the identical name. Early in their careers, they made an agreement that the one, our archdiocesan attorney, would use the name Francis; the other would be known as Frank. In order to be properly identified, both adhered strictly to this usage.

Francis X. Gallagher had achieved a brilliant career as a student at Loyola High School, Loyola College, and as a student and part-time professor, first at Johns Hopkins and later at the University of Maryland. Even before he graduated from law school he had become interested and active in politics and had before him a most promising career in that field. At the age of twenty-nine, however, he had decided to give up politics to devote himself completely to the private practice of law and the rearing of his children. In 1960, on the death of William Galvin, Archbishop Keough invited Gallagher to be attorney for the archdiocese. This invitation he accepted at considerable personal sacrifice, as became evident at the time of his death. In 1961, when I succeeded to Archbishop Keough, I asked him to continue in that capacity. One is tempted here to go into the detail of the many outstanding achievements of his career.

The frequency with which his name has appeared in these pages, has, I believe, given ample testimony of the important role he played in the conduct of archdiocesan affairs from the year 1960 down to the time of his death; and the great publicity given at that time to his whole career makes further comment here unnecessary. I wish only to add my own deep sorrow at the loss of a friend so dear and a helper so able and so valuable. His memory will be preserved for all time in the Archdiocese of Baltimore.

Toward the end of this period of discouragement and depression, I became involved in a most unusual episode that was highly publicized in the newspapers of the time. On January 2, 1973, shortly after we had finished our evening meal, I received a telephone call from the head of the local office of the Federal Bureau of Investigation informing me that an attempt had been made to hijack an airplane of the Piedmont Airlines. The hijacker was holding two young women, hostesses of the plane, at gunpoint. The exit from the plane was covered by armed agents of the FBI and members of the Maryland State Police. The hijacker had refused all pleas to release the two hostages and to turn himself over to the FBI. He had asked to speak to Lawrence Cardinal Shehan and Dr. John R. Lyon, a psychiatrist on the staff of University of Maryland Hospital. Would I be willing to go and speak to the man? I answered that I was ready to go immediately, if transportation could be supplied. I was assured that an FBI agent would be at the front door of the Basilica rectory within less than fifteen minutes. Monsignor Love, rector of the Basilica, who initially had taken the call and trans-

ferred it to me, joined me in my study before my conversation with the
FBI official had ended. He insisted on accompanying me. We put on
our topcoats and waited at the front door. Actually, two unmarked
automobiles came within ten minutes. I entered the first car and he
the second.

On the way to the airport I was briefed concerning what had
happened. The hijacker, a young man apparently in his thirties, seemingly through inadequate security procedure, had boarded the plane
at the Washington Airport. Shortly before the plane landed in Baltimore,
he had entered the restroom at the rear of the plane and had locked the
door from within. He waited until the plane had landed and the passengers and flight crew had left the plane. He then came out brandishing
an automatic pistol, taking hostage the two hostesses who then were
alone in the plane, and ordering them forward to the exit at gunpoint.
There he kept them, demanding that one of them use the radio-telephone to reach the head official of the airport and give him this message: supply a new unarmed flight crew and sufficient fuel to take him
to Toronto, Canada, where he wished to settle a personal problem. If
any tricks were attempted, he would first kill the young women and
then himself. All efforts of the FBI to induce him to release the hostages and surrender himself had failed. Any further developments
would be supplied to me after our arrival at the airport.

Hardly had these details been presented to me when we arrived,
closely followed by the automobile containing Monsignor Love. Dr.
Lyon arrived a few minutes later. He seemed deeply concerned, as well
he might be, for he was still a comparatively young man who had a
wife and three or four children dependent upon him. I, on the other
hand, had no one dependent on me, although my sister and other close
relatives would have grieved if anything tragic had occurred. One
important development had taken place before our arrival: Mr. Thomas Farrow, the head of the Baltimore FBI office, had placed himself in
a spot where he was plainly visible to the hijacker, had removed all
his clothing except his underwear, and had put on denim trousers
which he was able to show had no concealed weapon. He had announced
he was coming aboard the plane to talk to the man. After a brief conversation in which the hijacker refused to make any change in his
original demand, the agent had offered to take the place of the two
women as a hostage. I have no way of knowing just what the agent said
to him, but he must have brought home to him that, in their highly
emotional state after more than three hours being held captive at
pistol point, anything could happen to them and was bound to happen

if their ordeal were prolonged, and that they were in fact an ever-increasing liability. In any event, it later was learned that the gunman had first offered to release one of the hostesses, but each refused to leave without the other. At length, after forcing one of them to tie the agent's hands securely behind his back, he let both of them leave the plane. They had finally emerged leaning on each other and visibly upset by their long ordeal. They refused to be interviewed or make any statement beyond the fact that they had suffered greatly from the experience and wished to be left alone.

A moment or so later I used the radio-telephone to announce my name, said that I had come at his request to talk with him, and that I would proceed to a place from which he could see me and then would enter the plane to talk with him. After boarding the plane and having a brief conversation with him in the presence of Farrow, I asked the agent to withdraw far enough to be out of hearing distance. I gave the hijacker the opportunity to say whatever he wished and then pointed out that my one purpose in coming was to be of help to him. I said that there was only one way he could come out of his present dilemma alive: that was to release Farrow and to turn himself over to the authorities. I told him I was in a position to assure him that, if he acted according to my advice, he would not be injured in any way, that he would first be given the treatment which he obviously needed. Since he had committed a felony in attempting to hijack the plane, he would have to stand trial, but he would have a lawyer acceptable to himself for his defense. From time to time he raised an objection to what I was offering him. After about half an hour, however, he decided to do what I had asked him to do .Still holding on to his pistol, he permitted me to unbind Farrow's arms and allowed him to leave the plane. Then, stuffing his pistol conspicuously in the belt of his trousers, he quietly came with me. The purpose of the pistol, I suppose, was to show that he was not simply surrendering in the ordinary sense. He was acting on my advice and placing the responsibility on me. When we reached the administration building, two nearby FBI men suddenly pinioned his arms and a third grabbed for the pistol. After a brief tussle, again showing that this was no ordinary surrender, the hijacker quietly went with the officers. Thus undramatically ended what in its beginnings had been a scene full of drama, and even possible tragedy.

The next day the newspapers gave full coverage to the episode. The ending came too late Monday evening to be reported in full in the morning edition of *The Sun*. The *Evening Sun*, however, gave all the details. A deep black headline spread across the front page: "SHEHAN, FBI

AGENT TALK HIJACKER INTO SURRENDER AT FRIENDSHIP." The *Baltimore News-American* in an equally prominent headline announced "SHEHAN FOILS HIJACKER HERE," and on an inside page the article was continued under a three-column heading: "HIJACKER FOILED BY SHEHAN." A friend sent me a clipping from the *San Francisco Chronicle* of January 3 with a five-column spread entitled: "CARDINAL'S ROLE: HIJACKER TALKED INTO SURRENDER," and a picture of me faced with a battery of microphones. Another friend sent similar clippings from the *New York News* and the *Chicago Tribune*. It almost seemed that I had become a national "hero for a day."

Later Baltimore Mayor William Donald Schaefer sent me a scroll with the words: "City of Baltimore Citizen Citation to Lawrence Cardinal Shehan," and signed by himself. The Vatican paper *L' Osservatore Romano* also carried a picture and the story.

A touching aftermath of the incident is that, even to this day, the saintly father of the would-be hijacker comes to see me at least twice a month to give me a report on his son, to express his gratitude, and receive some words of consolation and encouragement. After more than six years of incarceration and treatment, the son has finally been released on parole and is trying to make his own living. This was one of the final episodes of that period of my ministry before I reached the actual date of my retirement.

I hope that I do not give the impression that I thought what I had done deserved such praise and so much notice. But after living for the better part of three years in an atmosphere of frustration and of gloom, I could not but take satisfaction in what seemed like a small break in the clouds that let the sunlight come through.

Pontificia Fotografia Felici

Elevation to the Cardinalate, February 2, 1965.

Cardinal Shehan with Pope Paul VI.

Pontificia Fotografia Felici

Eucharistic Congress Committee and Advocate Press

As Papal Legate to the International Eucharistic Congress, Melbourne, 1973.

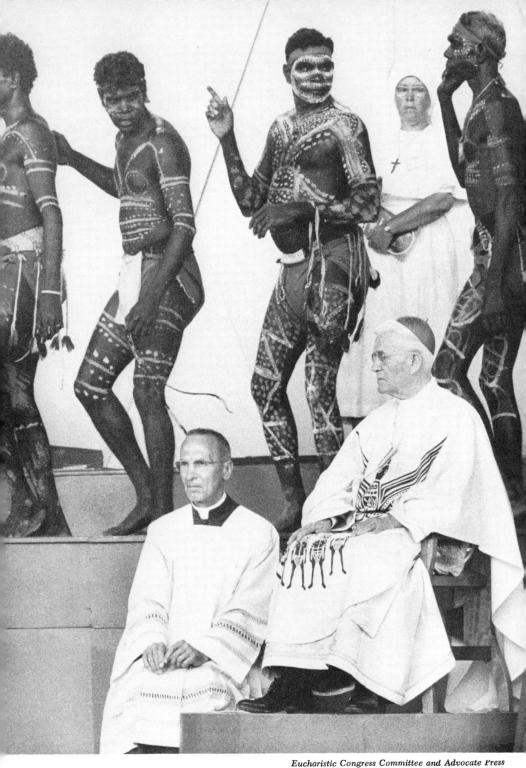

Eucharistic Congress Committee and Advocate Press

Northern tribal dancers perform at Aboriginal Liturgy during Melbourne Congress. The Cardinal wears a chasuble bearing Tiwi design from Bathhurst Island.

St. Joseph's Day celebration at St. Martin Home for the Aged, 1974. Megan Wheltle pulls the cord!

Henry J. Knott, Cardinal Shehan, Marion Burk Knott (Mrs. Henry J.), and Archbishop Borders at dedication of the Burk Building of Mercy Hospital.

Archbishop Borders and Cardinal Shehan depart for Rome, 1975, for the canonization of Mother Elizabeth Seton, who founded the Daughters of Charity in Emmitsburg, Md.

Baltimore Catholic Review

Greeting Pope John Paul II in Washington, D.C., 1979. At far right is Egidio Cardinal Vagnozzi.

12. The Final Years

ALL OF US, I SUPPOSE, have memories of late summer days overcast by clouds, when unexpectedly, the sun appeared beneath the dark western sky to throw a pleasant glow over the landscape. In my memory the years 1968-1973 remain like such a gloomy day of late summer, overcast by clouds that arose from racial tensions and conflict, from the growing burden of financial problems that I would have to pass on to my successor, from the Statement of Dissent and its aftermath, and from the widespread crisis of faith, which had grave effects on Catholic education and Catholic life in general and gave rise to the sad spectacle of a number of priests leaving their ministry at a time when their services were most needed in the Church. At the beginning of a previous chapter I have mentioned several sources of deep satisfaction that remained with me during that period, but the overall impression is that of a gloomy day in the declining year. Then suddenly occurred an event of great importance to me, which seemed like a burst of light from the sun just before it sinks beneath the western horizon.

About the middle of January 1973, I received a telephone call from the Apostolic Delegate, Archbishop Luigi Raimondi, asking if it would be possible for me to see him that afternoon if he were to come to Baltimore. Since I now held the rank of Cardinal, I knew it was useless to offer to go to Washington, so I simply assured him that I would be happy to see him at whatever time it was convenient for him to come. When he arrived, I greeted him and accompanied him to my study. Before we were seated, he placed in my hand an envelope addressed to me, saying: "I am pleased to bring you this communication from our Holy Father by which he appoints you his Legate to the International Eucharistic Congress to be held in Melbourne, Australia, beginning

Sunday, February 18." On opening the envelope I saw that the communication was signed by the Pope and was in the form of an Apostolic Brief. It began:

To our Venerable Brother
Lawrence Cardinal Shehan
Archbishop of Baltimore

Venerable Brother,
Greetings and Apostolic Blessing.

As everybody knows, in the very near future the fortieth International Eucharistic Congress will take place in Melbourne, a great city on the Australian continent which now for the second time—after the Congress of Sydney—has been invested with this honour as well as responsibility. This Congress is being carefully and zealously prepared by Our Venerable Brother, James Robert Knox, the archbishop of that city, with the help of experts, in such a way—and especially through pastoral renewal—that it is easy to foresee it will be a Congress noted for its religious fervour, its efficient organisation and most successful outcome. . . .

We are desirous to strengthen and confirm these programmes and objectives by Our own authority and presence, as it were. Consequently, Venerable Brother, as you have the dignity of a Cardinal, and are the Archbishop of Baltimore as well as the energetic President of the Permanent Commission for the promotion of International Eucharistic Congresses, We choose and appoint you as Our Delegate, and charge you with presiding over the Melbourne International Eucharistic Congress as Our representative. We are confident that you will carry out with success and profit, the task entrusted to you, according to the burning love which you yourself have for the mystery of the wondrous Sacrament of the Altar, in which Christ the Redeemer offers himself in an unbloody manner, in which he feeds souls and, apart from the sacrifice, is truly, really and substantially present under the Eucharistic species.

Finally We pray God that this impending Eucharistic Congress may really bring an abundance of spiritual graces, which are expected, and that these fruits may rebound to the good of Australia —of which We cherish a fond memory—and the entire world.

It is with these sincere wishes that We impart to you, Venerable Brother, to the Cardinals, Bishops, priests religious and all the faithful, who will be present at the Eucharistic Congress,

Our Apostolic Blessing, as a pledge of heavenly grace and consolation.

From Rome, at Saint Peter's, 25 January 1973, in the tenth year of Our Pontificate.

Paulus PP. VI

After I had read the brief, the Delegate and I discussed the chief duties that would be mine as the official representative of the Pope. It would be difficult to exaggerate the height of my surprise or the depth of my emotion caused by the visit of the Apostolic Delegate. A few days later, the Vatican made the public announcement of my appointment as Papal Legate to the coming Congress.

As I have mentioned, I had been a member of the Permanent Commission for the Promotion of International Eucharistic Congresses since 1960, and in that capacity had attended the Congress in Munich and the one in Bombay. Then as one of the Vice Presidents, five years later I attended the Congress at Bogotá, Colombia, to which again Pope Paul VI had come for part of the Congress. It was after that Congress that I had been named President of the Commission and in that position I would not fail to go to Melbourne.

Before my appointment as Legate Mr. Clemens Dietze, of a local travel agency, asked if he could arrange a pilgrimage for a group of Baltimoreans who, he felt confident, would want to accompany me to Melbourne for the Congress. Meanwhile, it had also been decided that Monsignor J. Francis Stafford would act as my secretary during the journey. On the day of the Vatican's announcement, I received a cablegram from Archbishop (soon to be named Cardinal) Knox, the Ordinary of Melbourne, congratulating me on my appointment, and it was followed by a letter giving details of the arrangements there.

Stafford and I decided we would accompany our group of Baltimoreans as far as Sydney. The travel schedule provided for a brief stay at Tahiti, with an overnight stop at the nearby island of Moorea, made famous by the film *South Pacific*. Because the sky was overcast, Stafford and I decided not to go with the rest of the group on that excursion. Before their small boat reached the island, a sudden tropical storm struck, marooning the group on that island for two full days. Meanwhile, our plane for Sydney arrived, and in order to be sure to arrive on schedule, Stafford and I decided we would have to take it, leaving in the hands of Divine Providence the continued journey of our group.

At Sydney we were met by the Honorable E. G. Whitlam, the Premier of Australia, who had arranged for us to transfer to the official aircraft of the Commonwealth of Australia for the last leg of our trip. In Melbourne we were greeted by Cardinal Knox; the Governor of Victoria. Sir Rohan Delacombe; Mr. R. J. Hamer, Premier of Victoria, and a large group of Australian and visiting prelates.

After the introductions and the customary exchange of courtesies, we learned that Cardinal Knox, in my name, had accepted the Governor's invitation that Stafford and I be his guests that afternoon and evening and remain with his family overnight. Accordingly, we were escorted to the Government House, a magnificent stone residence set in the midst of a beautiful, carefully tended park. It was a very formal English household presided over by the Governor and his gracious wife. A manservant took charge of our traveling bags, evidently prepared to unpack at least mine, to have my extra suit pressed and other clothes laid out. At the thought of the condition of the interior of my suitcase, rather carelessly packed, at the end of some five or six days of travel, I was somewhat embarrassed. Monsignor Stafford must have sensed it immediately, for he rescued me by telling the servant that he was accustomed to render this service for me and would give him the suit that needed pressing.

Shortly after our arrival, we had luncheon with the Governor and his wife. After a pleasant and informative conversation with them about the best features of Australia, their adopted home, we were informed about the time for tea and late dinner, and left pretty much to ourselves to rest, to read, to stroll about the beautiful gardens. Guests of rank had been invited to the very formal evening dinner. Thus passed our first day in Australia and the formal welcome from the Commonwealth of Australia to the Legate representing the head of the Vatican State.

On Sunday morning, Stafford and I, accompanied by Sir Rohan, were driven to Raheen, the residence of the Archbishop of Melbourne. It had been built by Cardinal Knox's predecessor, Archbishop Mannix, who had presided over the Archdiocese of Melbourne from 1917 to 1963. Much to our satisfaction, we found things far less formal at Raheen. We had luncheon with Cardinal Knox and the members of his household. There I met for the first time Monsignor Ian Burns of Sydney, who was to read the Apostolic Brief of my appointment as Papal Legate at the opening ceremony of the Congress, and Doctor John Horan, a prominent Melbourne physician and equally prominent layman of the archdiocese, both of whom had been appointed by our

Holy Father to represent the Vatican during the Congress and were to become my friends.

The opening ceremony took place at five o'clock Sunday afternoon in the beautiful Cathedral of St. Patrick, which, like Raheen, is a memorial of the labors and zeal of Archbishop Mannix. For it were gathered all the important officials of the state of Victoria and the city of Melbourne, all the Cardinals, Bishops, and priests who had arrived for this official opening, and members of the laity to the full capacity of the large cathedral. The ceremony was a simple one, consisting of music, the singing of appropriate psalms and hymns interspersed with instrumental pieces, the reading of the Apostolic Brief by which the Congress was officially inaugurated under the authority and patronage of Pope Paul VI.

Then Cardinal Knox gave his short but to me very touching welcome. Referring to the early relationship between the Archdiocese of Baltimore and the Archdiocese of Melbourne during its beginning days and early history, he said:

> May I . . . say that the place of Baltimore in the development of the Church in the United States of America and its influence in the English-speaking world made it particularly appropriate that the Cardinal Archbishop of Baltimore should be chosen as the Papal Legate to the 40th International Eucharistic Congress.
>
> Senior priests in Australia are familiar with the Baltimore Ritual and the catechisms. The Provincial and the Plenary Church Councils held in Baltimore influenced those held in Australia. It is sufficient to recall that Baltimore had already held its Third Provincial Council before the First Council of the Australian Province was held in Sydney in 1844.
>
> Once again, Your Eminence, a heartfelt welcome and may your stay in our midst be a happy and memorable one, coming as it does after the celebration of your Golden Jubilee of priesthood, for which we offer you our sincere, heartfelt congratulations.

To this, I gave my previously prepared response.

Although the Congress had officially opened on Sunday afternoon, the real opening, as far as the great masses of Catholic people of the Archdiocese of Melbourne and the many visitors from all parts of Australia and the rest of the world were concerned, took place late Monday afternoon in the huge Cricket Ground, in which the city properly takes so much pride. The field is a large circular one. Around its edge runs a cinder-covered road some fifteen feet wide, and just beyond the road rise banks of seats capable of accommodating 100,000 people. Before time for the ceremony of Monday, these seats were filled to capacity. Arriving at the entrance of the field some minutes before 5 P.M., Cardinal Knox and I transferred from the automobile which had brought us to a sleek black Rolls Royce, which evidently was provided by the civil government for such occasions. The rear part of it was fitted with a carpeted platform on which we stood while holding firmly to the highly polished metal bar before us.

At the moment of 5 P.M., we were driven through the entrance to the field and there our automobile took its place behind the cavalcade of eight handsome gray steeds, mounted by uniformed riders, each bearing a ten-foot spear topped with a small triangular flag. The cortege moved around the perimeter of the field to the strain of the Australian national anthem as Cardinal Knox and I waved in acknowledgment of the warm and long greetings of the people. Such was to be the introduction to every major ceremony at which, accompanied by Cardinal Knox, I presided at the Cricket Ground.

After we left the automobile and donned the vestments for the Mass, the procession moved across the field to the great platform on which the main altar of the Congress had been erected. To help to supply the music of the Congress, Cardinal Knox had brought the Vatican Choir from Rome. They alternated with the vast congregation in chanting the Gloria and the Creed, and sang religious motifs at appropriate intervals in the sacred Liturgy. The sound amplification system was excellent, every word of each speaker could be clearly heard and understood throughout the whole area.

It would be pointless to attempt to give even an inadequate summary of the many impressive events that crowded the week. The large ninety-six page memorial brochure gives the highlights of the Congress. The two ceremonies of which I have already spoken will always be indelibly inscribed on my mind. For me, the most moving ceremony of the week, however, was the Children's Mass. From all over the state of Victoria and beyond, in what seemed almost a miracle of transportational efficiency, 100,000 school children were brought into Melbourne by railroad trains. By noon, the whole throng was quietly in place. It was by far the most colorful of all the events— these almost countless young people in their bright summer clothes, with their even-brighter faces and voices. As the cavalcade of prancing horses entered the stadium with Cardinal Knox and myself following and waving to the people, there was a spontaneous roar of greeting.

The youngsters sang loudly, joyfully, and seemingly in perfect unison, throughout the Mass. They listened attentively to Father Harold Winston s homily, which was based on an allegory of one of Australia's best loved writers, Alan Marshall. In pleasing contrast with their loud and joyous singing was the reverence of their hushed silence during the moments of the consecration and elevation of the Sacred Host and the Precious Blood. After the words, "Lord, I am not worthy," more than two hundred priests streamed from the sanctuary across the field to bring Holy Communion to this huge throng.

So moved was I by the whole experience that, although I was not scheduled to speak at the Mass, as the Pope's representative I seized the opportunity to talk briefly to these young people during the few moments of silence following the distribution of Holy Communion. I spoke to them as the hope of the future of the Church of Australia. Who could look upon this vast sea of young faces of those just united with Christ in His Eucharistic Presence and not see in them Australia's future hope? I no longer remember the exact words of my talk, but whatever I said came from deep in my heart. Judging from the burst of immediate applause, I believe it was the shortest but most successful speech I ever made—perhaps the best, because the central idea was so clear and certain in my mind and the feeling that brought it to expression was so fresh and deep. After the Mass, Cardinal Knox and I quickly changed to our choir robes, and mounted our automobile behind the waiting cavalcade. As we circled the field waving our arms in farewell, there was a prolonged uproar of cheers and clapping—this time I didn't know whether it was for us or for the prancing steeds, but whether for the horses, for us, or for both, it was all in honor of Christ Jesus in the Eucharist and his Vicar on earth whom we represented, Pope Paul VI.

By far the most moving of the many speeches given that week was that of Mother Teresa of Calcutta, delivered in the subdued but distinct words of her ever-great earnestness. Because her words have such relevance today, almost ten years after they were uttered, I am tempted to quote them here. They are, however, carefully preserved in their fullness in the memorial brochure of the Congress. It is to be hoped that her talks bearing on the different aspects of her work will one day be gathered in book form and made available to the world. For her work is, I believe, the most important of the present-day Church—with one exception, that being the great work of worldwide evangelization that our present Holy Father, Pope John Paul II, has undertaken and has carried out with almost incredible vigor.

Other events of that week that stand out in bold relief were the Mass for the Aborigines, that for the sick, that for the deaf. Because of my commitment to another event, I was unable to be present at the Mass for youth, held at the Music Bowl. The author of the memorial brochure calls it an "inspiring occasion." Not all my commitments, however, were to Eucharistic Liturgies. Thirty thousand people attended the ecumenical prayer service, in which leaders and people of virtually all the major churches of Australia participated.

During the final days of the Congress, our Permanent Commission held its meeting. This, as I recall, took place on Friday morning in the building which housed the staff of St. Patrick's Cathedral, the Chancery office, and other archdiocesan offices. After an opening prayer and the reading of the minutes by Father Missaglia, the Secretary of the Commission, we immediately got down to the main business—the list of the dioceses we were to present to the Holy Father as possible sites for the next Congress. At the Congress at Bogotá several members of the Commission had expressed the hope that one of the larger dioceses in the United States would offer to host the Congress following that of Melbourne. It had become evident that the Commission was looking to me as its President to find such a site. I, therefore, had checked the possibilities and was now happy to tell them that one U.S. diocese had offered to act as host to the next International Eucharistic Congress. This was the Archdiocese of Philadelphia, which in my opinion offered many advantages as the site for the next Congress. It was one of the larger archdioceses of the United States; Cardinal Krol, the present Archbishop, was well known to many of the Bishops of the world, since he served in the Second Vatican Council as the English-speaking member of the General Secretariat. The archdiocese, in my opinion, had the resources to conduct such a Congress without outside help, and the city itself was well supplied with facilities that would be made readily available for the large outdoor Liturgies. Cardinal Krol, however, had attached one condition to his invitation: the Congress would have to be held in 1976, the year of the bicentennial celebration of the founding of the United States of America.

The members generally expressed satisfaction at receiving Cardinal Krol's generous offer. Several, however, raised two objections: first, it had been customary to hold the International Congresses at four-year intervals, and now I was suggesting only a three-year interval between Melbourne and Philadelphia; second, a fear was expressed that the holding of the Congress in Philadelphia during the national bicentennial might give it a political or national overtone which could be misunderstood. To these objections, I replied: first, the four-year interval, while generally desirable, has been a rather modern development and can hardly be regarded as a fast rule. In fact, at Melbourne we were already well into the fifth year since the Bogotá Congress of 1968. Second, given the United States policy of separation of Church and State, there was, in my opinion, no danger that the purely religious character of the Congress would be affected by the national celebration. I saw no serious reason why Cardinal Krol's offer should not be accepted and many good reasons why it should be. I further expressed my firm conviction that if the invitation were not accepted, it might be many years before another suitable U.S. diocese would offer to act as host for such a Congress. By a virtually unanimous voice-vote, the Commission decided to recommend to the Pope that he name Philadelphia as the site of the next Congress in 1976.

Without doubt, the most important and impressive Eucharistic Liturgy of the Congress was the *Statio Orbis* of the following Sunday with which the Congress came to its climax and to its solemn closing. For this ceremony, the planning committee had, to use a popular phrase, "pulled out all the stops." The huge crowd of far more than 100,000 not only filled the banks of seats but also spilled over onto the Cricket Ground proper. The very greatness of the congregation inspired the Vatican Choir, the Melbourne choirs, and the congregation itself to produce music that fully measured up to the importance of the occasion.

It had been only at the middle of the week that Cardinal Knox had informed me that I would be expected to give the homily at the final Liturgy. Perhaps he had delayed that information so that, instead of attempting to compose my homily for the *Statio Orbis* before I left Baltimore, I should wait to savor the full flavor of the Melbourne Congress. This, at least, was what happened. As the subject of my homily I chose "The Eucharist, the Light of a New Hope." As we faced the end of the twentieth century, we were all conscious of the fact that the century thus far had been dominated by the two greatest and most destructive wars of history. The one thing we all longed for was peace, peace for the whole world. War is the product of hate and the expression of hate. Peace can only come from love and is the expression of love. My theme, then, was the Eucharist, the sacrament of love and peace.

The whole Congress was for me a unique and inspiring experience. Coming as it did, almost at the end of my administration, after a period of so much distress and so many disappointments and discouragements of the previous four years, it seemed like a special dispensation of God's goodness and mercy to me. I hope I again may be pardoned if I quote the commendatory words of Cardinal Knox in his foreword to the memorial book on the Congress:

> I am especially grateful to His Holiness, Pope Paul VI, for his many signs of benevolence towards the congress and its organisers, and above all for sending His Eminence, Cardinal Shehan, as his Legate. We were disappointed, of course, at the Holy Father's inability to be with us in person, but he could not have chosen a more worthy and gracious representative than Cardinal Shehan. After a week of intense activity in which he was completely unsparing of himself, the Papal Legate paid a generous tribute to the hospitality of the people of Melbourne. He saw the fervour and the happiness of all who took part in the liturgies and the conferences as signals that people can love one another in accordance with the New Commandment. And he spoke of his abiding impression "that nothing is impossible when people work together for the good of their neighbors, inspired by faith and love." His Eminence believes—and I fully concur with his judgment—that the congress may be seen as a light of real hope for the Church.

After the closing of the Congress, Monsignor Stafford and I spent the night at Raheen. We stayed long enough to have our pictures taken with different groups of those who had worked in preparation for the Congress, for inclusion in the memorial book, and then we departed for Sydney. Cardinal Gilroy, whom we visited, had recently retired as Archbishop of Sydney and was living in a home for retired priests that he had founded. His successor, Archbishop Freeman, was obliged to be away from Sydney at the time, but he invited us to accept the hospitality of the Archbishop's House. There we stayed for the better part of two days, visited the beautiful Cathedral, had a good opportunity to see the magnificent harbor, claimed by the citizens of Sydney to be the greatest and most picturesque in the world, and had one of the very early guided tours through the fantastic limestone Opera House, designed to resemble a great sail boat, situated on the small peninsula that juts into the sea.

After the second day in Sydney, Monsignor Stafford and I started toward Rome, where I would make my report of the Congress to the Pope and present to him the large bronze cast of the symbol of the Congress that had been entrusted to me for that purpose by Cardinal Knox. We had decided to make two stopovers in our flight to Rome: one at Bangkok, the other at Athens. We found Bangkok interesting and picturesque, but nothing which, under the circumstances, would detain us more than the day. Athens, our next stop, was very different. I had had a brief glimpse of that most interesting city of pagan antiquity on my way back from Istanbul, but only enough to whet my appetite for more. Stafford had never been there and was eager to see as much of it as possible in the rather brief time we could allot to our visit.

There were still several hours of daylight left when we arrived at Athens, so as soon as we were settled in our hotel, we went off to the Acropolis and we were still there when twilight began to fall. In the morning after Mass and breakfast, we returned to the Acropolis for several hours, and then spent the rest of the day visiting the relics of ancient Athens, the Agora where Paul had disputed with Stoic and Epicurean philosophers with discouragingly meager results, the nearby Aeropagus where Paul was summoned before the ruling Council to give an account of his teaching, the temple of Zeus, the Dionysian theater where the tragedies of Sophocles and Euripides had been performed. The next morning, we went by automobile (about one hour) to Corinth, that ancient city of sin to which Paul went after he had been expelled first from Philippi and then from Thessalonica, and after his discouraging experience in Athens. Here it was that Paul had spent eighteen months founding the most famous of his churches, the one that caused him his greatest concern, to which he addressed two of his most famous letters. Such a brief visit was far from sufficient, but it at least gave us an opportunity of paying our homage to St. Paul by visiting this scene of his so-important labors, and of imprinting its image indelibly on our memories.

That afternoon we took the plane to Rome, for I felt I could delay no longer my appearance before the Pope to render the account of my stewardship as his Legate to the Melbourne Eucharistic Congress. The Pope received the report with his unfailing graciousness and an expression of gratitude. To me, personally, the most treasured picture that appears in the memorial book of the Congress is the photograph of Pope Paul VI and myself gazing at the large bronze symbol of the Congress, which has become a permanent article of display in the Vatican Museum. With the presentation of my report, this unique, most consoling and encouraging experience of serving as the Pope's Legate to the Fortieth Eucharistic Congress came to an end.

When Monsignor Stafford and I returned to Baltimore, we were well into the month of March. The eighteenth day of that month would be my seventy-fifth birthday, the regular time for the retirement of all Bishops and Archbishops, adopted in conformity with the documents of the Second Vatican Council and subsequent Vatican pronouncements. Accordingly, on that day I sent a letter to the Holy Father submitting my resignation from the position of Archbishop of Baltimore at any time he decided to accept it. In the course of the letter, however, I explained that the Good Samaritan Hospital, which was of great importance to both the archdiocese and the city of Baltimore and of whose board the Archbishop of Baltimore is *ex officio* chairman, was in the process of making a difficult and delicate change of administration. The temporary administrator had already received his recall to Bon Secours Hospital and the newly employed administrator would not arrive until April 1. It might be awkward if there were a change of the Chairman of the Board at the same time. It would be helpful if I could remain until the new administrator had settled into his post, a process that would not take longer than a month or two. The Holy See responded promptly, extending my term of office by one year.

The new administrator, Mr. James Oakey, who came from a similar position in New Jersey, had the close cooperation of the outgoing temporary administrator and fitted into his new post rapidly and efficiently. In the late summer I again addressed a letter to the Holy Father, informing him that the process of change had been successfully completed and that I was ready to retire whenever he would see fit to accept my resignation. The Holy See, however, adhered to the extension of one year. On April 2, 1974, the Vatican announced that Pope Paul VI had appointed the Most Reverend William D. Borders, Bishop of Orlando, to the Archdiocese of Baltimore. Archbishop Borders set June 26 as the date for his installation at the Cathedral of Mary Our Queen. Meanwhile, I was named Apostolic Administrator, with responsibility of continuing to preside over the archdiocese until Archbishop Borders should arrive.

Farewell tributes, I believe, are almost always suspect. In the nature of things they are one-sided, praising what has been praiseworthy, but glossing over weaknesses and defects. At the same time they are always deeply appreciated as signs of respect, goodwill, and friendliness. Mine was no exception.

When Archbishop Borders announced the date of his installation,

Henry Knott and a group of my friends decided to honor the occasion of my retirement by arranging a testimonial dinner at the Civic Center. For such an occasion as that, the capacity of the Civic Center is 3,500. It turned out to be a tribute not only from my Catholic friends, but also from my Protestant and Jewish well-wishers. As the climax of the event, Henry presented me with the sum of $450,000, which he and his committee had raised for the establishment of the Lawrence Cardinal Shehan Scholarship Fund to provide tuition to Catholic inner-city schools for students in need. It was indeed a handsome sum under any circumstances, but particularly in view of the short time at the disposal of Henry and the members of his committee, and in the absence of any publicity or fanfare. While the proceeds from the fund have continued each year to supply as many scholarships as possible to poor children of Baltimore, the fund itself, by prudent investment and additions, has increased to $800,000. Such a sum, although still a long way from meeting all the educational needs of the poor of the city, was, in its establishment, a step in the right direction.

The whole event was for me a gratifying occasion. Particularly appreciated were the remarks" of Bishop Gossman, who had been my Urban Vicar since his consecration in 1968. There were just three speeches on the occasion: that of Henry Knott, which was typically brief, and right on the mark; that of Bishop Gossman; and my own response, which appeared almost in its entirety on the Op-Ed page of the morning *Sun*. Here I take the liberty of giving that of Bishop Gossman, because it is a picture of me as he saw me at close range during the years he lived with me at the Basilica rectory, and because he was—and remains—my close friend. I warn the reader, however, it is a picture seen through very friendly eyes. I quote it in full because it is reasonably short and it gives me occasion to make some hopefully pertinent remarks about myself, and to bring this book to a more or less fitting end. The script of his speech is entitled simply: "Remarks by Bishop Gossman at Testimonial Dinner—May 21, 1974."

We know him as a churchman, an ecumenist, and a champion of justice on a national and international scale. I rise now to speak some other words about Lawrence Shehan, about the man behind the scenes—the man many of you have never really known and probably never will.

He is a man without pretense or guile; and is basically rather shy. Though he is probably considered as a man of power simply because of his position, I have never known him to act with a sense of his own power or importance. He does not underestimate his position; it simply never occurs to him to use his power. Yet he is a man of substance and strengths; no one works longer hours than he does. He sets a pace and a tempo that exhausts those years younger than himself. He is steadfastly dedicated to his pastoral duties, in season and out, in good times and bad, even though his faithfulness has, on occasion, brought him anguish, uncertainty, and the distinct possibility of failure. On more than one occasion in matters of controversy, Lawrence Shehan has stuck by his priests even when doing so may have risked bringing him disfavor or even embarrassment.

He has a charm and a wit all his own that are rarely seen in public. Nobody laughs quite like he does; his laugh is infectious—from deep down inside it bubbles up and is something to behold. I remember the time he said, "Joe, they took all the fun out of being a Bishop"—and he was right!

At the same time, he brings to all he does a deep sense of history and of his own rootedness in the past. His messages and sermons frequently speak to us of our own unique past and remind us that Lawrence Shehan probably has forgotten more history than many of us ever knew.

Lawrence Shehan is a man who became a bishop in a world where everything was certain, and a cardinal in a world where nothing was. Many people seem to expect a bishop to be omniscient, and some bishops seem to think themselves so endowed. But not Lawrence Shehan. He has struggled often with difficult, tough decisions. Again and again, he has shown himself willing to deal with demands of transition and change in an institution not especially known for either. He welcomes the opinions and views of others with openness and honesty. He is a man who really listens, and *sometimes* he is not too proud to change his mind.

As we might suspect but never be sure of, he has his moments of confusion and uncertainty in the face of the complex problems of today. In spite of his many achievements, he has even confessed at times to feeling himself almost a total failure.

And so, tonight we honor a man who is remarkable in many ways and for many reasons, and yet one with whom we can all identify in terms of our own frailty and uncertainty. I have deliberately tried not to draw a picture of him that is larger than life. Lawrence Shehan is a great man not because he is without frailty, but because he has been able to overcome frailty. It is with deep personal affection for Lawrence Shehan, the man and the priest, that I conclude by saying that he is indeed, and always will be, a great and good and gentle man, and for me a true friend and father.

I cannot leave the remarks of Bishop Gossman without making several observations. The first is to repeat what I said at the start: It is a picture of myself as seen through friendly eyes. The second is: I cannot comprehend my own words to him: "They have taken all the fun out of being a Bishop." I never had found any "fun" in being a Bishop. I had found many moments of deep satisfaction in doing the *work* of a Bishop; a constant feeling of deep gratitude to Almighty God in choosing me, unworthy as I was and am, to be a "successor to Christ's own Apostles"—but never any fun. Third, where I am quoted by him as saying on occasions that I felt I had been *almost* a complete failure; I might just as well have left out "almost," for there had been times, particularly during the period of 1968 to 1973, when I felt that, in view of the opportunities that had been given to me, and the honors that had been bestowed upon me, I had been a complete failure.

Lastly, when in his final sentence Bishop Gossman uses the word "great," I must say I have never seen in myself any element of greatness, except perhaps in the very limited sense that, as I have advanced in age, I have developed a sense of great, I may say total, dependence upon the goodness, love, and mercy of God, and the redemptive value and power of the sufferings, death, and resurrection of Our Lord and Saviour, Jesus Christ.

Most of us, I believe, are conscious of a regrettable shortcoming or defect in our life of prayer. Few of us have achieved the depth and intensity of prayer that we should have wished to see in ourselves; I must confess that I am among the many. Although I hope I have lived a prayerful priestly life in the general sense of that term, I have never seen myself as a person of deep and prolonged prayer. As I have advanced in age I have found it very difficult to change the habits of life acquired over so many years. This has caused me to turn more and more to the goodness and love of God and to His mercy revealed in our Lord and Saviour.

This, I suppose, is the logical place for me to speak somewhat more explicitly of my life of prayer and spirituality. Here I would say that, as one might suspect, my prayer life has centered about my daily offering of the Sacrifice of the Mass and my recitation of the Liturgical Hours of the Church, with the daily recitation of the rosary as a mark of my continuing devotion to Mary, the Mother of God. Throughout my whole life I have been an early riser. It is not unusual for me to awaken at 4:30 A.M., sometimes even earlier. The first thing I have done after rising is to recite the Morning Prayer. As a rule, my daily Mass has been offered at seven o'clock in the church or Cathedral to which my residence was attached, unless a special engagement required me to offer Mass at some other time and place. In Bridgeport after it was necessary for me to acquire my own residence, I said daily Mass in the private chapel, and the same was true during my rather brief residence at the new Cathedral rectory after my return to Baltimore. In both places, however, I made a practice of offering Sunday Mass with homily in the Cathedral. Generally speaking, I have always preferred to offer Mass for the people rather than to say Mass privately, and I have never been without at least a small but devout congregation. The time between my early rising and Mass has offered a convenient opportunity for prayer and for such study and writing as may be considered an extension of prayer. Much of this book, for instance, has been written during that time and in the late hours of the evening. I have made a habit of reciting the Evening Prayer in the late afternoon and the Office of the Readings in the late evening.

As I look back over the years, I would like to think of my life as priest and Bishop as an intertwining of prayer and ministry. The successes and failures in ministry may be said to be a measure of success and failure in prayer life—and I assure the reader that I am very conscious of my failures. I suppose it is hardly necessary to say that from the beginning of my priestly life I have always made regular and fairly frequent use of the Sacrament of Penance, except that in view of the attitude of many professed Catholics of the present day concerning the reality of sin and the importance of the Sacrament of Penance, it may be proper to recall this practice. Finally, I may say that I have always had a deep interest in and strong love of Sacred Scripture, and it has been one of the regrets of my mature life that I did not have the opportunity to pursue higher Scripture studies.

Finally, I believe I can truthfully say that always throughout my adult life I have considered the priesthood, established by Our Lord at the Last Supper and bestowed on me, as the central fact of my life. Ever since I began my studies for the priesthood I have had no other objective in life and have always considered my ordination the most important event of my life. Everything of significance that has happened to me since has been an addition to, or development of, my priesthood. I have not been unmindful of the essential importance of the initiating Sacraments of Baptism and Confirmation or that central treasure of Christian life, the Eucharist, but in the end I believe I shall be judged primarily as a priest. May God have mercy on my soul!

After my retirement I continued to reside in the Basilica rectory, the old "Archbishop's House" that adjoins the Basilica itself. There I have led as far as possible the life of a parish priest. Each morning I offer the early Mass in the Basilica in the presence of a small, devout congregation; I offer Sunday Mass with homily, and take my turn regularly in the confessional. Once a month I go to the new Cathedral to offer Sunday Mass with homily there. In his ever-kind thoughtfulness Archbishop Borders has included me in the schedule for the administration of the Sacrament of Confirmation in the various parishes of the archdiocese. On rather infrequent occasions I am called upon to administer the Sacrament of Priestly Ordination to the candidates of the Order of the Most Holy Trinity, one of whose younger priests helps us out quite regularly at the Basilica on weekends. The exercise of these functions of the episcopate continues to be a source of deep satisfaction. But I must say that my most enduring satisfaction arises from the possession and exercise of Christ's own priesthood, and from the privilege of living here at the Basilica under the edifying and inspiring leadership of Monsignor Paul Love, who directs a household so orderly and well cared-for, is so careful to maintain the dignity of the liturgical norms and customs, and who instituted and maintained for many years a most generous program of charity. Many poor and hungry people of downtown Baltimore came daily to the rectory to receive their generous ration of sandwiches and hot soup or coffee; they knew that Monsignor Love would never fail them.

One of the limitations of this program as it operated over so many years arose from the fact that the facilities of the Basilica rectory were not extensive enough to permit the applicants to come inside. They had to receive their rations at the basement door and then stand on the pavement outside to consume them. Happily, in very recent times, with the encouragement of Archbishop Borders, Associated Catholic Charities under the leadership of Mr. Harold Smith, its able Director, purchased a desirable and pleasing house with a storefront on Franklin Street. It is within the same city block as the Basilica and its rectory, and thus near enough to permit us to retain a certain fictitious sense of proprietorship. Here in these more spacious and appropriate quarters, the number served has increased from the maximum of 200 that Monsignor Love and his group were able to take care of, to a present 400, with indications of additional growth. A number of the parishes have willingly taken responsibility for providing the lunch one specific day each month. Appropriately, the facility has been named "Our Daily Bread," for it operates every day of the week, including Sunday. It is a source of satisfaction to have even a remote connection with such a project.

One of the most treasured elements of my life of retirement has been the continuing friendship of persons like Bishop Gossman of Raleigh and Bishop Mardaga of Wilmington, who were my former Auxiliary Bishops and shared with me living quarters at the Basilica rectory; the present Auxiliary Bishops: T. Austin Murphy, who often joins me at lunch; J. Francis Stafford, who was my most helpful and pleasant companion at the Melbourne Eucharistic Congress and is now the Urban Vicar; P. Francis Murphy, who for some years was my secretary and is now Vicar for Western Maryland.

The oldest and without doubt the dearest friend among the Bishops is John J. Russell of Richmond. Our friendship, as I have said previously, began in boyhood, has grown through all the years since, and remains down to this day. The Bishop to whom I owe most during the years of my retirement has been Archbishop William Donald Borders, who, by the will of the Holy See, succeeded me when my term of office came to an end. His thoughtfulness, his kindness, and his genuine concern have ever since been a daily experience of my life. Had they not been there during the days of my rather recent serious illness and the many months of convalescence, I probably would not have survived long.

From all the members of the hierarchy of this country, including those I have already mentioned as being in a special category, I have always been conscious, from that day long ago when I entered their ranks, of their sympathetic friendship and support. Outstanding in this respect has been John Cardinal Dearden, worthy successor of Edward Cardinal Mooney who did so much to encourage me in the early days of my priesthood and, if it were possible, still more during the early years of my episcopate. Much the same thing, I must say, is true of Terence Cardinal Cooke and his predecessor, Francis Cardinal Spellman; Timothy Cardinal Manning and his predecessor, James Francis Cardinal McIntyre, in spite of our many verbal battles during the time I was Chairman of the NCWC Department of Education—battles inherited from my friend and predecessor in that position, Bishop Matthew Brady of Manchester; Umberto Cardinal Medeiros of Boston, and his predecessor, Richard Cardinal Cushing, whose affection I always enjoyed and reciprocated; Patrick Cardinal O'Boyle of Washington, whom I have had many occasions to mention when treating of those difficult times beginning in 1968, and his successor, William Cardinal Baum, now Prefect of the Sacred Congregation for Catholic Education; and John Cardinal Carberry of St. Louis, like myself now living in retirement; John Cardinal Krol of Philadelphia. There is indeed a special bond that unites the members of the College of Cardinals. I must say that I have never ceased to be conscious of that special bond of affection.

Of the other members of the American hierarchy, I should place in a special category Archbishop Joseph Bernardin, recently named Archbishop of Chicago, whom I first came to know when he was a very young priest beginning his ministry under my friend Bishop Russell (then of Charleston, South Carolina) and from whom I received so many marks of kindness and consideration during the years he served as General Secretary and later President of the U.S. Catholic Conference and the National Conference of Catholic Bishops. In much the same class I would place Archbishops Philip Hannan of New Orleans; James Hickey of Washington; Edward McCarthy of Miami; John May of St. Louis; Thomas McDonough (recently retired) of Louisville, and his successor, Thomas Kelly, O.P.; Bishops Cletus O'Donnell of Madison, James Malone of Youngstown, and Theodore McCarrick of Metuchen—but here I must stop, since it would be impossible to mention all those Bishops from whom I have received special marks of kindness and friendship over so many years. I must not, however, fail to mention Archbishop Martin J. O'Connor, whom I first came to know when we were students together at St. Mary's Seminary and at the North American College, and from whom I received countless signs of friendship during all the years he was rector of the North American College.

The oldest priest-friend I claim undoubtedly is Monsignor I. Mitchell Cartwright, retired, a real contemporary, whom I have known since childhood. From long-time priest-friends of the generation below my own, I mention first Monsignors John Toomey and the recently deceased George Curtiss of Bridgeport, my Chancellor and Secretary respectively, who visited with me for several days not long ago; Monsignor Paul Love, rector of the Basilica, whose daily kindness and thoughtfulness I continue to experience; Melville Taylor, close friend since his boyhood; Anthony Dziwulski; the late Clare O'Dwyer; Porter White, whom I have had so many occasions to mention; Austin Healy; Bob Armstrong; Paul Cook; "Pete" Stallings; Eddie Lynch; Jerry

Kenney, Bill Newman, who, to the delight of so many priests and people was recently appointed rector of the Cathedral of Mary Our Queen; of the still-younger generation: Fathers Brian Rafferty, Richard Cramblitt, Michael Spillane, Joseph Barr, Glenn Byrne, Jeff Toohey, Joseph Bonadio, S.S., and Damian Anuszewski, O.SS.T., Jim Barker—all of whose kind thoughtfulness and concern are particularly touching to me. Last but not least, Michael Schleupner, whose kindness and thoughtfulness have seemed to increase with his burdens of the Chancery.

In a special category I should place Monsignor John Tracy Ellis (already mentioned in my prologue as author of the two-volume life of Cardinal Gibbons), whom I came to know when he was beginning his distinguished career in American Church history. In the same category I would place Father James Laubacher, S.S., of whom I have already spoken in connection with the Second Vatican Council. Here, too, I should mention Father J. Carroll McHugh, S.S., former rector of St. Mary's Seminary House of Philosophy, who became my confessor and spiritual director after Father Laubacher's transfer. To these names I should add those of Father Robert Leavitt, S.S., president-rector of St. Mary's Seminary, and Father Edward Frazer, S.S., Provincial of the Sulpician Fathers. Looking back over these many years, I believe I can say that since my youth I have never lacked devoted and treasured friends among the Sulpician Fathers.

Although my close association with the Jesuit Fathers does not go back so far, yet not less deep is the debt of gratitude and affection I owe them. Staunch have been the friends I have found among them, particularly during the years when I was serving as Bishop of Bridgeport and Archbishop of Baltimore. As friends who have been particularly dear to me I mention Father Joseph Sellinger, S.J., who during the many years of his presidency has done so much for Loyola College and for the archdiocese and city of Baltimore, and his immediate predecessor, Father Vincent Beatty, S.J. Nor should I fail to mention Father Leo Murray, S.J., who served as president of the CYO of SS. Philip and James parish while I was its pastor and who is now pastor of the parish of St. Ignatius in Baltimore.

Nor can I fail to make special mention of dear friends among the laity: the everfaithful Henry J. Knott and his wife, Marion; Henry Irr (recently deceased and much lamented) and his wife, Katherine; Dr. Richard Ferguson and his wife, Jeanne, who were so kind and thoughtful of my sister Mary during her later years; Francis A. Gunther, Jr., and his wife, Mary Ellen; Pierce Flanigan and his wife, Mary Ann; John Evelius, first partner and later successor of Francis X. Gallagher as Attorney for the Archdiocese of Baltimore, and his wife,

Mary; the always-ready and helpful Fred Saffran and his wife, Clara.

In a class all by herself is Betty Sweeney, who, shortly after I was advanced to the post of Archbishop, became my secretary. (I will call her my "lay secretary" to distinguish her position from that of P. Francis Murphy, who became my priest secretary after the end of the Second Vatican Council.) The services Betty has rendered have gone far beyond those of an ordinary secretary, and many of those services she has continued to fulfill after my retirement. One of the most important has been that of supervising the typing of the entire text of these memoirs. In carrying out this sometimes difficult task—since my hand-writing, never particularly good, has deteriorated as my age has increased—she has not only read the complete text many times, but she has also made important suggestions.

Almost in the same class with Betty Sweeney, I would place Nellie (Mrs. J. Erle) Baumgartner, long-time and faithful friend of my sister, who did so much to brighten the last years and particularly the last days of her life and whose lasting and devoted friendship I continue to share. Nor can I fail to mention Elizabeth Mulholland, who, as case-work supervisor of the Washington Catholic Charities more than forty years ago, rendered such invaluable service to me as Director of that organization, to those who worked under her, but especially to the poor people of that city. Even now, after all these years, but even more frequently since my recent serious illness, she never fails to send a periodic reminder of a friendship that began so many years ago.

Since the days of St. Elizabeth Ann Seton, the Daughters of Charity of Emmitsburg have been in a very special class in the Archdiocese of Baltimore. In a very real sense, the Sisters Provincial of that community can be said to be the direct successors of their sainted foundress. I suppose every Archbishop of Baltimore has looked upon each of them in turn as a very dear friend. When I returned to Baltimore in that capacity, Sister Isabel Toohey was Sister Provincial. She was to me a very dear friend, as was also, and still remains, her successor, Sister Eleanor McNabb. I hope I do not presume too much in calling the present Sister Provincial, Sister Mary Clare Hughes, a very dear friend

As I have already noted, to no community of Sisters do I owe a greater debt than to the School Sisters of Notre Dame. That debt of gratitude goes all the way back to Sister Cantia, under whom, at the age of five, I began my schooling; and particularly to Sister Mary Euthemia, who, I have no doubt, can be regarded as God's instrument in fostering within me the idea of a vocation to the priesthood and in helping me to turn my footsteps toward the altar. Throughout the years,

I feel that I owe many things to that community. In more recent years, their many Sisters have been symbolized to me by the person of Sister Kathleen Feeley. I first came to know Kathleen about forty years ago, when I was Auxiliary Bishop of Baltimore and pastor of the parish of SS. Philip and James. She was the youthful president of the CYO of that parish. At the end of her term of office, she entered the religious life, carrying with her an already acknowledged gift of leadership and an admirable spirit of religion. More than a decade ago, she was named President of the College of Notre Dame of Maryland. Wonderful have been the things that have happened under her leadership—growth, development, and an ever-enhancing reputation. At the time she took office, it was being said that the day of the women's college was gone, particularly the Catholic women's college in Baltimore. Now, no Baltimorean, especially no Catholic Baltimorean, would dare say that the day of the Catholic women's college is past. Through it all, she has remained "my very dear friend, Kathleen."

In the forefront of my Sister-friends I unhesitatingly would place Sister Mary Thomas, R.S.M., President and Administrator of Mercy Hospital. Through her extraordinary gift of administration, including her sound judgment, prompt decisiveness, and ever-calm and pleasing personality, Mercy Hospital ranks among the leading hospitals in this city, which is blessed with so many excellent hospitals. During this past year, through a set of special circumstances, she has become to me an even closer friend than before. For some time I had been under treatment of one of Mercy's leading specialists for what I would now call a relatively minor ailment. Then one late Sunday afternoon (to be specific, June 28, 1981), I was taken with a rather sharp abdominal pain. From its type and location I knew it had nothing to do with the ailment for which I was being treated. I decided, therefore, not to call the specialist, and, owing to the inconvenience of the hour, to call my personal physician early the following morning, meanwhile relying on such medication for pain relief as I had on hand. As the evening advanced, the pain became so severe as to seem almost unbearable. I finally decided to call Sister Mary Thomas and ask her advice. She promised to arrange for me to receive proper medication for relief from my present pain and to have me brought to the hospital as soon as possible. My telephone conversation with Sister Mary Thomas that evening of June 28 was the last thing of which I have clear remembrance for well over a full month. When in the early part of August I returned to full consciousness, I was informed that I had undergone two major intestinal surgical operations and two relatively minor complementary surgeries. Through her sound judgment and prompt decisiveness, Sister Mary Thomas probably had saved my life. Through the efficient care she provided throughout a prolonged period of convalescence, I have returned to a life of at least partial usefulness and of preparation for the real end that cannot be far away. I take it, therefore, that it is not strange that I should feel toward her a friendship far closer than before.

Besides Sister Mary Thomas, there is also Sister Veronica Daily, R.S.M., a friend since childhood days in St. Ann's School. Having entered religion and the nursing profession, she had made her way up through the ranks, became Local Superior, President of Mercy Hospital, and Provincial Superior; then returned to the ranks in Mercy to be useful in any way that presented itself. She is indeed a strong character and a loving personality to claim as a friend. Nor can I fail to remember her niece, Sister Elizabeth Anne Corcoran, whom, as well as Sister Kathleen Feeley, I have known since my pastorate at SS. Philip and James Church. From my observation, she is the "right hand" of Sister Mary Thomas, and to me she remains a very dear friend. Finally, among my friends of the Mercy community I hail Sister Louis Mary Battle, who, having come north from her homeland in the South, for many years now has been the superb Administrator of Stella Maris Hospice. She has been largely responsible for the enlargement and the steady improvement of that institution of the aging and for the excellent reputation which Stella Maris enjoys.

There are many Sisters of other communities to whom I owe a debt of gratitude not less than that which I have endeavored to pay to those I have mentioned. Here, those I have noted by name must stand as symbols of all the Sisters to whom I owe a debt so deep.

Of my immediate family, all that I need say here is that all of my brothers had died before I reached the age of retirement: William, August 14, 1961; Thomas, December 30, 1963; Dan, September 5, 1972; John Brooke, October 16, 1972. Only my sister Mary survived, retaining for me all that devotion she had manifested during all the many years of her life.

In September 1975, Mary accompanied the group of our Baltimore people who, under my leadership, had gone to Rome for the canonization of St. Elizabeth Ann Seton. There she met with a strange and fatal accident. She had gone with friends to a religious article store and had just emerged from the store when two young men on a motorcycle sped by. One grabbed the shoulder strap of her handbag. She fell and was dragged until the strap broke, when the young ruffians made off with the bag containing her wallet. The fall and the dragging caused her body to be severely bruised. She traveled home with the group, but shortly thereafter she died suddenly, October 5, 1975, as a result of a blood clot caused by the bruises.

Of all my brothers, Dan was closest to me in age, in disposition, and—many have remarked—in appearance, but also in mutual brotherly attachment. While still in high school, as I have previously noted, Dan chose dentistry as his profession and became a successful practitioner and part-time professor at the University of Maryland Dental School. He married Josephine Manfuso and, completely devoted to each other, they raised their equally devoted family of five children. As soon as they felt they could afford it, they purchased a lovely but unpretentious home on Taplow Road in Homeland, just east of where the new Cathedral was to be built.

Their oldest child, Daniel, Jr., having completed his education just as this country became involved in World War II, joined the U.S. Navy. There he became associated with Mary Meier, an excellent Catholic young woman from Riverside, California, who served in the same branch of the Armed Forces. At the end of the war they married and went to live at Riverside, where they raised their seven children.

Their next son, John, married Ann Reilly. When Dan and Josephine decided to move into an apartment, John and Ann took over the Taplow Road family home, and there they continue to live with their three children. Dan's youngest son, Robert, after graduating from Loyola College, married an excellent Catholic young woman, Judith Ward. Several years ago Bob took a promising position with a young firm in the recycling industry and he and Judy with their family, moved from Oklahoma back to Baltimore, where he established his headquarters, vowing never to leave again. They have a beautiful home not far from the new Cathedral.

Closest to me of all the children and Dan and Josephine are their two lovely daughters. Mary Frances, the older, married John Macsherry, of a well-known Baltimore Catholic family. They and their children live in the Roland Park area of North Baltimore. Joanna, the younger, married William J. Baird, Jr., a fine young Catholic businessman, who seems to be doing very well indeed. They and their eight children live next to the Cathedral rectory in the former home of Dr. Ferguson. All four of these families are devoted members of the new Cathedral parish.

These four children of Dan and Josephine who have remained in Baltimore have, with their mother and their spouses, kept alive the

Shehan family spirit and tradition. On each of the great feasts of the year, one or another never fails to arrange a joyous family reunion, to which I am always invited and go.

Of the five children of John Brooke, who married Peg Anderson of Wilmette, Illinois, only the youngest son, George, has remained in Baltimore. He and I manage to see each other from time to time. The other four, Brooke, Jr., Thomas, Mary Ellen, and Laurie, are scattered over the country, and for many years I have rarely had an opportunity to see any of them. Will, my youngest brother, married Ella Jackson. After Will's death, his only son, William, Jr., with his wife and family, and later his mother, moved to Salisbury on the Eastern Shore of Maryland.

I should add a few words about the family of Tom, my oldest brother. Married to Katherine Kohler, he had become a business partner with my father. While he was still a young man, he had an opportunity to establish a business of his own in Philadelphia. He, his wife and children, all still in grade school, moved to that city, where he founded a business that seemed to give good promise. He and Katherine established a pleasant home in a good neighborhood. Once the Depression struck, however, the tailoring business and everything connected with it suffered a rapid decline. Tom somehow managed to keep going and was able to give his four children a complete Catholic education, including college. Lawrence, the oldest, named after me, married an excellent young Catholic woman, Mary Gallagher. Katherine, his oldest daughter, married Bernard Tucker, brother of Father Eugene Tucker, S.J. His second daughter, Betty, married Francis Horstmann of the well-known Philadelphia Catholic family of that name. Patricia, the youngest, married Bernard Carey, a promising young Catholic lawyer. All of them quite understandably established their families in the Philadelphia area. Meanwhile, however, Tom had a hard struggle, and the time came when he had to close down his business. He was able, nevertheless, to obtain employment and continued to work down to his last illness and death at the age of sixty-eight. Through all the years, in spite of the distance that separated us, the Baltimore and the Philadelphia branches of the Shehan family managed to stay very close. By the time of Tom's death, I had become Archbishop of Baltimore. Accompanied by Bishop T. Austin Murphy, George Hopkins, and Porter White, I went up to Philadelphia to celebrate his funeral Mass and to conduct the burial ceremony.

With this, I bring the family chronicle and my memories of the past to an end.

Epilogue:
In Tribute to Pope John Paul II

IN THE EARLY EVENING of October 16, 1978, shortly after the traditional white smoke, rising from the Sistine Chapel, had signaled to the city of Rome and to the world that the election of a Pope had taken place, I, with two companions, Archbishop Rembert Weakland and Father Michael Spillane, stood in the Piazza of St. Peter, awaiting the drama that soon would unfold on the portico of the great Basilica. As soon as the Cardinals, wearing their red robes, had taken their places in the north balcony, Cardinal Felici advanced to the microphone that was placed in the middle of the balustrade of the central balcony and said in a loud, clear voice, "I bring you news of great joy. We have a Pope. He is Karol Wojtyla of Cracow in Poland. He has taken the name of John Paul II." Few in that vast audience recognized the name of Karol Wojtyla, and the few who did were so surprised that, for the moment, they forgot to applaud.

Immediately, the Pope, garbed in his white papal robes, strode to the microphone. "Praised be Jesus Christ," came the now everywhere-familiar greeting. "Now and forever," came the prompt response. Then, in what seemed to me to be perfect Italian, the Pope began his first public speech. It was so short that here I give it in its full English translation:

> My beloved brothers and sisters. We are all still profoundly saddened by the death of our beloved Pope, John Paul I. And behold, now the most eminent Cardinals have called a new Bishop to Rome. They have called him from a far-away nation— far away, but also very near in the communion of faith and Christian tradition.

With fear I received this nomination. But I did so in a spirit of obedience to Our Lord and with total trust in His mother, Our Most Holy Lady.

I don't know if I can express myself well in your—our—Italian language. But if I make a mistake you will correct me.

And so I present myself to all of you to confess our common faith, our hope, and our trust in the Mother of Christ and the Church, and to begin anew on the road, the road of history and of the Church, with the help of God and with the help of people.

With that, the Pope immediately pronounced the introductory versicles and went on to give the Apostolic Blessing to the city and the world (*Urbi et Orbi*): "May the blessing of Almighty God, Father, Son, and Holy Spirit descend upon you and be with you forever." "A-men," came the loud response, followed by thunderous applause. By his impressive presence and those few simple words, spoken in a resonant voice, the Pope seemed to have won over all members of that great audience. Then, for a moment, the Pope stood there silent, with arms extended in an all-embracing gesture. Now after four years of his action-filled papacy, as I recall that scene it seems to me that in the gentle Italian twilight there had dawned upon the Church of Christ the light of a renewed faith and strengthened hope.

What seems to justify the use of these words in connection with the papacy of John Paul II is the totality of papal events during the past four years. Four things in particular stand out in my mind: the twelve great journeys of evangelization, the three important encyclicals, the instantaneous worldwide reaction to the almost fatal assassination attempt, and the Pope's unique appeal to the youth of today and their response.

Within the restricted scope of this Epilogue it is impossible to give a detailed account of all twelve journeys or even the first of them. Here I shall choose three which are of special importance in themselves and at the same time can serve as types or examples of all the rest: the journey to Mexico, becuase it is the first and sets the scene for, and throws a special light on, the others; that to West Germany (Federal Republic of Germany), because of the circumstances under which it was undertaken and because of one particular discourse which is especially relevant to the world of science, technology, and acceler-ated production in which we live; and that to the Far East (to the

Philippines and Japan), again, because, in the great discourse delivered at Hiroshima, the Pope most effectively deals with the world of the immediate future, over which hangs the threat of nuclear warfare.

On January 25, 1979, the Pope set out on his journey to Mexico. Leaving Rome by airplane, he landed at Santo Domingo, where Columbus had landed on his first voyage of discovery, October 12, 1492, and had caused the first Mass to be celebrated in the New World. There, too, the Pope offered his first Papal Mass in the Americas. In his homily, he said: "I have come to these American lands as a traveler of peace to participate in an ecclesiastical event of evangelization, inspired by the words of the Apostle Paul: 'Yet preaching the Gospel is not the subject of a boast. I am under compulsion and have no choice. I am ruined if I do not preach it.'" Thus, at the very beginning of his first journey, the Pope announced what would be the purpose of all the journeys that would follow: evangelization.

From Santo Domingo, the Pope flew directly to Mexico City. There, in the Shrine of Our Lady of Guadalupe, he concelebrated Mass with the Latin American Bishops, and thus formally opened their Third General Conference. In his homily, which he entitled "Medellin—After Ten Years," he noted that the Second Conference had been held shortly after the Second Vatican Council. Its primary purpose was to apply the directives of the Council to the Church in Latin America. "The evangelizing intention of that Conference had been quite clear, but ten years have passed since then. Interpretations have been given that have been at times contradictory, not always correct, not always beneficial to the Church. The Church, therefore, is looking for new ways that will enable her to understand more deeply and fulfill more zealously the mission she has been given by Jesus Christ."

The next day, he and the Bishops went to Puebla, where he initiated the actual proceedings of the Conference with his main discourse of the journey. Here he may be said to have taken up where he had left off in his homily of the preceding day. He made it clear that there are three elements that are necessary to correct the false interpretations he had noted: the truth about Christ; the truth about the nature and mission of the Church; the truth about man. Here one is tempted to give a detailed analysis of that discourse, together with some of its striking passages. But no analysis, however detailed, and no series of quotations, however striking, can do justice to the whole discourse. The reader is urged to obtain a copy of the pamphlet "The Pope in Mexico," published by the U.S. Conference of Catholic Bishops, and read carefully all the speeches the Pope gave in that country, especially that given at Santo Domingo, that in the Shrine of Our Lady of Guadalupe, and above all that given at Puebla. The whole journey, I repeat, is a fitting introduction to all twelve, and throws important light on those that followed.

The second journey that I cite is that to West Germany (the Federal Republic of Germany). The Pope undertook the journey in answer to the invitation of the German Bishops to preside at the celebration of the 700th anniversary of the death of St. Albert the Great. But that year, the German Protestants were celebrating the 350th anniversary of the Augsburg Confession. When the Pope announced his intention, the news media forecast serious tensions and conflicts that would be caused by the papal visit. None of these dire predictions came true. On arrival, the Pope was cordially greeted by President Karl Carstens and later by the Prime Minister, and he was confronted nowhere by any unpleasantness. In my judgment, the outstanding speech of that journey was to an audience of scientists and students (estimated at 6,000) in the Cologne Cathedral on the subject of "The Connection between Scientific Thought and the Power of Faith in the Search for Truth." In his five stops in Germany, it is estimated that the Pope addressed one and a half million persons, besides the millions who saw and heard him through the medium of television or read his speeches in the press. The journey to Germany must be considered one of the most successful of the twelve.

The third journey to which I give special attention is that to the Far East: the Philippines and Japan. In the Philippines, a nation said to be 95 percent Catholic, everywhere great crowds turned out to greet him and hear him speak. In the city of Bacalog, near the sugar-growing plantations, where for several years there had been tension between the landowners and the workers, 500,000 were reported to have turned out to hear the Pope deliver his final talk on "The Land and Justice." In Japan, where the Pope had been invited to speak in the university founded by the United Nations at Hiroshima, the first city to have been destroyed by an atomic bomb, he spoke to scientists, technologists, and students on the subject of "Moral Choices of the Future," to which might be appended the subtitle, "Science, Technology, and Conscience in the World of the Future." It was a most appropriate discourse for a world living under the threat of nuclear warfare and the possible destruction of civilization.

Besides these three journeys, the Pope has made nine others: to Ireland, September 1979; to the United States, October 1979; to Turkey (Ecumenical Pilgrimage), November 1979; to Africa, May 1980; to

France, May-June 1980; to Brazil, June 1980; a second journey to
Africa (Nigeria and neighboring nations), February 1982; to England,
Scotland and Wales, May-June 1982; to the Argentine, June 1982.
All these journeys have been characterized by huge crowds which
have greeted him with enthusiasm wherever he has gone. They have
constituted a mission unique in the whole history of the Church.

Important as were the twelve journeys of evangelization, almost
of equal importance, from the long-range point of view, were the three
encyclicals which have been published by Pope John Paul II to the
present point of time. The first of these, *Redemptor Hominis*, published less than five months after his election, he began with these
words: "The redeemer of man, Jesus Christ, is the center of the uni-
verse and of history." It was eminently proper that the Pope, who had
already begun those great journeys of evangelization to spread the
good news of redemption by Jesus Christ, should devote his first
encyclical to the Redeemer of man and should begin this document
with His name and the title that most intimately relates Him to the
human race. The two main theses of this encyclical are the mystery
of redemption and the situation of the redeemed person in the modern
world. Human rights and dignity, religious freedom and the search
for the meaning of life in a world of scientific discovery and technological development are scrutinized. The Pope discusses the value of
collegiality and shared responsibility and pledges commitment to ecumenical goals. The Church must remain the Church of the Eucharist
and of penance. The Eucharist must not be regarded as simply the
occasion to express Christian brotherhood. In penance, the importance of individual confession, of sorrow and the intention to amend
must not be minimized. The Church's fundamental function in every
age is to point the consciousness and the experience of the whole of
humanity toward God. The Pope calls for appreciation of priestly
celibacy. He devotes the final section to Mary, the mother in whom
we trust.

The second encyclical is titled *Dives in Misericordia* (Rich in
Mercy). Obviously, it is closely related to the first, for the infinite
mercy of God may be said to underlie the mystery of man's redemption. The Pope, in the first chapter, gives us two special reasons for
treating the mercy of God here. On the one hand, modern man, who
through science and technology has attained dominion over the earth,
seems opposed to the very concept of mercy. So wide is that dominion

that there is no room for mercy. On the other hand, man is threatened more today than at any other time. He needs God's mercy. That mercy is made visible in the Person of Jesus Christ. In the second chapter, the Pope tells us that Christ makes God's mercy known through the Messianic message. That message Christ proclaimed in the synagogue of Nazareth and in His response to the Baptist: "Go and tell John what you have seen and heard: the blind receive their sight; the cripples walk; lepers are cured; the dead are raised to life; the poor have the good news preached to them." Christ transmits that message, especially through His life-style and His actions, His miracles for the poor and suffering, the blind, the lame, the deaf; through His preaching—for example, His parables of the Prodigal Son, the Shepherd and the Lost Sheep, the Good Samaritan—in every aspect of His ministry portrayed in the Gospels. In the third chapter, "The Old Testament," the Pope presents God's mercy in His care for His chosen people, foreshadowing the fullness of that revelation in the New Testament. In the fourth chapter, the Pope gives us a profound and detailed commentary on the Prodigal Son. The fifth chapter gives us the fullness of revelation of God's mercy in the Paschal Mystery of the Cross and Resurrection of Christ. The sixth, "Mercy...From Generation to Generation," mirrors the modern world in its present favored position, with its many possibilities, but also with sources of deep uneasiness. The seventh chapter treats the mercy of God in the mission of the Church, whose function is to profess and proclaim the mercy of God and to seek to put mercy into practice in her own life and in the lives of the faithful. This leads us into the final chapter, "The Prayer of the Church of Our Times." That prayer is a loud cry to God for mercy. The second encyclical can be fully understood and appreciated only as the Pope's profound meditation on the mercy of God, who is rich in mercy.

The third encyclical, *Laborem Exercens* (On Human Work), owes its origin to the fact that on May 15, 1981, we would be celebrating the ninetieth anniversary of *Rerum Novarum*, the definitive encyclical of Leo XIII, the great Pope of the "social question." In view of the social problems following upon World War I, Pope Pius XI had published his encyclical *Quadragesimo Anno* (After Forty Years) May 15, 1931; because of further problems that had arisen in the wake of World War II, John XXIII had published *Mater et Magistra* (Mother and Teacher) May 15, 1961. Anticipating the social and economic changes, which, according to many experts, are to take place as a result of new discoveries of science and further developments of technology, Pope John Paul II decided to issue a new social encyclical on May 15, 1981.

The work was finished and in the hands of the printer when, on May 13, the near-fatal shot was fired. Publication had to be deferred until the following September 14.

In the first chapter of the encyclical, the Pope tells us that, in reference to the anticipated changes, four main factors are involved: the widespread introduction of automation in the field of industry and production; the increasing cost of energy and raw materials; the growing realization that the heritage of nature is limited and is being intolerably polluted; the emergence on the political scene of peoples who, after centuries of subjection, are demanding their rightful place among the nations and in international decision-making. These conditions will require a reordering and adjustment of the structure of the modern economy and of the distribution of work. The Pope tells us that it is not for the Church to analyze scientifically these changes. The task of the Church is to call attention to the dignity and rights of workers, to condemn situations where that dignity and these rights are being violated, and to help to guide these changes so as to ensure authentic progress of man and society. It is not the intention of the Pope to take a line different from that of his predecessors, but to be in organic connection with the whole of the Church's tradition and her past activity. Nor is it his intention to repeat all that has been taught in the past, but rather to point out that work is at the center of the social question and, following the words of the Gospel, to bring forth from the Church's treasures "what is old and what is new." Work is part of "what is old." Nevertheless, the general situation of man in the modern world calls for the formulation of new tasks that in this sector face each individual, each family, each country, the whole human race, and the Church herself.

After having given this general background relative to work in the modern world and his own purpose in publishing this encyclical, the Pope then goes on in Chapters 2, 3, and 4 to discuss every important aspect and problem of work in the modern world: the permanent ethical order derived from reason and Scripture (especially the creation texts of Genesis); capitalism as a threat to that right order; worker solidarity as a just and spontaneous reaction to the abuses of capitalism; the profound changes brought about by worker solidarity to safeguard the dignity of the worker and the welfare of the family and nation; the conflict between capital and labor; the priority of labor; the errors

of communism and economism; work as the basis of private owner-
ship; the right of workers to a just wage and other social benefits;
the rights of women workers; the dignity of agricultural work; the
right of the disabled person to suitable employment; work and the
emigration question.

Chapter 5, "Elements for a Spirituality of Work," is of particular
importance because it is original and unique. It is original in the sense
that such a spirituality is not found in any of the encyclicals of previous Popes; unique in the sense that, so far as I am aware, it has not
been mentioned by any previous writer in the whole field of Christian
spirituality. But its main importance derives from its contents: elements for a "spirituality of work." These elements are three in number: work as a sharing in the activity of the Creator; work as an
opportunity for, and means of, closer union with Jesus Christ, the Man
of Work; the light shed on work by the Paschal Mystery of the Cross
and Resurrection of Christ. Because of the unique character and the
importance of its contents, this fifth chapter deserves a far more detailed treatment than I can give it here.

These three encyclicals are not simply important documents of
the present, to be read, laid aside, and finally to be forgotten. They,
like the other great encyclicals of the modern Popes, are part of the
Church's literary treasure upon which she continues to draw for inspiration, guidance, and edification.

As I have noted, the Pope had arranged for the publication of his
third encyclical on May 15, 1981. Meanwhile, however, he had scheduled a public audience for five o'clock on the afternoon of May 13. On
that day, the Pope left the Vatican shortly before five in the special
vehicle he used on these occasions, accompanied by his driver, his
priest-secretary and a plainclothesman. Proceeding to the gateway of
the Arch of the Bells, he had entered the Piazza of St. Peter precisely
at five. He had made one complete circuit of the awaiting crowd, estimated at 15,000, and was coming to the end of the second, headed for
the podium from which he intended to address the audience. Suddenly
there was a series of shots. For a moment the Pope stood erect and
silent; then he slumped into the arms of his secretary. He had been
wounded three times: one bullet had struck his right arm; a second
had gazed his left arm and shattered one finger of the left hand; the
third had struck his lower abdomen, passed through his body and out
through his lower left back. For a moment the driver zigzagged the

automobile to keep the Pope out of the line of fire in case other shots would follow; then he made straightway for the gate through which the Pope had entered a few minutes earlier. There the Pope was transferred to the ambulance that was always waiting during these audiences, and he was sped immediately to the Clinico Gemelli, Rome's newest and best equipped hospital. Within minutes he was stretched on the operating table, and the five-and-a-half hour repair surgery had begun. The bullet almost miraculously had missed three vital organs, the pancreas, the abdominal aorta, and the spinal cord.

By then the news had long since burst upon the world. Throughout the world, the outpouring of anger, outrage, and sympathy for the stricken Pontiff was all but universal—even more extensive, said *Time*, than it had been for President Reagan six weeks before.

> The reaction of world leaders went far beyond the official statements. . . .Said Reagan: "I'll pray for him." Soviet President Leonid Brezhnev cabled to the Pope: "I am profoundly indignant at the criminal attempt on your life." Dismayed West German Chancellor Helmut Schmidt exclaimed: "I feel I have been hit in the abdomen myself." Outgoing French President Giscard d'Estang, who escaped a terrorist bomb in Corsica the previous month, sent a wire to the Vatican expressing "profound emotion," and obviously he did not exaggerate. An associate, who was conferring with Giscard when the news came, reported that the French President, who is noted for his icy reserve, experienced "an enormous shock." Indian Prime Minister Indira Gandhi told reporters: "I am too shocked for words. What more can I say?" (*Time*, May 25, 1981)*

I have chosen to repeat the above portion of the *Time* article, because its news sources are worldwide and I consider its statements reliable. Twelve days after the near tragedy, both *Time* and *Newsweek* carried unprecedented lengthy lead articles, illustrating, it seems to me, the fact that in our present world Pope John Paul II stands forth as the most eminent personage of our era and the world's most important and most widely recognized spiritual leader, unparalleled in any field.

---

* Copyright 1981 Time Inc. All rights reserved. Reprinted by permission from *Time*.

One of the most noteworthy features of the twelve journeys of the Pope and, in fact, of his whole papal ministry, has been his constant concern for youth, his direct and effective appeal and challenge to Catholic youth everywhere and their response to him. This, perhaps, was most noteworthy in the visit to France, where it was least expected. It has been reported that in France some of the leaders of the Church attempted to dissuade the Pope from his announced plan of holding a special meeting with youth. It was thought that because of the apparent indifference of French youth to Christ, to the Church, and to the teaching of the Gospel, so few would attend that the meeting would prove to be a fiasco that would cast a pall of indifference over the other planned meetings of the Pope with the people of France. John Paul, however, insisted on going through with his original plan. So great was the outpouring of young people that they exceeded the capacity of the arena that had been reserved for the meeting. So enthusiastic was their response that the Pope found it difficult to bring the meeting to an end in time to attend the next event. John Paul's meeting with youth became the outstanding event of the whole French visit.

Much the same thing had happened in the Pope's meeting with the youth of the United States in Madison Square Garden, New York. Both of these meetings became typical of the response of Catholic youth to the Pope. Even more remarkable in some ways was the meeting of the youth of various nations at St. Peter's in Rome, called by the Ecumenical Community of Taizé. Twenty-five thousand from different parts of the world gathered within and outside the great Basilica (since St. Peter's was said to have been unable to accommodate all of them) to hear the Pope's message to them on December 30, 1980, in which, according to *L'Osservatore Romano*, the Pope used eight languages. To them, the Pope spoke on the subject, "The Soul of All Ecumenism: Conversion of Heart, Holiness of Life, Prayer." He spoke of the teaching of Christ on unity and the importance of full unity among the followers of Christ.

Even as I write this, there arrives the May 17, 1982, English edition of *L'Osservatore Romano*, which describes a meeting of the Pope with more than 100,000 young people of Bologna and the region of Emilia-Romagna. To them the Pope spoke of the "Power of Truth and Love to Change the World." We have to ask ourselves: is there another leader in the whole world who, through his personal appeal and without the slightest external compulsion, can draw together a crowd of more than 100,000 young people to honor him and to hear him speak?

What is significant in the Pope's attitude toward and his appeal to youth is the openness of youth everywhere to the Pope's appeal and the response, particularly of Catholic youth, to that appeal. This is one of the hopeful aspects of the Church, as she faces the end of the twentieth century.

Now, as we stand on the eve of the fourth anniversary of the Pope's election and gaze back on all that he has accomplished in these past four years—the twelve great journeys of evangelization, the three important encyclicals, the crowded public audiences held in the Piazza of St. Peter's, the daily appearance to recite the Angelus, his many meetings with important ecclesiastical and civil personages, his constant openness to persons and groups of every class and description, his relationship to Catholic youth and their ready response to him— as I consider all this, I unhesitatingly repeat the words with which I began: with the election of Pope John Paul II, "there dawned on Christ's Church the light of renewed faith and strengthened hope."